Cambridge Studies in American Literature and Culture

The puritan–provincial vision

Cambridge Studies in American Literature and Culture

Editor
Albert Gelpi, Stanford University

Advisory Board
Nina Baym, University of Illinois, Champaign-Urbana
Sacvan Bercovitch, Harvard University
Richard Bridgman, University of California, Berkeley
David Levin, University of Virginia
Joel Porte, Cornell University
Mike Weaver, Oxford University

Other books in the series
Peter Conn: *The Divided Mind*
Patricia Caldwell: *The Puritan Conversion Narrative*
Barton St. Armand: *Emily Dickinson and Her Culture*
Marjorie Perloff: *The Dance of the Intellect*
Albert Gelpi: *Wallace Stevens*
Richard Gray: *Writing the South*
Lawrence Buell: *New England Literary Culture*
Sacvan Bercovitch and Myra Jehlen: *Ideology and Classic American Literature*
Steven Axelrod and Helen Deese: *Robert Lowell*
Jerome Loving: *Emily Dickinson*
Brenda Murphy: *American Realism and American Drama*
Warren Motley: *The American Abraham*
Brook Thomas: *Cross-Examinations of Law and Literature*
Lynn Keller: *Remaking it New*
David Wyatt: *The Fall into Eden*
George Dekker: *The American Historical Romance*
Lothar Hönninghausen: *William Faulkner*
Tony Tanner: *Scenes of Nature, Signs of Men*
Robert Lawson-Peebles: *Landscape and Written Expression in Revolutionary America*
Margaret Holley: *The Poetry of Marianne Moore*
Robert Levine: *Conspiracy and Romance*
David Halliburton: *The Color of the Sky*
Michael Davidson: *The San Francisco Poetry Renaissance*
Eric Sigg: *The American T.S. Eliot*
David Miller: *Dark Eden*
Richard Godden: *Fictions of Capital: The American Novel from James to Mailer*
Alfred Habegger: *Henry James and the "Woman Business"*
Charles Altieri: *Painterly Abstraction in Modernist Poetry*
John McWilliams: *The American Epic*

Published by the Press Syndicate of the University of Cambridge
The Pitt Building, Trumpington Street, Cambridge CB2 IRP
40 West 20th Street, New York NY 10011, USA
10 Stamford Road, Oakleigh, Melbourne 3166, Australia

© Cambridge University Press 1990

First published 1990

Printed in Great Britain at the University Press, Cambridge

British Library cataloguing in publication data

Manning, Susan
The Puritan–provincial vision: Scottish and American literature in the nineteenth century. – (Cambridge studies in American literature and culture).
1. English literature. Scottish writers, 1800–1900. Scottish literature, 1800–1900. Influence of Puritanism
2. English literature. American writers, 1800–1900. Influence of Puritanism
I. Title
820.9'382

Library of Congress cataloguing in publication data

Manning, Susan.
The Puritan-provincial vision: Scottish and American literature in the nineteenth century / Susan Manning.
  p.   cm. – (Cambridge studies in American literature and culture)
Bibliography.
Includes index.
ISBN 0-521-37237-2
1. Scottish literature–19th century–History and criticism.   2. American literature–19th century–History and criticism.   3. Literature. Comparative–Scottish and American.   4. Literature. Compartive–American and Scottish.   5. Puritan movements in literature.   6. Regionalism in literature.   I. Title.   II. Series.
PR8550.M27   1990
820.9'9411–dc20   89-35787 CIP

ISBN 0 521 37237 2

SE

The puritan–provincial vision
Scottish and American literature in the nineteenth century

SUSAN MANNING
Newnham College, Cambridge

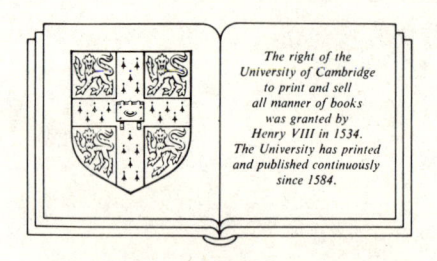

CAMBRIDGE UNIVERSITY PRESS

CAMBRIDGE
NEW YORK   PORT CHESTER
MELBOURNE   SYDNEY

Contents

Preface	*page*	vii
Acknowledgements		xi
1 Calvin's theology and the puritan mind		1
2 After Armageddon: Jonathan Edwards and David Hume		26
3 From puritanism to provincialism		47
4 The pursuit of the double		70
5 Spectators, spies and spectres: the observer's stance		106
6 'Is anything central?'		147
Notes		195
Bibliography		211
Index		238

Preface

This book starts from the observation that nineteenth-century Scottish and American literatures embody certain styles, subjects and preoccupations which characteristically distinguish them from English literature of the same period. Its purpose is to investigate, describe and account for these qualities, and to examine their critical consequences in some of the major works of fiction written by Scottish and American writers between 1800 and 1860. My initial assumption is that the writing of Calvin provides a focus – though not necessarily a source – for the distinctive features of Scottish and American literature; the argument proceeds by considering the modulations sustained by the language of puritanism between the sixteenth and nineteenth centuries, from theological to philosophical to political and finally to literary contexts. From these I derive the contours of what I have called the puritan–provincial mind.

It is perhaps necessary to stress at the outset that this is an essay in literary criticism, not literary history, the history of ideas or a comparative study of influences. Historical influence is not, in the main, at issue from one writer to the next, or even from puritanism to all of the provincial attitudes I identify in later writing. The primary concern is rather with a particular use of language and with the literary consequences of the assumptions that lie behind it. The early chapters, therefore, are not 'background', but integral to the inquiry. Calvin's language in the *Institutes of the Christian Religion* reflects and expresses a view of life just as Hawthorne's or Scott's fictional prose does; indeed, as I argue, the way his language organises the world has profound similarities with the shape and concerns of their fiction. The evidence for this reading is there in the writing itself. The language and phrasing of quotations is crucial; in these lie the echoes, continuities, development of implications. In what remains one of the most suggestive approaches to one half of my subject, *Studies in Classic American Literature*, D.H. Lawrence said 'Never trust the teller, trust the tale.' The 'tale' told by puritan–provincial writing is to be found less in the way I tell it than in its own words. Some of the implications of puritan thought which emerge – excessive introspection and self-questioning, for example, or the division between event and significance – were foreseen and warned against by Calvin himself, but they nevertheless remain tendencies inherent in his description of reality.

The many scholars to whose work I am indebted have proposed other models and other readings of particular aspects of this material which carry their own coherence and conviction. I am not offering new scholarship in these areas, but a larger interpretation which, in characterising this puritan–provincial bent of mind, seeks to illuminate Scottish and American nineteenth-century literatures in their relation to English literature as other readings have not. My accounts of Calvinism, of puritan thought and of provincialism are critically selective; they aim to trace a coherent line through a large amount of diverse writing in different literary forms. Necessarily, some aspects of theology, some subjects, some ways of writing and thinking about experience are emphasised at the expense of others. Analyses of specific works are exemplary rather than exclusive; the design overall is to be suggestive rather than comprehensive. That such major American texts as Franklin's *Autobiography* and *Moby-Dick* or Scottish works like *Waverley* or *Sartor Resartus* receive only passing comment in the book is not a sign that they do not 'fit' in the puritan–provincial framework – all in fact seem to me to ground themselves fully in the concerns of these chapters – but rather a consequence of the particular structure of my argument. Indeed, the discussions are intended to bring to mind further examples and modulations in Scottish and American or other literatures.

In a similar way, 1860 may be regarded as something of an arbitrary end point. At every turn, the writing of Henry James reflects and enlarges upon the provincial predicament of observation and distance, and the motif of the journey to the centre is perhaps more characteristic of his work than of any other writer. From 'The Passionate Pilgrim' (1875) to *The American Scene* (1906), by way of *The Bostonians* (1886), his art seeks to come to terms with and to embody the provincialism of America with respect to Europe's centrality. Robert Louis Stevenson, too, not only in the obviously puritan-based *Weir of Hermiston* or the intensely realised evil which aligns 'Thrawn Janet' with Hogg's *Confessions of a Justified Sinner*, but also in the South Sea tales, which are more than a footnote to Melville, takes up the nexus of puritan–provincial terms as the very foundation of his art.

The focused discussion of early nineteenth-century Scottish and American literatures belongs, then, in a more general context of enduring states of mind and ways of representing the world in words. By extension, 'central' does not equal 'English'. 'Provincialism' is not a question of nationality, political or geographical, nor puritanism solely a matter of religious persuasion. Poe for example pre-eminently possessed this puritan–provincial cast of thought, and yet he is quite outside the New England theocratic nexus and is also mid-nineteenth-century America's least parochial critic. The ways of thinking and the corresponding use of language which I define as puritan–provincial predate Calvin and the Reformation (they are clearly visible, for example, in some of the writings of St Paul and St Augustine), and they persist in much of the literature we know as 'modern'. And, as I argue, they characterise some works of English literature – singular masterpieces like *The Tempest* or Godwin's *Caleb Williams* which spring up periodically through the mainstream of English literature to reflect in their context apparently anomalous modes of apprehension.

However, for a variety of reasons, these qualities are peculiarly focused in Scottish and American literature of the eighteenth and nineteenth centuries. They take particular shape and doctrinal form from Calvin's *Institutes* and are codified into a powerful imaginative synthesis which underpins much of this literature. The comparison (which for reasons of space and unwieldiness has to remain largely though not altogether implicit here) with another literature – English – which is not so underpinned, shows its literary consequences. It is these which are, finally, the central concern of this book. What is the source of the seemingly disproportionate emotional power which such writing exerts over its readers, and what are the literary and human limitations of the structure of thought characteristically exemplified in puritanism?

A word about terminology. Calvinism is a proper noun, referring to the doctrine set out by Calvin's *Institutes*, and as such is capitalised throughout. Puritanism I have defined as a way of thinking and of living rather than a body of doctrine; puritans are those who find Calvin's formulations to be an adequate description of reality and who embrace the co-ordinates of existence entailed by attempting to live within the implications of his doctrine. Both terms are used in this special, non-dogmatic sense; neither, therefore, is capitalised here. Similarly, 'provincial' and 'puritan–provincial' are intended to define an outlook and a use of language, not as terms of derogation or dismissal implying second-rateness. This may indeed sometimes be the consequence of writing from within this framework of assumptions and procedures, but it is not necessarily so. Some of the works considered succumb to the negative aspects of puritan–provincialism; others, avoiding the twin dangers of what I have called 'alienated imitation' and 'egocentric idiosyncrasy', which threaten the provincial outlook, find a way to write non-provincially about life perceived from this point of view. It should become apparent that I regard *The Heart of Midlothian*, for example, as one of the great works of nineteenth-century fiction. I make no apology, however, for the critical judgements which do emerge from my comparison of provincial and 'central' literature.

Acknowledgements

Any work of criticism and synthesis such as this owes an enormous debt to previous scholarship in the field. My field or fields have been wide; much excellent criticism and fascinating research have already been achieved, and this has been a constant stimulus to my own work. I cannot acknowledge all these influences individually, either here or in the body of the book, and must allow the Bibliography to stand as a record of general and particular indebtedness. It is a great pleasure to record the generous help given by friends and colleagues during the preparation of this book. I am grateful, firstly, to Professor Mary Ann Radzinowicz and Dr Howard Erskine-Hill for their guidance in the early stages of my work on Scottish and American subjects. The Cambridge University Library and the National Library of Scotland have been continuing points of reference throughout my research; the staff of both institutions have been consistently knowledgeable and helpful. An important part of the work for this book was undertaken during the tenure of a Harkness Fellowship at the University of Virginia in Charlottesville, between 1978 and 1980. I am grateful to the English Department of the University of Virginia for the welcome extended to me during this time and for the instructive seminars on American literature in which I was privileged to participate. I have been most particularly glad, then and since, of the opportunity to make the acquaintance of Professor David Levin. His encouragement and assistance, and the example of his scholarship, have greatly influenced the conduct and completion of this study. I owe much, too, to colleagues and friends in Newnham College and the University of Cambridge. Kate Fullbrook has stayed with it from its first muddy beginnings until now; her consistent enthusiasm for and stringent criticisms of the project have constantly challenged me to sharpen my own ideas. Jane Bastin has given valuable time freely to practical details which might otherwise have overwhelmed me; her less tangible influence on my thinking and writing has been yet more important. Professor Andrew Hook of the University of Glasgow and Dr Tony Tanner were generous and constructive examiners of the Ph.D dissertation from which this book comes; I am grateful to Dr Tanner in addition for his continuing support of my work and for many stimulating discussions of American literature. I owe a great deal to Jean and Richard Gooder, as teachers, colleagues and friends. It would be impossible to acknowledge adequately the generosity and variety of their support over many years; I merely record it warmly here. My final acknowledgements, to my family, are the hardest to describe. Without them, this book might have been completed sooner; it is far more likely that it would never have happened at all. The book is dedicated to my parents.

1

Calvin's theology and the puritan mind

> Calvinism is the natural theology of the disinherited; it never flourished, therefore, anywhere as it did in the barren hills of Scotland and in the wilds of North America. (H.L. Mencken)[1]

Puritanism is not a body of doctrine but a state of mind. John Calvin's *Institutes of the Christian Religion* (1536–59) was the authoritative codification of Reformation theology; it set out doctrine not merely for the puritan sects but also for the 'Elizabethan Settlement' of 1559, which established the Church of England. Theologically, therefore, little separates Anglicans from Calvinists; the distinctions lie all in the way these doctrines are held: they are matters of emphasis, of temper and tone, of degrees or assent or dissent – matters which are finally more susceptible to literary than to theological, historical or political definition. These impalpable turnings of inclination and temperament combine to define two distinct understandings of the nature of man and his relationship to what lies beyond himself, and they determine the contours of what I shall describe as the 'central' and 'provincial' minds.

Calvin's theology provided a satisfyingly complete and distinctive world picture for those who lived in obedience to its strictest precepts, a picture so powerful that, even after the religious tenets on which it was founded had lost their compulsion, it shaped the imaginations of those brought up in its shadow. The way Calvin formulates Reformation principles at once reflects and enjoins an attitude towards these principles which establishes the puritan mind in embattled opposition to the centres of experience in the world.

CALVIN'S THEOLOGY

Calvinism is based upon an emphatic, ever-present consciousness of Original Sin and the consequently 'fallen' nature of man, which taints not only his every action but all his perceptions and aspirations. 'Infidelity', according to Calvin, 'was at the root of the revolt': Original Sin represents Adam's failure of faith in respect of a promise made to him by God.[2] This first transgression of God's law and disobedience to His will entails the total corruption of man's nature and the ruination of his hopes: 'For our nature is not only utterly devoid of goodness, but so prolific in all kinds of evil that it can never be idle' (*Institutes*, I, 218). Insistence on the positive force of evil in human nature is an initial term in the oppositions and polarities which structure Calvinist theology: 'Our souls are a very abyss of iniquity', Calvin wrote to Protector Somerset in 1548.[3] Failure of faith distances and estranges man from God; he simultaneously yearns after God's mercy and flees before His righteous ire. He seeks shelter, but fears vengeance. Through Adam's transgression all men are reprobate, doomed to eternal perdition.

Man's nature, Calvin stresses, manifests through the Fall such rank infidelity and propensity to evil that the sentence of universal reprobation is exactly just. But God is merciful as well as just, and decrees that some few shall be saved. These are the elect, and their salvation is as immutable as the damnation of the reprobate. Calvin insists that election must be arbitrary if it is to avoid being payment of a debt to man: God's choice is not a reward for good works, but free grace.

By admitting the arbitrariness of God's election, man abrogates the right to pry into causes, to make 'reasons' or to attempt to explain what never can be understood. Calvin and his followers distrust the speculative intellect and believe that man's reason is irremediably corrupted by the Fall; faith in God's 'Word', the Scriptures, is now the only means of apprehending His will. In a passage whose echoes can be heard right through to the fiction of the nineteenth century, Calvin says

> Let it be our first principle that to desire any other knowledge of predestination than that which is expounded by the word of God, is no less infatuated than to walk where there is no path, or to seek light in darkness. Let us not be ashamed to be ignorant in a matter where ignorance is learning. Rather let us willingly abstain from the search after knowledge, to which it is both foolish as well as perilous, and even fatal to aspire . . . There is good reason to dread a presumption which can only plunge us headlong into ruin. (II, 204)

To pursue knowledge unlawfully is to court the vengeful pursuit of God, to be 'engulfed in [the] profound abyss' (II, 242).

Salvation by faith alone was the central tenet of that aspect of Reformation theology which attempted to counter both corrupt papal practices and the heavy emphasis laid by the Catholic Church on 'works' as a means to salvation; a complete trust in the redeeming saviour characterises the Lutheran Church. Calvin holds the same theological position, but places much more emphasis on the absoluteness of God's predestination. At this point the paradoxes begin to proliferate. Calvin's injunction to acquiesce in God's inscrutable will is balanced by his belief that the elect must take an active part in their own salvation by becoming aware of their state and undergoing 'conversion'. He makes faith the subject of investigation: the individual, burdened by the knowledge of his own corrupt nature and the inevitable distortion of all his perceptions, has nevertheless a duty to discover the true state of his soul. Only the elect can redeem Adam's failure of faith by finding a renewed true faith in God; only the truly faithful can come to a consciousness of their own election. The circularity of the formulation means that any security is always liable to turn back on itself. The Calvinist may never be sure of his own faith, as all its outward manifestations are treacherous (I, 478). 'Ye have to prove yourselfs quhither ye be in the faith or not', as the Scottish Calvinist Robert Bruce would put it.[4]

With such traps awaiting the unwary inquirer, Calvin places the burden on the individual, not in action itself but in the unremitting self-scrutiny which must accompany action. He defines faith as 'a firm and sure knowledge of the divine favour toward us' (I, 475); the mark of its truth is *assurance*: 'So true is this, that the term *faith* is often used as equivalent to *confidence* . . . the goodness of God is not properly comprehended when security does not follow as its fruit' (I, 483–4). But 'so long as we are pilgrims in the world' and therefore 'involved in the mists of error' (I, 471), even this confidence must be constantly affected by doubt and insecurity: 'believers have a perpetual struggle with their own distrust' (I, 484).

A theology of absolute predestination tends away from action towards passivity before the immutable will of God. While this does seem to be an inevitable implication of the doctrine, Calvin himself refutes vigorously any suggestion that passivity is the lot of the believer; on the contrary, 'conversion' is but the beginning of a strenuous life of toil against the snares of worldliness; again Calvin's language is pregnant with implication for later writers:

> though purged by [God's] sanctification, we are still beset by many vices and much weakness, so long as we are enclosed in the prison of the body. Thus it is, that placed at a great distance from perfection, we must always be endeavouring to make some progress, and daily struggling with the evil by which we are entangled. (I, 520)

Consciousness of election only intensifies man's sense of the *distance* between himself and God; it turns his life from a passive wallowing in the mire of his own sinfulness to a journey, a pilgrim's progress towards Sanctification. The shape of life, from being a static tableau of Original Sin, becomes a dramatic narrative.

But Calvin was not explicit about why works are necessary when saving grace comes by faith alone; or, rather, he established the paradox without indicating a way to make it livable. Assertion was sufficient as long as faith supported the believer across logical gaps, but doubt bred a demand for reasons and for assurance that God's absolute transcendence was not utterly without care for human effort, that inscrutability did not equal tyranny. In transforming the theology of the *Institutes* into a rule for living, practising Calvinists needed to make God more accessible to human apprehension and more amenable to the 'laws' of nature and of reason. It was in this climate that 'covenant theology' developed in the seventeenth century.

Covenant teaching mitigated the arbitrary nature of men's fates and seemed to restore to them some measure of autonomy; it stressed God's mercy and His particular interest in mankind above His inexorable justice. The covenant was a bargain freely entered into on both sides: men could be confident that if they fulfilled their part, God would keep His. There were, according to seventeenth-century theologians, two covenants: the first was the Covenant of Works, made with Adam and all his posterity, that in return for leading a righteous and obedient life, man would be rewarded by eternal bliss. This law, the law of nature, was implanted in man's heart; it was codified in the commandments given to Moses on the mountain (the Law of the Old Testament). However, the corruption of all men in Adam's original disobedience meant that righteousness was no longer possible to man, that it was beyond his capacity to fulfill the Covenant of Works.

God therefore, said the covenant theologians, was no longer bound by His promise to save mankind; but in His mercy He proffers man the New Law, or Covenant of Grace, first adumbrated in Genesis, revealed repeatedly in His particular care of the Jews and fulfilled in Christ's Incarnation. Whereas the Covenant of Works assumed that man can by willing virtuous action accomplish it, the Covenant of Grace takes account of the corruption of human will through Original Sin. Under the dispensation of grace, the Christian is able to accept that his efforts to save himself are unavailing and, in an act of faith ('I believe You can save me if You will'), to give up to God the responsibility for his salvation. The Old Law demanded obedience; the New requires faith; its seals are the sacraments of Baptism and the Eucharist. The New Law does not render the Old obsolete: the commandments given to Moses were both absolute *and* unattainable; as Jonathan Edwards would put it, 'men, being sensible of these things, might ... know how impossible it is for them to obtain salvation by the works of the law, and be assured of their absolute need of a mediator'.[5]

Although Calvinism stressed that faith not works was the only way to salvation, the Old Law remained in operation to show how the elect must try to live once they are called. John Cotton and other New England divines, perceiving that the obligation of man was to act morally in a world where – because of Original Sin – right action was no longer attainable, developed a theology of the 'Middle Way' which set forth a combination of 'diligence in worldly business, and yet deadness to the world; such a mystery as none can read, but they that know it'.[6] The hint of exclusiveness in that final clause which refuses to resolve the elements is potentially threatening to any who might dare to question the premise, but to these early New Englanders such a paradox was observed, experienced *fact*, and quite livable. Covenant theology was, essentially, a promise of *meaning*: by reducing the inscrutability of God and rendering Him amenable to rational exchange, it gave the Calvinist believer scope for action and confidence in its efficacy. The early historians of the Colonies – William Bradford, John Winthrop and Cotton Mather – did not find this uncertainty about human behaviour incompatible with their discernment of divine mission in the whole enterprise.

Covenant theology developed subsequently to the *Institutes*, but in refuting Catholicism's sacrificial theory of the Eucharist (whereby through transubstantiation the elements of bread and wine actually become the body and blood of Christ), Calvin describes the sacraments as 'pactions, by which God enters into covenant with us, and we become bound to holiness and purity of life, because a mutual stipulation is here interposed between God and us' (II, 505–6). In this notion, Calvin attempts to reconcile divine grace to human action, faith to active virtue. The Sacraments are thus the embodiment of the Word rather than the substance of God:

> an external sign, by which the Lord seals on our consciences his promises of good-will toward us, in order to sustain the weakness of our faith, and we in our turn testify our piety towards him, both before himself, and before angels as well as men . . . [The sacraments are] a visible sign of a sacred thing . . . a visible form of an invisible grace. (II, 491–2)

Calvin's language deliberately introduces a division between language and the substance or reality it refers to, *as a tenet of doctrine*. Crucially, the need for *faith* to bridge the gap between the Sacraments as symbols and the actual presence of the Holy Spirit in them means that the efficacy of the Sacrament is dependent upon the election of the partaker.

THE PURITAN MIND

> The essence of Calvinism and the essence of Puritanism is the hidden God, the unknowable, the unpredictable.[7]

Calvinism is a theology of crisis. Born of opposition and persecution, its spirit was apocalyptic and absolute. What distinguished the puritan most signally from the Anglican who shared his 'reformed' theology was insistence on the letter of the law, a doctrinal intransigence (or 'purity') which resolved spiritual dilemmas by appeal to an authority at once internal and absolutely transcendent. Puritan defensiveness ('coming ... out of the fiery furnace of Romish persecution, they were jealous of everything that had once passed the Pope's fingers, lest it might be too hot for them') set up a structure of thought which dealt in oppositions and absolute antipathies, and which found the Manichaean side of St Augustine most hospitable to its polarising mentality. Puritans positively welcomed the idea of 'two societies of human beings, one of which is predestined to reign with God from all eternity, the other doomed to undergo eternal punishment with the Devil'.[8]

The World of Light and the World of Darkness locked in eternal and issueless conflict seemed a fitting image for the puritan struggle at its revolutionary moment of crisis. Calvinist polarities demand that the mind work simultaneously within contradictory frames of reference: no single vocabulary is adequate to describe its experience. The puritan finds release from the deadlock of contemplation only in action. A paradox lived is a constant conflict: the more strenuous and extended the combat, the more purifying its effect, as Milton describes in one of the most famous products of English puritan confidence:

> Good and evil we know in the field of this World grow up together almost inseparably . . . It was from out the rinde of one apple tasted, that the knowledge of good and evill, as two twins cleaving together leapt forth into the World. And perhaps this is that doom which Adam fell into of knowing good and evill, that is to say of knowing good by evill . . . I cannot praise a fugitive and cloister'd vertue, unexercis'd & unbreath'd, that never sallies out and sees her adversary, but slinks out of the race, where that immortall garland is to be run for, not without dust and heat. Assuredly we bring not innocence into the world, we bring impurity much rather: that which purifies us is triall, and triall is by what is contrary.[9]

Milton's prose reflects his confidence that he is at the centre of things, involved: in active controversy he forces the paradoxical theory to yield up its contradictions to experience. At such moments of crisis absolute faith is possible; the principles of justification and exclusivity carry the reformer forward on a high wave of confidence. It is only once the moment passes that the polarities of the puritan mind press themselves forward as oppositions to be resolved by reasoned argument.

Anglicans were both less absolute and less exclusive in their approach to reform. Hooker, in *Of the Laws of Ecclesiastical Polity* (1593 et seq.), advocated a caution which infuriated his puritan adversaries: 'the change of lawes, especially concerning matter of Religion, must be warily proceeded in. Lawes, as all other thinges humaine, are many times full of imperfection... no doubt but to beare a tollerable soare is better than to venter on a daungerous remedie'.[10] When good and evil are the only counters, a middle position such as this cannot exist: there is neither concept nor language to describe the spectrum of possibilities which plays between the polarities. Hooker denied infallibility to *any* created power; his willingness to concede that the benefits of religion may not be exclusive to any single persuasion allows his writing a latitude and a tolerance which are denied to the puritan. Calvin's theology entails radically different views of the world depending on how far the doctrinal position is taken to be a complete description of reality.

The conceptual structure of polarities determines both the nature of Calvin's doctrine and the psychological state it induces in the believer. Division was introduced into God's harmonious universe by the Fall: man and God are divided by man's rebellion against his Creator's righteous anger. In 1726 the American puritan Samuel Willard described this state of alienation in language which would resonate through many mutations of context and purpose. Fallen man, he said, 'is held in passive subjection to the law, though he doth not actually conform unto it. He is not properly an outlaw, or put out of reach of it, but a rebel'.[11] Division becomes the structuring principle of life. Man and nature are divided because the Fall has distorted man's vision so that he can no longer see God directly in His works; Nature now becomes to him a series of inscrutable signs to be 'interpreted' for their possible significance. Man and man are divided one from another by the absoluteness of the distinction between elect and reprobate. Man is, finally, divided from and within himself; he becomes a battleground of warring faculties: the intellect against the will, the head against the heart, reason against faith.

> The believer finds within himself two principles: the one filling him with delight in recognising the divine goodness, the other filling him with bitterness under a sense of his fallen state; the one leading him to recline on the promise of the Gospel, the other alarming him by the conviction of his iniquity; the one making him exult with the anticipation of life, the other making him tremble with the fear of death. (*Institutes*, I, 486)

Such abrupt swings of the emotional pendulum from joy to despair, with no central resting point, are characteristic of the puritan mind; the absoluteness of the distinction between election and reprobation allows no provisional judgement. Although Original Sin and the Fall of Man are at the centre of Anglican theology too, there the doctrine is held much more experimentally. Lancelot Andrewes, for example, plays on the word 'fall' in his sermons, showing how we are bruised and soiled, but not killed by it. The mildness of his imprecation, 'Our Nature is not right in joynt',[12] with its hopeful possibility of amelioration, could scarcely be further from the wilful destructiveness which Calvin understands by the Fall.

All churches descended from St Augustine taught predestination, election and reprobation; it was a feature of the 'Thirty-nine Articles' (perhaps the nearest the Church of England came to a statement of official doctrine). What is unique to Calvinism is, firstly, its exclusiveness: Christ's death, in Calvin's system, is the pledge of salvation to the predestined elect alone; secondly, its finality: the individual had been decreed elect or reprobate from and to all eternity without possibility of alteration. Calvin has a much more present sense of reprobation than Hooker, and the Calvinist feels a sense of 'special privilege' associated with his own election which sets him apart from the mass of men.[13] Calvin's God is Just rather than Loving; his religion is compounded of faith in his redemption and fear of God, and its primary sin is unbelief, lack of faith or *confidence*.

Hooker, on the other hand, holds that it is the Christian's duty to hope that all may be saved, and not to restrict the workings of God's mercy and grace to the elect (*Laws*, II, 202–3). He is willing to countenance degrees of belief and of holiness and holds that 'feare worketh noe mans inclination to repentance, till somewhat else have wrought in us love alsoe' (III, 9). The primary thought is of God's love in Christ: 'Salvation to all that will is nigh', as John Donne would put it, emphasising the inclusiveness of grace rather than whether the sinner is able to 'will' it.[14]

As a way of life, then, puritanism struggles with the legacy of Original Sin; everything is entailed in man's initial rebellion from God's will. Distance and disinheritance define the self: theologically, from God; psychologically, from Nature (the world), from other men, from one's own better self and from meaning. Man, the disinherited heir of God, is rebellious and resentful; he simultaneously yearns towards the Father and hates Him for His righteousness. Man pursues knowledge and certainty unwisely and is in turn pursued for his presumption. He is at odds with life, and persecution and exile define his relationship to the world. Before this is theology, it is a state of mind, one which Calvin letters show to have dogged him throughout life:

> Whenever I call to mind the state of wretchedness in which my life was spent [in Geneva], how can it be otherwise but that my very soul must shudder when any proposal is made for my return? I pass over entirely that disquietude by which we were perpetually tossed up and down, and driven from one side to

another... I know indeed from experience, that wheresoever I might turn, all sorts of annoyances were strewn in my way; that if I would live to Christ, this world must be to me a scene of trial and vexation; the present life is appointed as the field of conflict.[15]

Calvinists find no rest in the world; they are, in the words of St Paul which were so important to St Augustine, 'strangers and pilgrims on the earth'.[16] To live in, but not of, the world is the aim of all protestants; characteristically, Calvinist doctrine pushes the thought to its extreme of opposition, as it gives a first – and immensely powerful – theological codification to an enduring state of human consciousness. Although modern historical research is tending to qualify the supposition that the puritans of the Elizabethan and Jacobean church were natural radicals and to emphasise rather their conservatism and centrality in social and political affairs, Hooker as early as 1593 found a stance of *opposition* to characterise the Calvinist reformers (*Laws*, I, 43). To be a stranger is not merely not to belong to one's surroundings, to be distanced from their meaning, but to be estranged and set at odds with them. The Calvinist, passing through this world, demands that it yield up its secrets and give him tidings of his Maker; the world looks blankly back.

The puritan universe is anxious and insecure because of the distance which the Fall has interposed between man and God, which prevents man from perceiving God directly in Nature. God is mysterious and inscrutable; His universe is full of evidence about His nature, but man's corrupt vision is unable to read it reliably. The result is an obsessive search for significance, a relentless interpretation of 'clues'. Despite this ineluctable Mystery at the centre of things, man cannot rest content at the periphery, for he is enjoined to discover the state of his soul, in defiance of what Ralph Waldo Emerson would later call the unreliability of his instruments.[17] The puritan's perception is burdened by the consciousness that everything has designs on him, is a 'sign' of his state. Nothing in the world is innocent of intention, but the messages are all in code. Where the faithful possess the mystery, the unregenerate are driven to *solve* it with the aid of the only tools available to them – reason and nature – whose inefficacy had been roundly demonstrated by Calvin in Book I of the *Institutes*. Paradoxically, and as if to overcome by sheer power of assertion, the Calvinist is both an obsessive observer and an obsessive rationalist. His reason is constantly at work, ordering, constructing, offering up 'explanations' to a world which absorbs them with silent impassivity.

This oscillation between the poles of observation and ratiocination exemplifies the puritan's difficulty in pitching the relationship of the individual to the world, of the self to the other. Merely to observe, to wait for evidence to present itself, is to be passive and to empty the self of positive aspiration; to reason with the world and with God is to be presumptive, over-active. For the puritan there is no stable middle term between self-abnegation and self-assertion. In their reaction against the extravagant rationalism of Aquinas and the Thomists, Calvin and Luther swung to an opposing extreme of irrationalism, although they reached this position (in one of the central paradoxes of Calvinist thought) through a triumphant exercise of the powers of human reason.

More temperate reformers admitted the logic and virtue of much of the Calvinist case but sought to mitigate its absolutism and to win back a place for human reason in the divine scheme of things. Recoiling from the stringency of Calvin's anti-rationalism, Hooker, for example, declares that there is a code of behaviour – Natural Law – which is directly available to human reason: 'the lawe of reason or humaine nature is that which men by discourse of naturall reason have rightly found out themselves to be all for ever bound unto in their actions' (I, 89). Reason is 'the director of mans will by discovering in action what is good' (I, 79). Reason and the natural laws (themselves decreed by God) are not displaced by Divine Law or by revelation, but merely supplemented by it in spiritual matters (I, 139).

Of the Laws of Ecclesiastical Polity devotes itself to refuting Calvin's view that Scripture, directly apprehended by faith, is man's only access to knowledge of God. On the contrary, Hooker argues, there are many routes to knowledge, and none should be exalted at the expense of another. God's intentions as revealed in the Scriptures are mediated for the individual by the collective authority of that consensus of human reason which is the Church. This consensus is an important guarantor of meaning for the individual: 'The generall and perpetuall voyce of men is as the sentence of God him selfe' (I, 84–5). Calvinism finds no such consolation in collective reason: the individual is alone with God's Word, his only mediator the faith which God's Grace may have bestowed upon him to approach it. The existence and the quality of that faith must therefore be the primary inquiry for the Calvinist believer.

Hooker's appeal to reason and tradition as necessary checks to the excesses of individual 'affection' attempts to temper the intensity and isolation which pressurises puritan faith; the idea that 'of things once receyved and confirmed by use, long usage is a law sufficient' (I, 165) is what the puritan (and, as I shall suggest later, the provincial) *must* dispute. Hooker is clear, however, that to speak of knowledge and experience rationally is quite different from attempting to *control* one's relation to the world through reason; where his language finds a tenable position of partial and provisional understanding, puritan rhetoric is driven to penetrate the hidden secrets of God. Fearful punishment awaits such presumption.

The conscience played a vital part in the puritan's 'conversion', his coming to consciousness of election. He was bound to dispel any doubts he might have about his election, because 'From doubtings, ariseth trouble of mind, and terror of conscience', and only the reprobate have terrified consciences:

> Their doubtings are condemning, and condemned: and directly opposed to faith . . . He that will not beleeve, shall be damned, destruction shall be upon them: and flaming vengeance . . .
>
> Remember, God hath allowed none to doubt or despaire of their election. Neither hath he allowed any to beleeve the certaintie of their reprobation. None can gather the persuasion of their reprobation from themselves, for all men are liers.[18]

The burden of proof of election falls on the self-investigating conscience, but its findings might be radically untrustworthy. Where the spaciousness of Hooker's writing allows room for uncertainty *within* faith, the puritan tends – in his life and his writing – to strive always to eradicate doubt by sheer force of self-scrutiny. To this end, Calvin says, God has appointed the conscience as an internal observer, 'a witness which allows them not to conceal their sins, but drags them forward as culprits to the bar of God . . . following him on even to conviction'. Even more ominously, Calvin likens the conscience to a 'kind of sentinel' set over man 'to observe and spy out all his secrets, that nothing may remain buried in darkness' (*Institutes*, II, 141).

The bifurcation of the puritan personality into actor and observer was a tenet of doctrine; Calvin's own training as a lawyer fosters a rhetoric of oppositions and a structure of thought which resounds through contexts far removed from his discussion of election and reprobation. Samuel Willard's account of the workings of conscience suggests the power which these images of division, legalistically expressed, held over the puritan imagination. He describes its functions successively as a 'statute book' of the natural moral law, a 'register' in which are indelibly recorded all the acts of man's life, a 'witness' to his most secret sins which 'dares not withold its testimony, when God commands it to declare', and an 'accuser' which 'will haunt [men] with its reflections, and give them no rest'. Next, conscience is a 'judge' which 'keeps a court in the man'; finally, it is an 'executioner' which 'falls upon the man, and rends and tears him', and 'a guilt apprehended that torments them, and makes them feel a hell in their own breasts; they start and fly at the shaking of a leaf, and would run away from themselves, if possibly they could'.[19] The excessive violence of the language and the perceived inadequacy of its images suggest the puritan's anxiety as he confronted the imperfect practice of his own life with the intransigence of the theory that claimed to contain and describe it.

Puritan writing lacks the means to express not merely provisionality but acquiescence: the giving up of self to God obtains – in the prose – no release through spirituality or self-forgetfulness. In a passage like this (from Jonathan Edwards' *Personal Narrative*) even the puritan's submission seems willed:

> when I ask for humility, I cannot bear the thoughts of being no more humble than other christians. It seems to me, that though their degrees of humility may be suitable for them, yet it would be a vile self-exaltation in me, not to be the lowest in humility of all mankind.

The point is not that Edwards' experience of grace does not involve joyful acquiescence, but that in setting it down he is bound, by the conventions of the model of puritan conversion, to justify its authenticity by resorting to a rhetoric of *absolute* self-abasement. There is a significant distance – one which later writers would exploit as a lever on their fiction – between experience and the language which may describe it.[20]

The natural consequence of the doctrine of total predestination is complete passivity before the will of God. But Calvinist faith was dynamic, and the progressive stages of conversion, from Effectual Calling through Justification to Sanctification, emphasised the *narrative* understanding of faith as it revealed itself in the actions of the convert: 'A Man's whole Life is but a Conversion.'[21] Here, in the telling of one's own story, was a potential escape route from the stalemate of dogma, a route which would release the puritan–provincial imagination of nineteenth-century writers from the constraints of their own logic. But because of the distancing effects of Original Sin, the story of the Calvinist convert's life is not itself simply descriptive of his increasing closeness to God. His physical experiences are *emblematic* of the stages in his spiritual regeneration; individual events in his life ('natural facts' as Ralph Waldo Emerson would later say) symbolise 'spiritual facts'.[22] The narrative of the life of the convert from birth to death is the *allegory* of the soul's journey towards salvation.

Emblem, symbol, allegory: these emphasise the doubleness of the puritan vision, the compulsive need to *interpret* the experience in terms of something else, to discover 'meaning' in 'fact'. The truth of the word, like that of nature, is not directly available to the unregenerate imagination. 'The word itself . . . is a kind of mirror in which faith beholds God' (*Institutes*, I, 474): the word reflects the reality, but (in consequence of the Fall) does so indirectly, at a distance, as allegory or symbol. The Word mirrors God, actions mirror the Word; the puritan plays his actions onto the mirror of the Scriptures hoping to 'read' one Word in terms of the other.

The puritan spiritual autobiography tells the story of the soul's progression from the first stirrings of grace in the unregenerate mind through strivings, doubts and backslidings to eventual assurance. It both follows a predestined route and creates one for the reader himself to follow. But it also, in the retelling, involves itself in a continual interrogation of events. The problem, enacted repeatedly in puritan spiritual autobiographies, is to unite the particular 'natural fact' with the 'spiritual fact' of which it is the symbol: what did the event *mean*? Was it true evidence of salvation, or merely that 'vain confidence' by which the devil tempts us to perdition (*Institutes*, I, 211)? Can the 'natural' and 'spiritual' facts be adequate and complete reflections of one another; how is experience to be translated into writing about experience? These, and related questions, would inform Scottish and American writing well beyond the reach of direct influence.

Covenant theology appealed to the side of the puritan mind which was always tempted to drive a bargain with God. Two aspects reveal the particular bent of the puritan mind. Firstly, the 'Law' – Old and New – was held to reveal absolute truth. Puritans refused to concede Hooker's distinction between the Law which was the direct Word of God, eternal and unchangeable, and the 'lawes positive', which had a more local and contingent force and were framed with 'regard had to the place and persons for which they are made' (*Laws*, I, 250–1). For the puritan there is nothing which we might properly call a *historical* truth; the apocalyptic framework in which he operates puts him in direct contact with the eternal, or it throws him into Calvin's 'abyss'. It is this which helps to give a peculiarly abstract, unrooted air to a work like Jonathan Edwards' never completed *A History of the Work of Redemption* (posthumously published in 1774); the absoluteness of Edwards' exegesis makes no attempt to establish its eternal conclusions within a framework of historical change. Temporal – contingent – narrative considerations are powerless to mediate between the instant and the infinite. There may be, as Emerson puts it later, 'only two absorbing facts, I and the Abyss'.[23]

The puritan's refusal to countenance a local dimension to truth is a further symptom of this polarised view of reality: as long as he feels himself to be at the centre, at the generating focus of eternal truth, his faith is absolute, and he may move mountains. But take this confidence away, suggest that truth may be provisional or partial, and he will veer at once to the opposite extreme of scepticism, where all is relative and any centre of stability seems at an unapproachable distance. To a large extent the inner or psychological history of puritanism is the story of its attempts to fight off the consciousness and the consequences of this failure of confidence which I shall call provincialism. In chapter 2 we shall see Hume grappling with this problem in a philosophical context; here we may note that the a-historical stance, and the tendency to swing from eschatological confidence to absolute scepticism are attitudes towards life which are inherent in and codified by the puritan viewpoint before it becomes the provincial one.

A second feature of covenant theology also demonstrates this characteristic way of thinking. The practice of explaining every historical event in relation to God's covenanted will for man reinforced the puritan's belief that no incident is neutral, that everything which happens is a sign to be 'read' for its significance, as being either something commanded by God, or something which breaks a commandment. Hooker insisted that some things in life are *not* tied to keeping or breaking of a covenant, but are 'free in their owne nature and indifferent' (*Laws*, I, 154). In his confidence that 'signes must resemble the thinges they signifie' (II, 33), Hooker's primary commitment to reality over theology is an important feature of what we may call the 'central' mind. The strict Calvinist's primary allegiance to the absolute truth of the Word and mistrust of the veracity of appearances tend on the other hand to favour abstraction over actuality and to insist that reality be brought to square with theory.

Where Calvin understood the sacraments as seals of the Covenant, Hooker stressed their value as *participation* in Christ. The difference hinges once again not on a doctrinal point, but on the way meaning is seen to reside in the elements of the Eucharist, and how this may be received by the believer. Calvin held that faith gives the sign meaning as the spiritual gift of Christ's redemption. Without this faith the sign empties itself of meaning and becomes a vessel without content. Calvin describes the hollowness of the Word if it is not received faithfully:

> a Sacrament is so separated from the reality by the unworthiness of the partaker, that nothing remains but an empty and useless figure. Now, in order that you may have not a sign devoid of truth, but the thing with the sign, the Word which is included in it must be apprehended by faith ... the office of the sacrament differs not from the word of God; and this is to hold forth and offer Christ to us, and, in him, the treasures of the heavenly grace. They confer nothing, and avail nothing, if not received in faith ...
> All signs become null when the thing signified is taken away.
>
> (*Institutes*, II, 502–3; 509)

The puritan unsure of his own election finds himself in a world of empty, unreadable symbols, a threateningly inscrutable surface whose depths he cannot plumb. Outer and inner, symbol and significance, word and thing become part of the Calvinist structure of polarities, and part of the puritan–provincial rhetoric of distance.

For Hooker, on the other hand, meaning is inherent in the elements *as* sacraments: the bread and wine are vehicles of grace which are not dependent upon the state of mind of the receiver. They may not be efficacious if received in the wrong spirit, but 'the elements and words have power of infallible signification, for which they are called seales of Gods trueth' (III, 85). The verbal contrasts between the two accounts of sacramental meaning reflect fundamentally divergent understandings of the nature of reality:

> For wee take not baptisme nor the Eucharist for bare resemblances or memorialls of thinges absent, neither for naked signes and testimonies assuringe us of grace received before, but (as they are indeed and in veritie) for meanes effectuall whereby God when wee take the sacraments delivereth into our handes that grace available unto eternall life, which grace the sacramentes represent or signifie. (II, 247)

While for the Anglican the sign and what it signifies are in coherent and constant relation – 'our souls may receive and possess Christ as truly and certainly as the material and visible signs are by us seen and received' – for the Calvinist, the relationship is always precarious and threatens to overturn received meaning in favour of unapprehended 'significance'.[24] Just as the signified tended to overwhelm the sign for the Roman Catholic believer in transubstantiation, so the Calvinist swung to the opposite extreme in insinuating the domination of the sign over what it signified. In both cases, this undermines the confidence with which the sacraments may be received as '*pledges* and *assurances* of the interest which we have in the heavenly things which are represented by them'.[25]

SELF AND OTHER: PURITAN CHURCH AND COMMUNITY

Hooker's notion of communion in the sacraments may be summed up by St Paul's phrase, 'we being many are one bread, and one body; for we are all partakers of the one bread' (1 Corinthians 10: 17). Both otherness and relationship are preserved here as they cannot be in puritan theology, which leads always in the direction either of alienation from or subsumption in the other. The typological and allegorical frame of mind does help to mitigate the individual's sense of being at sea in a world of threateningly significant but seemingly random facts, but paradoxically this same frame of mind is also responsible for the sense of isolation. In his quest for significant information pertaining to the state of his own soul, the Calvinist is unable to imagine the 'other' as anything but a message to him, a distorted reflection of something within. For all its insistence on the transcendence of God and the littleness of man, Calvinism takes an ineluctably anthropocentric view of the universe. One reason for the terrifying aloneness which man feels in this world is that he simply fails to *see* that which is beyond himself, to apprehend and accept otherness.

Everything is a reflection, an emblem of his inner state – or it is nothing. The puritan community structured itself on principles of exclusion and mutual observation: the elect watched the unconverted and defined themselves in opposition to them; the unconverted watched themselves, nature and each other (for signs of election), and the elect (for guidance); an inscrutable God watched all men.

Self-investigation was not of course peculiar to Calvinists in the seventeenth century: contemplation of the self by the self is the leading feature, for example, of the meditations of Donne, Vaughan and Thomas Browne. Again, it is the attitude towards the act that distinguishes them: the Calvinist scrutinises his soul in all seriousness, as it were – and indeed, what he finds there is a matter of eternal life or death to him – while the Anglican can catch himself in the act, can eavesdrop on his own self-questionings; can, in short, find a perspective from which to view his own littleness without belittling it, by recognising a centre beyond himself.

The other potential danger of there being no 'middle term' between the soul and God – again one which covenant theology attempted to mitigate, with partial and temporary success – was relativism: without an externally constituted authority, no man's judgement could be subject to that of another. While Hooker placed much importance on consensus, and allowed nature, reason and tradition to support the Word of Scripture, for Calvin obedience was enjoined to God's properly constituted authorities only through His decree, and the individual was left alone with his own uncertainty. The unresolvable conflicts of viewpoint to which this 'freedom' could lead delighted anti-puritan satirists of Elizabethan and Jacobean England. John Selden, for example, caricatured the position of the puritan who 'would be judged by the Word of God: if he would speak clearly he means himself, but that he is ashamed to say so; and he would have me believe him before a whole church, that have read the word of God as well as he. One says one thing, and another another; and there is . . . no measure to end the controversy.'[26]

The thought (as Selden put it) that 'disputes in religion will never be ended' was one that the Anglican could cheerfully concede; but everything in Calvinism abhorred such willingness to suspend judgement: toleration would lead to laxity, and it presaged moral and spiritual degeneracy. The pattern of conversion recorded in the spiritual autobiographies was a *necessary* one, and deviation from the right path meant certain disaster, as the companions of Bunyan's Christian found when they chose other routes which better suited their temperaments:

> But when they saw that the Hill was steep and high, and that there was two other ways to go; and supposing also that these two ways might meet again, with that up which Christian went, on the other side of the Hill: Therefore

they were resolved to go in those ways; (now the name of one of those ways was Danger, and the name of the other Destruction). So the one took the way which is called Danger, which led him into a great Wood; and the other took directly up the way to Destruction, which led him into a wide field full of dark Mountains, where he stumbled and fell, and rose no more.[27]

Puritans, then, demanded resolution of 'disputes in religion' and the establishment of the one true Church, even as their habits of mind rendered consensus unattainable. Otherness was a threat unless it could be colonised for the self; the pressure on individual consciousness was such that to observe something which did not fit one's own pattern of meaning was to jeopardise the precariously held order of that pattern.

The powerful attraction of the Calvinist towards monovalency – the right path, the one true Church – was partly a response to the deep divisions which structured his perceptions. This dualism struggled always towards resolution, a resolution which could be pursued as long as there was confidence that a 'transcendent signified' – God – was at the centre controlling the generation of meaning; but once the confidence which held the first puritans in an undeviating principle of knowing God's will gave way to doubt, nothing remained to check the oscillations of mood and interpretation.

Although puritans lived always in the balance of extremes, not all puritans were extremists; from Calvin himself pastors enjoined men to 'observe a mean' (*Institutes*, II, 31) and to believe that Grace was necessarily accompanied by Works, while theologians fought a continuing battle against 'heretics' within the system who exploded the precarious paradox and carried its logic in opposing directions. *Either* man is saved by grace alone and his salvation is absolutely predetermined by God and independent of civil or moral laws (the Antinomian position, held for example in Massachusetts by Anne Hutchinson and in fiction, much later, by James Hogg's Robert Wringhim (see chapter 4), *or* works *are* efficacious, which suggests that man can be saved by his own efforts and may prejudice the divine dispensation towards him (the position of the Arminians, who repudiated extreme predestination and believed that Christ died to enable salvation for *all* men and that salvation can be resisted or refused).[28] Both the spiritual 'inner light' of the eighteenth-century Awakenings and the liberalising theology are here: from the beginning, Calvinism constantly threatened to polarise towards Antinomianism and Arminianism in one guise or another. For the believer (drawn as he always was to take one step further in the direction of a definable position, a logical certainty) the middle ground was a slippery and uncertain foothold; the dangers of hypocrisy – of living in the flesh *and* being of it – of presumption and of immorality were ever present.

The 'British Church', as George Herbert put it, displayed 'A fine aspect in fit aray, / Neither too mean nor yet too gay'; it was characterised by its position between the 'hills' of Rome and the 'valley' of the puritans.[29] The middle ground is essentially a non-doctrinal position; it has nothing to prove, no territory to stake out for its own. For the puritan, such ground is always hard won, because he knows the extremes more intimately in his own experience. The poised holding of opposites, when it does occur in puritan writing, is correspondingly rarer, more striking. It takes the form of the ability to hold 'either/or' steadily in the mind as 'both/and', to perceive intuitively the meaning of oxymorons like 'strenuous passivity' and the connection between predestination and free will. Where the Anglican seeks participation in Christ through reason and action, the thrust of puritan endeavour is always towards knowledge: the discovery of the predestined will of God. His desire is to move from observation to possession.

PURITANISM IN SCOTLAND AND AMERICA

In Old Testament theology, God's original covenants were made with the Jews, the 'chosen people' whom He promised to lead to salvation. Making covenants with the deity confirms the sense of specialness, apartness, of small and threatened communities on the fringes of a more powerful 'central' culture. It is self-definition by opposition, exclusion and *purpose*. This sense of communal election was re-enacted by both Scottish and American Calvinists as they thought about their mission to restore the Church of Christ to its original purity. For the Scots it was a new application of a ferociously maintained national self-image dating back to the St Andrew legends and made explicit in the Declaration of Arbroath (1326), whose conclusion (resounding like an early Declaration of Independence) refuses 'to submit to the rule of the English, for it is not for glory we fight, for riches, or for honours, but for freedom alone, which no good man loses but with his life'.[30] The first formal Scottish Covenant was compacted in 1557; in it the 'Congregation of Christ' bound itself to resist the 'Congregation of Satan': it drew up the boundary lines of inclusion and exclusion. Declaring religious freedom, it also reinforced a pattern of division and opposition.

The National Covenant of 1638 aimed to secure the unique purity of the reformed Scottish church against the papistical innovations of Charles I. This was at once a defensive and a divisive measure: pledging itself to uphold what seemed the incompatible imperatives of King and Presbyterianism, it sought religious unity and national integrity by force of declaration. Reality was muddier, and the upshot was eventually civil war – not only between England and Scotland, but within Scotland itself; but the Covenants of 1557 and 1638 reflect a mood of assertive nationalism and the confidence of being 'centred' by national 'election'.

The sense that the eyes of the world were upon the activities of the chosen nation also determined the self-image of the American puritans, who in their 'Errand into the Wilderness' set about establishing a 'happy *Israel* in America', a 'new Zion' where God's will could be accomplished and biblical prophecies fulfilled.[31] In the post-reformation flush of confidence, Scotland and America (sure of the salvation of their elect communities) saw their social and church covenants as mirrors of the divine Covenant of Grace. The communal bond asserted by the Presbyterian and Congregationalist churches of Scotland and America contrasted with the individual seclusion of English puritans after 1660 and confirmed theocratic power over the Calvinist communities. The absolute division between inclusion and exclusion was controlled and codified: acceptance of the Church covenant was, along with internal assurance of one's own salvation, the prerequisite for membership of the community of the elect.

The Calvinist pastorate in both Presbyterian Scotland and Congregational New England repeatedly called for boundaries to be established between the elect and the reprobate. This was the burden of John Knox's fearsome sermons on predestination, and was codified in the Scottish 'Confession of Faith' in 1647. The solidarity and strong sense of identity of these covenanted communities established them in their own eyes as islands of virtue in a sea of sin. When, later, loss of confidence in the divine mission and falling church membership contributed to making subscription to the covenant a *substitute* for conviction of faith, the balance between Grace and Works was disrupted. But so long as Scots and Americans believed that they were indeed chosen people, a shining light to the rest of the world, covenant theology held the opposing strains of activism and passivity in viable tension.

In this first flush of activity and 'mission', the Calvinists' energies were other-directed, the enemy to be fought external and easily recognised. God's will seemed clear, and the strait way to salvation was well lit. This is not to say that Calvinist individuals did not doubt and search their consciences anxiously for 'signs' of election, but that collectively the Scottish and American Calvinist communities were operating at the active end of their emotional pendulum swing, and that in so doing they were able to resolve – or sometimes to evade – the logical paradoxes of their theoretical position.

In Scotland, the Reformation proceeded from the beginning in opposition to crown and court; Presbyterianism had to fight for both its birth and its right to live. The puritans who fled from religious oppression in England to the perils of the American wilderness also defined everything they did and wrote in opposition to the corruption and evil which constantly sought to engulf them. But both Scottish and American puritans had Calvin's own testimony to the sanctity of persecution as a special mark of God's favour (*Institutes*, II, 20), so opposition was in fact a confirmation of divine mission. It became a principle of action, a habit of mind and a form of writing. The worst thing that could happen to the Calvinist who defined himself either as God's chosen example to the world or as His soldier was that the world should take no notice of his paradigm or of his antagonism. This was exactly what did happen to the Scottish and American puritans as they became increasingly isolated from the hub of English life. The sense of distance from the centre and the accompanying loss of confidence in the special destiny of his mission sowed the seed of doubt in the puritan's mind. Perhaps, after all, he was not chosen; perhaps he was one of the reprobate, doomed to struggle unnoticed at an infinite distance from God. It was the mark that – the sustaining moment of crisis having past – the puritan was becoming a provincial.

So the emotional pendulum swung back as historical events confirmed the cast of mind. Scottish Presbyterians were forced further and further into opposition and isolation by what they saw as the apostasy of their English puritan allies during the Civil War. With the political provincialism which followed the Union of Crowns in 1603, the Scottish reformed church became increasingly identified with defensive nationalism, particularly after the savage repression of the Covenanters following the Restoration. As it became less outward looking, the characteristic puritan point of view swung from action to passivity: its hallmark became observation of and resistance to the actions of the distant, oppressing centre.

In America, the confidence of the first settlers in the centrality of their mission was shaken when they realised that – far from all eyes being on them in their errand to save Christianity in England – they were ignored. Conceived originally as the radical spearhead of reformed religion, the American puritan community was forced to watch events in England during and following the Civil War by-pass its position and leave the new Zion stranded high and dry on its hill. The New England puritans were no longer active pioneers observed by the world, but passive observers of the real theatre of action in England.

Deprived of the possibility of action to define and project their self-image, Calvinists found the paradoxes and divisions of their doctrine reflected inwards: because of its affinity with reprobation, any state of enforced passivity was extreme torment for the puritan, who was driven thereby to find within himself the poles of spiritual conflict and to become the living embodiment of a paradox. Without an external antagonist, the soul alone became God's battleground; in the passivity of his provincial distance the puritan's mind tended to bifurcate treacherously, to reveal the inherent tensions of will and spirit. He became two selves – an observer and an actor, a saint and a sinner, regenerate and reprobate – two selves utterly opposed and yet (to the external view and the corrupted conscience) perhaps indistinguishable.

The tensions and tendencies of inward-turned Calvinism are perhaps best illustrated by the horrifying witch trials of the later seventeenth century in which both the New England and the Scottish churches attempted to exorcise their inner demons and purify their societies of the elect. These events bring into disastrous prominence the paradoxes and contradictions of the Calvinist absolutes, the uncertainties of self-observation and the dangers of observing others. These are the contours of puritan–provincial perception which continue to haunt Scottish and American writing into the nineteenth century.

Witchcraft and witch hunts were a recurring feature of mediaeval society; they seem to have operated to release unmanageable tensions of all types, religious, social and sexual, and as a means of containing the damage which these might otherwise do. Historians and sociologists now study them as an index of values and of how a society perceives itself at a particular moment. The most important witch trials in New England were notably late: in Boston in 1688, and in Salem in 1692. In Scotland there were several national witch hunts from 1590 until 1662, but the closest parallels to the New England outbreaks are to be found in the local panics in East Lothian in 1678 and in Paisley in 1697. In Scotland, after the departure of James VI to the English throne in 1603 had deprived the people of a divinely ordained focus for their loyalties, the periodic witch hunts became a way of reaffirming defensively the precarious theocratic solidarity of the Scottish nation. Occurring as they did less than forty years before the repeal of the Scottish Witchcraft Act in 1735, these late manifestations show many similarities to the Boston and Salem incidents, not least in the response by the society as a whole, and its ministers in particular, to the crises. Cotton Mather's *Memorable Providences, Relating to Witchcraft and Possession* (1689) and his *Wonders of the Invisible World* (1693) turned the events to account in his fulminations against backsliding and the disintegration of the society of the elect: New England was scourged by demons in retribution for its apostasy from God. In both Scotland and America a sense of provinciality manifested itself as a fear of assault from without and a corresponding disintegration of the personality from within.

Witch hunts characteristically re-established the boundaries between those inside the community and those beyond the pale. The particular form of the late seventeenth-century Scottish and American witch trials reflected the insecurities of puritan–provincial societies; theocracies become passive and defensive, self-questioning rather than self-assertive. In these trials a form of testimony called 'spectre evidence' assumed crucial importance, to the extent that it became itself the focus of scrutiny and inquiry as events unrolled inexorably and seemingly without limit. 'Spectre evidence' was in essence a logical extension of Calvinist doctrine, an extension liable to present itself at a point of waning confidence. It marks, in the terrifying epistemological void which is opened by questioning the nature – and then the existence – of truth beneath appearances, a significant moment in the evolution of the provincial viewpoint from the puritan one. Calvinist theology insisted that no fact or event was neutral; everything was a 'sign'. Normally, therefore, any evil which occurred to one's body or property was an indication of particular or general depravity; those who continually suffered misfortune or ill health were understood by their neighbours to be – justly – on the sharp end of God's wrath. In times of witchcraft, however, the equations did not seem as simple: personal and social ills (the 'signs') could be attributed to the malice of the Devil, and the individual absolved from responsibility for the affliction. The same might by extension be true for a whole society. The normal relationship between cause and effect, sign and significance, was disrupted and the Calvinist set adrift again in a terrifying world of meaningless clues.

The question of responsibility was central to these Calvinist witch trials. If the man whose cattle died or the girl who was tormented with hysterical fits was not experiencing retribution and was not therefore responsible for these evils, did demonic possession absolve the possessed of moral responsibility for the evils he or she caused to others? 'Spectre evidence' turned on this question: was the visible appearance of a person's 'spectre' (on the testimony of the accuser or a witness) in an incriminating situation reliable evidence that that person had entered a compact with the devil – that is, become a witch? 'Spectre evidence' was for some time admitted by the judges in the New England trials as valid testimony against the accused, despite Cotton Mather's protest that ordinarily malicious people 'may unhappily expose themselves to the judgement of being represented by devils, of whom they never had any vision, and with whom they have much less written any covenant', a sentiment echoed by the Scottish minister John Bell of Gladsmuir in 1703; 'no doubt Satan can go of, and for himself, where he hath no League with the Witch'.[32]

In Scotland, the 'spectre' who haunted the afflicted in the shape of the accused was just one form of the 'familiar' or spirit by which the devil assisted the witch in evil doings; the witch herself often confessed to a polarisation of good and evil into independently acting entities within herself. At this point Calvinist theology reinforced pagan folk beliefs about the 'coimhmeadh' (co-walker) or *doppelgänger* of Scots-Irish mythology: 'every way like the man, as a twin-brother and companion, haunting him as his shadow . . . whit[h]er to guard him from the secret assaults of som of its own folks, or only as a sportful ape to counterfeit all his actions'.[33] It would prove a potent image of inner division for puritan–provincial fiction.

The extravagancies by which the afflicted gained and kept the attention of the community turned the investigations into something of a spectator sport: observers were temporarily distanced from the dangers of their own position as they watched Martha Goodwin ride an invisible horse up and down the stairs of Cotton Mather's house or listened fascinated to the confessions of the notorious Scottish warlock Major Weir. The Calvinist community divided into the possessed, the 'actors', and those who observed them, the 'spectators'. This too would become a crucial feature of later Scottish and American writing.

Mather's observations of the bewitched state were part of a larger purpose to accumulate '*evidence* and *argument* as a critical eye-witness to confute the Sadducism of this debauched age'.[34] The observer's stance was dignified, made objective and 'scientific'; this tone informs contemporary accounts, both Scottish and American, which aim to explain the events to an outside audience. Importantly, such narratives were largely composed with an eye to an English audience and received their first publication in England. In Scotland there was at first no readership for these works, while Cotton Mather's *Memorable Providences* (published in Boston in 1689) was written as a contribution to English debate on the subject and republished in London in 1691. (It also had an Edinburgh republication in 1697, the year of the Paisley trials.)

The witchcraft narratives are provincial documents based in puritan presuppositions whose characteristics re-emerge, transformed, in later Scottish and American writing, as philosophy, politics and, finally, fiction: they are carefully composed literary works for a non-local audience, designed to explain mysterious happenings and to justify actions; they anticipate incredulity, misunderstanding, and criticism; they fear ridicule. The author of such a work, be he Cotton Mather or an anonymous Scottish minister, claims impartiality and objectivity as his literary credentials: he is the sympathetic observer, the distanced recorder, and hopes thereby to gain access to the 'centre'.

It was natural that the recording minister or lawyer as author should stand aloof, judge as he was of the evidence represented by others, but (more significantly) it was also *dangerous* to declare an interest in a witch trial, or to become involved in any way. To speak for the defendant risked accusation as a witch's accomplice (and ministers were implicated in some of these trials); to speak against the evidence invited reprisals from the Devil. Observation was safe, participation perilous.

The witchcraft trials brought into the open the fragility of the synthesising faith which made the Calvinist polarities livable by holding them to the 'middle way'. Applying pressure to that synthesis at a point when confident action could not be sustained, these late trials exposed the implicit consequences of the 'either/or' mode of perception for both the Calvinist individual and his society. They were not so much a cause of later events or attitudes as a magnifying glass which brought the inner tensions of puritan–provincial assumptions into an uncomfortably sharp focus. In the shadow of these monstrous events, the absolute separability of appearance from reality might become a daily problem of living; the insecurity engendered as husband accused wife and neighbour gave evidence against neighbour destroyed the illusion of social coherence, of the unification and common interests of the community of the elect. No relationship could be taken for granted; it became clear that the individual was threatened with living in absolutely literal terms the spiritual isolation to which his theology consigned him. Under conditions of such intense and defensive observation the relationship of self and other became increasingly problematic.

As usual, the puritan could go either way: he either fell back upon the absolute separation between man and man, which despite its awful aloneness had its consolations (at least it was clear that every other was potentially a betrayer and an enemy), or he entertained the possibility that self and other might be interchangeable, that to 'sympathise' with another meant to become that person, to know his inmost thoughts, and that one's own self was liable to similar invasion or colonisation. Such a view seemed inherent in the 'evidence' the witch trials provided that the mind might be possessed by an alien, satanic will. This brought into question the nature of the relationships between passivity and action, between action and responsibility, between responsibility and freedom.

The witch trials translated a theological and philosophical debate directly without an imaginative transformation into the terms of a human life, with intolerable consequences and unleashing almost unthinkable possibilities. For the puritan, action is an emblem of moral condition, but that moral condition is undermined if the action may have been prompted by a possessed will. Observation too is untrustworthy when it is at the mercy of diseased and corrupted perceptions. These events also revealed how useless was reason as a substitute for faith in bridging the gap between word and truth, self and other, free will and predestination as these seemed to structure the boundaries of human life. How could reason mediate between the conflicting claims of accuser and accused, or draw meaningful inferences from the evidence when it was itself *so obviously* tainted and bewildered by the corruption it pretended to judge? As long, that is, as human reason was interpreted in a strictly Calvinist sense.

But the witch trials not only reveal the inherent tensions and paradoxes of strict Calvinism; they also mark the beginnings of its decline as a theocratic power over men's lives. By the end of the seventeenth century, the witch hunt as a collective rite of purification and an affirmation of communal solidarity was a tradition *épuisé* in western culture; its late resurgence in Scotland and America was related to its peculiar alignment with puritan and provincial uncertainties. Despite signalling a nadir of confidence, the Scottish and American outbreaks at the turn of the eighteenth century did not on the whole have catastrophic consequences for their societies: that the implications of the Calvinist witch trials *remained* largely implicit indicates that the disjunction between the principles and the practice of living was increasingly being accommodated by a softening of Calvin's inexorable logic.[35] Men might still pay lip-service to the concept of Original Sin, but at the dawn of an 'Age of Reason' they were becoming unwilling to concede that this entailed the absolute untrustworthiness of the rational faculty. But the discontinuous viewpoint of the puritan persisted into eighteenth- and nineteenth-century Scottish and American thought to structure it around polar oppositions of observation and action, alienation and possession, emptiness and absolute significance. The provincial continued to find it difficult, as the puritan had done, to bring the sign and what it signified into a meaningful relation which preserved the identity of each, to accept the contingent and to rest in participation.

2

After Armageddon: Jonathan Edwards and David Hume

> For if these [Calvinist] doctrines, in the whole length and breadth of them were relinquished, he did not see, where a man could set his foot down with consistency and safety, short of Deism, or even Atheism itself; or rather universal Skepticism. (Samuel Hopkins on Jonathan Edwards)[1]

Eighteenth-century attempts to accommodate Calvin's theology to the visible achievements of reason are the strongest currents of continuity between puritanism and provincialism. No longer carried high on the triumphant confidence of the critical moment, puritans were brought to reckon with forces which indicated other 'centres' of experience beyond the grasp of their apocalyptic dogma; the exclusive qualities of Calvinist faith made it unable to coexist with the claim of reason to be a source of knowledge and belief, but demanded confrontation and either dominance of or submission to these claims.

Against the increasing consciousness of eccentricity which marks eighteenth-century Calvinism's struggle to find a place for itself in the 'Age of Reason', two voices stand out at opposite ends of the anti-rational spectrum. Jonathan Edwards was the strongest spokesman for orthodox Calvinism bred by New England; David Hume was a Scot who, relinquishing his Calvinist upbringing, set his foot down – with consistency if not with safety – at the other extreme of 'universal Skepticism'. Both, through the unwavering clarity and confidence with which they perceived the contours of the puritan mind, maintained a poise of detached participation which holds their writing tautly on the near side of provincialism.

The 'Awakenings' in New England operated like the witch trials to re-establish clear principles of social identity by exerting the pressure of communal scrutiny on individual behaviour. In this case the aim was to convert the 'observing' members of the community enlisted under the Half-Way Covenants to fully participant 'saints'. The Half-Way Covenants were introduced by a synod in 1662 to counteract the falling numbers of communicants without acceding to the 'open' policy of communion offered by Edwards' grandfather Solomon Stoddard. They implied a two-tier system which divided society into potentially elect 'observers' and actually saved 'participants', and seemed to many to blur insidiously the boundary line between elect and reprobate. The new 'rational' Calvinists who supported the temporising methods of the Half-Way Covenants increasingly aligned themselves with the liberalising propensities of the English and European Enlightenments and declared their trust in human reason as a way to God. In opposition to this softening, the fundamentalist Calvinist George Whitefield stressed the *depravity* of human reason and found a route back, in the religious 'Awakenings' of the 1730s and 40s, to religious belief through the affections – the 'heart' – alone. By inciting the Half-Way members to declare themselves finally one way or the other, he sought to re-establish the absolute dividing lines of the theocratic society. People queued up to declare their sinfulness, and extravagance and sensationalism inflated the language of depravity until words were superseded by frantic tears, shakings, stampings and fainting fits. The symptoms hardly differed from those of the 'possessed' victims of witchcraft less than fifty years before. There was a strong pull in the puritan psyche towards emotional release, and the new mood seemed another mark of God's special favour to New England, 'a very *extraordinary* dispensation of providence'.[2]

In these circumstances Jonathan Edwards stepped in to confront the Calvinist paradoxes exposed by the witch trials and subsequently debated in the intervening years of theological controversy. With uncompromising orthodoxy his writing attempts to re-enact the synthesis of faith under new conditions. His most famous sermon, 'Sinners in the Hands of an Angry God', riding high on the tide of revivals already begun, provoked a new wave of hysterical conversions at Enfield in 1741. It is easy to see why; Edwards' language exposes all the most terrifying aspects of Calvinist uncertainty: the hollow confidence of the unconverted, 'natural' man's distance from meaning, and the slim comfort that the 'mere arbitrary will and uncovenanted, unobliged forbearance of an incensed God' is all that stands between man and the abyss.[3] Edwards reiterates the theme of estrangement and exclusion (which seventeenth-century covenant theology and eighteenth-century rationalism were attempting to mitigate) in his sermon, 'The Christian Pilgrim' (1733), where he picks up the image (endemic to puritan literature) of the Christian as a stranger on earth, a traveller or sojourner on his way to a heavenly home. The motif would structure a significant number of nineteenth-century Scottish and American fictions:

> A traveller is not wont to rest in what he meets with, however comfortable and pleasing on the road. If he passes through pleasant places . . . his journey's end is in his mind . . . these things are not his own . . . he is but a stranger . . . There is but a very imperfect union with God to be had in this world . . . a very imperfect conformity to God, mingled with abundance of estrangement.[4]

But Edwards' orthodoxy is not atavistic, a mere restatement of Calvinist dogma: its concerns and its manner are drawn from a thoroughly eighteenth-century desire to reconcile the facts of experience to the structures of belief, and in his writing at its best life and thinking about life cohere in an act of faith which can, defeating the powers of reason, turn an inhuman thought into a beautiful one.[5] The basis of this synthesis in Edwards' prose is a unique combination of sensationalist epistemology and Calvinist dogma; he attempts to shore up faith against the temporising claims of reason and to establish the puritan temper as an universal psychology.

The theological and epistemological questions which motivate his subsequent writing were initially posed for Edwards, as matters of urgent practical observation and problems of behaviour, by the religious Awakenings in Northampton. Edwards welcomed the effects of the revival on his community while deploring and being deeply worried by its excesses. Congregations were vast, sermons once more had visible effect and immorality all but disappeared from the town. But there were, as he would put it later, 'false Appearances' and 'corrupt Mixtures' in the leaven of conversions which *seemed* to testify to the salvation of such a large number of souls. Many conversions were only temporary; the authenticity of others looked questionable from the beginning. When was a conversion not a conversion? How could one tell? Edwards' own *Personal Narrative* (written around 1739 at the height of an earlier local wave of revival) embodies just such an anxiety, which rapidly becomes a matter of verbal and semantic insecurity, as to the precise *meaning* of spiritual movements felt in the soul. As Edwards saw it, this had to do with the way in which the relationship between the perceiver and experience could only be expressed through a language designed (or so he understood Locke) to be descriptive of *external* phenomena. Such a language had no tools to distinguish the true from the false in an experience which was entirely internal.

In a letter to Benjamin Colman of Boston (a sceptical observer of the 'Surprising Work of God') in 1737, Edwards voiced some of the difficulties:

> There have indeed been some few instances of impressions on persons' imaginations, that have been something mysterious to me, and I have been at a

> loss about them; for though it has been exceeding evident to me by many things that appeared in them, both then (when they related them) and afterwards, that they indeed had a great sense of the spiritual excellency of divine things accompanying them; yet I have not been able well to satisfy myself, whether their imaginary ideas have been more than could naturally arise from their spiritual sense of things. However, I have used the utmost caution in such cases; great care has been taken both in public and in private to teach persons the difference between what is spiritual and what is merely imaginary.[6]

There are two keys notions in this passage: the absolute difference between the spiritual and the imaginary, with the difficulty of making this distinction reliably from observation, and the idea that the veracity of a conversion is determined by the presence of a 'spiritual sense' of things. Although the distinction between the spiritual and the imaginary may be imperceptible to the observer, it is a real one, and the 'sufferer' – if we may call him that – can be taught its marks. But the 'spiritual *sense*' (defined in opposition to 'imaginary *ideas*') has absolute authority and is completely internal to the believer. The pastoral advisor found his authority increasingly questioned as the fervour of the Awakenings augmented. It was easy for Edwards to feel that he had lost control of his congregation and become a passive observer of manifestations whose meaning could not be fathomed.

The implications were ominous, but Edwards himself, in a series of sermons delivered prior to the first Northampton Awakenings, had preached reliance on this internal sense as the only true test of salvation. In 'A Divine and Supernatural Light' (1734), he drew a distinction between a rational belief in something and a felt apprehension of its reality. This opposition of head and heart allows him to bridge the puritan gap between corrupt perception and absolute truth. At this point, before the worrying evidence of the Revivals, Edwards confidently makes a direct analogy between the way faith reaches the soul and the way the puritan writer may give the reader access to truth, the 'meaning' behind the words. Both believer and reader must be able to *feel* that truth, not merely assent rationally to it:

> Thus there is a difference between having an opinion that God is holy and gracious, and having a sense of the loveliness and beauty of that holiness and grace. There is a difference between having a rational judgment that honey is sweet, and having a sense of its sweetness. A man may have the former, that knows not how honey tastes; but a man cannot have the latter unless he has an idea of the taste of honey in his mind. So there is a difference between believing that a person is beautiful, and having a sense of his beauty. The former may be obtained by hearsay, but the latter only by seeing the countenance. There is a wide difference between mere speculative rational judging any thing to be excellent, and having a sense of its sweetness and beauty. The former rests only

in the head, speculation only is concerned in it; but the heart is concerned in the latter. When the heart is sensible of the beauty and amiableness of a thing, it necessarily feels pleasure in the apprehension. It is implied in a person's being heartily sensible of the loveliness of a thing, that the idea of it is sweet and pleasant to his soul; which is a far different thing from having a rational opinion that it is excellent.[7]

Edwards' argument liberates a suprarational 'sense' which is the sign of a direct apprehension in the perceiver's soul. The passage is logical and demands rational assent to its progression: 'Thus ... So ... When ... necessarily ... It is implied in ... that ...' The pace is tightly controlled by the parallel layering of its opposed clauses: three times 'the former ... the latter' are formally balanced against one another. And yet through this comes a quite different language which tends always to suggest that the mind (as Edwards puts it elsewhere) is blind, and to oppose thinking *about* something to sensuous apprehension of that thing. Whereas the mind fragments, the 'sense' is unitary and unifying: that single word is opposed successively to 'opinion', to 'rational judgment', to 'believing', and to 'mere speculative rational judging'. And then the connotations of 'sense' are built up: it is associated with 'heart', and then merges through the transitional 'heart is sensible' to compound in the 'heartily sensible'. It is then associated with loveliness, with ideas of the 'sweet' and the 'pleasant' gathered into his 'soul'; the rational mind is carried by the language of the Psalms and the Song of Solomon out of its grammatically ordering propensities to the unmediated sensuous apprehension of qualities. Subject, verb and object dissolve and mingle in the expansive immediacy, the naming power of the noun: 'God is holy and gracious' becomes, simply, 'holiness and grace'; 'honey is sweet' becomes 'sweetness'; 'person is beautiful' becomes 'beauty'. The reader is called to experience directly, to bypass thought and move in to know the quality by filling himself full of it.

It is a brilliant passage, which manages to walk the tightrope of its oppositions with a control which neither falters nor constrains. Edwards never (here or elsewhere) denies the value – indeed the necessity – of reason in human apprehension of the world, but he is clear not only (as an Anglican would also be) about its insufficiency, but also about its *irrelevance* to grace. The 'divine and supernatural light' bypasses all efforts to deflect it into the mind and shines directly into the soul. The prose enacts this, its rational framework providing only a structure to 'contain' the meaning, which is luminous through it. For Edwards, as for Calvin, the word is an emblematic vessel of meaning; the 'supernatural light' of experienced truth pierces the masking adjectival 'holy', 'gracious' and 'sweet' to the essential 'sweetness' and 'grace'.

In this sermon Edwards conveys the essence of conversion as an experience. He relies heavily on words like 'sweetness', 'beauty' and 'amiableness', but their tightly held place in the patterning of the prose rescues them from abstraction or evasiveness. Edwards is one of the few puritans whose writing demonstrates the necessary relationship between the word and the truth it contains while remaining faithful to the Calvinist symbolising, which insists on the division between the sign and what is signifies. To read this passage is to perform something like the transition between thinking about sweetness and tasting honey: Edwards provides an analogy for the qualitative change in perception which prepares the heart to receive God's grace. If the 'spiritual sense' can be understood to be like the sense of taste or of sight, then the 'sweetness' or 'beauty' of its perceptions may seem similarly available to description.

Edwards' own conversion narrative continually returns to the double question of 'what is a conversion?' and 'how can it be described?' in ways that draw on, but frequently also appear to undermine, his more analytic writings *about* the conversion experience. In the puritan universe theory and practice must be made to confirm each other; but they frequently do so only under some strain. Edwards' *Personal Narrative* does not clearly signpost the 'stages' of experience charted in conventional spiritual autobiography, although all of these are recognisably present. Instead, what *happens* is to an unusual extent synonymous with 'how can it be described?'; the inadequacy of language points to something at the very heart of the experience itself. What is required of the puritan 'saint' is an emptying of self, not a self-projection, and this sits uneasily with the role of autobiographer.

The *Personal Narrative* insists from the outset on the absolute separateness of grace from will and action. Here is the frustration of the Calvinist: the necessity of doing everything to encourage, to facilitate the entry of grace into the heart, in the full knowledge that such efforts are not merely useless but may themselves testify to the continuing corruption of the soul. Striving after virtue is necessary to avoid falling into despair and apathy, but it plays no part in salvation.

By casting his account in personal terms, Edwards inevitably involved himself in a narrative 'I' and put himself, the self-questioning sinner, at the centre of the stage. His own mind is the theatre of God's unfolding plan for him and, emblematically, for the world. The questing will cannot simply deny itself. Even in self-abasement it enacts the paradox of willed will-lessness:

> I love to think of coming to Christ, to receive salvation of him, poor in spirit, and quite empty of self, humbly exalting him alone; cut off entirely from my own root, in order to grow into, and out of Christ: to have God in Christ to be all in all; and to live by faith on the Son of God, a life of humble, unfeigned confidence in him.[8]

This begins to suggest how the 'empty self' which comes later to be at the heart of puritan–provincial Scottish and American literature is actually profoundly egotistical. Wilfully denying an inviolable centre of self – a self centred outside itself, in God – and yearning for deracination from the soil of this world (thereby refusing a steadying social dimension), Edwards' image enacts the paradox of will, 'organised and disciplined and inspired . . . quiescent in rapt adoration or straining in violent energy, but always will', which R.H. Tawney defines as the quintessence of puritanism.[9] As Edwards recounts the successive forms of his search for salvation, it becomes apparent that he can neither eradicate nor circumvent will. Even the moments of visionary rapture only take their place in the narrative with an overlay of willed significance. As soon as the mind begins to reflect on its experiences, the will orders them in accordance with its desires. For the puritan, the emblematic nature of events assures this.

The Calvinist's will is his greatest burden: he has to live with its pervasive corruption, knowing that it is this which interposes between the self and God's grace. But it is also his chief glory; it is the tragic self that rebels against the immutable justice of its fate, that affirmation of otherness which refuses to be absorbed, displaced or possessed by the general good. The will's refusal to renounce its claims in defeat turns the static state of predestination into a dramatic narrative and keeps alive the tension of crisis and conflict in the puritan–provincial mind.

The opposition of self-directed will and quiescent spirit means that Edwards' *narrative* can never quite bring his experience to the point of definition. Its emotional force tends always to dissolve under pressure from his subsequent analytical scrutiny: 'My experience had not then taught me, as it has done since, my extreme feebleness and impotence, every manner of way; and the bottomless depths of secret corruption and deceit there were in my heart' (p.182). Each new low (or high) point touched by the narrative is rendered provisional and inadequate in the retelling by a subsequent knowledge of even lower (or higher) states, until language itself is exhausted of superlatives and reduced to a litany of incapacity: 'I know not how to express better what my sins appear to me to be, than by heaping infinite upon infinite, and multiplying infinite by infinite. Very often, for these many years, these expressions are in my mind, and in my mouth, "Infinite upon infinite – infinite upon infinite!"' (p.187). In this respect Edwards (like many Calvinist writers) makes a virtue of his frustration at the impossibility of *forcing* the word to give up its meaning, of rendering 'truth' directly on the printed page.[10] Calvin's own rhetoric rises to heights of metaphorical eloquence as he attempts to evoke the torments of reprobation, but his analogies are insistent and coercive, and provide no space into which the reader may move to grasp hold of their meaning. Assertion cannot overcome the distance between rhetoric and experience. It is the dilemma of Melville's Ahab, in *Moby-Dick*:

> All visible objects . . . are but as pasteboard masks. But in each event — in the living act, the undoubted deed — there, some unknown but still reasoning thing puts forth the mouldings of its features from behind the unreasoning mask. If man will strike, strike through the mask! . . . That inscrutable thing is chiefly what I hate . . .[11]

With the events of the Revivals clearly in mind, Edwards produced his major theoretical study of conversion, *A Treatise Concerning Religious Affections* (1746). The *Religious Affections* investigates the nature, apprehension and effects of the 'spiritual sense' and in the process throws Calvin's distinction between words and things into a thoroughly eighteenth-century arena. The excessive emotionalism of the Revivals combined with recent memories of the mind's delusion by 'spectre evidence' in the witch trials to make moderate Calvinists doubt the wisdom of denying a place to reason in estimating the quality of an impression when it seemed that it was 'not above the power of Satan to suggest thoughts to men; because otherwise he could not tempt them to sin'.[12] The *Religious Affections* addresses the problem of how accurately phantoms or appearances mirror reality, and (by extension) asks how the mind can ever 'know' reality. Edwards — refusing to countenance the claims of reason — bases his defence of the legitimacy of the movements of the heart on the distinction (most conveniently expounded by Locke) between primary sense-impressions and the mind's combination of these to form complex ideas.

Locke considered the integrity of the personality as unquestionable; to suppose the soul to 'think' and the mind not to perceive it would be, he said, 'to make two Persons in one Man' — and that 'would be suspected of Jargon'.[13] What was 'Jargon' to Locke, and would have been 'cant' to Samuel Johnson, was perfectly congenial to the puritan–provincial outlooks of Edwards, Hume and Adam Smith: for them, the potentially divided personality was a ready-made Calvinist metaphor for the workings of the mind.

Edwards, then, divides the mind into 'two faculties': an observer 'capable of perception and speculation' and a more active faculty which is 'some way inclined with respect to the things it views or considers' (p.96). The first faculty, or *understanding*, is 'an indifferent unaffected spectator'; the second, or *inclination*, is a participant (p.96). When expressed in action, the inclination is called *will*; when felt strongly in the mind alone it is called *heart*. Intellect and feeling are opposed as they had been in 'A Divine and Supernatural Light'. A true 'religious affection' may be distinguished from a 'passion' – which might be false, or even emanate directly from the devil – in that the mind is not overborne by the strength of the impression, but is always in control and able to choose. The moral freedom of a religious affection contrasts not only with the passions, which coerce the will, but also with the passivity of the understanding, which can only receive sense-impressions and record them without either judging or acting. The two faculties are integral: the individual is always both observer *and* actor; but they also divide the self. A perception may be analysed as either one of the mind or of the heart.[14]

Calvinist notions of division and distanced (alienated) observation also structure Edwards' probing of contemporary empiricist thinking about the distinction between words (as signs) and the things they represent. Where Locke assumed that things in nature and ideas in the mind are linked by the words that describe and symbolise them, Edwards suggests that in the absence of faith, words as the product of the corrupt perceptions of the mind are unstable arbitrary symbols of the realities they claim to represent. For the unregenerate, living with words or signs alone interposes a distance between them and reality; they stand aloof from the world, observing and eavesdropping on real experience. 'The mind', says Edwards, 'makes use of signs instead of the ideas themselves.'[15] The 'rhetoric of distance' which describes this position is that of the rational believer in the sweetness of honey who has never experienced its taste; it is the stance too of Hawthorne's Coverdale, the compulsive observer of the real lives of others.

Emotional apprehension (as in 'A Divine and Supernatural Light') involves divine grace; reuniting the word with the thing, it allows the self to become *involved* with the objects it contemplates. The word, passionately apprehended, is truth. For Edwards, the reunion takes place entirely from within, dissolving distance and alienation: we know reality, through grace, internally. God 'acts *upon* the mind of a natural man, but he acts *in* the mind of a saint as an indwelling vital principle ... he doth unite himself to them'.[16] Regeneration re-establishes the direct congruence between an idea in the mind and the object it refers to; conversion clears the imagination of the veil of corruption which the Fall had interposed between perception and reality. Signs are firm and interpretable, stablised, as it were, by God.

In Part II of the *Religious Affections*, Edwards investigates the reliability of self-observation and the observation of others as indices of true religious inclination and salvation. He concludes that outward signs such as 'fluent, fervent and abundant ... talking of the things of religion' cannot confirm either 'that affections are truly gracious affections, or that they are not' (p.135). He asserts on the other hand (p.151), that we cannot reason backwards from the *effects* of grace as they are felt in the heart to the *means* by which it entered, or to its nature. The uncertainty in outward signs of grace also denies access to another's soul (p.181). Although a man has a duty to discover 'experimentally' (by the guidelines laid down in Part III of the *Religious Affections*) whether or not he is saved, his observations of others may not lead to any final judgement as to the state of *their* souls. The tests he is to apply reiterate that the observer (or the 'conscience') is *internal* to the self and has no external legitimacy. The communal sanctions which held the early societies of the elect together were so weakened by witchcraft and by the self-justifying emotionalism of the Revival that authority seemed now to come from the self, and, in acting, to return to the self. This marks a further stage in the evolution of puritanism into provincialism.

For Edwards, conversion seems to approximate more closely to an aesthetic than to a moral experience. The inadequate snatches of language amount to a glimpse of the beauty of holiness, a new way of perceiving the world and one's place in it. In his review of Soame Jenyns' work on the origin and nature of evil, Samuel Johnson insists that 'it is the consequences ... of all human actions that must stamp their value'.[17] Edwards has no confidence that an action *can* be judged on its consequences: throughout the *Personal Narrative* the value of virtuous action is undermined by its origin in natural (and therefore corrupt) rather than spiritual impulses. The test of experience, which to Johnson is always the great winnower of theory, cannot be applied, and Edwards is left with the imperfectness with which language can render his *sense* of an inner change.

The *summa* of Edwards' thinking about grace is his posthumously published work, *The Nature of True Virtue* (written 1755–8), which describes conversion in terms of harmony between individual being and Being in general, a kind of concord which anticipates the transcendental unity. The beautiful harmony of grace is a gift bestowed quite independently of virtuous action, and to speak of it requires the passive voice. The concept of harmony also modifies significantly the isolation of the self-observing consciousness implicit in the *Religious Affections* and the writings of the Awakenings: the elect are drawn to one another by sympathy of spirit. This, says Edwards, is our only means of mutual understanding:

> We have no other ways to conceive of anything which other persons act or suffer, but by recalling and exciting the ideas of what we ourselves are conscious we have found in our own minds; and by ... substituting ourselves in their place.[18]

The idea of setting the self outside itself to observe others and to enter their experience by sympathetic identification significantly anticipates

Adam Smith's *Theory of Moral Sentiments* (to be discussed below). Even more significant, however, is Edwards' concept of self-disagreement, which suggests that exactly the same process of doubling and observation takes place in the operations of conscience *within the self*:

> when a man's conscience disapproves of his treatment of his neighbour, in the first place he is conscious, that if he were in his neighbour's stead, he should resent such treatment from a sense of justice . . . And then in the next place, he perceives that therefore he is not consistent with himself, in doing what he himself should resent in that case; and hence disapproves it, as being naturally averse to opposition to himself.[19]

Sympathy is irresistible: it may neither be willed towards the unregenerate, nor refused to the fellow-saint. Edwards believed, however, that sympathy (through God's grace working in the saint) could *induce* regeneration and salvation in another: he who could see the beauty described by the preacher, for example, was thereby prepared to receive grace and be converted. When John Witherspoon (the evangelical Scots Calvinist who became President of the College of New Jersey) lectured on 'Eloquence', he secularised this transcendent ethical sympathy into an aesthetic principle: the 'excellence' of eloquence, he said, lay 'in making another perceive what I perceive, and feel towards it as I feel'.[20] The simultaneously passive and coercive qualities of this Calvinist-derived notion of sympathy continue through the work of Hume and Adam Smith and have important consequences for Scottish and American nineteenth-century fiction.

Edwards subjects the question of passivity and action to a fundamental reconsideration in his other major theological treatise, *A Careful and Strict Enquiry into the Modern Prevailing Notions of . . . Freedom of the Will . . .* (1754). In this work he reasserts against the Arminians the uncompromising Calvinist principle of absolute predestination and demonstrates that determinism is incompatible neither with free choice nor with moral responsibility. In redrawing the boundary lines between the polarities of action and passivity, Edwards distinguishes between necessity and compulsion: the will chooses to act and is able to act as it chooses, but the grounds of its choice are determined. Moral responsibility is founded in the *engagedness* of the will: our actions are praiseworthy or blameworthy 'not so properly because they are *from* us, as because we are *in them*, i.e. our wills are in them; not so much because they are from some *property* of ours, as because they are our *properties*'.[21] Once again the puritan viewpoint makes *possession* rather than *participation* the consequence of abandoning neutrality by the act of will. Volition is determined by our inclination towards or against the objects of the understanding; the will always chooses to act on the basis of what it perceives to be the greatest good. Freedom, Edwards says, is to act within the constraints established by divine order; those who attempt to deny them are enslaved to the arbitrary and corrupt motions of their fallen natures.

Discussing the will's initiation of action on the basis of prior passive observation by the understanding, Edwards as an orthodox Calvinist questions man's ability to reason backwards from an action to its 'cause'. In any case, he doubts the stepping-stone sequence of causality and prefers to see the connection between an act and its determinant as 'antecedence': part of the harmonious web of universal relationships in the unchanging mind of God (p.180). Edwards continues to believe in causation as events in the world obey God's will, but (like Hume) he holds that perception rather than *a priori* relation determines human beliefs about cause and effect. Causation is a human construct born of man's need to introduce an intelligible middle term between the events he perceives and wills and their determining source in God's will. It is a product of human frailty, a 'covenant of meaning' which brings the time-bound into relation with the eternal:

> if once it should be allowed, that things may come to pass without a cause, we should not only have no proof of the being of God, but we should be without evidence of the existence of any thing whatsoever, but our own immediately present ideas and consciousness. For we have no way to prove anything else, but by arguing from effects to causes: from the ideas now immediately in view, we argue other things not immediately in view: from sensations now excited in us, we infer the existence of things without us... If things may be without causes, all this necessary connection and dependence is dissolved, and so all means of our knowledge is gone. (p.183)

The relationship between the individual's partial knowledge and experience of an event and God's encompassing foreknowledge and determination of that event can only be defined provisionally, and with respect to the point of view of the perceiving consciousness. Where we shall see Hume accepting the principle of causation as one of the mind's necessary fictions, and none the less finding space for moral action and personal responsibility, Edwards redeems his position from scepticism by reasserting the external Covenant of Grace whereby God grants man a vision of absolute truth through faith. Despite the partiality of the individual viewpoint, there exists a 'centre' beyond the self, in God.

In both cases, however, radical solipsism is a mere doubt away. Hume and Edwards, with their Calvinist backgrounds, move swiftly into the gap between objective reality and the perceptions of the mind which Locke's *Essay* insouciantly exposes. Where Locke assumes a direct correlation between the two, Edwards and Hume accept that there may be no connection whatever and that the objective world may be forever inaccessible to the perceiving consciousness. In these conditions, the mind is not the master of its environment; it is a bundle of impulses and desires, defined by its responses to sensations whose generation may be entirely internal. Edwards calls this the condition of Fallen man, and has recourse to Original Sin and the possibility of Redemption to explain it. Hume, discarding theological Calvinism while retaining its mode of reasoning, travels a stage further into the thought processes which would characterise the provincial mind.

DAVID HUME

As a lapsed Calvinist brought up and writing in a puritan and provincial society, Hume developed a philosophical *oeuvre* which is strikingly reminiscent, though quite independent, of Edwards' thought. Both writers agree that their theory – as theory – cannot be lived, but they find different ways to accommodate it to life. Edwards attempts to convey the unpalatable religious truths intuitively: his prose works to make us *feel* and *taste* them as through faith. To know truth thus is not merely to believe it, but to delight in it through the operation of a 'religious affection', as Edwards himself came to rejoice in the conviction of God's sovereignty. Hume makes it clear that philosophy and life do not cohere logically: as a philosopher he observes life; as a man he lives or participates in it. Although men cannot live *as* philosophers (or *as* Calvinists), they do not, Hume shows, escape the consequences of their theories in the *way* they live. I shall be concerned here with three aspects of Hume's writing: firstly, with the connection between his philosophy and Calvinist thought; secondly, with the transitions of his writing between the language of puritanism and the self-image of the provincial distanced from the 'meaning' and involvement of the 'centre'; thirdly, with the way his prose enacts the poise which can make the philosophy livable, the poise which lives from a centre of self without being self-centred and which finds a place for mind within a philosophy that declares mind to be evanescent and a fiction.

Hume's *A Treatise of Human Nature* (1739–40) moves from Locke's principles that 'all our ideas are copy'd from our impressions' and that it is 'by EXPERIENCE only, that we can infer the existence of one object from that of another', to demonstrate the impossibility of knowledge about the world other than that provided by the mind's perceptions:

> Let us fix our attention out of ourselves as much as possible: Let us chace our imagination to the heavens, or to the utmost limits of the universe; we never really advance a step beyond ourselves, nor can conceive any kind of existence, but those perceptions, which have appear'd in that narrow compass. This is the universe of the imagination, nor have we any idea but what is there produc'd.[22]

Here is a potent image of self-pursuit, with the imagination at once the seeker and the sought. The Calvinist finds the Fall to account for the gap between subjective perception and objective realities; Hume shows that the mind creates the categories 'subjective' and 'objective' as polarities, and that we have no way of telling whether these correspond to a real ontological division. In a note to Book I of the *Treatise* he says that the attempt to penetrate from 'appearances' to 'reality' is futile, because the mind (the Fallen mind?) has no access to truth beyond its own partial perceptions. Book I proceeds with devastating logic to show the minimal place that reason occupies in human knowledge and behaviour. Strict Calvinists insisted upon the absolute separation of reason and faith; Hume, making the paradox explicit, at once calls into question all intellectual support of belief (by demonstrating that rational attack on faith is nonsensical) and refuses to relinquish reason. It is 'that very suspense or balance, which is the triumph of scepticism'.[23]

He demonstrates with a chain of reasoning very similar to Edwards' that free will is most properly understood as a feeling on the part of the actor; to an observer the same action would look determined. The *position* is in complete agreement with Samuel Johnson's 'all theory is against the freedom of the will; all experience for it', but whereas for Johnson the self-evident primacy of experience makes theorising futile, Hume brings the paradoxical oppositions of theory and practice into confrontation, suggesting that his reader look steadily and simultaneously at both.[24]

Belief as opposed to reason is the vital component in causation, too: when events are observed to be 'constantly conjoined', the mind comes to expect that the appearance of one will be followed by that of the other, and to infer a causal connection between them, although 'the powers, by which bodies operate, are entirely unknown. We perceive only their sensible qualities: and what *reason* have we to think, that the same powers will always be conjoined with the same sensible qualities?'[25] Causality is, then, strictly the *interpretation* of events by the human mind, philosophically unjustifiable but psychologically necessary. It is like the Calvinist's desire to make an inscrutable universe 'mean'. Hume breaks this covenant of meaning by suggesting that the movement from observed conjunction to reasoned causation is purely a 'transition of the imagination', and 'meaning' is forever hidden from our view. When he then rephrases this as 'all we know is our profound ignorance', Hume begins to sound like a strict Calvinist.[26] His stress on the passivity of reason before the impressions of the senses seems to preclude the possibility of mind standing in active relation to its environment, unless – swinging to the opposite extreme entirely – the mind *creates* its environment. Again, in the absence of a stable relationship between the two, there is no means of telling.

Indeed the mind itself – empirically conceived – is only a convenient fiction, 'nothing but a heap, or collection of different perceptions, united together by certain relations, and suppos'd, tho' falsely, to be endow'd with a perfect simplicity and identity' (*Treatise*, p.207). This teasing word 'heap' gives a hint that Hume is playing philosophical games with his reader. The sceptical conclusions are very similar to those of the Calvinist, but in the absence of divine sanctions and the guilt associated with the split between appearance and reality, Hume can allow his mind to play freely over the implications of its own non-existence. Without a hint of anxiety, he carries his rational arguments to their supremely anti-rational conclusions. In 'the universe of the imagination', the only proper subject of investigation can be the mind itself: Hume turns Locke's empiricism back onto the perceiving mind to ask 'how far we are *ourselves* the objects of our senses' (p.189)? Without fundamental, 'objective' integrity, the mind can only catch itself by perceiving its own perceptions, by observing itself in action. In a passage of immense suggestiveness for Scottish and American fiction, Hume transfers the image of the uninvolved spectator observing the world at a distance inwards to an act of self-observation:

> The mind is a kind of theatre, where several perceptions successively make their appearance; pass, re-pass, glide away, and mingle in an infinite variety of postures and situations. (p. 253)

To account for man's sense of personal identity, Hume adduces memory and imagination, which associate isolated perceptions to produce an illusion of coherence and continuity through time; he revitalises the Calvinist division of the consciousness into a self which perceives and acts, and a self which observes these perceptions and actions. The self-observation by which we establish our own identity is directly analogous to the way we come to a sense of others:

> suppose we cou'd see clearly into the breast of another, and observe that succession of perceptions, which constitutes his mind or thinking principle . . . 'tis evident that nothing cou'd more contribute to the bestowing a relation on this succession amidst all its variations . . . the memory not only discovers the identity, but also contributes to its production, by producing the relation of resemblance among the perceptions. The case is the same whether we consider ourselves or others. (p.260–1)

Discovering ourselves is like seeing into the breast of another: the boundary line between observation and invasion is dangerously pliable.

The 'observer's stance' from which we view the theatre of the mind as memory is similar, too, to the detached interest with which the historian views the spectacle of the past:

> what more agreeable entertainment to the mind, than . . . to see all the human race, from the beginning of time, pass, as it were, in review before us;

appearing in their true colours, without any of those disguises, which, during their life-time, so much perplexed the judgment of the beholders. What spectacle can be imagined, so magnificent, so varied, so interesting?[27]

In the absence of an 'eternal' dimension such as structured Edwards' *History of the Work of Redemption* and gave meaning to the continuum of history, there would seem to be nothing to anchor the temporal, which becomes purely relative: a 'spectacle' to interest the detached puritan–provincial observer. But, says Hume, something more is demanded of the historian than the 'general abstract view of the object' taken by the philosopher, which 'leaves the mind so cold and unmoved that the sentiments of nature have no room to play'. 'History' keeps 'in a just medium' between the extremes of observation and possession; its practitioners 'are sufficiently interested in the characters and events, to have a lively sentiment of blame or praise; and, at the same time, have no particular interest or concern to pervert their judgment'.[28]

Similarly, in matters of taste, Hume finds that the best critics combine the impartiality of the detached observer with sympathetic entry into the imaginative universe of the original audience. The writer 'must free his mind from all *prejudice*', and 'forget, if possible, [his] individual being and [his] peculiar circumstances. A person influenced by prejudice ... obstinately maintains his natural position, without placing himself in that point of view, which the performance supposes.'[29] Clearly, 'distanced observation' and 'sympathetic possession' do not cohere as aspects of a single critical stance: to observe properly is to shed one's own prejudices merely to adopt those of another. The self-containment implied by distanced observation seems to be undermined by the sympathy demanded of the observer. The 'proper point of view' is vital, but crucially unspecified.

The coherence between observation and possession, judgement and sympathy, is that between analysis and sense, reason and feeling: it is that intuitive sense of wholeness by which a man may consider himself 'a man in general', with access to what Hume calls a 'true standard' (p. 277). The 'true standard' is a sort of base line of human nature: the aesthetic or moral judgement to which all men, when shorn of contingent prejudices, will assent; it thus has an important communal – participatory – dimension. The true standard is what would be perceived by the ideal critic; the ideal critic is he who, discarding his local prejudices, has access to the true standards of art and morality. Hume is enough a man of the Enlightenment to resolve the circularity of the equation by appealing to his reader's common experience: are there not things which everyone accepts as beautiful, or good, and do we not call these things true? Such an appeal is sustainable while a consensus can be publicly posited; to watch Hume's confident appeal to his audience making rational resolution of a paradox seem unimportant is to wonder what happens when such an appeal is no longer possible. Hawthorne, in provincial America, takes up Hume's very terms to ask questions about observation of and participation in a work of art when the artist cannot count on an accepted distance from which his audience will make their aesthetic judgement. Chapter 5 will consider this fully; here we may note that Hume has given new currency to the puritan division between observation and possession and has accommodated it by substituting social *confidence* for religious *faith*.

'Of the Standard of Taste' evokes 'sympathy' as the means by which the observer spans the distance between himself and what he observes and comes to possess its meaning. Jonathan Edwards described 'sympathy' as a way of inducing religious affection in an observer outside the fold; but we have also seen how the puritan under pressure retreats from the dangers of involvement to the safety of distanced observation. Sympathy, Hume says, involves a forgetting of self; as such it mitigates self-centred isolation, but its implications for the selfhood of the observer may be more ominous. As Hume goes on to say, sympathy in fact involves an *emptying* of self, perhaps forcibly: a person influenced by 'prejudice' has not 'imposed a proper violence on his imagination, and . . . forgotten himself for a moment' (p.277). The difficulty (which is merely implied in Hume's terms, and is firmly controlled by the public poise of his writing) is one of relationship: of maintaining one's own centre of self without imposing it on another and of responding to another's centre of self without being absorbed into it. The dilemma of relationship is characteristic of the puritan who lives from a shaky centre of self, unsure of his 'status'; it is also the dilemma of provincial society as it confronts the 'centre'.

'Sympathy' was a key term for many eighteenth-century moral philosophers. The difference between the 'moral sense' thought of Shaftesbury and Butler and the writings of Edwards and Hume is, like the difference between Calvinism and Anglicanism, largely a matter of temper and tone, of emphasis rather than of basic doctrinal disagreement. Both the English moral sense philosophers (Shaftesbury by way of the Cambridge Platonists and Butler through his Presbyterian lineage) and the puritan–provincial line of Edwards and Hume were fundamentally biassed towards Calvinist structures of thought; again, the degree of tenacity with which they were prepared to follow the implications of their thinking to a logical (though perhaps unsustainable) conclusion helps to characterise the difference between the two positions.[30] All these writers based their ethical analyses on a division between action and observation; Shaftesbury and Butler derived their notions of moral judgement from the *agent* (the doer of the deed which is to be judged); Hutcheson, Hume and Adam Smith, on the other hand, built moral theory around the observations of the *spectator*, not the actor, and thereby introduced an inherent distance from the event. To observe is not to experience, but it does give a perspective from which to pass judgement as long as we recognise that such judgement can only be of appearances, not of realities.

Observation of others, Hume says, produces in the spectator the sense either of sympathy or judgement. Sympathy is 'the chief source of moral distinctions' (*Treatise*, p.618); both it and moral judgement (based on the inclinations and disinclinations which sympathy activates) are passive before impressions made on the senses. The self cannot help but be swayed by its sympathy with another (p.592); the observer's judging stance and his distinct existence are threatened by the sympathetic movements of his senses. There is the present danger that sympathy will become empathy, that the observer will be swallowed up by the actor – or the province subsumed in the centre:

> where, beside the general resemblance of our natures, there is any peculiar similarity in our manners, or character, or country, or language, it facilitates the sympathy. The stronger the relation is betwixt ourselves and any object, the more easily does the imagination make the transition, and convey to the related idea the vivacity of conception, with which we always form the idea of our own person. (*Treatise*, p.318)[31]

The ease with which neutral observation becomes sympathy with the observed suggests that for Hume the stances are not polarised in fact as they are in theory: we do not *live* as observers any more than we do as philosophers. The 'observer's stance' is a fiction in morality as in aesthetics, a posited ideal, like that of the perfect critic, which enables us to retain a perspective on our actions even as we are immersed in them.

Hume is not suggesting that we can or ought to become the impartial observer, but that we may think about ourselves as though we could. Man's glory is that his mind's perceptions are *not* limited to sensory experiences and that the interest of his thoughts is not undermined by their (philosophical) unreality. To this extent, to posit the observer's stance is to become for a moment that 'superior being', the sceptic, who is not locked into the chain of sensations which is all he *knows* he is, who 'can easily exalt his notions and conceive a degree of knowledge, which, when compared to his own, will make the latter appear very contemptible'.[32]

The contradictions and oppositions which structure Hume's philosophy are finally – as he himself is fully aware – not resolvable in intellectual or logical terms. In 1739, at the beginning of his career as a writer, Hume wrote to his mentor Francis Hutcheson:

> There are different ways of examining the Mind as well as the Body. One may consider it either as an Anatomist or as a Painter; either to discover its most secret Springs & Principles or to describe the Grace & Beauty of its Actions. I

imagine it impossible to conjoin these two Views. Where you pull off the Skin, & display all the minute Parts, there appears something trivial, even in the noblest Attitudes and most vigorous Actions: Nor can you ever render the Object graceful or engaging but by cloathing the Parts again with Skin & Flesh, & presenting only their bare Outside. An Anatomist, however, can give very good advice to a Painter or Statuary: And in like manner, I am perswaded, that a Metaphysician may be very helpful to a Moralist; tho' I cannot easily conceive these two Characters united in the same Work.[33]

It is as though someone offered to 'conjoin' Swift with Keats in one work; it cannot be done – at least if we imagine conjunction to involve a kind of Coleridgean unity, a 'reconciliation of opposite or discordant qualities' which will subsume all distinction into itself.[34] The 'anatomist' and the 'painter' are both real for Hume, and they are opposed, and there is no higher, transcendent position, no 'mind of God' from which perspective they might be seen to coalesce in a larger whole. Instead, they have to learn to live side by side: the anatomist must participate, the painter observe, but they will not in so doing *become* each other or lose their distinctness through sympathy.

Hume's writing in the *Treatise* conveys a sense of what it is to look steadily at two utterly inconsistent realities; furthermore, his means as an artist of mastering the puritan mental universe are intimately derived from the terms of that universe. His prose demonstrates the ability he posits of the human mind to look at *and* beyond or through the reality of the senses. *This* is the 'dignity of human nature'. In the audacious wit of his own style, which even at its most confiding and beguilingly personal is taut and ready to spring away again from the reader, Hume evades (and encompasses) the logic of his philosophical position and meets the paradox of its Calvinist antecedent: that we strive to know, and know that we cannot know.

This is the meeting point of theology and literature. In no way abating the rigour of the position, but conceding everything to its untenability, Hume makes it joyously livable. It is only at the high points of Scottish and American provincial fiction that we may look for such a perfect poise of distanced participation, such absolute marriage of the Calvinist faculties of action and passivity. Hume holds and handles these polarities with a lightness of touch which is profoundly serious; by adding *pleasurable* doubt to the Calvinist co-ordinates he establishes a position which has profound affinities with the fiction of Scott, Hawthorne and Melville.

The essay 'The Sceptic' is a scarcely disguised embodiment of Hume's own way of living with the disparity between man's limitations and his aspirations. Its style exposes the utter futility of philosophising in the act of justifying its pursuit:

human life is more governed by fortune than by reason . . . While we are reasoning concerning life, life is gone; and death, though *perhaps* they receive him differently, yet treats alike the fool and the philosopher. To reduce life to exact rule and method, is commonly a painful, oft a fruitless occupation: And is it not also a proof, that we overvalue the prize for which we contend? Even to reason so carefully concerning it, and to fix with accuracy its just idea, would be overvaluing it, were it not that, to some tempers, this occupation is one of the most amusing, in which life could possibly be employed.[35]

There is something very much of the *salons* about Hume's disengagement: an ease, a charm, a just valuation of its own lightness reminiscent of Pope's description of the French belletrist Vincent Voiture, who 'wisely careless, innocently gay,/Chearful, he play'd the Trifle, Life, away.'[36] But Hume's writing contains also an element of endurance, almost of stoicism, whose presence gives the game a sombre tinge. The modesty of the claim Hume makes for his activities is both a graceful acknowledgement of the value of civility over pedantry and an unblinking look at the vanity of human wishes. The effect is not, however, quite the resting lightly on surfaces that Pope describes; at moments in Hume's writing the engulfing emptiness of the sceptical position becomes a journey to the heart of darkness, a Calvinist quest for the meaning hidden at the centre of significance:

> The *intense* view of these manifold contradictions and imperfections in human reason has so wrought upon me, and heated my brain, that I am ready to reject all belief and reasoning, and can look upon no opinion even as more probable or likely than another. Where am I, or what? From what causes do I derive my existence, and to what condition shall I return? Whose favour shall I court, and whose anger must I dread? What beings surround me? and on whom have I any influence, or who have any influence on me? I am confounded with all these questions, and begin to fancy myself in the most deplorable condition imaginable, inviron'd with the deepest darkness, and utterly depriv'd of the use of every member and faculty.   (*Treatise*, pp.268–69)

Hume pictures himself deprived of the social comforts of moral consensus ('expell'd all human commerce': p.264), cast adrift in the fathomless ocean of his own speculations. This is the ruin and shipwreck with which Calvin threatened the seeker after forbidden knowledge.[37] Even here, describing the very brink of human desolation, Hume manages a disengagement which does not insult the reader's involvement; the reality of the experience and the detachment of the voice are simultaneously present. There is nothing alienated – or alienating – about this; neither does it draw the reader improperly far into an intensely private realm. The relationship between experience and the way it is described, between participant and observer, is tantalising; we can never quite catch Hume as one or the other.

But it is not so much the journey to the heart of darkness itself which defines Hume's stance – or will define Scott's, or Hawthorne's – but the nature of the messages the traveller brings back on his return. The passage above continues immediately:

> Most fortunately it happens, that since reason is incapable of dispelling these clouds, nature herself suffices to that purpose, and cures me of this philosophical melancholy and delirium, either by relaxing this bent of mind, or by some avocation, and lively impression of my senses, which obliterate all these chimeras. I dine, I play a game of backgammon, I converse, and am merry with my friends; and when after three or four hour's amusement, I wou'd return to these speculations, they appear so cold, and strain'd, and ridiculous, that I cannot find in my heart to enter into them any farther.
>
> Here then I find myself absolutely and necessarily determin'd to live, and talk, and act like other people in the common affairs of life. (p.269)

The diction relaxes from the abrupt, non-sequential self-questioning of the first paragraph, which seems to refer inwards to a private world, to the expansive, confiding tone of geniality which beams outward from the second. The deep-delving puritan has become a *raconteur*; the story he tells is a public one, the truth – but only the available, shareable truth. The sheer riskiness of the wit which controls this crucial turn from despair to faith reveals the extent of Hume's self-possession as he accommodates human reasoning to the irrational extremities of experience. With a glorious audacity, Hume accepts Calvin's challenge in Calvin's terms and declares himself the man who will defy the odds to 'seek for truth'[38]:

> Methinks I am like a man, who having struck on many shoals, and having narrowly escap'd ship-wreck in passing a small frith, has yet the temerity to put out to sea in the same leaky weather-beaten vessel, and even carries his ambition so far as to think of compassing the globe under these disadvantageous circumstances. (pp.263–4)

And yet of course – as Hume knows full well already, though his reader does not at this point – the whole thrust of the *Treatise* is to deny such absolutism, to win back a provisional viewpoint, a livable doubt, from the extremes of light and dark, possession of knowledge and alienation from it. Hume's *philosophical* position of 'universal Skepticism' is at the opposite end of the spectrum from Jonathan Edwards' 'Calvinist doctrines'; their *writing* has the task in each case of making the stance tenable. Edwards makes a transcendent appeal beyond language, Hume a comic appeal to a shareable affirmation of incongruity. These are the co-ordinates which persist to preserve the distinctive character of puritan–provincial writing through the multifarious influences which in the eighteenth century continued to modify its expression and tone.

3

From puritanism to provincialism

> Edwards' great millstone and rock
> of hope has crumbled, but the square
> white houses of his flock
> stand in the open air,
>
> out in the cold,
> like sheep outside the fold.
> Hope lives in doubt.
> Faith is trying to do without
>
> faith. In western Massachusetts,
> I could almost feel the frontier
> crack and disappear.
> Edwards thought the world would end there.   (Robert Lowell)[1]

Adam Smith (Hume's friend and another Scot of Calvinist background) is not a writer of Hume's complexity, but his first book, *The Theory of Moral Sentiments* (1759), develops the concepts of sympathy and of the 'impartial spectator' in ways which simultaneously reaffirm their connection with Calvinism and extend their literary possibilities as 'non-central' ways of looking at the world.

Adam Smith took a broader view of sympathy than Hume: he defined it as 'our fellow-feeling with any passion whatever', and synonymous with 'humanity' – which thereby became passive and *re*-active, rather than vital and initiatory, although its demands on the individual were irresistible.[2] Sympathy was a social bond: spectators placed themselves in the situation of the actor or sufferer and shared in his emotions, and the agent had *his* emotions modified by sympathising with the spectators and imagining how he would feel if he too were watching his own actions (p.22). Smith saw these sympathetic ties as the basis of moral judgement; they became the criteria for participation in or exclusion from the community. This thought has great psychological power: describing its implications, Smith's tone assumes the familiar Calvinistic ring of extremity; his language sheds its characteristic coolness to become highly charged and emotionally coercive:

> The violator of the more sacred laws of justice can never reflect on the sentiments which mankind must entertain with regard to him, without feeling all the agonies of shame, and horror, and consternation ... By sympathising with the hatred and abhorrence which other men must entertain for him, he becomes in some measure the object of his own hatred and abhorrence ... He dares no longer look society in the face, but imagines himself as it were rejected, and thrown out from the affections of all mankind. He cannot hope for the consolation of sympathy in this his greatest and most dreadful distress. The remembrance of his crimes has shut out all fellow-feeling with him from the hearts of his fellow-creatures ... But solitude is still more dreadful than society ... The horror of solitude drives him back into society, and he comes again into the presence of mankind ... loaded with shame and distracted with fear, in order to supplicate some little protection from the countenance of those very judges, who he knows have already all unanimously condemned him. (pp.84–5)

The plight of the wretched, predestinated reprobate lies very close to the surface of such a passage.

Positing an *impartial* spectator to decide which actions were worthy of sympathy made *objective* judgements possible in an affective framework of morality. It was also the way (as Adam Smith understood it) that the individual developed self-command. Humanity (sympathy for others) and self-command (control of oneself) together constituted the wholeness and perfection of human nature.[3] Smith's impartial spectator was, like Hume's, a fiction, a theoretical observer whose lack of involvement in the action or emotion of the agent enabled him to appraise it without prejudice. Distance was crucial: 'The partial spectator is at hand: the impartial one at a great distance' (p.154). A 'real' observer's judgement will always, Smith says, be prejudiced by his emotional or physical involvement in the action he observes; the impartial spectator becomes once again a *necessary* fiction to fend off utter relativism in justice and morality.

Scottish critics, following Adam Smith, extended the categories of observation and sympathy to aesthetics. Alexander Gerard, in *An Essay on Genius* (1774), describes the sympathetic imagination as a necessary ingredient of artistic success; without it, he says, the poet becomes 'a spectator' whose detachment from the scene he describes makes him incapable of imparting it to his audience; 'coolly imagining' his subject, 'he feels not the passion, he has not force of genius or sensibility of heart sufficient for conceiving how it would affect a person who felt it, or for entering into the sentiments which it would produce in him'.[4] Such, as I shall suggest in chapter 5, is the plight of many a puritan–provincial artist in nineteenth-century Scottish and American fiction, from James Hogg's Spy to Hawthorne's Coverdale.

Keats' 'negative capability' derives directly from the idea of aesthetic sympathy; Coleridge's 'Dejection: An Ode' is its obverse. For the Scottish or American Romantic writer, the failure of imaginative sympathy is more fundamentally threatening in its intimate connection with moral shortcoming: it is not merely an unhappy fact, but a sign of 'reprobation'. Conversely, the provincial writer is also drawn, as the central English writer is not, to consider the invasive colonising tendencies which might accompany such a 'sympathetic' entering of another's experience. The 'aesthetic' position cannot be held unanxiously by the provincial writer: it dissolves immediately into questions of identity and relationship which polarise at the extremes of alienation or assimilation.

Adam Smith extends the notion of observation to self-scrutiny: to posit an impartial spectator as we regard our own actions would, he writes, vanquish self-deceit, 'this fatal weakness of mankind . . . the source of half the disorders of human life'. He proposed that such introspection should accompany every action: 'If we saw ourselves in the light in which others see us, or in which they would see us if they knew all, a reformation would generally be unavoidable. We could not otherwise endure the sight' (pp.158–9). Robert Burns' echo 'O wad some Pow'r the giftie gie us / *To see ourselves as others see us!*', in a poem directed at Calvinist hypocrisy, is a reminder of how close Adam Smith's theory still is to the theological stance of self-scrutiny.[5] The connection gains further resonance in his identification of 'two selves', an observer and an actor:

> We can never survey our own sentiments and motives, we can never form any judgment concerning them; unless we remove ourselves, as it were, from our own natural station, and endeavour to view them as at a certain distance from us. But we can do this in no other way than by endeavouring . . . to examine our own conduct as we imagine any other fair and impartial spectator would examine it . . . We suppose ourselves the spectators of our own behaviour, and endeavour to imagine what effect it would, in this light, produce upon us. This is the only looking-glass by which we can, in some measure, with the eyes of other people, scrutinize the propriety of our own conduct. (pp.110, 112)

Adam Smith calls the self-scrutinising faculty the conscience. The conscience is not merely the mirror of society turned inwards; it is also 'the vice-regent of God within us' (p.166): conscience is the judge; the acting self is in the dock. Although there is little likelihood of direct influence, Adam Smith's image here is identical to that of Samuel Willard's puritan manual; it is also a measure of his distance from 'centrality' and from Locke's disbelief in the possibility of 'two Persons in one Man'. The self-observing conscience and the self-directed will may oppose one another and instruct the man to act in conflict with himself. Smith solves this problem by stressing the need for self-command: the imaginary impartial spectator within the self must be allowed to take precedence over the more immediate demands of the acting self.

The division between agent and conscience almost disappears as the imagined self controls the real one. The impartial spectator is conjured internally in response to the *sense* of virtue in the individual: the 'vice-regent of God within us' has access to the divine through intuition; it is not accessible to rational analysis. In response to this intuition the imagination evokes an ideal way of looking at reality, distancing conscience from this social foundation in the observations of others. The half-hidden question (which does not arise with Smith because he is confident that the observer's stance is objective, but which would become pressing to the unconfident provincials of subsequent generations) is, how can one share Keats' confidence that 'What the imagination seizes as Beauty *must be* truth'?[6] How, in other words, do we *know* that it is the 'vice-regent of God' and not the agent of Satan who thus prompts our responses? Desire for assurance in these terms is itself a mark of the provincial's inner division and insecurity.

The individual's imaginative quest for personal integrity has a further important consequence. The ideal internal spectator enables the agent to distance himself from his own passions and to control them, thereby overcoming or avoiding 'excessive' emotion, which is, in Smith's view, socially distasteful because others cannot sympathise with it in its full magnitude. The sufferer distances himself from his own immediate experience by imagining how an impartial spectator would view his sufferings; this makes his emotion available for sympathy by real observers. The self-observer alienates himself from his own emotions in order to reduce the distance between himself and other men.

Adam Smith himself makes explicit the connection between this distanced, impartial stance and the provincial's relationship to life at the centre. 'Of all the corrupters of moral sentiments', he says, 'faction and fanaticism have always been by far the greatest.' 'The real, revered, and impartial spectator ... is, upon no occasion, at a greater distance than amidst the violence and rage of contending parties' (pp.155–6).[7] This suggests some of the *virtues* of the provincial position; *The Theory of Moral Sentiments* gives perhaps the most extensive positive account of the 'rhetoric of distance'.

The advantages of 'distance' would also become an important element in American political rhetoric in the post-independence years, at a time when the nation's imaginative writers were preoccupied, in literary terms, with its effect on the 'covenant of meaning'. Benjamin Franklin, for example, declared that 'Americans are a kind of Posterity' in relation to English writers, because 'being at too great a distance to be bypassed by the Fashions, Parties and Prejudices that prevail among you [English]', Americans can 'read their Works with perfect Impartiality'; later the American historian George Bancroft wrote in *The North-American Review* that 'the voice of America, deciding on the literature of England, resembles the voice of posterity more nearly than anything else, that is contemporaneous, can do'.[8]

The distance between Boston or New York or Edinburgh and London had both a psychological and a metaphorical dimension. Observation rather than experience, distance rather than immediacy, passivity rather than action were the terms in which Scots and Americans perceived their provincial relationship to the centre, terms which were directly analogous to the predicament of the unjustified individual under Calvinist theology. Like puritans, provincials felt language – the word – to be at once the source and the manifestation of their predestined passivity and distance from the heart of experience. Disjunctions between manner and matter, the word and its meaning, were explained by their failure any longer to 'possess' the language of the centre, although they had no other. It was their inheritance, but they had been dispossessed.

John Witherspoon wrote a series called 'The Druid' which considered the problems of language and expression in America. 'The word Americanism', he said, 'is exactly similar in its formation and signification to the word Scotticism'; both denote peculiarities of idiom inevitable because 'we are at a great distance from the island of Great-Britain, in which the standard of language is as yet supposed to be found'.[9] The Scottish distance from the centre of significance was, he felt, the consequence of its 'fall' from nationhood into dependency: 'by the removal of the court to London, and especially by the union of the two kingdoms, the Scottish manner of speaking, came to be considered as provincial barbarism; which, therefore, all scholars are now at the utmost pains to avoid'.[10]

Adam Smith, who had considered the ethical advantages of distance, picked up the metaphor again in his *Lectures on Rhetoric and Belles Lettres* delivered to Glasgow students in 1762–3:

> We in this country are most of us very sensible that the perfection of language is very different from that we commonly speak in. The ideal we form of a good

> stile is almost conterary [sic] to that which we generally hear. Hence it is that we conceive the farther ones stile is removed from the common manner it is so much the nearer to purity and the perfection we have in view. Shaftesbury who keeps at a vast distance from the language we commonly meet with is for this reason universally admired.[11]

The Scottish literati put themselves to endless pains to correct what Hume called the 'very corrupt Dialect of the Tongue which we make use of' in their published work: Adam Smith's lectures are themselves a case in point; Hume had his English vetted before publication; Scotsmen compiled lists of ostracised 'Scotticisms' and flocked to learn correct pronunciation from R.B. Sheridan's Irish father; the rhetorician James Beattie described the positive dangers of using a language one does not 'possess', whose authority has been alienated: 'we handle English', he wrote, 'as a person who cannot fence handles a sword; continually afraid of hurting ourselves with it, or letting it fall, or making some awkward motion that shall betray our ignorance'.[12] Here is an invidious degree of self-consciousness in using language, a paralysing defensiveness about not being 'at home' which kills spontaneity. 'When a Scotsman therefore writes', declared Henry Mackenzie in 1780, 'he does it generally in trammels. His own native original language, which he hears spoken around him, he does not make use of; but he expresses himself in a language in some respects foreign to him, and which he has acquired by study and observation.'[13] The structures of Calvinism evoke the plight of the provincial: distance from direct experience, the 'trammels' of fate which prevent free and natural expression of meaning, and alienation from one's natural origins.

In America the sense of distance from the realities represented by the English language became part of a quest for distinctively 'American' literature. The stance and idiom of English literature (which were only too available as models for both American writers and readers) were 'at home' in a world the newly independent American was trying to shake off. Pride and policy required the rejection of old forms and old meanings; the problem was that although 'American' experience did not seem to be like 'English' experience, its only means of expression was rooted in 'English' realities. It was a matter of 'honor', wrote Noah Webster, that America should have 'a system of [its] own, in language as well as government'. He continued with the argument which would become a favoured staple of nationalistic rallying calls: 'Great Britain, whose children we are, and whose language we speak, should no longer be *our* standard; for the taste of her writers is already corrupted, and her language on the decline. But if it were not so, she is at too great a distance to be our model, and to instruct us in the principles of our own tongue.'[14]

Other writers were less sanguine about the *possibility* of a creative language whose freedom from old traditions would reflect the political assertions of the 'Declaration of Independence'. Perhaps, after all, American literature would bear the burden of division and disinheritance:

> [English] is the product of a foreign soil, and notwithstanding it is transplanted into a region, where there is no danger, that its native vigor will decay, or beauty be marred, yet it cannot in the nature of things supply those strong motives to intellectual exertion, which it would, if it were growing up with our growth, and receiving in its very front the deep marks of our national character and pecularities... we do fear, that our literature, the literature of the imagination and the heart, will be cramped by the language, which is prescribed as the measure of its stature and its strength, that it will creep too servilely in the track, which thousands have trod, and be too long a slave to foreign models and foreign caprice.[15]

The matter of the American writer seemed divorced, distanced, from the manner of its embodiment. This dilemma of the artist condemned to write in a medium to which he does not 'belong' and which does not belong to him has become familiar in the context of another provincialism through the musings of Joyce's Stephen Daedalus, or Seamus Heaney's sense of the 'pre-occupation' of all literary language:

> Our pioneers keep striking
> Inwards and downwards,
>
> Every layer they strip
> Seems camped on before....
> The wet centre is bottomless.[16]

This is a thoroughly Romantic notion of originality, of colonising virgin territory to the self; but it is also the provincial dilemma: at a distance from the 'centre' of meaning, thoughts polarise into opposing manner and matter. For the Scottish or American puritan–provincial writer, salvation lay in unified perception; division was the mark of the damned. The task of the provincial, like that of the Calvinist, was to reunite word and thing, symbol and signified.

At this point, Common Sense philosophy stepped in to reassure Scots and Americans that the gulf which seemed to have opened onto Calvin's abyss was illusory, that their perceptions (despite Edwards and Hume) could after all be trusted, and that the good and the true were accessible to all. It was not an easy task: Hume's *Treatise* was strictly empirical; its sceptical conclusions were coherently derived from widely accepted Lockean principles, principles which, as Thomas Reid wrote to Hume, 'I never thought of calling in question, until the conclusions you draw from them ... made me suspect them. If these principles are solid, your system must stand.'[17] Reid was the most eminent of the Scottish writers who in refusing Hume's scepticism found themselves denying his premise: he turns Hume's 'all we know is the evidence of our senses' into the strongly assertive statement that we know the world *because* our senses tell us about it. His *Inquiry into the Human Mind, on the Principles of Common Sense* (1763) extends the thinking of Hutcheson and the Moral Sense philosophers to posit an epistemological 'sense' which is shared by all men, is rather variously defined as knowledge, the faculty of Reason and the 'Light of Nature', and which *knows* directly the external world and its relations. Reid significantly evoked Hume's sceptical epistemology in terms of the magical insubstantiality of Shakespeare's *Tempest*; 'upon this hypothesis', he wrote, 'the whole universe about me ... all things without exception, which I imagined to have a permanent existence ... vanish at once; "*And, like the baseless, fabric of a vision, Leave not a tract behind* [sic]"'.[18] To Reid the idea is patently absurd. Nineteenth-century Scottish and American writers who invoked the play to describe their sense of the unstable relationship between thought and 'reality' would be (as chapter 5 will suggest) less unequivocal.

Reid's work (like that of his fellow Scots Dugald Stewart, Thomas Brown and Alexander Gerard) was immensely popular in circumventing the implications of Hume's philosophy. Asserting a physiological justification for perception, 'Common Sense' writing also appropriated the lay meaning of common sense and cast Hume in the unattractive light of a closet intellectual:

> Such a popular opinion as this, stands upon a higher authority than that of philosophy; and philosophy must strike sail to it, if she would not render herself contemptible to every man of common understanding. For though, in matters of deep speculation, the multitude must be guided by philosophers, yet, in things that are within the reach of every man's understanding, and upon which the whole conduct of human life turns, the philosopher must follow the multitude, or make himself perfectly ridiculous.[19]

Hume, of course, would concede all of this without giving one inch of his sceptical ground. Insisting on 'life' *at the expense of* 'thought', the Common Sense writers unscramble Hume's double perspective into two very much simpler positions. Much of what Reid affirms to support his anti-sceptical stance had already been fully canvassed by Hume himself. On memory, for example, Reid 'concludes farther, that it is no less a part of the human constitution, to believe the present existence of our sensations, and to believe the past existence of what we remember, than it is to believe that twice two make four'.[20] Hume would agree entirely, but his discussions of memory and the sense of personal identity provide the additional bearing of the sceptical mind reflecting on its own beliefs. What we cannot help but believe is not therefore necessarily *true*.

Common Sense philosophers found themselves unable to assail the logic which led Hume to his sceptical conclusions and could only refute him by intuited counter-assertion based on the mind's 'sense' of itself; they initiated late eighteenth-century philosophy's distrust of the speculative mind *per se*. Hume exercised the full range of intellect while remaining in the world of 'common sense'; the poise of his writing balances experience and thought as not only compatible but inseparable, and rescues the life of the mind from abstraction. All this is lost to the Common Sense writers. After the riches of Hume they seem philosophically simplistic, humanly a little thin. Defensiveness gives Common Sense writing that air of provinciality which Matthew Arnold described as characteristic of the English Nonconformists who defined themselves against the Established Church; Common Sense takes its whole being from *opposition* to Hume, and exclusion of rather than hospitality to ideas.[21]

Despite its defensiveness and the rather weak compromise it offered between the philosophical polarities of rationalism and empiricism, Common Sense thought enjoyed an enormous vogue in Scotland and America in the years surrounding American independence. The reasons, in a climate of revolutionary unrest and political consolidation, are not far to seek. The 'common sense' of Common Sense philosophy made it very welcome to a revolutionary experiment which declared human equality. Observation-based knowledge suggested a democracy of facts against the hierarchical fictions of the speculative metaphysician; it also assumed equal access to this knowledge for every man, however limited his philosophical pretensions. But if America's adoption of Common Sense principles was superficially radical in its rejection of hierarchies, it was more fundamentally conservative. As in Britain Reid and his successors developed Common Sense to defend established categories of moral behaviour against the anarchy of rampant solipsistic sensationism, so in America it guarded the new Republic against the dangers of radical speculation and tended to set experience *against* thought. Founded on the self-evident truth of 'facts', Common Sense lent order and coherence to the new country; indeed, it may be said to have given America its justification for existing at all.

Common Sense philosophy dominated education in both Scotland and America until the middle of the nineteenth century. The writers whose work I discuss in subsequent chapters were educated in its shadow, if not directly by its proponents. None, except Fenimore Cooper, accepted its tenets wholeheartedly, but none avoided its influence. Hawthorne pays evasive, equivocal and sceptical homage to it; Poe plays with it; Melville scorns its gentility; Hogg tries to adopt it but finds it profoundly alien; Scott encompasses it with cavalier freedom. At issue, however, is not influence so much as analogous modes of perceiving the world – and their literary consequences. Whatever their local differences in attitude towards Common Sense philosophy, all these writers share a common literary concern: their fiction finds the relationship between sense-based 'facts' and thought-based 'ideas' complex, problematic and fascinating. This makes them all, in quite distinct ways, very self-conscious writers who look for a resolution of the conflict between facts and thoughts in the development of the fictional voice itself.

Hume, by reducing everything in the realms of knowledge to self-consciousness, by refusing to distinguish between mind and matter (in that matter may exist only as perceived by mind), paradoxically freed the mind from obsessive self-consciousness. 'Mind', as it appears in the *Treatise*, is not embattled (as Common Sense philosophy makes it) against materialism or external necessity, because it is everything, and nothing, and plays freely over the nature of its own assumptions. Thomas Reid, insisting in the name of divinely ordained truth on the distinction between mind and matter, attempted to preserve freedom of action against determinism. Hume's and Common Sense thought share a common puritan derivation; once again, distinctions turn on tone and emphasis. Hume's scepticism has an affinity with Edwards' fundamentalism; Common Sense aligns with the religious moderates who dominated the eighteenth-century Scottish Church and who helped to create American Unitarianism. Scottish Moderates from John Simson and Francis Hutcheson to Reid himself united Common Sense to the main line of eighteenth-century 'moral sense' philosophy.

For these writers, as for Hume, ethics was based not in ideas or in reason, but in sense. The moral sense inbuilt in every man was a faculty like touch, taste or any other, which received impressions from the external world and directed action. Like the other senses, too, the moral sense could function well or badly in any individual case. Evil under this system became a mere bodily malfunction, a disease of the moral sense.[22] This seems a far cry from Calvin's insistence on natural depravity and the innate corruption of all human perception, but in an important way the positions are continuous. James McCosh, a nineteenth-century Scottish President of the college of New Jersey, and himself a late exponent of Common Sense, wrote an account of the 'Scottish School' which shows how closely its principles mirrored puritan expressions of division and the self-observing conscience:

> *It* [the 'Scottish School'] *proceeds throughout by observation . . . It observes the operations of the mind by the inner sense – that is, consciousness.* In this philosophy consciousness, the perception of self in its various states, comes into greater prominence than it had ever done before . . . they thought that the mind could observe the world within by consciousness more directly and quite as

accurately as it could observe the world without by sight, touch, and the other senses.[23]

This is Calvinist in all but its *trust* in the evidence of the senses, internal or external, moral or physical: it is Calvinism without Original Sin. The relationship between the observer and the self it scrutinises is not one of antagonism but of information; its product is 'facts'. This shift from the experience-based thinking of Hume to the sense-based observation of the Common Sense philosophers changes the meaning of experience. For Hume as for Edwards, to experience is also to recognise that the evidence of the senses is at best provisional, at worst delusive; for Reid and his followers experience has become synonymous with 'facts' and 'observation'; direct access to truth is assumed. This flattening of consciousness has important consequences for the scope which the mind allows to its own perceptions:

> Because we are not furnished with observations sufficient to decide this question... the hypothesis... proceeds to another; that moisture is unfriendly to animal growth. The truth of this is inscrutable to us by reasonings a priori. Nature has hidden from us her modus agendi. Our only appeal on such questions is to experience; and I think that experience is against the supposition ... But when we appeal to experience, we are not to rest satisfied with a single fact. Let us therefore try our question on more general ground.[24]

This passage, which reads like the work of a Common Sense philosopher, comes in fact from Thomas Jefferson's *Notes on the State of Virginia* (1784). Both as philosopher and as politician, Jefferson upheld the principles of Common Sense and distrusted speculative thought. Even in the wide-ranging correspondence which he resumed late in life with his old political opponent John Adams, Jefferson refused to indulge in 'speculations and subtleties' and (implicitly reproving Adams' free-ranging thoughts) declared sententiously, 'when I meet with a proposition beyond finite comprehension, I abandon it as I do a weight which human strength cannot lift: and I think ignorance, in these cases, is truly the softest pillow on which I can lay my head'.[25] Jefferson does not distinguish between scepticism about the ultimate status of human speculations and scepticism about the speculative act of mind itself. Hume never makes us feel that this is so. For Jefferson, observation is the sole legitimate source of knowledge about the world; the tangible (which included everything available to the senses, moral and physical) provides the only basis for epistemological confidence. When, therefore, he came to define his sense of America in response to the enquiries of a French diplomat, Jefferson embodied it (in the *Notes on Virginia*) as a series of observations on the boundaries, seaports, climate, constitution, manufactures, and so on: the quantifiable phenomena of the land as a physical entity.

More crucially, however, it is these principles which lie behind Jefferson's earlier attempt to define America, 'The Declaration of Independence' which he drafted at the behest of the Continental Congress in June 1776. Writing to a correspondent many years later, Jefferson recalled his aims in terms which resonate intriguingly with the tones of *Caleb Williams* or *Edgar Huntly*, 'William Wilson' or *Redgauntlet*:

> When forced ... to resort to arms for redress, an appeal to the tribunal of the world was deemed proper for our justification. This was the object of the Declaration of Independence. Not to find out new principles, or new arguments, never before thought of, not merely to say things which had never been said before; but to place before mankind the common sense of the subject, in terms so plain and firm as to command their assent, and to justify ourselves in the independent stand we are compelled to take. Neither aiming at originality of principle or sentiment, nor yet copied from any particular or previous writing, it was intended to be an expression of the American mind, and to give that expression the proper tone and spirit called for by the occasion.[26]

'Common Sense' is invoked here in both its semi-technical and its lay meanings: both its ordinariness and its emotional appeal are important. So is its essential conservatism: Jefferson stresses that the 'Declaration' merely stated universally accessible truths which were bound to command assent. Even more interesting, however, is the nexus of necessity and freedom, compulsion and independence within which Jefferson describes the 'Declaration' taking shape, terms which draw us back to the puritan roots of his Common Sense rhetoric and complicate its confidence that a 'truth' plainly stated will draw all men to right a perceived injustice. The appeal to the 'tribunal' of the world, like the appeal of the criminal to his judge, or the sinner to his conscience (the 'vice-regent of God' within him), or fallen man to his maker, is a self-justification which calls both necessity and freedom to witness. Americans, in Jefferson's terms, were 'forced' and 'compelled' to declare their independence and freedom from constraint. They are in an important sense justified sinners. As we saw in chapter 1, adversity was literally heaven-sent to the puritan: it spurred him on to virtuous action in confidence that he was amongst God's chosen people. Here was another revolutionary moment which concentrated puritan–provincial energies into positive self-definition, and Jefferson was not slow to exploit the galvanising potential of inbred Calvinist structures.[27]

The first sentence of Jefferson's draft 'Declaration' declares its origin in pragmatic empiricism, not philosophical speculation: 'When in the course of human events it becomes necessary for one people to advance from that subordination in which they have hitherto remained ...'[28] The language of necessity here is Newtonian rather than Calvinist:

'causes ... impel them to the change' (p.423). But as a 'separating' document, the 'Declaration' simultaneously renounces a covenant ('dissolving' bands of relationship), and proclaims a new Confession of Faith as it announces a new mission. In its confident belief that a new start *can* be made – optimistically assuming that *declaring* independence is equivalent to *becoming* independent and that if the past cannot be denied it can be left behind – this seems to be Calvinism in its 'active' revolutionary phase, asserting rather than doubting, overcoming opposition and division rather than succumbing to it.

Despite this positive thrust, the document is full of troublesome discontinuities. Its underlying assumptions are not unequivocally hopeful; both where they derive from the radicalism of Tom Paine and where their source is the language of Common Sense and moral sentiment, the defensive aspects of the puritan temper threaten always to overset them by insinuating a counter-polarity. The effect is a whole spectrum of tones which make much heavier emotional demands than at first appears.

The 'Declaration' is, as Jefferson says in his letter, a 'justification', justification for an act which may look to the world like rebellion from legally constituted and traditionally sanctioned authority (a Calvinist Fall, perhaps?). Against this, Jefferson presents his case: 'let facts be submitted to a candid world, for the truth of which we pledge a faith yet unsullied by falsehood' (p.424, Jefferson's draft). These anti-platonic, self-evident truths are brought to a world 'white', unprejudiced and open to evidence – in short, a world of impartial spectators freely responsive to the claims of the common sense. At this bar of judgement the colonists pledge their own innocence: asserting their prelapsarian purity clearly opposes them to the guilt of the tyrannous king. A cumulative toll of details – 'facts' – specifies how the 'father' has abused his paternal authority and exercised arbitrary, irresponsible power over the hapless colonists, who are distanced from the meaning and source of his decisions. Against his absolute decrees, their every impulse and action towards justice is rendered powerless; enforced passivity makes them vulnerable to all his tyrannies:

> He has dissolved Representative Houses repeatedly, for opposing with manly firmness his invasions on the rights of the people. He has refused for a long time, after such dissolutions to cause others to be elected; whereby the Legislative powers, incapable of Annihilation, have returned to the People at large for their exercise; the State remaining in the mean time exposed to all the dangers of invasion from without, and convulsions within.
>
> (p.430; as adopted by Congress)

Active verbs characterise the king; passive reactive constructions are the colonists' lot. Against the cumulative determinism which Jefferson's rhetoric re-enacts in its recitation of the king's iniquities, there is a gathering consciousness of the *separate* identity of Americans; the language of the 'Declaration' evokes the process of self-definition by opposition as the repeated 'he has' begins to find an answering echo in 'our' and 'us':

> He has combined with others to subject us to a jurisdiction foreign to our constitution, and unacknowledged by our laws; giving his Assent to their Acts of pretended Legislation: For Quartering large bodies of armed troops among us... For imposing Taxes on us without our Consent: For depriving us of the benefits of Trial by Jury: For transporting us beyond Seas. (p.431)

The king himself has first renounced the covenant with his people by abdicating government in America and 'declaring us out of his Protection'. To the removal of his presence he has added positive destruction: 'he has plundered our seas, ravaged our Coasts, burnt our towns, and destroyed the Lives of our people'. This litany of wantonness turns authority into oppression, abandonment to vengeance; in the face of it, the colonists' self-justification and their demand for justice become synonymous. Every plea from the victims to their master *within* the covenanted relationship of ruler and subject, father and child, centre and colony, has proved unavailing: 'our repeated Petitions have been answered only by repeated injury'.

This is much more than the breaking of 'political bands' announced at the beginning of the 'Declaration'; the coming into existence of a new nation in an act of opposition and secession carries with it undertones far removed from the assertive empiricism of enlightened confidence. As 'an expression of the American mind' the 'Declaration' is replete with a kind of negative suggestiveness which threatens the democratic optimism of its final pledge of unity.

The act of separation is simultaneously a *natural* occurrence, a revolution like the revolution of the spheres, and a profoundly *un-natural* one which sunders forcibly the ties of human relationship. The 'natural' expression of the Newtonian universe governed by rational, ascertainable laws of cause and effect is directly juxtaposed with the Common Sense rhetoric of sensation and sympathy: the final British injustice to the colonists offends not their reason, but their feelings of 'consanguinity'; once the bonds of the heart have been violated, there can be no return. 'These facts have given the *last stab to agonising affection*, and manly spirit bids us to renounce for ever these *unfeeling brethren*' (p.427, Jefferson's draft; my emphasis). Natural affections are ruptured by an impossible either/or choice which leads to alienation and the emotional gulf expressed in what I have called the 'rhetoric of distance'. In 1783 Ezra Stiles described, similarly, how 'Britain forced upon America the tremendous alternative of the loss of liberty or the last appeal, either of which instantly alienated and dissolved our affections, never more to be recovered'.[29] Jefferson's language changes key entirely in the latter part of the 'Declaration' to accommodate the emotional justification for secession: there is, for the provincial asserting his identity in opposition to the centre, no continuum between ideas and feelings. Jefferson's 'expression of the American mind' establishes that mind, stylistically, as a discontinuous one, divided between an enlightened rational optimism and a violated sensibility.

The act of separation is a Fall into Division, from which point only a new start, a new assertion of freedom in a freshly covenanted relationship, can save them: 'and for the support of this declaration we mutually pledge to each other our lives, our fortunes & our sacred honour' (p.427, Jefferson's draft).[30] Lockean pedagogy provided the Patriots with a secular version of the 'Fortunate Fall' which justified these revolutionary political actions: the old patriarchal authoritarianism which sustained puritan society was dissolved, and 'children were henceforth to have freedom to choose their own, worthier "parents"'.[31] But the discontinuous styles of the 'Declaration' imply that this optimistic creed would always, in puritan–provincial expression, be shadowed by its negative antagonists – guilty rebellion and eternal reprobation. Questions about how far a new start is ever possible, about whether separation means flight and flight entails pursuit or return, and whether asserting new relationships can compensate for the sundering of old are posed by those who ponder what it means to be American, from Hawthorne and de Tocqueville to Henry James and beyond. They are also the questions which puritan–provincials put to the world. As Melville's *Mardi* enacts, to rupture the ties that hold one in 'place' may be to cast out beyond reach of redemption. As he considered the awful possibility of breaking 'covenants of meaning', Jonathan Edwards warned that 'if things may be without causes, all ... necessary connection and dependence is dissolved, and so all means of our knowledge is gone' (*Freedom of the Will*, p.183; see above, p.37). Jefferson's 'Declaration of Independence' makes a sublime bid for the possibilities of freedom *within* the stabilising structures of causation, but its divided rhetoric and assumptions are those of a predetermined, postlapsarian universe of division.

From the 'Declaration' onwards, the act of separation came to have immense symbolic potential, both political and spiritual, for Americans. Politically, the distance established between American and European affairs was a crucial element in the new nation's sense of itself. European war provoked President Washington to early expression of the policy of non-intervention in his Farewell Address of 1796: 'Europe', he said, 'has a set of primary interests, which to us have none, or a very remote relation . . . it must be unwise in us to implicate ourselves.'[32] This sentiment was codified and hardened into the 'Monroe Doctrine' of 1823; in addition, the evangelical nationalism of the early years of the century insisted that America continue to define itself as a 'city on a hill', a shining example *from afar* to the rest of the world.[33]

Refusing relationship and finding safety in distanced observation are familiar ingredients of the puritan–provincial outlook. Such political and nationalistic non-intervention was doubly defensive: it did not risk involvement in the world, and it was seen as a form of self-reliance, proof that America could indeed – against all Europe's scepticism – stand alone; the rest of the world was not necessary to it. Self-reliance, both national and individual, became an article of American faith expressed with richly ambivalent defensive assertion in the writing of Emerson and the Transcendentalists.

Emerson was the product of the 'liberal Christianity' of Unitarian Boston. He was raised, like the others of his generation, on the principles of Common Sense and Scottish aesthetics: the *Rhetoric and Belles Lettres* (1783) of Hugh Blair, the *Elements of Criticism* (1762) of Lord Kames, Archibald Alison's *Essays on the Nature and Principles of Taste* (1790). In 1832 he resigned as pastor of Boston's Second Church, and began to speak out against the coolness and insipidity of the rational Unitarians; his writing rediscovers the spiritual fervour of the early puritans but infuses it with a tincture of optimistic Romantic nationalism and German transcendental thought. It has become a cliché of criticism that Emerson is a Calvinist with Original Sin left out.

The continuities with Calvinism run through Emerson's work, however, not directly from puritan language and thought but muted by Common Sense, which modifies as it reinforces the characteristic puritan–provincial habits of mind. Successive reactions against and transformations of Calvin's theology – Evangelical, Sceptical, Common Sense, Unitarian, Transcendentalist – all flow from a similar perception of the world: that structure of polarities and oppositions outlined in chapter 1. When George Santayana notes that Emerson is not merely a victim but an early exponent of the 'genteel tradition', he identifies a general characteristic of nineteenth-century American literature: it 'only half escape[s]' the systems of which it is critical.[34] The state of mind exemplified by Calvinism is so powerful that even when its individual terms can no longer compel, the framework survives to structure the thought of those born in its shadow. Critical as Hawthorne, Poe and Melville were of Emerson's optimistic Transcendentalism, his writing none the less shows clear affinities with their expression in fiction of similar preoccupations and problems.

Emerson's essay 'Self-Reliance' (1841) picks up the separatist train of thought from the 'Declaration of Independence': 'Trust thyself: every heart vibrates to that iron string.'[35] The essay exudes confident radical meliorism, but it is underscored by nostalgic primitivism in the familiar puritan–provincial mode: society has distanced man from his true impulses; integrity is to be found only amongst 'children, babes, and even brutes!', because 'that divided and rebel mind, that distrust of a sentiment . . . these have not. The mind being whole, their eye is as yet unconquered, and when we look in their faces, we are disconcerted' (p.50). Emerson would have it both ways: the myth of the Fall into Division which structures this thought is countered by his belief that the purity and integrity of a prelapsarian world *are* recoverable by an act of will. But the world of self-reliance is a world which denies relationship; if every heart 'vibrates to that iron string', it does so in isolation: 'what have I to do with the sacredness of traditions, if I live wholly from within? . . . No law can be sacred to me but that of my nature' (p.52). 'I will have no covenants but proximities' (p.72). What Santayana calls the 'systematic subjectivism' of Transcendentalism is unequivocally celebrated in the non-participant voice of 'Self-Reliance'.[36] External, public sanctions and codes of behaviour ('covenants') fade before the internal tribunal of the self-observer; Calvinist 'conscience' is secularised (as in Common Sense philosophy) to 'consciousness', while the legalism of its original framework remains:

> the law of consciousness abides . . . I have my own stern claims and perfect circle. It denies the name of duty to many offices that are called duties. But if I can discharge its debts, it enables me to dispense with the popular code. If any one imagines that this law is lax, let him keep its commandment one day.
>
> (pp.73–4)

In 'The Transcendentalist' (1842), Emerson proclaims this creed as the new Idealism; for the Idealist, he says, 'mind is the only reality, of which men and all other natures are better or worse reflectors. Nature, literature, history, are only subjective phenomena.'[37] Emerson shares Hume's scepticism about knowing the external world as other than the product of the perceiving mind, but (drawing an inference which Hume refused) he employs the Calvinist rhetoric of distance triumphantly to overcome the consciousness of division between subject and object by denying objects:

> It is very unhappy, but too late to be helped, the discovery we have made that we exist. That discovery is called the Fall of Man. Ever afterwards we suspect our instruments. We have learned that we do not see directly, but mediately, and that we have no means of correcting these colored and distorting lenses which we are, or of computing the amount of their errors. Perhaps these subject-lenses have a creative power; perhaps there are no objects.[38]

The self-consciousness of this position is fundamental and all-embracing; it does not fear division between self and other because self may absorb and subsume other. Asserting this universal unity, the Transcendentalist pins all his faith on 'spiritual perception' rather than sensuous perception: this is Edwards' 'divine and supernatural light' immediately available to all. Now and eternity, self and nature, are the same thing in the moment of transcendent perception. Without this leap of faith, as Emerson put it in his Journal,

> I am kept out of my heritage. I talk of these powers of perceiving & communicating truth, as my powers. I look for respect as the possessor of them. & yet, after exercising them for short & irregular periods, I move about without them ... Always in the precincts – never admitted.[39]

It is the plight of the distanced provincial; Emerson reveals it as a state of mind. Heaven opens, and the natural and transcendent cohere in a mystical vision of unity which overcomes division:

> mine is a certain brief experience, which surprised me in the highway or in the market ... and made me aware that I had played the fool with fools all this time, but that law existed for me and for all; that to me belonged trust, a child's trust and obedience, and the worship of ideas, and I should never be fool more. Well, in the space of an hour probably, I was let down from this height; I was at my old tricks, the selfish member of a selfish society ... These two states of thought diverge every moment, and stand in wild contrast ... The worst feature of this double consciousness is, that the two lives, of the understanding and of the soul, which we lead, really show very little relation to each other; never meet and measure each other: one prevails now, all buzz and din; and the other prevails then, all infinitude and paradise; and, with the progress of life, the two discover no greater disposition to reconcile themselves. Yet, what is my faith? What am I? What but a thought of serenity and independence, an abode in the deep blue sky? Presently the clouds shut down again; yet we retain the belief that this pretty web we weave will at last be overshot and reticulated with veins of the blue, and that the moments will characterize the days.[40]

Compare this passage with the moment in Hume's *Treatise* (quoted above, pp.45–6), when the two halves of the 'double consciousness' are brought together in the mind, which is, as Emerson puts it in his Journal, 'the author of both parts of the dialogue'; here are two very different responses to a similar sense of division.[41] For Emerson, the 'brief experience', the mystical, spiritual vision, is the only true reality; it reveals ordinary life for the common, uninspired tawdry affair it is. The world and the spirit are opposed and never meet. The pathos of the human condition is that spiritual possession is so involuntary and fleeting: chased to no avail, it comes unsought to the passive mind and departs again as suddenly, leaving the mind questioning and bewildered: 'what is my faith? What am I?'

Hume's 'double consciousness' is reconciled *narratively*, through time, and not as a subsuming 'moment' when the earthbound body drops away from the transcendent soul, leaving it in unclogged and spiritual splendour. For Hume, the same self is at one moment the speculative, sceptical intellect, the distanced observer, at another the participating, sociable being, eating and revelling with friends. The two positions are inconsistent, but both true; they are united in the mind of the writer who accepts both as equally of himself. Narrative — story-telling — may negotiate the dangers of solipsism for the puritan–provincial. Temporal and timeless 'explanations' of perception do not compete; the paradox of free will and determinism may be sustained for as long as it can delay resolution into either/or. The 'story' for Hume, as (I shall suggest) later for Hawthorne, Melville and Scott, may provide ties, relationships and responsibilities which anchor the self beyond its own perceptions.

If Hume's writing contains its own polarities by accepting both equally, Emerson's seeks to deny their opposition by aspiring always to an absolute perspective, from which distance everything dissolves into Unity:

> One key, one solution to the mysteries of human condition, one solution to the old knots of fate, freedom, and foreknowledge, exists; the propounding, namely, of the double consciousness... So when a man is the victim of his fate ... he is to rally on his relation to the Universe, which his ruin benefits. Leaving the daemon who suffers, he is to take sides with the Deity who secures universal benefit by his pain... Let us build altars to the Blessed Unity which holds nature and souls in perfect solution, and compels every atom to serve an universal end... Let us build altars to the Beautiful Necessity. If we thought men were free in the sense that in a single exception one fantastical will could prevail over the law of things, it were all one as if a child's hand could pull down the sun. If, in the least particular one could derange the order of nature, – who would accept the gift of life?[42]

As a statement of the rightness of necessity and Calvinistic predestination, Jonathan Edwards could scarcely fault this. It lacks, however, the anchor of Original Sin, the consciousness of complicity with life's imperfections which holds man to earth and forces him to face the doubleness of human nature. There is no sense, either, in this writing of a life lived *in* the world which does not always seek to transcend it. Emerson is the secular successor of the puritan 'pilgrim and stranger'. Unless human limitations can be incorporated, made present in the writing, the 'double consciousness' easily resolves itself under pressure into a single world-denying vision of transcendent beauty, which for Emerson is the act of imagination, 'ever attended by pure delight'. It is for him the only means to overcome distanced observation and inhabit again the creating centre of experience, to 'ascend' 'from an interest in visible things to an interest in that which they signify, and from the part of a spectator to the part of a maker'.[43] Redemption is strictly secular, but it is conceived and expressed from within the puritan–provincial nexus.

The puritan was always drawn to resolve the felt conflict between world and spirit by denying the world. 'The solid seeming block of matter', as Emerson puts it in *Nature*, 'has been pervaded and dissolved by a thought.'[44] Emerson's Transcendental poet is not brought up short by the real; he uses 'things or visible nature' as 'types or words for thoughts' ('Poetry and Imagination', p.24). For him knowledge is possession, and possession is power: he subdues otherness by subsuming it; 'unfix[ing] the land and the sea, [he] makes them revolve around the axis of his primary thought, and disposes them anew. Possessed himself by a heroic passion, he uses matter as symbols of it. The sensual man conforms thoughts to things; the poet conforms things to his thoughts' (*Nature*, p.56).

In the Calvinist universe, uninterpreted signs threaten and coerce: 'For every seeing soul there are two absorbing facts, I and the Abyss', as Emerson confided to his Journal in 1866.[45] Unless the perceiver can dominate by interpretation (colonise otherness to his own powers of imposing meaning), that otherness – full of unpossessed significance – threatens to define *him* as one of the reprobate, excluded from significance and salvation. The quintessentially Emersonian poem is the enigmatic chant of the riddling 'Sphinx': 'who telleth me one of my meanings, / Is master of all I am'.[46] For obsessively self-referential provincials, Nature only exists to carry messages from Spirit; spiritual 'facts' are more concrete than natural 'facts':

1. Words are signs of natural facts.
2. Particular natural facts are symbols of particular spiritual facts.
3. Nature is the symbol of spirit. (*Nature*, p.31)

The 'symbolising' frame of mind exercises great fascination over the imaginations of Hawthorne, Melville and Carlyle. All three consider whether – and how – 'Nature' can truly be said to be 'the symbol of spirit'. Carlyle evokes a truly Calvinist scepticism (shared by both Hawthorne and Melville, and by the Emerson of 'Experience' if not of *Nature*) when he confers the doubleness of 'concealment' as well as 'revelation' on symbols.[47] In Carlyle's cosmology, 'Heroes' alone can read the 'open secret' of the universe; they are the elect who – as Melville would put it – have the ability to 'pierce through the pasteboard mask' of symbolic appearances to the reality behind.[48]

Emerson's confidence in the 'radical correspondence between visible things and human thoughts' (p.34) tends to collapse the distinctions between self and other, observer and the world. Most importantly for the writer, the 'other' is his audience. In his act of interpretation, in carrying the 'message' of spirit to the soul of the reader through the medium of language, puritan–provincial writers have constant designs upon their audience. They lay siege to our attentions and demand our assent: the contract or covenant is absolute. Accepting the writer's right to interpret for us, we surrender our own powers of judgement. Such writing offers no negotiation; it coheres on its own terms, but these terms may not be questioned: the reader accepts and enters, or rejects and remains outside. This re-enacts the relationship of absolute dominance and submission between God and man with all the intransigence of Calvinism.

Emerson's *Nature*, with its evasive verbal equivocations, may seem a long way from the coercive appeal of a hell-fire sermon, but it is a virtuoso performance which attempts to colonise assent by appealing to 'feeling' abstracted from reason, seducing the readers into agreeing with his propositions before they quite understand or possess them. It systematically subverts the traditional vocabulary of belief, sliding, for example, smoothly from 'God' to 'some god' to 'the soul', until we realise that somehow we have assented to the thought that 'God' and 'self' may by synonymous (pp.52–3). His doctrine of 'Idealism' is introduced by an astonishing passage which suggests that it does not matter whether Nature is 'real' or 'ideal', whether the external world exists or is entirely a figment of the human imagination:

> In my utter impotence to test the authenticity of the report of my sense, to know whether the impressions they make on me correspond with outlying objects, what difference does it make, whether Orion is up there in heaven, or some god paints the image on the firmament of the soul? The relations of parts and the end of the whole remaining the same, what is the difference, whether land and sea interact, and worlds revolve and intermingle without number or end ... or whether, without relations of time and space, the same appearances are inscribed in the constant faith of man? Whether nature enjoy a substantial existence without, or is only in the apocalypse of the mind, it is alike useful and alike venerable to me. Be it what it may, it is ideal to me so long as I cannot try the accuracy of my senses. (pp.52–3)

From here it is the merest step (as though it had been argued), to assert that the ideal *is* the real: 'ideal affinities ... only are real' (p.59). Hume never makes it a matter of *indifference* whether or not the external world has an existence apart from our sense-perceptions of it: to say that we cannot finally know something is not at all the same as saying that because we cannot know we do not care. In fact, of course, Emerson's rhetoric is inveigling the reader to move from the sceptical position to the Idealist one – to colonise all manifestations of otherness as creations of the self. The implication (which is smoothly arrived at from a starting point of 'indifference' as to the existence of the external) is an undervaluing of experience and a negation of everything but the express products of mind, sensibly conceived. Emerson's response to the harshness of experience is to deny it reality; this is how the puritan–provincial mind defends itself against what it cannot subdue:

> We dress our garden, eat our dinners, discuss the household with our wives, and these things make no impression, are forgotten next week; but, in the solitude to which every man is always returning, he has a sanity and revelations which in his passage into new worlds he will carry with him.[49]

Emerson's own title, 'Experience', challenges the reader to set this against Montaigne:

> My selfe who but grovell on the ground, hate that kinde of humane Wisedome, which would make us disdainefull and enemies of the bodies reformation. I deeme it an equall injustice, either to take naturall sensualities against the hart, or to take them too neere the hart ... One should neither follow nor avoyd them: but receive them. I receive them somewhat more amply and graciously, and rather am contented to follow naturall inclination. We need not exaggerate their inanity: it will sufficiently be felt, and doth sufficiently produce it selfe.[50]

It is worth pausing over the relationship between Jefferson's appropriation of Montaigne's 'soft pillow of ignorance' in support of 'experience' against theory and Emerson's inclination to dispose of the physical world in favour of the spiritual. If they are poles apart – Jefferson plants his feet firmly on the *facts* of experience and refuses to speculate; Emerson wonders 'How long before our masquerade will end ... and we shall find it was a solitary performance?' ('Experience', p.81) – that very polarity gives them an affinity which sets them apart from the central stance of their model. Jefferson appeals to experience against theory; Emerson appeals to it for evidence of its insubstantiality. Montaigne, on the other hand, is not appealing to experience *for* anything: 'One should neither follow nor avoyd [naturall sensualities], but receive them.' He is neither distanced from it nor immersed in it. Here, self-consciousness is a voice confidently participating in all its own ironies and inconsistencies, and enjoying the impossibility of resolution:

> Philosophicall inquisitions and contemplations serve but as a nourishment unto our curiosity. With great reason doe Philosophers address us unto natures rules: But they have nought to doe with so sublime a knowledge: They falsifie them, and present her to us with a painted face, too-high in colour and over-much sophisticated; whence arise so many different pourtraits of so uniforme a subject. As she hath given us feete to goe withall, so hath she endowed us with wisedome to direct our life. A wisedome not so ingenious, sturdy and pompous as that of their invention; but yet easie, quiet and salutairie. And that in him that hath the hap to know how to employ it orderly and sincerely, effecteth very well what the other saith: that is to say naturally. For a man to commit himselfe most simply unto nature, is to doe it most wisely. *Oh how soft, how gentle, and how sound a pillow is ignorance and incuriosity to rest a well-composed head upon.*[51]

This is less a declaration of independence than a declaration of common cause. It accepts 'nature' but makes no attempt to subdue or define it.

Montaigne is an important figure for Hume as well as for Emerson and Jefferson: for puritan–provincial writers, his sceptical stance represents the possibility of mediating between polarities. As Emerson put it in his lecture on 'Montaigne; or, The Skeptic' (1845), between 'the abstractionist and materialist . . . there arises a third party to occupy the middle ground', who 'finds both wrong by being in extremes. He labours to plant his feet, to be the beam of the balance.'[52]

Set the passage from Montaigne himself against Hume's portrait of 'The Sceptic' (quoted above, p.45): this 'middle ground' is *occupied*, lived in, by Hume and Montaigne as it never is by Emerson, whose very description of the position implies a resolution, a unification of opposites, and whose own rhetoric tends always to favour the 'abstract' over the 'material'. Indeed, the polarised structure into which Emerson approvingly drops Montaigne – 'nothing so thin but has these two faces, and when the observer has seen the obverse, he turns it over to see the reverse. Life is a pitching of this penny, heads *or* tails' (p.143; my emphasis) – finds a suggestive resolution in a position more comforting to the puritan–provincial observer then free sceptical thinking:

> The final solution in which skepticism is lost, is in the moral sentiment, which never forfeits its supremacy. All moods may be safely tried, and their weight allowed to all objections: the moral sentiment as easily outweighs them all, as any one. (p.174)

Montaigne and Hume, on the other hand, inhabit a humanly complex position which is utterly simple in its ability to know the truth about itself and not need to do anything with it. It is 'that acceptant view which is comic in its profoundest sense, which is part reconciliation, part knowledge of eternal disparity'.[53] In Emerson's writing, the puritan–provincial outlook reaches consummate expression: theological Calvinism is secularised to a thoroughgoing philosophical Idealism which sweeps away anxieties and tensions inherent in the puritan polarities. Faith in the 'transcendent signifier' (God) – which controlled the early Calvinists' tendency to interpretative solipsism – has been replaced by a serenely subjective self which transcends the problems of relating temporal and eternal, word and meaning, appearance and truth in a single unifying vision untroubled by its own solipsism.

Scottish and American imaginative writers of the nineteenth century characteristically find their subject matter in the range of experience associated with the same puritan–provincial dichotomies; but at their best, Irving, Poe, Hawthorne and Melville, and Scott, Hogg, Lockhart and Carlyle all reject the unifying vision to search for an equivalent in fiction to Hume's poised scepticism. The following chapters appraise some of their attempts to accommodate mutually excluding oppositions in a more expansive vision of reality.

4

The pursuit of the double

By inquiring out of the proper way, I mean when puny man endeavours to penetrate to the hidden recesses of the divine wisdom... in order that he may understand what final determination God has made with regard to him. In this way he plunges headlong into an immense abyss, involves himself in numberless inextricable snares, and buries himself in the thickest darkness.

(John Calvin)

For this is the nature of a guilty conscience, to fly and to be terrified, even when all is safe and prosperous, to convert all into peril and death.

(Martin Luther)

[I] feel that every thought, every cause, is bipolar & in the act is contained the counteract. If I strike, I am struck. If I chase, I am pursued. If I push, I am resisted.

(R.W. Emerson)[1]

The paradox of the puritan–provincial mind is that it knows it cannot know the hidden truth of the 'centre', and yet must strive for knowledge. Inscrutable appearances both torment and fascinate. The centre of significance seems always veiled by the surfaces of nature and of language; truth and knowledge are forbidden secrets which must be fathomed in *opposition* to the tyrannous will at the heart of things. The puritan's or the provincial's search for knowledge is thus also a bid for independence, an attempt to shed the abject state of distanced ignorance and to live apart from the forces which seem to control existence. He desires, though, to gain knowledge without losing innocence, which in a Fallen world is impossible; the result is that his perception divides, the one half capitulating to the 'experience' of the centre with its connotations of degeneracy and decadence, the other half standing aloof

The pursuit of the double 71

to maintain its radical innocence. Within the puritan, this bifurcation corresponds to the division of conscience and will; within the provincial, it is the simultaneous desire to emulate and to be independent.

Appealing from theory (or theology) to experience is complicated for puritan–provincials, because the relationship between mind and the world it observes is always positively in question: reason and feeling or belief never simply cohere. The active rationalising faculty and the reactive sympathetic capacities of response are at odds within the individual; the Calvinistic heritage means that this division is associated with guilt. Pursuing the knowledge which would represent integrity, identity or independence also entails flight from the consequences of involvement with experience; the pattern of flight and pursuit doubles and interlocks the puritan–provincial's fate with the aroused passions of the centre. The distinction between self and other blurs and may be lost. In this binary pattern of oppression and rebellion, dominance and submission represent the only conceivable form of relationship.

Division within the self reproduces the doubling without: confrontation becomes self-confrontation, pursuit becomes soul-searching. In their narratives of flight and pursuit Scottish and American writers give temporal extension to a state of mind. The conflict between actively rational and sympathetically responsive aspects of the self becomes dramatic as the fictions juxtapose the mutually contradictory accents of reason and of feeling whose polarisation was described in chapters 1 to 3. Behind both radical and reactive viewpoints is the rhetoric of Calvin strengthening the ties and the mutual antagonism between them. Combined in this way, their emotional power is highly compelling. These fictions abound in echoes and re-expressions of Calvin's formulations; both language and structure testify to the continued vitality of puritan–provincial perception. Living a life and telling a tale unfold in parallel as the self-justifying voices of these narratives attempt to dominate the sympathies of their audience. The results can be claustrophobic, enclosing the reader so tightly within the puritan–provincial mind that no wider horizon is visible. But they may also be critical, illuminating the state without becoming trapped within it. A question which must be asked of these tales – because it defines the difference between provincial fiction and fiction about provinciality – is whether and how the author is able to imply the existence of a world beyond the co-ordinates of the divided mind.

Puritanism and provincialism relate primarily not to a body of doctrine, a geographical location or a political affiliation, but to a state of mind, a predisposition to view the world in certain ways. The structure and expression of Scottish and American fiction in the first half of the nineteenth century characteristically exemplify this mode, but although it is pre-eminently visible here because of intense reinforcement from all the cultural forces which impinge upon literature – and is therefore best revealed by this context – the puritan–provincial outlook is not in any sense confined to it. The most suggestive avenue into the Scottish and American fictions of flight and pursuit is the work of an Englishman whose writing adopts a defiantly eccentric stance towards the typical concerns of the English novel.

William Godwin was a lapsed dissenting minister, a political radical and the author of an influential anarchist tract when in 1794 he published *Things as They Are; or, the Adventures of Caleb Williams*. It had immediate and lasting effects on Scottish and American fiction, far disproportionate to its influence on English literature but commensurate with its puritan–provincial rationale. A provincial lad, Caleb Williams, enters the employment of a courteous but mysteriously melancholy master, Falkland. Caleb becomes convinced that Falkland's dejection is the consequence of a guilty secret and resolves to know the truth. His curiosity drives him to open a private trunk in defiance of Falkland's express injunction:

> Thus was I hurried along by an uncontrollable destiny. The state of my passions in their progressive career, the inquisitiveness and impatience of my thoughts, appeared to make this determination unavoidable ... I had always reverenced the sublime mind of Mr. Falkland; I reverenced it still. My offence had merely been a mistaken thirst of knowledge.[2]

Falkland pursues him relentlessly for this 'sin', and he becomes an outcast from society. But Caleb is also 'chosen', picked out by Falkland: elected for service, he *cannot* leave, and as the 'adventures' of Caleb's flight from the vengeful master develop, the fates of protagonist and antagonist become strangely interlinked. Having broken one covenant by his disobedience, Caleb tries to bargain for another from a position of utter weakness:

> I was prepared for an amicable adjustment of interests; I would undertake that Mr. Falkland should never sustain injury through my means; but I expected in return that I should suffer no encroachment, but be left to the direction of my own understanding ... [Falkland replies:] You little suspect the extent of my power. At this moment you are enclosed with the snares of my vengeance, unseen by you, and at the instant that you flatter yourself you are already beyond their reach, they will close upon you. You might as well think of escaping from the power of the omnipresent God, as from mine! (p.144)

Caleb's accommodating tones of common sense propose a genteel compromise which is starkly countered by the Calvinistic determinism of Falkland's response. 'That is my will', he declares (p.153); his despotism is absolute, and his powers of surveillance and pursuit seem to

Caleb not only inexorable but super-human. But Falkland is also a being of superior goodness, looked up to 'with veneration' (p.7) by his servants, including Caleb himself. Godwin's language ensures, somewhat obtrusively, that Calvinism provides the primary terms for the novel's action.

The idioms of Calvinism and of radicalism are closely allied: besides being the story of Caleb Williams, the novel was a propagandist tract for the Jacobin age. When Caleb is imprisoned, and again when he escapes, his reflections blend religious anguish and self-justification, anger at social and political injustice and a characteristically provincial sense of distance from the heart of events:

> I was astonished at the folly of my species, that they did not rise up as one man, and shake off chains so ignominious and misery so insupportable... I resolved ... to hold myself disengaged from this odious scene, and never fill the part either of the oppressor or the sufferer. (p.156)

However, determinism finally proves the more powerful force; Caleb's resolution of disengagement is thwarted at every point as his life and Falkland's become increasingly embroiled. Caleb never finds a position from which to stand outside his apparently predestined fate of eternal flight and pursuit, and nothing in the book's language or shape can suggest what such a stance might be. The oppositions, polarities and doublings of the novel's structure so closely reflect the Calvinist frame that its radical intentions are simply swamped. Caleb continually tries to act as though he were the Godwinian free agent proclaimed by *Political Justice*, but his curiosity is a passion which subverts all reason; possessed by and not in possession of his own fate, he is 'advancing to the brink of the precipice'. He had, he says, 'a confused apprehension of what I was doing, but could not stop myself' (p.113).

The radical idiom none the less provides a way of opposing the characters of Caleb and Falkland and the worlds to which they belong. Caleb is pre-eminently – and disastrously – rational: his whole being works on logical principles of observation and inference. Starting from an utter confidence in 'facts', he searches obsessively for the truth which will dispel the mysteries which surround him. Caleb's voice is forthright and matter-of-fact; his radicalism declares a vigorous unanswerability reminiscent of Tom Paine. By contrast his master and victim, pursuer and double, is a gothic figure from a degenerate and anachronistic aristocratic world – the world of the oppressors – whose characteristics reveal themselves in conventional terms. Godwin arranges dramatic clashes between two utterly opposed vocabularies and ways of life:

> Villain, cried he, what has brought you here? I hesitated a confused and irresolute answer. Wretch, interrupted Mr. Falkland with uncontrollable

impatience, you want to ruin me. You set yourself as a spy upon my actions. But bitterly shall you repent your insolence. Do you think you shall watch my privacies with impunity? I attempted to defend myself. Begone, devil! rejoined he. Quit the room, or I will trample you into atoms. (p.8)

These worlds begin to impinge on one another as Caleb's 'innocent' radicalism dissolves in the murky gothic pool of 'experience' with a compelling psychological verisimilitude which creates in the reader 'an impression as if the events and feelings had been personal to himself'.[3] The source of this power is neither radicalism nor gothicism, but the language of 'feelings'. Here are Adam Smith's involuntary sympathies overriding both rationality and principle; they reassert a psychological determinism which reinforces the Calvinist temper without being bound by its theological dimensions. This rhetoric of sympathy completes the puritan–provincial matrix which at once defines the book's structure of dualities and accounts for its emotional compulsion. 'Facts' – the basic counters of the rational mind – continually prove to be at odds with the beliefs or 'affections' which control the workings of that mind. The inherent contradiction of an empirical psychology of sensation or 'feeling' in pursuit of rationalist ends (already seen in the writings of the Scottish Common Sense philosophers) receives dramatic embodiment in the narrative of *Caleb Williams*. Caleb's actions are governed by association and sentiment; he becomes aware of the 'magnetical sympathy' (p.112) between himself and Falkland and feels that he 'perfectly understood his feelings' (p.126). Indeed, *all* relationships in the novel are governed by sympathy, which tends to 'double' parallel occurrences and characters rather than differentiating between them; pursuer and pursued become two aspects of a single character at war with itself. This fusion, which is also a division, has religious, psychological and political dimensions; it marks a transition from the terms of objective truths to those of subjective impressions. Confrontation becomes self-confrontation, and thought slides continually into self-consciousness: 'Why should my reflections perpetually centre upon myself? self, an overweening regard to which has been the source of my errors!' (p.325).

It is the plight of the provincial. Caleb is a candid youth who 'had had no intercourse with the world and its passions; and, though [he] was not totally unacquainted with them as they appear in books, this proved to be of little service to [him] when [he] came to witness them [him]self' (p.106); in Falkland he confronts moral and psychological complexities for which he has simply no resources. The theory of his innocent state cannot accommodate the experience of continuing life. With this vulnerability, to discover Falkland's secret is for him to be in turn possessed by it. Falkland's 'inheritance' has made him what Matthew Arnold (describing the historical Falkland who may have been Godwin's model) calls 'a man in the grasp of fatality'; this is precisely what Caleb himself is aware of becoming through his uncontrollable curiosity.[4]

Caleb's confirmation of Falkland's guilt marks an epoch which irrevocably divides in his life 'what may be called the offensive part, from the defensive which was the sole business of my remaining years' (p.134). For both men, *offence* throws the sinner into *defensiveness*, passivity and evasion: an action undertaken to assert independence at once entails and makes manifest the pitiful subjection of the individual:

> I was incapable of any resolution. All was chaos and uncertainty within me. My thoughts were too full of horror to be susceptible of activity. I felt deserted of my intellectual powers, palsied in mind, and compelled to sit in speechless expectation of the misery to which I was destined. (p.134)

Caleb's story is a parable of the Calvinist Fall and a dramatic evocation of the plight of the provincial. Distance and the absence of relation co-ordinate his universe. His position is impossible: innocence is also ignorance which demands to be educated into knowledge. Knowledge of the centre's secrets is the fall which enables the provincial to see his (lost) innocence for what it was, but it simultaneously structures his world as a series of polarities. He knows these to be inadequate to the truth of experience as *lived at* the centre, but can find no sufficient language for its complexities. Caleb's dilemma poses anew Milton's rhetorical question: What kind of good is that which only exists through ignorance of evil? To know why something is forbidden one would have to know the forbidden thing itself; Calvinists are enjoined to accept or to reject the prohibition *because* it is arbitrary. Either submit to the secrets of the Divine will or attempt to dominate that will by penetrating its decrees: there seems no possible path between the extremes of action and passivity.

Throughout the book, Caleb defines himself always in opposition to Falkland: by 'proving' Falkland's guilt, he both infers and vindicates his own innocence. As Caleb begins to confront his own guilt or complicity, Falkland comes to seem less so, until in the final scene where Caleb renounces passive flight and turns to attack his pursuer, their ethical positions appear to undergo an instant and complete reversal:

> I proclaim to all the world that Mr. Falkland is a man worthy of affection and kindness, and that I am myself the basest and most odious of mankind! . . . In thus acting I have been a murderer, a cool, deliberate, unfeeling murderer. (p.323)

At this point, even more strangely, Falkland throws himself into Caleb's arms and submits to *his* dominance: 'you have conquered!' (p.324).

Unaccountable though it is, this dramatic *dénouement* stays entirely within the terms which are established by, and then come to control, the rest of the narrative. Just as Caleb, to the end, cannot find anything to replace the moral polarities of guilt and innocence, so Godwin himself can offer nothing better than 'ambiguity' (Caleb's own term) to relate the mutually contradictory idioms which coexist in the book. And 'ambiguity' – implying confusion or unclarity between two *opposing* interpretations, one 'right', the other 'wrong' – is itself merely a momentary resting place, a slippery middle ground between the heights and the depths.[5] *Caleb Williams* remains two books which coexist in just such an 'ambiguous' relationship. It is a radical, revolutionary novel which sees the centre, the enemy, as beyond itself, graspable and conquerable, a novel in which, right to the end, the pursuit is a 'pursuit of happiness'. This is the novel of active Calvinism, of 'truths assured of ultimate triumph'.[6] But it is also (and to modern readers more compellingly) a pessimistic novel of psychological determinism in which the enemy, the other, is within. The battleground is the soul in which antagonistic elements of the self are locked in predestined and issueless conflict. This is the novel of passive, defensive or 'provincial' Calvinism. Each book is at once the double and the polar opposite of the other, and Godwin offers no key to unlock them from each other's grip.

This coercive framework extends even to the relationship between narrator and reader. The colonising voice of the self-justifying (and, later, self-accusing) narrator Caleb demands, with Poe-like intensity, the reader's assent to the truth of his tale. As with Calvinism itself, no negotiation is possible in this relationship: the reader who refuses to swallow Caleb's clearly unstable interpretation of events whole is offered no alternative standpoint (either within the tale or from a narrative voice) from which to reach a more reliable assessment. In this case the book itself becomes a tantalising repository of unpossessed secret meanings. Caleb has an interest in perpetuating the rhetoric of opposition and oppression, which avoids the need to take responsibility for his actions; asserting his passivity before events is excellent defence: predestination can take the blame. What Caleb (and Godwin) cannot realise for the reader is the way in which the assumption of 'experience', 'guilt' and responsibility may be simultaneously a declaration of freedom. Not only is Godwin's language trapped in the puritan–provincial nexus of his conflicting idioms; the plot also fails to use the progressive unfolding of narrative in time – telling the story – to stand outside the compulsively repetitive swings of the Calvinist pendulum. The obsessive catalogue of flights and pursuits has itself all the claustrophobic tensions of the divided mind. It required greater imaginative capacities than Godwin possessed to transform the puritan–provincial trope of doubled flight and pursuit into an account of the present real possibilities of being through the act of narration itself.

One of Charles Brockden Brown's literary ambitions was 'to finish a work equal in extent to Caleb Williams'.[7] He most nearly achieved this in *Edgar Huntly; or Memoirs of a Sleepwalker* (1799), a narrative of flight and pursuit in which two first-person accounts increasingly reflect one another and threaten to collapse into a single nightmare of internal division. The preface sees a specifically American potential in the mingling of narrative and psychological dimensions, or as Brockden Brown describes it, 'a series of adventures, growing out of the condition of our country and connected with one of the most common and most wonderful diseases or affections of the human frame'.[8] The nature of this 'connection' is powerfully suggested by the novel's coercive puritan–provincial idiom, but it is not fully controlled by Brockden Brown's thought. The power of the writing exerted an influence on Poe and Hawthorne: these writers were able to relate the internal disorders of the mind to the external 'story' of America with a subtlety of implication which evades the polarities and oppositions that are its controlling structures. But Brockden Brown's unformed apprehension of the American possibilities in his Godwinian model makes a fascinating prelude to the achievement of these later writers.

The young American hero Edgar Huntly suspects a melancholy European, Clithero Edny, of murdering his friend and determines to penetrate the secret of the other's evident derangement:

> Henceforth this man was to become the subject of my scrutiny. I was to gain all the knowledge, respecting him, which those with whom he lived . . . could impart. For this end I was to make minute inquiries, and to put reasonable interrogatories. From this conduct I promised myself an ultimate solution of my doubts. I acquiesced in this view of things with considerable satisfaction. It seemed as if the maze was no longer inscrutable. (pp.39–40)

But Huntly's pursuit of the truth is hampered by his 'limited and uniform' experience, gained mostly from books; 'I found', he says, 'that to be a distant and second-hand spectator of events was widely different from witnessing them myself and partaking in their consequences' (p.100).

Huntly feels himself a 'chosen' American, absolved from the guilt of his European quarry's past and confident of his benevolent motives and reasoning powers. Not realising that his 'innocence' is merely ignorance, he thinks himself with what Brockden Brown elsewhere calls 'all the subtilties of ratiocination' into disastrously erroneous conclusions.[9] Such unwarranted tracing of hidden causes from observed effects implicates Huntly himself in Clithero's crimes and condemns him to re-enact Clithero's fate. He becomes like his 'conductor' a sleepwalker through the American wilderness, poised over the Calvinistic abyss to whose brink he has been brought by the unlawful wish to penetrate the truth of another soul. His 'sympathy' with Clithero is unsatisfied until it achieves empathic self-identification, and until 'appearance' has succumbed to 'significance'.

Aggression and defensiveness become inextricable as pursuit turns into an emblem of inner division; both Clithero and Huntly find their conscious wills overridden and made passive by the activated conscience. A confused and nightmarish web of doublings and oppositions directs the narrative until Huntly's Calvinist origins reveal themselves in pessimistic exhaustion which desires nothing but an end to self-consciousness: 'Was I born to a malignant destiny never tired of persecuting?' (p.176). Despite Clithero's bitter indictment of his egotistical self-gratification, Huntly remains to the end unaware of the disproportion between his good intentions and their disastrous outcome. He continues to reason on puritan principles which repeatedly prove inadequate to experience, and his benevolent impulse towards another can only express itself in a relation of dominance and submission: 'it shall be my province to emulate a father's clemency, and restore this unhappy man to purity and to peace' (p.54).

Obsessively recapitulating Clithero's experiences, Huntly equates thought with self-consciousness in an image that anticipates Poe: 'Consciousness itself', he says (meaning *self*-consciousness), 'is the malady, the pest, of which he only is cured who ceases to think' (p.249). The psychological power of the puritan rhetoric at once masks and exposes the self-enclosed fixation of the mind that employs it; these tones will be struck again through Hogg's *Confessions* and Hawthorne's 'Young Goodman Brown':

> All within me was tempestuous and dark. My ears were accessible to no sounds but those of shrieks and lamentations. It was deepest midnight, and all the sounds of a great metropolis were hushed. Yet I listened as if to catch some strains of the dirge that was begun. Sable robes, sobs, and a dreary solemnity encompassed me on all sides. I was haunted to despair by images of death, imaginary clamors, and the train of funeral pageantry. I seemed to have passed forward to a distant era of my life. The effects which were to come were already realized. The foresight of misery created it, and set me in the midst of that hell which I feared. (p.90)[10]

This is Clithero at the scene of the murder which is his fall, and, proximately, Huntly's too. It is a moment which telescopes time and continuity into the instantaneous consciousness of the perceiver: intense self-awareness is crucial here, but set beside comparable moments in Poe it looks curiously artless. It has analogies with the moment of outraged sensibility in Jefferson's 'Declaration of Independence': there is no continuous emotional register in *Edgar Huntly* to connect the languages of mind and heart. Brockden Brown's narrative finds no Middle Way – either in the story or its telling – between the polarised extremes of rationalism and terror, but, unlike Poe's, his prose does not relish the disjunction and exploit it for effect. Brockden Brown handles his gothic machinery with utter seriousness; he lacks the means to insinuate uncertainty or to suggest the untrustworthiness or self-dramatisation of the first-person narrator.

The problem is compounded by the narrative dimension of flight and pursuit which arises directly from the moment of guilt: it doubles and enforces this kind of perception without finding any external correlative which might comment implicitly on its narrow angle of vision. The caverns, torrents, panthers and ferocious Indians which Huntly encounters in his headlong rush through time and the pages of the book obsessively re-enact his state of mind. Huntly's mind does not develop, and his actions cannot release him from the predestined mould of his self-conscious perceptions. Inner and outer mirror one another in *Edgar Huntly* with a claustrophobic intensity which sorts oddly with a world which none the less clings (like Godwin's 'radical' *Caleb Williams*) to the possibility of rational explanation. Such rampantly solipsistic rationalism in the face of threateningly contradictory experience is the puritan–provincial ego's disguised attempt to dominate and subdue its surroundings.

The effect is curiously static and finally redundant: it seems a subject more suited to a short story than to the narrative extension of Brockden Brown's treatment.[11] Like Huntly, the author cannot allow anything to remain mysterious within the novel. In the dreamlike inconsequentiality of events are many initially inexplicable incidents which undermine Huntly's naive rationalism and suggest that the 'facts' he trusts so implicitly are merely a small part, if that, of the complexity of truth. There is in the end always a rational explanation forthcoming for such mysteries, but, as W.H. Prescott noted in 1834, attempts 'to account for the marvels of the story by natural or mechanical causes . . . are very seldom satisfactory, or competent to their effect'.[12] The problem lies in the circularity of explaining events themselves introduced to undermine the narrator's confident rationalism in rational terms, even at the 'higher' level of authorial narration. As with the spontaneous combustion of a character in Brockden Brown's earlier novel *Wieland* (1798), Edgar Huntly's somnambulism seems emotionally inadequate as an 'explanation' of many mysterious events, but the text leaves no room for further interpretation. Brockden Brown exposes the shortcomings and the dangers of a mentality which searches always for 'significance' behind appearances, but he has written a book whose emotional coerciveness creates this appetite in its reader *and* – quite naively – attempts to satisfy it. We must look to Hawthorne, Melville and Poe for something which unmasks the puritan–provincial viewpoint without succumbing to it, and to Scott and Hogg for a historical and narrative framework which circumvents 'explanations' to reunite thought and feeling and to give the inexplicable in human nature a place inaccessible to reason's claims. Where Brockden Brown is anxiously circumstantial about his mysteries, his successors are, in different ways, reticent.

James Hogg's *The Private Memoirs and Confessions of a Justified Sinner* (1824) tells what purports to be the same story twice, in versions whose accounts are quite irreconcilable. The initial doubling of the twice-told story is reflected at every turn in the narrative itself, which is a complex tale of pursuit: the pursuit and eventual murder of the 'Enlightened' hero George Colwan by his Calvinist brother Robert Wringhim; the pursuit of Wringhim by his satanic 'double' Gil-Martin; the pursuit of Wringhim simultaneously by the forces of law and the demons of Scottish folklore. Both Wringhim's own narrative and that of the Editor who attempts later to piece together the story are pursuits of the 'truth', the 'facts' behind the appearances of events. The 'Sinner' Robert Wringhim's account is a spiritual autobiography which describes his inquiry into the clues that external occurrences may afford about the state of his soul. The Editor is an Enlightenment Scot whose version of the story uses 'nature, utility, and common sense' to establish empirical facts behind the contradictory traditions which surround the strange events of Wringhim's life.[13]

The languages, suppositions and intentions of these narrators are utterly opposed; both are, finally, found wanting as complete or objective accounts. But neither do they complement one another and between them reveal the 'truth' to the reader: *The Westminster Review* said in exasperation that 'the author has managed the tale very clumsily, having made two distinct narratives of the same events; and, however true it may be in mathematics, it certainly does not always hold in story-telling, that two halves are equal to one whole'.[14] Nor does Hogg ever intend that they should. For if the Editor and the Sinner represent diametrically opposed viewpoints, they are also facets of the same puritan–provincial mind. Both search for unassailable truth beyond inscrutable appearances; both 'interpret' these appearances through a series of polarities, doublings and oppositions. Having projected this structure onto the world, they then find that events, as they 'read' them back, confirm it. The idioms of the Editor and of the Sinner work respectively on natural and supernatural assumptions: one belongs to the provincial moment of Scottish history, the other to its puritan phase. Their outlooks have a fundamental similarity which gives the book as a whole consistency and imaginative coherence; it is the fullest evocation of the puritan–provincial temper in all the literature of this period.

The Editor's narrative describes the relationship of George Colwan and his brother or half-brother Wringhim as one of flight and pursuit.

The pursuer or (as the Editor says) 'persecutor', Wringhim, 'a devilish-looking youth' who 'knew no other pleasure but what consisted in opposition', attended the attractive and carefree Colwan 'as constantly as his shadow', demanding to be spurned and persecuted (pp.34,21). Wringhim's 'constant' and 'inexplicable' attendance on Colwan has the effect – according to the Editor – of making his brother an outcast: 'at last George was fairly driven from society, and forced to spend his days in his own and his father's lodgings with closed doors' (p.37). The existence and the nature of the two men are defined by their antagonism, and after Colwan's death Wringhim is apparently haunted by a 'familiar' in the shape of his murdered brother. Each, perhaps, is the conscience of the other. Despite his vaunted rationalism and spirit of enlightened inquiry, the Editor does not hesitate to describe Wringhim's apparently uncanny knowledge of his victim's movements as 'like the attendance of a demon on some devoted being that had sold himself to destruction' (p.37).

Wringhim's narrative begins 'I was born an outcast in the world' (p.97);[15] he is a 'pilgrim and stranger' whose tale attempts to coerce the reader's acquiescence in an interpretation of events which would support his 'election'. His pattern of doublings and oppositions is the mirror image of the Editor's account of George Colwan's troubles, couched now in the self-justifying terms of the Calvinist autobiographer rather than the rationalising tones of the Common Sense antiquarian. Like Caleb Williams, the Sinner has a sense of the specialness of his fate, 'without which, this detail of my actions would have been as a tale that hath been told . . . in short, a thing of nothing' (p.114). Because of his election, however, his story has significance as a pattern for others. Like Caleb, too, the sense of his own righteousness sustains him through trials and pursuit, as he finds himself universally execrated for crimes he is not conscious of having committed. He is the living embodiment of Calvin's dictum that 'there is a singular consolation . . . when we are persecuted for righteousness' sake'.[16] Hogg also borrows the radical language of oppression to evoke the Sinner's sense of his plight: his tormenting mentor Gil-Martin becomes his 'tyrant', and the others his 'persecutors' (p.205).

The pursuit motif which structures the Editor's understanding of Colwan's and Wringhim's relationship also underscores Wringhim's own understanding of his mysterious consanguinity with Gil-Martin. At their first meeting, which takes place at the exact moment when Wringhim feels convinced that he is of the elect, but which may in fact be the moment of his Fall (through spiritual pride), he describes 'a sort of invisible power that drew me towards him, something like the force of enchantment, which I could not resist . . . he was the same being with myself!' (p.116). Gil-Martin declares, ironically echoing the dubious relationship between Colwan and Wringhim, 'I am indeed your brother, not according to the flesh, but in my belief of the same truths' (p.117), and reveals that his sympathetic powers compass both physical and psychological appropriation of another's identity: 'by contemplating a face minutely,' he says, 'I not only attain the same likeness . . . I attain the very same ideas . . . the possession of his most secret thoughts' (p.125). Here is the threatening potential of 'sympathy' over personal integrity made manifest.

The provincial Wringhim who 'lack[s] not the spirit, nor the will, but . . . lack[s] experience wofully', at first thinks that he would 'give worlds' to be able to emulate such 'a rare qualification' in his mentor, but soon comes to fear Gil-Martin in all his avatars: 'He was constant to me as my shadow, and by degrees he acquired such an ascendancy over me, that I was never happy out of his company, nor greatly so in it' (pp.156, 125, 132). The relationship comes to seem one of dominance and submission: Wringhim feels himself the 'prize' and the 'possession' of Gil-Martin (p.145). It is a relationship repeatedly enacted in Hogg's fiction: between the dwarf Merodach and the lady who abhors and is charmed by him in 'The Brownie of the Black Haggs', for example, or between Kendale and the 'Baron St Gio' who tells him that 'you must be sensible that you are now entirely in my power, and at my disposal, and that all your dependence must be on me'.[17]

Increasingly, Wringhim and Gil-Martin become inseparable: 'to shake him off was impossible – we were incorporated together – identified with one another, as it were, and the power was not in me to separate myself from him' (p.183). This is Locke's 'Two Persons in one Man' with a vengeance. The 'double' who first appeared to him at his moment of great spiritual triumph has become the burden of his life. If this is true of Wringhim's invocation of Gil-Martin, it may be equally true of George Colwan, who encounters Wringhim first as a mocking parody of the 'plaudits of approval' (p.20) which greet his prowess at tennis. In both cases, the continuing presence of the double threatens not only the protagonist's self-esteem but his very identity. For Wringhim, the protracted torment of being pursued through the Borders by Gil-Martin's demonic retainers causes him to long for release from self-consciousness in *utter oblivion*' (p.184).

More obviously (and less insidiously) than the Editor's, Wringhim's narrative convicts him of false logic, of inferring causes from apparent effects to accord with his presuppositions. Just as the enlightened Editor manages to prove to his own satisfaction that the 'explanation' for the events he records (many of which actually remain unexplained) is 'the rage of fanaticism' (p.93), so Wringhim persuades himself that Gil-Martin is none other than Czar Peter of Russia. The claims of 'reason' are most convincingly disposed of by making Gil-Martin its most accomplished and unanswerable exponent.

When the Editor returns in the final section of the book – following the emotionally coercive narrative of the Sinner – the insufficiency of his account becomes apparent: history and tradition prove altogether too slippery as a basis for 'facts' or the kind of truth he wants to find. Presented with dubious evidence, the rationalistic Editor decides to go and visit the Sinner's grave himself. The characters rely on the testimony of their senses throughout both parts of the narrative, but this empirical evidence continually raises problems of interpretation which Hogg suggests cannot be solved by ratiocination. The Editor is finally confronted by an absolute disjunction between reason and the 'facts'; needing to win the day for Enlightenment, his rational detachment disappears:

> Were the relation at all consistent with reason, it corresponds so minutely with traditionary facts, that it could scarcely have missed to have been received as authentic; but in this day, and with the present generation, it will not go down, that a man should be daily tempted by the devil, in the semblance of a fellow-creature; and at length lured to self-destruction . . . In short, we must either conceive him not only the greatest fool, but the greatest wretch, on whom was ever stamped the form of humanity; or, that he was a religious maniac.
>
> (p.254)

No one in the novel has, however, any more access to meaning than the Editor; evil is incontestably, palpably *there*, but most intractably mysterious. Hogg calls up all the resources of Scottish folk tale and demonology to evoke an evil simultaneously earthy and metaphysical. The devils which pursue Wringhim and provoke his eventual suicide belong both to his unconscious *and* to the public world of the fiction. The reader cannot choose between these as 'explanations'. The book is so terrifying, so effective in its emotional demands, because it is so intransigently inscrutable. Every exegetical attempt leads straight into a cul-de-sac: the psychological explanation which sees the doubling pursuit as a figment of a religious or a disordered imagination discounts the evidence of uninvolved witnesses, but to accept the actual, separate existence of Gil-Martin requires also some form of demonism – an explanation which immediately raises further unanswerable questions. In *The Confessions* there *is* no 'truth', only discordant points of view; the book seems to lead the reader to a sceptical acceptance of complete relativity.

The advantages of Hogg's reticence over Brockden Brown's explicative anxiety are plain. Hogg has a language available to him in Scots folk tradition to describe the irreducible evil which is both within and without the self, and he does not – as Brockden Brown must – dispel it by narrative evasion for ideological reasons. Guilt (which Brockden Brown was unwilling to associate with the American Adam of the New World, but which pursues him in the form of Indians from the untamed wilderness of the psyche) is in Hogg's tale firmly rooted in both individual and communal history, and, in the end, is unconquered by the present.

As though to endorse Hogg's refusal to allow 'facts' to be dominated by the interpretative activity of puritan–provincial scrutiny, the Editor implies that the narrative itself – the whole story – may be 'double' in the same way as all its elements, and suggests a 'puritan' way of reading:

> What can this work be? Sure, you will say, it must be an allegory; or (as the writer calls it) a religious PARABLE, showing the dreadful danger of self-righteousness? I cannot tell. (p.240)

The Editor's final resignation of responsibility for the work's meaning anticipates Carlyle's *Sartor Resartus* and, even more suggestively, Hawthorne's narrative 'formula of alternative possibilities'.[18] The firm placing of *The Confessions* in a Calvinist context establishes the basis of interpretative uncertainty; however, Hogg does not appear to be highlighting the allegorising process in order to make his readers question how they read. A full exploration of the provincial mentality, which involves an interpretation of the relationship between text and reader, must await Hawthorne.

Hogg's *Confessions* focuses the reader's attention onto the puritan–provincial mind with a ruthless and unremittingly steady gaze; it appears at once intolerable and inescapable. Gil-Martin's maxim near the end of the narrative that 'we are all subjected to two distinct natures in the same person' (p.192) is hard to resist after all that has gone before. This confrontation of the self with itself, and the falling away from the reader of all external relation, also characterises much of Poe's work, none more so than the short story 'William Wilson' (1840), which Thomas Mann described as the classic example in fiction of the *doppelgänger* motif.[19] Beside the powerful solidity of the *Confessions*, 'William Wilson' seems a shallow piece of virtuosity, but Poe's obvious fascination with ideas of pursuit and doubling makes comparison irresistible. The deliberate divorce between manner and matter in this tale suggests another way of treating the subject of inner division, a way implied in the eighteenth-century Scottish and American writings on language discussed in chapter 3.

William Wilson, 'outcast of all outcasts most abandoned', tells his own self-justifying tale of 'unpardonable crime'.[20] He attempts to wring sympathy from 'fellow men' to ease his isolation, but the nature of his account and the coerciveness of his tone demand nothing less of the reader than total moral surrender. As in the *Confessions*, 'sympathy' slides into 'empathy', transforming an ethical duty into a threatening psychological doubling for the reader. The madman who claims his audience's sympathy threatens their sanity.

William Wilson's is a tale of provincial life: abandoned in youth by his parents to 'the guidance of my own will', he connects his English school 'with a period and with a locality when and where I recognize the first ambiguous monitions of the destiny which afterward so fully overshadowed me' (p.320). The house (as often in Poe's work emblematic of both the narrator's mind and of his past) was 'old and irregular': it seemed to the young Wilson endlessly complex and fascinating (p.320). Like Caleb Williams, Edgar Huntly and Robert Wringhim, William Wilson feels superior to his fellow scholars; but his control is challenged, and the oppositional pattern of dominance and submission develops between himself and his 'double': the second William Wilson was the only one who

> presumed . . . to refuse implicit belief in my assertions, and submission to my will; indeed, to interfere with my arbitrary dictation in any respect whatever. If there is on earth a supreme and unqualified despotism, it is the despotism of a master-mind in boyhood over the less energetic spirits of its companions.
>
> (p.325)

Unable to accept any challenge to his autonomy, William Wilson taunts his adversary into opposition and pursuit, much as Caleb rouses Falkland or Wringhim courts Gil-Martin's attentions. As we might expect, a strange sympathy exists between pursuer and pursued: 'there were many points of strong congeniality in our tempers', so that 'to the moralist it will be unnecessary to say . . . that Wilson and myself were the most inseparable of companions' (p.327). Suspending for a moment the implications of this direct appeal to 'theory' – this challenge to admire the narrator's self-conscious command of his condition – we note that the sympathetic power of the second William Wilson, like that of Gil-Martin, apparently extends to physical appearance.

Provincially sensitive to infringements of his right to self-determination, Wilson resents 'the disgusting air of patronage which he assumed towards me, and . . . his frequent officious interference with my will' (pp.330–1). He decides to resolve the conflict by a flight into independence, but the pursuit once courted in defiance is inexorable:

> *I fled in vain*. My evil destiny pursued me as if in exultation, and proved, indeed, that the exercise of its mysterious dominion had as yet only begun . . . From his inscrutable tyranny did I at length flee, panic-stricken, as from a pestilence; and to the very ends of the earth *I fled in vain*.[21]

Finally, a 'stern and desperate resolution that I would submit no longer to be enslaved' (p.347) makes William Wilson turn and fight. But the final confrontation proves that the past cannot be denied or cut out of the self; as Hawthorne put it in 'Monsieur du Miroir' (1837), the fates of the antagonists are 'inseperably blended' – or, like the birthmark in another of Hawthorne's tales, the guilt (or moral sense) of William Wilson is embedded in his very self: destroying it, he ends his life.[22]

Or, at least, his tale. The blatantly clichéd form in which Poe's story enacts the language and motifs of Calvinist and Romantic alienation is its most striking feature. It is less in his use of the theme of the pursuer (of innocence, of independence) pursued (by his guilt, by his European past) as a parable of American experience that Poe is most 'American' than in the parodying impulse of an idiom which *distances* the enactment from the experience instead of approximating to it on either a literal or a psychological level. 'William Wilson' is no more a Germanic investigation of the unconscious at war with itself than it is a supernatural tale of demonic possession or a dramatisation of its narrator's insanity. The tale *purports* to be moral allegory: its epigraph reads ominously, 'What say of it? What say of CONSCIENCE grim, that spectre in my path?'[23] But there is nothing about Poe that we should be cajoled into accepting at face value. 'William Wilson' projects an extraordinary pastiche which transforms political, ethical and psychological positions into a series of rhetorical poses. It is perfectly appropriate that William Wilson's final confrontation with his double occurs at a masked ball where *no one* is his 'real' self.[24] The provincial's imitative style is parodied by the second William Wilson into absolute emptiness of identity; the *reality* of the way of life parodied nowhere appears.

This is not narrative so much as a succession of poses which direct and then confuse the reader's expectations in a series of circles around the central emptiness of the voice. The narrator is, in turn, the Wandering Jew whose 'unpardonable crime' has made him 'an object for the scorn, for the horror, for the detestation of my race' (p.317); the man of sentiment, who longs 'in passing through the dim valley, for the sympathy' of his fellow men (p.318); the nostalgic painter of lost childhood in another world; the Geoffrey Crayon-ish recorder of the picturesque – 'how quaint an old building was this! – to me how veritably a palace of enchantment!' (p.322); the pedant – 'encompassed by the massy walls of this venerable academy, I passed, yet not in tedium or disgust, the years of the third lustrum of my life' (p.323); the natural aristocrat borne down by vulgarity – 'the common property of the mob' (p.324); the rationalistic searcher for explanations – 'this is a somewhat remarkable coincidence; for the day is precisely that of my own nativity' (p.326); the evoker of the gothic *frisson* – '*and his singular whisper, it grew the very echo of my own*' (p.330);[25] the self-conscious provincial; the madman recollecting his delusions in a period of recovered sanity; the debauched Byronic hero – 'the vortex of thoughtless folly into which I there so immediately and so recklessly plunged, washed away all but the froth of my past hours' (p.335); the Godwinian victim of persecution – 'from his inscrutable tyranny did I at length flee, panic-stricken, as from a pestilence' (p.345); the fervent radical reformer – 'I now began to feel the inspiration of a burning hope, and at length nurtured in my secret thoughts a stern and desperate resolution that I would submit no longer to be enslaved' (p.347); the extravagant gothic villain mouthing the violences of the form – 'scoundrel! imposter! accursed villain! you shall not – you *shall not* dog me unto death! Follow me, or I stab you where you stand!' (p.348); and, finally, the quasi-biblical voice of conscience, of his 'other self' – '*In me didst thou exist – and, in my death, see by this image, which is thine own, how utterly thou hast murdered thyself*' (p.349).[26]

What is this farrago of voices? Is it the result of Poe's provinciality as a writer (the *Quarterly Review* said of J.K. Paulding's *Lay of the Scottish Fiddle* that 'the first effort of American wit would necessarily be a parody. Childhood is everywhere a parodist. America is every where a parody, a mimicry of her parents')? Or is something further involved?[27] Poe is rehearsing, quite without a 'message', a series of motifs to achieve a unified 'effect' on the reader: the state of obsessive self-consciousness and the consequent division of the personality. To put it another way, the provincial consciousness and its mode of defining itself against the world rather than in it is the subject rather than a characteristic of Poe's tale. This distance implies not only Poe's understanding of the provincial point of view, but also the existence of some world external to it. But when we look in 'William Wilson' for such a world, the poses of the prose surface remain opaque. Poe, like Brockden Brown's Carwin the Biloquist in *Wieland*, is a master of voices, of adopted points of view, but his writing permits no space for other voices than that of the moment, and no way through this to an outer world which might mitigate the claustrophobic effect of the monomaniacal tone. Poe's fiction threatens to colonise its reader by cutting off his access to meaning: its allusions are 'closed': they refer only to other literary poses – whether gothic, demonic, or Germanic – and never outwards to an independent reality which might give solidity to the 'effect'. Poe uses the terms of the puritan–provincial temper in a highly sophisticated and self-conscious manner; he is not in any sense trapped within them, but he is not their critic. For this, we shall look to Melville.

Poe's insistence on his theory of effect and on the separation of the surface of the work of art from 'life' makes his play with puritan–provincial poses seem at once too serious and not serious enough when we compare it with the more rooted understanding of the predicament displayed by Scott and Hawthorne. This rootedness derives in both writers from a sense of continuity through time and of contingent truths which mediate between the absolute and the completely relative. This *relationship* of past and present, which fiction pre-eminently conveys in narrative, is something which Poe's writing, with its 'temporal provinciality', cannot concede.[28]

Scott's *Redgauntlet* (1824) offers a complete contrast in method within similar puritan–provincial contours. It is also a story of a young man's search for independent identity and a place in the world, a story in which pursuit, doubling and predestination express a darker understanding of the Enlightenment's *Bildungsroman*. *Caleb Williams* and *The Confessions* are immersed in this Calvinistic idiom, and explore the range of its coercive power at it were from within; 'William Wilson' is a closed and enclosing rhetorical pastiche of these elements. *Redgauntlet* employs the same grim counters of experience expansively to tell a story which is simultaneously a masterpiece of story-telling.[29]

Scott acknowledged that 'few novels . . . excited a more powerful interest' for him than *Caleb Williams*; his pleasure in Godwin's telling of the tale overrode his 'sense of the fallacy of his arguments, of the improbability of his facts, and of the frequent inconsistency of his characters'; all this, Scott said, 'is lost in the solemnity and suspense with which we expect the evolution of the tale of mystery'.[30] 'Solemnity' because we know what will happen – the ending is predestinated in the manner of its telling – and 'suspense' because we also *don't* know – the author has apparent freedom to do anything he chooses. The covenant which binds the reader to the work of the author enacts the paradox of determinism and free will. But for Scott this relationship is never claustrophobic or passive, because telling a story always involves an appeal to another world outside that story. The two worlds do not compete with or contradict one another as they do in *Caleb Williams*, where the radical message which appeals to 'life' conflicts with the determinism of the fiction: finally, Scott always reminds his reader, the story is only a story. But it takes us to places which, although they make no claim to *be* life, comment on it from an angle which is not available *in* life. In *Redgauntlet*, this is true not only of the relationship which Wandering Willie's tale told within the book bears to the 'life' of Darsie Latimer, but also of the relationship of the novel as a whole to the life of Scotland in 1824.

Redgauntlet is Scott's most formally adventurous novel, and its different narrative methods function centrally in the unfolding of the story. The initial exchange of letters between Darsie and his friend Alan Fairford establishes the two young men, in their own eyes, as mutually complementary:

> we must each perform our separate destinies. I am doomed to see, act, and tell; thou, like a Dutchman enclosed in the same diligence with a Gascon, to hear, and shrug thy shoulders.[31]

They cast each other in opposing roles, comic self-dramatisations which are kept in control by the response of the 'double' who knows another part of the truth about the self. Obsessive self-consciousness is transformed in Scott's hands into fascination with creating one's own story and then living it, making one's place in things. Darsie Latimer, setting out to discover the secret of his origins, does exactly this:

> I am affected with a sense of loneliness, the more depressing, in that it seems to me to be a solitude peculiarly my own. In a country where all the world have a circle of consanguinity, extending to sixth cousins at least, I am a solitary individual, having only one kind heart to throb in unison with my own ... The necessary communication of master and servant would be at least a tie which would attach me to the rest of my kind – as it is, my very independence seems to enhance the peculiarity of my situation. (p.8)

Darsie is looking not for a single friend with whom he can empathise (he has this already in Alan), but for a place in the world, for ties of relation and responsibility which will allow him to escape the paradoxical puritan–provincial nexus of isolation and dependency. He combines Caleb Williams' curiosity with the passivity of the somnambulant Edgar Huntly. Forbidden by his guardian to visit England, he is irresistibly, though aimlessly, drawn towards the Border.[32] 'I resemble', he tells Alan, 'the poor tethered horse, which ... is always grazing on the very verge of the circle to which it is limited by its halter' (p.24). He awaits some clue to his identity and his fate: 'the anxious thoughts which haunt me began to muster in my bosom, and my feet slowly and insensibly approached the river which divided me from the forbidden precincts, though without any formed intention' (p.31). At this moment, on the brink of trespass, he is almost swept away by the treacherous advance of the tide, and is saved by the bold courage of a man whom he subsequently makes into a 'character' in his own 'story' for Alan:

> An air of sadness, or severity, or of both, seemed to indicate a melancholy, and, at the same time, a haughty temper. I could not help running mentally over the ancient heroes, to whom I might assimilate the noble form and countenance before me. (p.40)

It is the portrait of the gothic hero-villain: the fallen archangel or the noble penitent with a guilty past. It is Caleb's Falkland, or Wringhim's Gil-Martin. But Scott makes it clear (as Godwin and Hogg do not) that this characterisation of Redgauntlet is also a figment of Darsie's overactive imagination, which creates a tale of mystery out of very few 'facts': Alan's next letter accuses him of 'work[ing] mysterious and romantic heroes out of old cross-grained fishermen' (p.50).

Scott candidly exposes his own story-telling procedures: having introduced us to the rootless innocent, or unfallen provincial protagonist

Darsie (and his double, or conscience Alan), and sent him off in pursuit of his destiny, Scott involves him with a fittingly 'fallen' antagonist and creates the mystery which is that destiny. Redgauntlet *is* a gothic hero-villain – the story demands one – and Scott, through the eyes of his story-teller Darsie, unashamedly plays his villainous posturing to full effect. The unfolding of the narrative of pursuit and flight, dominance and submission, is exemplary: Darsie's curiosity about his mysterious 'preserver' (p.33) becomes indistinguishable from his desire to know his own identity; he 'invit[es] his fate' (p.158) by hovering in the forbidden ground, and is caught up in the machinations of the man of experience:

> When I had been thus snatched from destruction, I had only power to say to my protector, – or oppressor, – for he merited either name at my hand, 'You do not, then, design to murder me?' . . . 'Be silent . . . with questions or entreaties. What I mean to do, thou canst no more discover or prevent, than a man, with his bare palm, can scoop dry the Solway.' (pp.219–220)

Following Redgauntlet's display of inscrutability and arbitrary power, Darsie undergoes a period of drugged imprisonment; events become dreamlike and dislocated, and he is no longer able to distinguish rationally between the real and the imaginary. The balancing voice of Alan Fairford and the normal world are lost as the narrative changes (after a brief section of connecting third-person narration) to the first-person form of Darsie's journal, which takes it closer to the self-enclosed world of Caleb Williams or William Wilson. Events in this part of the story follow Godwin's novel quite closely, but at a stylistic remove which, if not quite parody, is certainly allusion rather than imitation:

> My story, long a mysterious one, seems now upon the verge of some strange development; and I feel a solemn impression that I ought to wait the course of events, to struggle against which is opposing my feeble efforts to the high will of fate. (p.225)

What solves the mystery, and what saves Darsie in the end, is this very passivity which distinguishes him so signally from Caleb Williams; he has the ability to await events instead of precipitating them. A comic trial scene which proves that 'justice' cannot help him (as it could not help Caleb Williams) does bring Darsie to confront and acknowledge his relationship with his persecuting protector Redgauntlet. Darsie at first declares his independence from the bond of dominance and submission which Redgauntlet proposes to the court: 'I cannot conceive', he says, 'by what singular tenure this person claims my obedience as a guardian; it is a barefaced imposture' (p.237). But Redgauntlet asserts his rights another way: Darsie is brought back under his power by a terrible frown which awakens in him an unnameable recollection of the past:

> angry at myself for my pusillanimity, I answered him by a look of the same kind, and catching the reflection of my countenance in a large antique mirror

> which stood before me, I started again at the real or imaginary resemblance which my countenance, at that moment, bore to that of Herries [Redgauntlet]. Surely my fate is somehow strangely interwoven with that of this mysterious individual. (p.248)

This relationship is involuntary and cannot be evoked at will. Nor can it be denied: Darsie and Redgauntlet are tied together by an ambivalent sympathy which suggests their consanguinity.

Scott does have a rational explanation (in the form of a belated Jacobite plot) waiting to account for the extraordinary behaviour of Redgauntlet. Darsie, it seems, is the head of the Redgauntlet family, and his countenance will be crucial in attracting support for the cause. But it is an explanation which does not pretend to be complete: Redgauntlet's account of how it is that he and Darsie come to have the mysterious horseshoe frown belongs to the legendary past; the tale he tells, in which 'the evidence of [a] father's guilt was stamped on the innocent face of the babe' (p.260), holds to an extreme form of fatalism:

> The privilege of free action belongs to no mortal – we are tied down by the fetters of duty – our mortal path is limited by the regulations of honour – our most indifferent actions are but meshes of the web of destiny by which we are all surrounded. (p.262)

Darsie refuses the implicit challenge in Redgauntlet's polar viewpoint to adopt the opposite position and contents himself with a prudent temporising which his uncle rejects with disdain:

> 'I will not – indeed I feel myself incompetent to argue a question of such metaphysical subtlety, as that which involves the limits betwixt free-will and predestination. Let us live honestly and die hopefully, without being obliged to form a decided opinion upon a point so far beyond our comprehension.'
> 'Wisely resolved,' he interrupted with a sneer – 'there came a note from some Geneva sermon.' (p.263)

But it is Redgauntlet himself, not Darsie, who has shown himself to be cast in the puritan–provincial mould. Darsie's acceptance of the unknowable separates him from Caleb Williams or Edgar Huntly and allows him to evade Calvin's 'immense abyss'. But he does not accept Redgauntlet's fatalistic suggestion that he too lies under the family doom, and the 'explanation' of their relationship provokes a new question, which is to be tested in the narrative: will he be able to break out of this fate which has been cast on the family for a sin committed in the past, or is he, too, doomed to be forever on the losing side? This is a question which is not susceptible of rational solution; the answer to it only becomes available through the telling and the outcome of the tale.

Darsie discovers that the chain of predestination cannot be broken by intemperate action, which would only enmesh him more fully in events he does not understand; he must instead await events while keeping faith in his own inner independence. He rejects the pattern of dominance and submission which Redgauntlet offers him as an ineluctable model by declaring 'My thoughts are my own ... and though you keep my person prisoner, these are beyond your control' (p.268). This is very similar to Caleb Williams' resolve to hold himself 'disengaged from this odious scene, and never fill the part either of the oppressor or the sufferer' (*Caleb Williams*, p.156), but unlike Caleb, Darsie can refuse to play the part Redgauntlet has created for him and manages to assert a form of freedom *within* his acceptance of the responsibilities which acknowledging his family relationship brings.

The story does seem at first to unfold on Redgauntlet's terms: he determines and forces the action while Darsie remains in passive subjection to his plans. As though to reinforce the point, Alan too, having resolved to act 'in pursuit of his friend' (p.277), doubles Darsie's experience and becomes a prisoner under the influence of the mysterious and powerful 'Father Buonaventure' (the deposed 'Father' of Scotland, Charles Stuart). But the activity of the Jacobites is finally and permanently quashed by the government's refusal to allow them to constitute a revolution: Redgauntlet's monomania, which gives him power over the opposing actions of less determined men, is impotent before a strategy of prudent passiveness. His cause (like that of the revolutionary puritans) cannot survive without confrontation, and Darsie's recognition of the need to avoid 'a dangerous and violent rupture with his uncle' (p.474) is supported by the conduct of the Hanoverian leader:

> 'His Majesty will not even believe that the most zealous Jacobites who yet remain can nourish a thought of exciting a civil war, which must be fatal to their families and themselves, besides spreading bloodshed and ruin through a peaceful land ...
>
> 'Then, gentlemen', said Redgauntlet, clasping his hands together as the words burst from him, 'the cause is lost for ever!' (p.487)

The passivity of the double protagonists Darsie and Alan is characteristic; Scott's 'chief characters', as he said himself, 'are never actors, but always acted upon the spur of circumstances, and have their fates uniformly determined by the agency of the subordinate persons. This arises from the author having usually represented them as foreigners to whom everything in Scotland is strange.'[33] As Scott's anonymous self-criticism recognised, the hero's distance from the initiating centre of action makes his tribulations in the unknown world of the unfolding fiction particularly accessible to the reader's sympathy. It allows for a measure of identification with the protagonist's uncertainty while ensuring that the relationship between author and reader remains the determining feature of the story: 'while [the author] is going into explanations and details which, addressed directly to the reader, might appear tiresome and unnecessary, he gives interest to them by exhibiting the effect which they produce upon the principal person of his drama, and at the same time obtains a patient hearing for what might otherwise be passed over without attention'.[34]

But these passive heroes are not merely a narrative sleight of hand; they are at the thematic centre of *Redgauntlet* and enact Scott's understanding of the possibilities and limitations of the provincial fate of Scots in post-Union Britain. Darsie's awaiting of events attempts to create something livable out of what is essentially – as Redgauntlet presents it – a creed of crisis and revolutionary opposition. The passive hero recognises both the responsibilities of his relationship to Redgauntlet and the responsibility he bears to the community of his upbringing; he reconciles these apparently opposed claims on himself by accepting prudently (as Robert Wringhim or William Wilson cannot) that his own self-determination must – and may – take place within the larger determinism of events which he cannot control. In so doing, he averts the doom on the house of Redgauntlet, aligns himself with the winning side and overnight comes into possession of relations, status and a purpose in life. Alan, who feels that 'the law is my vocation – in an especial, and, I may say, in an hereditary way, my vocation' (p.18), is also associated with this stance of wise passiveness. The law, as often for Scott, has a useful doubleness: it is, literally, a Scottish profession, and metaphorically a religious 'profession'. The smuggler Nanty Ewart, who is associated with Redgauntlet's illicit plot, has been 'outlawed' and deprived of all relation; he is the Calvinist castaway (p.470). The history of Scotland within the overall progress of eighteenth- and nineteenth-century Britain was for Scott a special example of how prudent acceptance of events might preserve and strengthen the essential aspects of national identity at a time when rebellious struggle against historical processes could only lead to confrontation with forces beyond local or individual control.

Passiveness, and observation of the actions of others, may be the provincial's lot, but it may also be the lot of all men; according to Scott self-limitation need not entail pessimistic determinism. The interpretation of history which Scott derived from his Scottish Enlightenment teachers allowed for limited personal freedom within an overall movement of social progress; to assert one's personal will against the 'historical will' was simply a meaningless activity, but its corollary was not the kind of passive fatalism to which Redgauntlet subscribed. Reversing the normal alignment of Calvinist oppositions, Scott associates passivity, observation and acceptance – the 'provincial' positions – with freedom; these alone can combat what John Buchan calls 'the iron compulsion of fate' which dominates the novel.[35] The structure of pursuit and counter-pursuit and the sympathetic resemblance between Darsie and Redgauntlet suggest not only that the past must recognise the claims of the present, but also that freedom in the present depends upon reconciliation with the past. Darsie's quest for his past results in his being pursued by that past for its own purposes; the comic ending suggests that the needless cycle of flight and pursuit is cut through not by confrontation but by accepting mutual interdependence and participating in a common fate.

But all this is to cast in alternative form what is fully contained within the narrative and the way it is told. *Redgauntlet's* great triumph as a novel – and what finally lends weight to its ideas – is that it does not take itself too seriously. It is content, in the words of Hogg's Sinner, to be a 'tale that has been told'. The telling is what makes it and what differentiates it from the novels of flight and pursuit considered so far in this chapter; Scott has seen the dramatic potential of the divided puritan–provincial mind, and exploits it so freely that Redgauntlet is at once a caricature of the gothic hero-villain Falkland and a creation of profound historical understanding. Not the least of the Calvinist paradoxes is how the same counters could satisfy such opposed imaginative impulses as those of Godwin and Scott.

The tale of *Redgauntlet* opens up a world rather than closing life down around the consciousness of the perceiving self as *Caleb Williams* does. Scott's voice within the tale is in this sense analogous to Hume's at the end of Book I of the *Treatise of Human Nature*: both create a public space within what seems the most private of relationships, that of the individual with himself. In *Redgauntlet*, the inset tale of Wandering Willie demonstrates in miniature the story-teller's art. As he entertains his audience, Wandering Willie reveals aspects of Darsie's experience and of the truth he seeks which are not accessible to rational explanation; indeed, are not explicable at all. 'Wandering Willie's Tale' is a virtuoso performance which adds another dimension to the novel's narrative of the pursuit of the double.

The blind fiddler Willie replaces Redgauntlet as Darsie's guide around the treacherous border of the Solway Firth. He regales his *protégé* with a story which Darsie then recounts in his next letter to Alan. Willie is in touch not only with Scotland's past in his tale of Darsie's ancestor but also with the 'other' worlds of the unconscious and the supernatural. The story of the trip to Hell and back reopens the irrational and mysterious possibilities of the theme of pursuit and counter-pursuit which structures the novel and puts it back into a context which vividly embodies its dark Calvinist origins in fallen man's illicit quest for forbidden knowledge and God's vengeful pursuit of his errant creature. The story's folk mode comfortably accommodates images of the supernatural and the unconscious, but Willie's narrative skill, and Darsie's constant awareness of it, ensure that they do remain 'other'. The audience steps aside from life to enter the magical precinct; but the voice of the story-teller is always between us and the reality of the experience:

> My gudesire's hair stood on end at this proposal, but he thought his companion might be some humoursome child that was trying to frighten him, and might end with lending him the money. Besides, he was bauld wi' brandy, and desperate wi' distress; and he said he had courage to go to the gate of hell, and a step further, for that receipt. The stranger laughed. (p.137)

Scott has caught the rhythms of the speaking voice to perfection, but they are also the rhythms of the conscious story-teller shaping and controlling his phrases for effect. Rich verbal surfaces and skilful modulations of tone remind us that this is 'Wandering Willie's Tale'. The ironies of his account of Steenie Steenson's meeting in the forest with the stranger are all accessible; the story-teller is careful to provide the possibility of a 'rational' explanation, which effectively gives the reader imaginative licence to indulge the alternative possibility. The supernatural is an integral part of Steenie Steenson's world; his tale invites us to make it part of ours.

What looks like a glimpse into the darkest depths of the soul in fact remains resolutely public; the messages brought back from the darkness by Steenie Steenson are only the shareable ones:

> But, Lord take us in keeping, what a set of ghastly revellers they were that sat around that table! My gudesire kend mony that had long before gane to their place . . . There was the fierce Middleton, and the dissolute Rothes, and the crafty Lauderdale . . . There was the Bluidy Advocate Mackenyie, who, for his worldly wit and wisdom had been to the rest as a god. And there was Claverhouse, as beautiful as when he lived, with his long, dark, curled locks streaming down over his laced buff-coat, and his left hand always on his right spule-blade, to hide the wound that the silver bullet had made. (p.138)

These are the recognisable folk memories of the darkest moments in the Scottish past; they are not the private demons of the soul, the ferocious Indians of the psyche, but the collective scapegoats of the community. They give a public dimension to Redgauntlet's tale of Alberick, the evil spirit who haunts his and Darsie's own past.

Willie's account of his ancestor's visit to Hell suggests a communal evil; it does not venture to communicate what it was like to be Steenie having that experience. We learn that 'muckle was the dool and care that came o't to my gudesire' (p.123), but the story-teller's presence between his experience and the reader removes the element of coercion which characterises the self-enclosed vision of *Caleb Williams* or Hogg's *Confessions*. Scott typically defines the relationship between 'author' and reader as one of dominance and submission, but (as he says in *Waverley*) 'scorn[s] to tyrannize' over the reader's passive subjection.[36] The tale ends on a note of triumphant openness as the sceptical story-teller's voice of Wandering Willie accommodates human reasoning (and the imaginative limitations of his audience) to the irrational extremities of experience:

> Sir John made up his story about the jackanape as he liked himself; and some believe till this day there was no more in the matter than the filching nature of the brute. Indeed, ye'll no hinder some to threap that it was nane o' the auld Enemy that Dougal and my gudesire saw in the laird's room, but only that wanchancy creature, the major, capering on the coffin... But Heaven kens the truth, whilk first came out by the minister's wife, after Sir John and her ain gudeman were baith in the moulds. And then my gudesire, wha was failed in his limbs, but not in his judgement or memory – at least nothing to speak of – was obliged to tell the real narrative to his friends, for the credit of his good name. He might else have been charged for a warlock. (pp.145–6)

The puritan's sense of the divorce of words from meaning, and of fallen man's distance from the heart of experience, becomes in provincial fiction a characteristic preoccupation with the gap between events or emotions and what can be communicated of these. Scott's stories, like Hawthorne's (and like Hogg's *Confessions*), tend to be 'twice told' and reach the reader framed by prefatory paraphernalia which remove them from the actuality of experience without preventing him from participating in the process of meaning. 'The Highland Widow' (1827), for example, is introduced as 'a story' of 'the state of the highlands'; the reader's distance from the widow herself is adjusted by the responses of Mrs Bethune Baliol (who retells the tale) to an earlier account of the same events. 'I heard the narrative', she says, 'with a mixture of horror and sympathy, which at once impelled me to approach the sufferer and speak to her the words of comfort, or rather of pity, and at the same time made me afraid to do so'. The ineluctable otherness of the widow is conveyed by her refusal to be touched by sympathy; the observer cannot possess her experience, and it seems impertinent to try:

> save from the half smile that seemed to intimate the contempt of a being rapt by the very intensity of her affliction above the sphere of ordinary humanities, she seemed as indifferent to my gaze as if she had been a dead corpse or a marble statue.[37]

This otherness, this refusal to succumb to sympathy and the breakdown of the boundaries of identity is, for both Scott and Hawthorne, an essential aspect of human independence and human dignity. Both writers are extremely alive to the equivocal aspects of 'sympathy', and for both an establishment of distance between manner and matter, between the truth of the story and the way it is told, is a way of keeping at bay an impending dissolution of distinction between the matter of the tale and the mind of the reader.

Distance helps to distinguish the tale from the 'real' events it describes, but Hawthorne shows that it may also be a *subject* of the fiction. In 'Roger Malvin's Burial' (1832), Reuben Bourne's sense of sin and his need to expiate his guilt arise not from having left his dying 'father' Roger Malvin in the forest; 'for that,' we are told, 'he felt he deserved no censure'. What bothers him is that because he cannot communicate to others *why* he left Malvin before the older man's death – the 'true story' of the original incident – it becomes impossible for Reuben to return and bury him. As so often in Hawthorne's work, it is the 'incommunicable thought', the distance between experience and how it can be represented, which erects barriers against sympathetic understanding.[38]

Hawthorne's 'Young Goodman Brown' (1835) is a supernatural tale of flight and pursuit to the depths of darkness and back whose enclosure in the mind of its experiencing protagonist would seem to place it much more with Hogg's 'Sinner's Narrative' or with the self-justifications of Caleb Williams or Edgar Huntly than with Scott's expansive third-person narration. Hawthorne seems to have chosen 'self' rather than 'other' as his subject matter; these, as Scott saw it, were the author's alternatives: 'poetry which treats of the actions and sentiments of others may be grave or gay according to the light in which the author chooses to view his subject, but he who shall mine long and deeply for materials in his own bosom will encounter abysses at the depth of which he must necessarily tremble'.[39] Hawthorne was accused in his lifetime (and since) of mining 'long and deeply for materials in his own bosom'. But his supposedly autobiographical 'Old Manse' preface to the volume in which 'Young Goodman Brown' was first collected reminds the reader that authorial self-revelations are really quite external:

> How little have I told! – and, of that little, how almost nothing is even tinctured with any quality that makes it exclusively my own! Has the reader gone wandering, hand in hand with me, through the inner passages of my being, and have we groped together into all its chambers, and examined their treasures or their rubbish? Not so. We have been standing on the greensward, but just within the cavern's mouth, where the common sunshine is free to penetrate, and where every footstep is therefore free to come. I have appealed to no sentiment or sensibilities, save such as are diffused among us all. So far as I am a man of really individual attributes, I veil my face. (pp.32, 33)

The real features of the author remain quite inscrutable to the reader's curiosity.

Hawthorne's sense of the unshareable is not merely an eighteenth-century decorum separating the public and private domains; his inaccessibility is teasing: it challenges us to know him, but bids us stop short at the mouth of the cavern wherein his 'real' self is located. He shows the entry, but refuses to conduct us further. For Hawthorne, as for the Calvinist, the self and the public world, reality and appearance, are utterly discontinuous; but – like Hume – he none the less finds a social voice to 'open an intercourse with the world'.[40] He shares with Scott a strong sense of what may and what may not be known to one man of another in a fallen world, of what messages may emerge from the heart and what must remain forever shrouded to the observer.

But Hawthorne's self-possession is different from Scott's: reticent to the point of inscrutability, he characteristically gives with one hand and takes away with the other. This balancing of opposed possibilities makes 'Young Goodman Brown' a perfect solution to the problem of how to portray a self-enclosed consciousness – the puritan–provincial mind – without becoming trapped, and trapping the reader, within it. Perhaps more than any other, this tale embodies the complete translation of Calvinist structures of thought into literature.[41]

Goodman Brown first appears on the 'threshold', about to undertake a 'journey ... forth and back again' (*Mosses*, p.74). The young man flees on a forbidden but inescapable quest through the forest to a witches' meeting, learns there of deep sin in the hearts even of those whom he most reveres, and returns to the daylight world 'a stern ... distrustful, if not a desperate man' (p.89). The 'knowledge' to which his curiosity, abandoning 'faith', leads him is incommunicable and spiritually blighting. The story is told in an apparently impersonal and objective third person, but the writing immediately involves itself in Goodman Brown's journey; the reader either joins his quest through the woods in all its horror or remains in the clearing, unmoved. The 'distance' between the reader and the subject of the tale seems to have collapsed into a nightmare vision of archetypal fears: the unconscious and supernatural connotations of *this* flight through the forest take us downwards and inwards rather than out of ourselves. The effect could hardly be more different from that of 'Wandering Willie's Tale'; Hawthorne internalises Scott's predetermining, distancing narrative voice to create a prose which does seem to have designs on its reader.

Deep into the abysmal darkness the hostile powers of the wilderness oppress the young puritan's soul: 'The whole forest was peopled with frightful sounds; the creaking of the trees, the howling of wild beasts, and the yell of Indians' (p.83); here is Edgar Huntly's nightmare world projected outwards from the haunted mind of the perceiver. The claustrophobic scene plays on the reader's worst fears of being trapped within his own consciousness: the incommunicability of Goodman Brown's experience is built right into the structure of the tale. It is a strategy which resembles nothing so much as a short story by Poe. But 'Young Goodman Brown' could never be mistaken for a Poe tale. The most obvious difference is that the reader feels able to say things about the nature of Goodman Brown's experience and the quality of his perceptions which, posited of a Poe narrator, would be quite meaningless. The story, that is, at the very moment when it colonises the reader's attention, does seem to refer outward to something beyond itself, something which can be brought to bear on its coercive vision. This is the central paradox whose tenure sustains the tale as a *literary* experience of Calvinism.

How is it, then, that we are able to 'possess' the story of Goodman Brown without being possessed by it? Hawthorne's narration incorporates two kinds of 'distance' from Goodman Brown's experience, both of which suggest affinities with Scott (and, further back, Hume) rather than with Poe. Firstly, the density of the narrative base contrasts strongly with Poe's essentially unanchored fictions, where things always have the slightly unreal quality of imported theatrical props. Hawthorne implicitly qualifies Goodman Brown's point of view by locating his journey into the forest precisely in both historical and theological circumstances. The Salem witch trials, the debate over the value of 'spectre-evidence' and the inveterate allegorising habit of the divided puritan mind all emerge as contexts which enable the reader to 'see' Goodman Brown's puritan–provincial mentality without being absorbed into his perceptions. He attempts to understand his world by assigning meaning on the basis of exact correspondences between observed events and spiritual significances:

> something fluttered lightly down through the air, and caught on the branch of a tree. The young man seized it, and beheld a pink ribbon.
>
> 'My Faith is gone!' cried he, after one stupefied moment. (p.83)

Goodman Brown's unstable allegorising mind is polarised: to him his wife Faith *is* purity. He cannot allow her (in his mind) to have any connection with evil; she is *either* 'a blessed angel on earth', *or* a 'polluted wretch' (pp.75, 88). The same discontinuity is revealed in his abrupt reversal of opinion about the virtuous villagers as, one by one, they become associated in his mind with evil. The self-righteous horror with which he observes the 'sinful' world is that of the provincial who equates ignorance with innocence but is none the less irresistibly drawn towards the complexities of experience. Unconscious curiosity drives him into the forest and traps him into enacting an allegory of Original Sin and the Fall. It is a dramatic embodiment of the puritan frame of mind in which formulation precedes, and determines, perception.

But it is Goodman Brown who does the symbolising, not Hawthorne. The forest of the pursuit is a narrative requirement of the story as well as a symbol of the unconscious. In his simultaneous flight away from and pursuit of knowledge, Goodman Brown enters a strange self-generating world where a mental doubt immediately separates itself from the perceiving consciousness and assumes the existence of a physical 'fact': 'what if the devil himself should be at my very elbow!' he speculates; he turns round, and there at his elbow is a 'second traveller... apparently in the same rank of life as Goodman Brown, and bearing a considerable resemblance to him' (pp.75, 76). The devil he conjures up is his double in everything but age – he is Goodman Brown's 'experienced', older self. The urbane, curiously underemphatic and commonsensical verbal surface seemingly endorses this apparition's objective status. But the reader's awareness of how such 'facts' have been generated prevents any attempt to 'read' them on Common Sense principles as evidence about the real nature of things. To recognise the puritan provenance of Goodman Brown's perceptions is not to interpret or explain them, even in psychological terms. The psychological explanation is a capitulation like any other to the rationalising desire to dispel mystery, to dominate by 'knowledge', just as Goodman Brown and the other protagonists of this chapter attempt disastrously to exert power over their victims by knowing the secret springs of their actions. As in all these tales of doubling and pursuit, a rational explanation is forthcoming: 'had Goodman Brown fallen asleep in the forest, and only dreamed a wild dream of a witch-meeting? Be it so, if you will' (p.89); but, as in 'Wandering Willie's Tale', the very willingness to concede it suggests that there is something more. Our possession of Goodman Brown's story through the distancing historical imagination which creates a space between the reader and the protagonist's experience involves accepting the absolute otherness of that experience.

The second way out of Goodman Brown's mind would seem to have been precluded by the absorption of the narrator into the consciousness of the protagonist. Wandering Willie's voice embellished his ancestor's experience with absorbing vividness but did not attempt to penetrate what it was like to *be* Steenie Steenson. Something similar happens, with consummate subtlety, in the language of 'Young Goodman Brown'. The 'sable form' of the warlock, under the pressure of Goodman Brown's provincial perceptions, elucidates the empathic, colonising view of 'sympathy': that penetration of the mystery of the human heart which undermines individual integrity. But this vision is qualified by the free-floating openness of the language, which consciously distances itself from *direct* experience of reality and sends out lifelines for the reader instead to the Bible, to Shakespeare and to Milton. As it evokes empathy, the prose deliberately excludes it: descriptive, allusive and evocative, it creates a space which simultaneously distances us from the actual 'deep mystery' desired and feared by Goodman Brown *and* suggests what it might be like to look at things this way:

The pursuit of the double 101

> 'This night it shall be granted you to know their secret deeds: how hoary-bearded elders of the church have whispered wanton words to the young maids of their households; how many a woman, eager for widow's weeds, has given her husband a drink at bed-time, and let him sleep his last sleep in her bosom ... By the sympathy of your human hearts for sin, ye shall scent out all the places – whether in church, bed-chamber, street, field, or forest – where crime has been committed, and shall exult to behold the whole earth one stain of guilt, one mighty blood-spot. Far more than this! It shall be yours to penetrate, in every bosom, the deep mystery of sin, the fountain of all wicked arts, and which inexhaustibly supplies more evil impulses than human power – than my power, at its utmost! – can make manifest in deeds. And now, my children, look upon each other.' (p.87)

The realities here are all verbal; it is intensely literary, giving rein to all the exuberance and rhetorical excess kept in check by the understated tones of the tale's beginning: 'whispered wanton words ... a woman eager for widow's weeds'. This is a language which deals in extremes of the unstatable: the '*deep mystery* of sin, the *fountain* of *all* wicked arts ... which *inexhaustibly* supplies *more evil* impulses ...' The self-consciously achieved effect of the words of the sable form is greater than any meaning which can be attached to them; Hawthorne exploits the capabilities of language to render 'explanation' inadequate and achieves deliberately what Brockden Brown's prose is trapped into unawares.

But if the divorce of manner from matter is a source of power in the writing, it is so in a way quite different from the designedly deracinated poses of Poe's writing, for the sable form's address is like a demonic inversion of Dimmesdale's Election Day sermon in *The Scarlet Letter*, to which 'Hester Prynne listened with such intentness, and sympathized so intimately, that the sermon had throughout a meaning for her, entirely apart from its indistinguishable words'.[42] In the over-writing of the sable form's sermon, Hawthorne intimates how the puritan–provincial mind understands the relation of words to reality.

The many echoes of *Paradise Lost* in this passage suggest that Goodman Brown's self-generating allegory of Original Sin may originate in Milton's cardinal literary expression of puritan consciousness. Goodman Brown's vision, initiated in necessitated freedom and consummated in self-willed compulsion, enacts (in the forest journey) the story of Adam and Eve's Fall through the temptations of Satan. 'This night' of the sable form's peroration is the fatal night on which Eve first hears the voice of the tempter:

> for I this night –
> Such night till this I never passed – have dreamed,
> If dreamed, not as I oft am wont, of thee,
> Works of day past, or morrow's next design,
> But of offense and trouble, which my mind
> Knew never till this irksome night.[43]

It is the night in which Goodman Brown (convinced like Hogg's Wringhim of the centrality of his individual experience) takes upon himself the destiny of the human race.[44] The sable form echoes Milton's rhetoric of perdition and the annihilation of 'Faith' (IX, 1073–1080), and culminates in a conscious assumption of the high Miltonic style to give, in 'the sympathy of your human hearts for sin', what amounts to a parody of the mutual disgust of the fallen angels:

> Sublime with expectation when to see
> In triumph issuing forth their glorious Chief;
> They saw, but other sight instead, a crowd
> Of ugly serpents; horror on them fell,
> And horrid sympathy; for what they saw,
> They felt themselves now changing.   (x, 536–41)

Goodman Brown's reality, in every sense, is a literary one. A paralysed, passive descendant of 'active' puritan forebears (p.77), his experience comes through the borrowed forms and idiom of an inheritance he cannot actively assume; he is a distanced provincial, alienated from both his language and his community. 'A stern, a sad, a darkly meditative, a distrustful, if not a desperate man, did he become, from the night of that fearful dream. On the Sabbath-day, when the congregation were singing a holy psalm, he could not listen, because an anthem of sin rushed loudly upon his ear, and drowned all the blessed strain' (p.89).

Paralysis and passivity are the salient characteristics of the protagonist of Melville's most famous short story. 'Bartleby the Scrivener' (1853) is impeccably structured on the puritan–provincial model of doubling and pursuit. The narrator and the 'unaccountable' scrivener who joins his office and 'prefers not' to work or to leave become locked in the familiar relationship of opposition, where passivity and action double as flight and pursuit:

> The passiveness of Bartleby sometimes irritated me. I felt strangely goaded on to encounter him in new opposition – to elicit some angry spark from him answerable to my own.[45]

The narrator swings between angrily desiring to 'forever rid me of this intolerable incubus' (p.45) and being pursued into exile and alienation by some fate connected with his mysterious double: 'fearful ... of being again hunted out', he drives about aimlessly, paying 'fugitive visits to Manhattanville and Astoria' (p.50). Bartleby's absolute, intransigent passivity exerts a strangely coercive influence on the bewildered narrator, who finds himself echoing Bartleby's very phrases. His anxiety is intensified by the other's absolute evasion of confrontation, by which the narrator might reinforce his dominant position in the relationship:

> again obeying that wonderous ascendancy which the inscrutable scrivener had over me, and from which ascendancy, for all my chafing, I could not completely escape, I slowly went down stairs and out into the street, and while walking round the block, considered what I should next do in this unheard-of perplexity . . . I resolved to argue the matter over with him again . . . He answered nothing. (pp.41-2)

Bartleby refuses even to constitute an opposition.

The 'sympathy' between them, the 'bond of a common humanity' which 'drew me irresistibly to gloom' (p.33), is a consequence of 'restless curiosity' (p.32) which drives the narrator to discover the source of Bartleby's mysterious behaviour. But, like Caleb Williams checked in his self-righteous desire to expose Falkland, the narrator finds himself unaccountably reluctant to dismiss Bartleby, despite all his apparent justification:

> I strangely felt something superstitious knocking at my heart, and forbidding me to carry out my purpose, and denouncing me for a villain if I dared to breathe one bitter word against this forlornest of mankind. (p.36)

There is something falsely theatrical about this style, something which reminds the reader of the empty poses of Poe's narrator as he adopts stances which have no substance. A few pages further on Melville clearly signals both where the narrator's language originates and how far removed it now is from that origin:

> Some days now passed, during which, at leisure intervals I looked a little into 'Edwards on the Will', and 'Priestly on Necessity'. Under the circumstances, those books induced a salutary feeling. Gradually I slid into the persuasion that these troubles of mine, touching the scrivener, had been all predestinated from eternity, and Bartleby was billeted upon me for some mysterious purpose of an allwise Providence, which it was not for a mere mortal like me to fathom. Yes, Bartleby, stay there behind your screen, thought I; I shall persecute you no more; you are harmless and noiseless as any of these old chairs; in short, I never feel so private as when I know you are here. At last I see it, I feel it; I penetrate to the predestinated purpose of my life. I am content. Others may have loftier parts to enact; but my mission in this world, Bartleby, is to furnish you with office-room for such period as you may see fit to remain. (p.44)

Like William Wilson, and (differently) Goodman Brown, Melville's narrator divorces manner from matter, 'doubling' word and theory; his voice dramatises the emptiness of rhetoric which sends words in pursuit of things. The narrator's comfortable gentility finds 'meaning' in the structures of Calvinism; the prose balances his genteel manner against the theological intransigence of the matter. 'At leisure intervals I looked a little . . . gradually I slid into the persuasion . . . not for a mere mortal like me to fathom . . . any of these old chairs . . . others may have loftier parts to enact... such period as you may see fit to remain': such is the ease with which the narrator accommodates '"Edwards on the Will", and "Priestly on Necessity"... all predestinated from eternity... mysterious purpose of an allwise Providence ... persecute ... predestinated purpose'. Triviality confronts immensity. We can hardly miss the inflated self-satisfaction of the rhetoric of submission as the narrator 'accepts' the predestinated purpose of his life: 'I am content. Others may have loftier parts to enact'; the self-conscious vocative – 'yes, Bartleby' – makes a mockery of this easy humility.

Once we begin to attend to the first-person voice in this way, it becomes clear that 'Bartleby' is a parody. Not exactly of the puritan structures of division and doubling – action/passivity, flight/pursuit, dominance/submission – but of the stance which can adopt them as structures divorced from theological content. This is the voice of Irving's Geoffrey Crayon, of J.R. Lowell's Hosea Biglow, of Hawthorne's 'd----d mob of scribbling women', and of the American reviews.[46] It is the provincial voice of genteel America, the voice of Common Sense, born when 'Calvinism ... lost its basis in American life'.[47] Melville makes it clear that the Common Sense manner *parodies* its puritan antecedent: it adopts its postures and its idiom devoid of the faith which justified them and gave them substance.

'Bartleby' exposes how Calvinist structures, which once had power to make the puritan's universe cohere, have become in mid-nineteenth-century America polite conventions and narrative devices with merely 'literary' ordering power. It is remarkably similar in this respect to Hawthorne's allegorical parody 'The Celestial Rail-Road' (1843) which satirises, in the 'progressive' voice of liberal America, the debased coinage which Bunyan's puritan vocabulary has become. Santayana calls this voice 'the tender echoes and quaint fancies' of 'a digestion of vacancy':

> It is a great, though incidental advantage, that the materials from the heart of the Hill Difficulty have been employed in filling up the Valley of Humiliation; thus obviating the necessity of descending into that disagreeable and unwholesome hollow.[48]

Both here and in 'Bartleby' puritan structures have become counters the narrator deploys to tell his story to a 'sympathetic' audience in an effective manner. The language of division and doubling and the narrative structure of flight and pursuit help Melville's narrator to subdue his fictional world to comfortable order. Because they are unanchored in experience, he can discard them at will: the sense of 'predestinated purpose' to shelter Bartleby is abandoned without comment and without consequence to the narrator when his friends query his judgement, and the outcome of the story seems to vindicate his irresponsibility. The double to whose fate his own has become linked just leaves – dies – and the narrator is left to moralise comfortably on the outcome: 'Ah, Bartleby! Ah, humanity!' (p.54). He finds or invents another story for Bartleby, an 'explanation' that belongs to the past and absolves him from responsibility for the scrivener's fate. The fatal doubling turns out to be no more than a convenient narrative device.

However, the tale itself escapes its narrator's anodyne influence. 'Bartleby the Scrivener' manages to be both a satiric parody and a haunting tale which remains finally enigmatic. We no more explain it by accounting for the manner of the narrator than he himself explains Bartleby by telling us that 'he had been a subordinate clerk in the Dead Letter Office at Washington' (p.45). It is more, that is, than one of Poe's consummate ventriloquistic poses or than the pastiche of American optimism offered by 'The Celestial Rail-Road'. As he parodies the attenuated religiosity of Unitarian America, Melville simultaneously re-affirms the *imaginative* vitality of the myth whose literal decadence he exposes. Beneath the empty rhetoric of the story's surface there is apparently some sombre significance. This is the most difficult aspect of the tale: it seems strangely to reassert the puritan paradoxes in the very act of satirising them. With a full religious and intellectual scepticism, and a complete literary self-awareness which is absent from *Caleb Williams* and *Edgar Huntly*, Melville has produced a work whose meaning seems to reside within the same puritan–provincial polarities as theirs do. It bears a relationship to them similar to that which Hume's philosophy bears to his Common Sense antagonists.

The story hinges on Bartleby's absolute otherness; the emptiness of the narrator's language is quickly enough plumbed, but this gains no more access to Bartleby. It seems as though the opaque surface of his passive presence holds the key to the truth or significance of the story, and (as most criticism of the tale demonstrates) the reader is driven impertinently to 'interpret' him in ways as vulgar as those of the narrator. If the narrator lives in Emerson's 'world of surfaces' and succeeds in the art of skating well on them, Melville seems to live suspended like Jonathan Edwards' spider over the abyss, in the terrifying Calvinist world of unfathomable significances, of meanings inaccessible to our corrupted faculties. The power of Bartleby's silence at the end of the tale, a silence like that of the apparently satanic Babo in 'Benito Cereno' which sends back no responses to the anxious inquiries of the reader, is the power of inscrutable nature over the imagination of Fallen Man: 'there is such a dumb blankness, full of meaning, in a wide landscape of snows – a colorless, all-color of atheism from which we shrink'.[49]

5

Spectators, spies and spectres: the observer's stance

> The mind is a kind of theatre, where several perceptions successively make their appearance; pass, re-pass, glide away, and mingle in an infinite variety of postures and situations.
> (David Hume)

> Ah that Distance! what a magician for conjuring up scenes of joy or sorrow, smoothing all asperities, reconciling all incongruities, veiling all absurdness, softening every coar[se]ness, doubling every effect by the influence of the imagination.
> (Walter Scott)

> We soon tire of things which we visit merely by way of spectacle, and with which we have no real and permanent connection. In such cases, we very quickly wish this spectacle to be taken away, and another substituted.
> (Nathaniel Hawthorne)[1]

The narrative of flight and pursuit dramatises the puritan–provincial search for 'unlawful' knowledge and its theological, psychological and literary consequences. This chapter considers the fallen state, the alienation and failure of faith which both unjustified puritans and provincials find in themselves. Once again the Calvinist structure of perception provides an analogy for the provincial viewpoint and a metaphor for the artist. In the provincial fiction considered in chapter 4, the concept of 'sympathy' tended always to undermine the boundaries between self and other. This chapter shows how the breakdown of the 'covenant of meaning' distances self from other and overemphasises the inscrutability of appearances until, to the observer, surfaces become entirely devoid of 'content'. This may occur within a fiction, or – even more crucially – between the narrator or author and reader. The puritan–provincial divorce of manner from matter (the 'rhetoric of distance') has a striking effect upon nineteenth-century Scottish and American fiction.

The Fall, as described by Calvin and explicated for a provincial society by Jonathan Edwards, opened a gulf between words and objects, an ontological distance which accounts for the failure of words to mean and of objects to reveal their 'significance'. For both puritan and provincial this is, threateningly, not so much a failure to signify — for to the excluded observer things seem ominously charged with significance – as a failure of confidence that the signs may be interpreted correctly. Both personal identity and human relationship dissolve in a world where passivity and observation are the norm and action and participation the unattainable desiderata of existence. In its provincial phase the coercive and critical rhetoric of Calvinism gives way to a vocabulary of alienation and distance: the world is reduced to an enigmatic spectacle, the self to a spectator and other people to spectres whose lack of solidity and uncertain significance continually entice and decoy the search for objective truth.

It is a dilemma which we may relate directly back to the problems posed by spectral evidence during the witch trials. Such evidence could be viable only as long as men were confident that God's purposes were consistent and directly revealed — so that guilt might infallibly be inferred from the operation of the accused's 'spectre' against another person. The spectre, in other words, was a 'sign' whose significance could be accurately known. But if the spectre might appear randomly or act independently of the will of its 'owner', then the ascertainable connection between them dissolved, and nothing could be deduced from a spectral appearance about the real state of the accused's soul. Chapter 1 suggested how the witch trials tended to polarise puritan communities into those individuals who were made spectral by possession and the spectators who observed them in order to re-establish for their society the connection between appearance and significance. Cotton Mather's record of these events established the spectator's stance of distanced observation as a characteristic and 'safe' voice for provincial authors confronting criticism from the 'centre'. It is a stance which appears to conform to eighteenth-century English literary tradition but which in nineteenth-century Scottish and American fiction diverges crucially from it to suggest the instability and untrustworthiness of the puritan–provincial spectator's voice when confidence in the controlling presence of a covenanted deity is lost. This chapter will trace the critical consequences of that divergence.

The Spectator (1711–13) of Addison and Steele created an audience from a new group of English readers, a 'middle class' as yet without a characteristic literary voice. *The Spectator* simultaneously formed and guided this audience through the stability and authority of its accent. The voice of 'Mr Spectator' is essentially impersonal, a transparent medium for observation and moral comment; it is devoid of idiosyncrasy and sufficiently open to allow the reader to step in and complete the character by his own involvement with the positions adopted. The rhetorical 'I' of the English periodical essay (be he Addison's 'Spectator', Johnson's 'Rambler' or Goldsmith's 'Citizen of the World') earns his authority through his impersonality: his characteristics colour the occasion just sufficiently to lend it authenticity – to establish the present reality of the subject – without obscuring its broader authority. The stability of the spectator's viewpoint gives a unified tone to the collected papers, and the observer's stance defines the man of good breeding and right thinking. The periodical voice assumes both the existence and the accessibility of stable values; it is clear, straightforward and confident.

The correctness and centrality of Addison's prose made *The Spectator* a pattern for Scots and Americans long after its importance as a model for English writers had declined. Samuel Johnson's dictum that 'whoever wishes to attain an English style, familiar but not coarse, and elegant but not ostentatious, must give his days and nights to ... Addison', had a special significance for provincial writers – especially after Hugh Blair's *Lectures on Rhetoric and Belles Lettres* (1783) had subjected Addison's prose style to intensive analysis designed to encourage imitation.[2] Henry Mackenzie's Edinburgh periodicals *The Mirror* (1779–80) and *The Lounger* (1785–6) were popular provincial successors in the genteel mode and earned their editor the soubriquet 'our Scottish Addison' from Scott, while in America Franklin and Freneau imitated *The Spectator's* intimate appeal to a non-learned audience as a model of approved English style consistent with the claims of democracy.[3] The Virginia lawyer William Wirt declared in his *Letters of the British Spy* (1803):

> Were I the sovereign of a nation, which spoke the English language, and wished my subjects cheerful, virtuous and enlightened, I would furnish every poor family in my dominions (and see that the rich furnished themselves) with a copy of the Spectator ... For one of the peculiar perfections of the work is, that while it contains such a mass of ancient and modern learning, so much of profound wisdom, and of beautiful composition, yet there is scarcely a number throughout the eight volumes, which is not level to the meanest capacity.[4]

Here was a vision – from a distance – of centrality, to which Scottish and American provincial writers constantly aspired, but which their fiction just as constantly refuses to endorse.

Wirt's *British Spy* was a periodical in the Addisonian mode whose impartiality depended on the absolute anonymity of its authorial voice and which claimed authority through an (editorially distanced) English narrator. At this provincial remove the spectator has, crucially, become a 'spy', an eavesdropping tourist who does not belong to the local scenery and manners he describes. The Addisonian model allows for diversity and lends weight to the sententious moralising papers, but *The British Spy* fails to hold a tone: the ventriloquistic narrative voice plays indecisively between the central Addisonian mode and the rhapsodic sentimental voice of Sterne or the formalised rhetoric of Burke. The device of the spectating spy comes to seem almost purely defensive: anonymity and distance protect the writer against criticism, but he fails to capitalise on this freedom. The imitative voice cannot establish any convincing relationship to its 'American' subject matter.

In 1802, Washington Irving adopted the *persona* of Jonathan Oldstyle to make his observations on New York society. This old bachelor speaks of himself, with the authority of his literary genealogy, as 'an uninterested spectator'.[5] As with many of the other literary voices who will feature in this chapter (William Wirt, for instance, also wrote a series of 'Old Bachelor' papers), Oldstyle's confirmed celibacy reflects his spiritual condition: 'un-attached' by personal or domestic ties to life, he is distanced from the most intimate human relationships.[6] Irving perceived a potentially interesting conflict between his voice and its subject matter to which Wirt is blind: Oldstyle's age and his 'Englishness' (his youth belongs to the pre-revolutionary Colonial period when America's values were still those of England) entirely *unfit* him to be a 'representative voice' of the new country:

> I often sigh when I draw a comparison between the present and past: and though I cannot but be sensible that, in general, times are altered for the better, yet there is something even in the *imperfections* of the manners which prevailed in my youthful days that is inexpressibly endearing. (p.5)

Oldstyle's relation to experience is more that of Sir Roger de Coverley than that of the Spectator. Instead of speaking from the centre of events, he is, as an 'English' voice, almost completely *alienated* from his American surroundings.

Irving could not handle the complexities of a fictional voice which simultaneously claims objectivity in its comments on society and reveals itself as naive and superannuated: Oldstyle's voice tends to swing between satire and comic buffoonery, thereby preventing the reader from adopting *any* continuing stance towards New York or its *mores*. Irving recognised his dilemma, however, and attempted to restore the authority of his *persona* by dividing it. The 'alienated' aspect of Oldstyle was separated from the corrective narrator by introducing a second voice, the 'honest countryman' (p.11). This new voice (developed from Franklin's homespun American *personae* Silence Do-Good and Poor Richard, and from Freneau's Robert Slender) relieves Oldstyle of the burden of naivety and misunderstanding and also steals his comic potential. Oldstyle's voice gains confidence and acquires the desired tone of authority as he explains the conventions of the theatre to the 'honest countryman'. Meanwhile, the 'American' characteristics of the countryman – comic self-depreciation, rustic humour, and common sense – all define themselves in opposition to Oldstyle's friendly condescension. The naive observation of the alien eye, with all its pastoral clumsiness, comes to carry more authority than the integrated bachelor-*persona* derived from the central *Spectator* tradition. Its superiority derives precisely from its alienation and distance from any form of cultural 'centrality'. Without an established position to maintain, the margin may – as we saw in chapter 3 – claim a greater objectivity in relation to reality than the centre.

But an observer's stance which articulates *non*-relation or the failure of relation between the observed world, the observer and the audience is highly ambivalent. The transition from 'spectator' to 'spy' marks an emotional shift from authority to emptiness and from involvement to alienation. The cautious imitativeness of Wirt's and Irving's periodical papers effectively neutralises the morally dubious connotations of the voyeuristic spy, but a close Scottish analogue, James Hogg's *The Spy* (1810–11), begins to explore the fictional interest of the observer's stance.

Hogg's first venture in a career-long quest for a stable literary voice is a curious hybrid of provincial *Spectator* essays heavily coloured by the intrusive *persona* of the observing Spy. The Spy's account of himself formalises Hogg's own first days in Edinburgh, when his plan was 'to begin a literary weekly paper, a work for which [he] certainly was rarely qualified', considering that he 'had never been once in any polished society – had read next to nothing ... and knew no more of human life or manners than a child'.[7] The Spy's claim to objectivity is based not on a lifetime's involvement with the society, but precisely on his strangeness to it; the social observer has become an alien, an outsider – and his very being is defined by the habit of observation:

> every thing here being quite new to me, any incongruity of taste or character will be much more ready to strike me, than such as have been used to witness the same scenes all their days. Besides, I am constantly on the look-out for singularities, and flatter myself that I have discovered great abundance of them ... I have spent such a long life in doing nothing else but making observations.[8]

The 'rare' qualification of unfamiliarity renders the Spy usefully invisible: 'though there is scarcely a single individual in Edinburgh who has not seen me, as have great numbers in the country besides, yet not one of a thousand amongst them know [sic] who I am, or what I am about' (p.1).

Invisibility becomes the mantle of Prospero which guarantees the Spy's immunity: 'Not one of them / That yet looks on me, or would know me'.[9] Set this beside the way Wirt's 'British Spy' draws the mantle of invisibility around himself in *his* first letter, and the complexities of the stance of the unobserved observer begin to emerge:

> I still continue to wear the mask, and most willingly exchange the attentions, which would be paid to my rank, for the superior and exquisite pleasure of inspecting this country and this people, without attracting to myself a single eye of curiosity, or awakening a shade of suspicion. Under my assumed name, I gain an admission close enough to trace, at leisure, every line of the American character; while the plainness, or rather humility of my appearance, my manners and conversation, put no one on his guard, but enable me to take the portrait of nature, as it were, asleep and naked. Beside, there is something of innocent roguery in this masquerade, which I am playing, that sorts very well with the sportiveness of my temper. To sit and decoy the human heart from behind all its disguises: to watch the capricious evolutions of unrestrained nature, frisking, curvetting and gambolling at her ease, with the curtain of ceremony drawn up to the very sky – Oh! it is delightful! (pp.99–100)

Hawthorne's later observers, Wakefield, Ethan Brand and Roger Chillingworth, bring out the latent portentousness of Wirt's language. The sense of 'exquisite pleasure' which the observer gets from 'playing' with his subjects, using the impenetrability of his masquerading disguise to catch them unawares 'asleep and naked', and through sheer 'roguery' and 'sportiveness' to strip from them all the protections of social 'disguise', strongly suggests Hawthorne's accounts of that unforgivable sin which consists in violating the sanctity of the human heart. Secure in his own invisibility, the spy uses the selfhood of those he observes for his own amusement. Indeed, the predatory observer only exists in the act of observing the unself-conscious identities of his 'victims'. The secret pleasures of spying give the observer a power and prestige over others which effectively substitutes for the privileges of birth or the centrality of participation.

The invisibility of Hogg's Spy is overtly that of emptiness and non-being: 'I am wholly intent on the behaviour of other people, and regardless of my own' (p.1). His description of a chequered career confirms that he is an 'empty' self, given body only by the various roles which he adopts and discards in succession; but, strikingly, egotism is the most salient feature of his account:

> I am now become an observer so accurate, that by contemplating a person's features minutely, modelling my own after the same manner as nearly as possible, and putting my body into the same posture which seems familiar to them, I can ascertain the compass of their thoughts, to a few items, either on the one side or the other, – not precisely what they are thinking at the time, but the way that they would think about any thing. (p.3)

For this voice (which importantly anticipates the empty malevolence of Gil-Martin in Hogg's later *Confessions*), others exist merely to be 'possessed' and colonised by the observer. Vampire-like, he proves his own superiority by encompassing and appropriating their vital reality. Like the 'Biloquist' in Brockden Brown's *Wieland*, the Spy acquires a temporary illusion of solidity through an act of holistic ventriloquism. This impersonation is compensation for the self's failure to possess experience directly. The Spy, like many of the figures of provincial fiction, belongs to a realm of artifice which is set self-consciously apart from life: 'It is the effect of anything completely and consummately artificial, in human shape', says Hawthorne, 'that the person impresses us as an unreality, and as having hardly pith enough to cast a shadow upon the floor'.[10]

But the suggestiveness of Hogg's authorial emptiness is limited by the provincial writer's personal search for a literary voice as he tries out roles which fail to stabilise in later numbers of the magazine. The passage quoted above slides immediately into an archly humorous account of the scrapes into which the Spy has been led by his ventriloquising propensities; interest fades from the *persona* itself until in the twelfth number (again, apparently, accidentally) Hogg lights as Irving had done on the possibility of dividing the voice. Hogg's version suggests, as Irving's fails to, the sinister implications of the observer's stance in the *frisson* – is it guilt? – of the observer surprised in the act of observation. The tables are turned. The Spy's challenger, who 'was equipt with a grey plaid, and staff, like a Nithsdale shepherd, and appeared extremely bashful and simple' (p.89), is unknown to him but seems quite familiar with the 'invisible' observer:

> I ken you weel enouch, for I hae seen ye baith at our house, and i' the kirk, an' my father kend ye weel, for I hae often heard him speaking o' ye. (p.90)

The mystery of this one-sided relationship is never resolved: we are dealing here not with a separate character but with another facet of Hogg's literary personality:

> With surprise and concern I learned his determination of devoting his whole life to literature; while from the little knowledge he had of the world, of books, men or manners, he seemed a person the least fitted for it of any that ever formed such a project. (p.90)

This glosses the Spy's earlier account of himself: Hogg has found it necessary (as had Irving with Oldstyle) to separate the voice of the traditionally authoritative Spectator – now alienated from his social medium – from the 'local' voice which is in contact with provincial life. The Spy's embarrassment at being surprised in the act of his *métier* puts him, as he recognises, at a disadvantage. He is no longer cloaked in protective invisibility; the observer's distance from experience is exposed in all its emptiness and vulnerability to solid reality. Hogg's secondary avatar (a Scots-speaking, commonsensical Nithsdale shepherd) invokes a national voice which seems more firmly rooted than that of the alienated 'English' voice of the Spy, but Hogg always has one ear attentive to the response of a superior and English-speaking audience and never quite grants his shepherd the eccentric authority of the margin which he claims. The voice of the Nithsdale shepherd eventually proves to be no less empty, no less divorced from its matter, than that of the Spy himself.

The empty authorial stance is not characteristic merely of the minor works of as yet little-known writers: Walter Scott (a much more confident and established member of the Edinburgh literati) also proliferated – with similar consequences – authorial voices designed to protect the impenetrability of his empty *persona* 'the Great Unknown'. When he came to explain his 'humour' in persisting with the fiction of anonymity long after the authorship of the Waverley Novels was an open secret, Scott adduced amongst other reasons the benefits of invisibility and personal concealment: like a 'spy', he 'could appear, or retreat from the stage at pleasure, without attracting any personal notice or attention, other than what might be founded on suspicion only ... the author of *Waverley* was in this respect as impassible to the critic, as the Ghost of Hamlet to the partisan of Marcellus'.[11] Authorial self-concealment permits his fictional self-projection in a series of masks or 'showmen' who introduce the various novels; they include the posturing rhetorical pedant Jedediah Cleishbotham, the antiquarian Dryasdust and his acolyte Templeton, and the aspiring provincial Addison Crystal Croftangry, who avers, 'with becoming modesty, that I do think myself capable of sustaining a publication of a miscellaneous nature, as like to the *Spectator* or the *Guardian*, the *Mirror* or the *Lounger*, as my poor abilities may be able to accomplish'.[12] There is also the retiring Peter Pattieson, a ventriloquistic stage manager who is 'cunning in counterfeiting of voices', and (like Hawthorne) 'fonder, on almost any occasion, of being absent than of being present': 'I confess, that, were it safe to cherish such dreams at all, I should more enjoy the thought of remaining behind the curtain unseen, like the ingenious stage manager of Punch and his wife Joan, and enjoying the astonishment and conjectures of my audience'.[13]

It is a veritable rogues' gallery of 'empty' provincial masks, all being disembodied projections of the 'Eidolon' or 'spectre' of 'The Author of Waverley' who flits in and out of their 'introductions', admonishing them when they get self-important and begin to imagine that they are real and substantial, and gleefully confounding the boundaries between fiction and fact. Several times in these prefaces, 'the Author' or one of his avatars suggests that insubstantiality is the condition of authorship: 'every anonymous writer is . . . only a phantom'; 'let fame follow those who have a substantial shape. A shadow – and an impersonal author is nothing better – can cast no shade'.[14]

When 'compulsory circumstances' caused him to abandon his anonymity, Scott suggested in his fable of the harlequin Arlechino who was persuaded by flattery to perform once without his mask and was never afterwards able to regain the magic of his masqued performances, that his fictions were only playable under the liberating disguises of his multiple *personae*. In the speech at the Theatrical Fund Dinner in 1827 in which he acknowledged authorship of the novels, Scott rose to the theatricality of the occasion and compared himself to the unmasked showman Prospero at the end of *The Tempest*: 'The wand was now broken, and the book buried. You will allow me further to say, with Prospero, it is your breath that has filled my sails.'[15] Shakespeare's showman exerts a peculiar influence over the puritan–provincial imagination. All the fiction considered in this chapter alludes openly or covertly to *The Tempest*, with its idealising vision and its manipulative, wilful protagonist. It will be important to examine the reasons for this affinity and to question its bearing on the characteristic form of provincial literature.

Like Hogg's Spy, and like Hawthorne's Coverdale later, Scott's protective mask of invisibility has an equivocal relation to the reality which it allows him to observe; it is not altogether 'safe to cherish such dreams', and his unmasking involves the 'shame of detection' at a clandestine activity.[16] The mask of invisibility puts a protective distance between the observer and life, but in Scott's writing it is not merely a defensive device. The showman creates and then operates within a realm where actions have no consequences in life; his purpose is to provide a bridge between reality and fiction which overleaps the normal relations of cause and effect, action and responsibility. Scott's masks do not, like those of Irving and Hogg, signal a *failure* of relation between the observer and the fiction or the present and the past; standing midway between the reader and the story, they suggest the possibility of a special kind of relationship which vanquishes – for the duration of the fiction – the logic of everyday.

It is fitting, then, that James Fenimore Cooper entitled his first attempt at an 'American' subject *The Spy: A Tale of the Neutral Ground* (1821). The novel is set just after the execution of the British spy Major Andre during the revolutionary War of Independence, and the romantic plot mirrors that historical event. Harvey Birch (the 'spy' of the title) is a double agent: actually a patriot working under 'Mr Harper' (George

Washington in disguise), he maintains his cover and retains his freedom to move invisibly through the enemy lines by selling unimportant secrets to the British. Masquerading as a pedlar, he maintains a studied neutrality. But conflicting rumours surround his activities, and he is hated and mistrusted by everyone except 'Harper', who knows his true identity. Birch, the professional observer, is alienated by his occupation from the normal sphere of human sympathies, but seems thereby to have a peculiar access to the 'mysteries of the human heart'. He is double in himself: both abstracted from experience, and at the centre of it.

Observation and its uncertainties are a major element in the plot; an atmosphere of ambiguity and distrust pervades the whole novel. Accurate observation, 'in a war, in which similarity of language, appearance, and customs, rendered prudence doubly necessary', is at once crucial to survival, and almost impossibly problematic.[17] All the clues appear to conflict and elude satisfactory interpretation. This state of civil war (as Cooper presents the conflict between the English and American sides) renders every man an observer, defined by the accuracy of his observations. There are clear analogies with Calvinism, which requires continual vigilance in observation to distinguish the elect from the reprobate and to penetrate the disguises of appearance to the reality beneath. The civil war, too, is a familiar metaphor for the divided condition of the individual puritan soul struggling towards conversion. As in Hogg's periodical (and as we saw from a different angle in the fictions of pursuit discussed in chapter 4) the observer observed in the act of observation looks like a spy – and spying, as the fate of Major Andre reminds us, is a dangerous activity. Observation may *seem* safer (because uncommitted) than action, but it courts the dangers of a spy's fate. Cooper's romantic hero Henry Wharton (a soldier on the British side) absents himself from the theatre of war and dons disguise to visit his family in the neutral territory. Before he can reveal himself to them, an officer of the patriot army arrives at the house. This close observer penetrates his masquerade and suspects treachery. The dangers of observation in a state of war extend to the concealment of one's true identity even for benevolent ends, and Henry Wharton is arrested as a spy.

His escape and final vindication are effected by the 'real' spy, Harvey Birch, who assumes the voices and forms of others with a virtuosity which renders his impersonation opaque to even the keenest observers. He has a hut (an 'observatory' as it is called) stocked with the costumes and properties of his masquerades. Cooper (like Scott) borrows from eighteenth-century aesthetic theories of the picturesque to lend visual emphasis by locating Birch at the 'correct' distance for observation of the action (p.112).[18] His physical distance and mental alienation from the book's more conventionally rendered figures and (after his father's death) his lack of human ties tend to empty him of personal characteristics. Birch's protean assumption of forms gives him, to other characters, the intangibility of a 'spectre' (p.260). The spy sinks his identity in the profession of observation.

The moral complexities of spying are suggested but undeveloped: Cooper evades the logic of Birch's trapped position as a double observer by means of the mysterious 'Mr Harper', who functions at crucial moments from beyond the fictional world as a *deus ex machina* to free the spy's tied hands for action and to make him an *agent* in the resolution of the plot. Harvey Birch's alienation is mitigated by his relationship with 'Harper': when he is asked whether he has no comrades, he replies, 'No – no, I am alone truly – none know me but my God and *Him*' (p.211). Like Bishop Berkeley's deity, Harper watching over his creature ensures Birch's continuing existence and (like Scott's narrators) by the constancy of *his* observation gives the spy a stable identity. 'Harper' is Washington, the new and true 'father' of America and guardian of his country. The disguised general's powerful presence from beyond the local plot prevents the more ambivalent aspects of the observing role from becoming resonant and allows Cooper to contain his narrative (at the cost of literary tact) within the framework of the romantic novel. The presence of a godlike figure *within* the fiction controls the polarising tendencies of its puritan–provincial structure.

Birch is eccentric, distanced from the romantic centre which organises the novel. He derives from Scott's structurally provincial but thematically central voices such as Edie Ochiltree in *The Antiquary* (1816); Wandering Willie is another. A patriotic American, Birch prefigures Cooper's own subsequent development of the lone, alienated figure of Natty Bumppo, who observes the progress of American civilisation as he is pushed passively westwards before it. Although Leatherstocking gains increasing thematic centrality in the series, Cooper never achieved an American *Heart of Midlothian*, in which the 'eccentric' or provincial protagonist who is at the heart of the novel works not in opposition to but in harmony with the movement of both the fictional story and the real history it enacts.

Intangible as a spectre, Birch's unexplained appearances at unlikely times and places in the novel invoke interpretative anxieties similar to those suffered by attendants of the puritan witch trials. When the empty voice of the provincial Spectator masks itself in invisibility, the spy becomes spectral, floating etherially across the scenes he observes, neither impinging on nor impinged upon by its reality. Indeed, in Scottish and American provincial literature, to set oneself up as a spectator is to risk becoming an unhoused spirit or an 'Outcast of the Universe'.[19]

Hawthorne's Wakefield is a very ordinary sort of man; his identity seems fixed, rooted, and solid: 'who could have anticipated, that our friend would entitle himself to a foremost place amongst the doers of eccentric deeds?' (p.131). But one day, on a whim, he leaves his wife and hurries off to 'lose his individuality, and melt into the great mass of London life' (p.133). He takes an apartment in the 'next street' to his own, at a distance from which he can observe the features of his old life, 'curious to know . . . how the little sphere of creatures and circumstances, in which he was a central object, will be affected by his removal' (p.134). The passing of a single night in his new role of detached observer 'wrought a . . . transformation' in his relationship to the reality which was his life, a transformation which the narrator represents as 'a great moral change' (p.135). For twenty years Wakefield, in heavy disguise, 'haunt[s] around his house' (p.137). He becomes, like the Spy, both invisible and alienated from human sympathies:

> He had contrived, or rather he had happened, to dissever himself from the world – to vanish – to give up his place and privileges with living men, without being admitted among the dead . . . He was in the bustle of the city, as of old; but the crowd swept by, and saw him not; he was, we may figuratively say, always beside his wife, and at his hearth, yet must never feel the warmth of the one, nor yet the affection of the other. It was Wakefield's unprecedented fate, to retain his original share of human sympathies, and to be still involved in human interests, while he had lost his reciprocal influence on them. (p.138)

By becoming an observer, Wakefield loses his place in the world; the gaps of affection close all too quickly around the emptiness left by his withdrawal. His eccentric act does not as he expects render him conspicuous and 'special' to the observations of others. Like the Calvinist in the long eras following the active revolutionary moment, he finds himself stranded on the unobserved periphery of events: 'Poor Wakefield: Little knowest thou thine own insignificance in this great world! No mortal eye but mine has traced thee' (p.133). Wakefield, in his invisibility, 'lives' only through the observations of the narrator who in retelling the story for the reader's edification tries to think himself into the circumstances that could have produced such an 'unexampled' incident (p.130). 'Wakefield' is a typically elusive Hawthorne tale whose underemphatic presentation and neat explanatory 'moral' seem quite incidental to the enigmatic events they describe. The narrator's cool re-creation of the wreck of two human lives, and the detachment with which he presents his characters, suggest that he may himself be guilty of the moral espionage for which he censures Wakefield:

> Now for a scene! Amid the throng of a London street, we distinguish a man, now waxing elderly, with few characteristics to attract careless observers, yet bearing, in his whole aspect, the hand-writing of no common fate, for such as have the skill to read it. (p.137)

If Wakefield has become a living spectre haunting his own life, the distanced narrator also haunts the lives of his characters, living for the reader only through his evocation of their story, but refusing to participate in the dilemmas he has created for them or to rescue them with a touch of 'reality' from the shadowy half-existence to which his 'distanced' narration has consigned them. Wakefield's sin, for which he is designated 'Outcast of the Universe', seems dangerously close to the observations of the narrator who distances experience in fiction. It is a thought which will be even more strikingly insinuated by the activities of Coverdale. These narrative voices are at once derived from and far removed in spirit from Scott's gleefully spectral surrogates.

The complexity of the multiple layers of observation is ambiguously suggested in 'Wakefield', and the narrator evades the censure he applies to Wakefield by deriving from his own observations a conventional moral which *seems* to lead outwards to 'life'. In 'The Man of the Crowd' (1840), Poe subjects the motivation of the observing, spectral narrator to detailed scrutiny. It is one of his most successful tales, in which the disembodied voice which characterises so much of his work is the perfect vehicle for the insubstantial pageant he creates.

The convalescent narrator is an idle but acute observer whose state renders him almost preternaturally perceptive. Emptied of pain, he seems to have no positive characteristics other than a generalised curiosity. From the window of a London coffee-house this detached American (as it emerges later) observes the crowds going by in the street, and amuses himself by imagining their professions and ranks in society, and their emotions. He has none of his own: 'I felt a calm but inquisitive interest in everything.'[20] Evening falls, and the interest of the scene increases as it becomes more theatrical in the garishly discriminating illumination of gas-lights. An individual catches his attention. This man appears to have something inhuman in his aspect: 'Retzch, had he viewed it, would have greatly preferred it to his own pictural incarnations of the fiend' (p.166). It is the face of knowledge. The observer is fascinated by its secrets, and 'a craving desire to keep the man in view, to know more of him' initiates his first action: he leaves what Poe calls his 'observatory' to join the crowd. He goes, however, not as a participant in its activities, but in order to observe his man without being himself observed: '[I] followed him closely, yet cautiously, so as not to attract his attention' (p.167). Heightened curiosity colours his perceptions, and he begins to construct his subject's story:

> I perceived that his linen, although dirty, was of beautiful texture; and my vision deceived me, or, through a rent in a closely-buttoned and evidently second-handed *roquelaire* which enveloped him, I caught a glimpse both of a diamond and a dagger. (p.167)

From this point, if not before, we are aware that the narrator's observations are not trustworthy. His insatiable desire to know what he describes as 'some secrets which do not permit themselves to be told' (p.159) lends an air of guilt to his own concern to avoid observation. The man searches for crowds and then wanders aimlessly amongst them; his pursuer begins to associate himself with his quarry ('a second turn brought us into a square, brilliantly lighted, and overflowing with life' [p.169]); his observations enable him to 'act' vicariously by following in another's footsteps. The existence of the other gives the observer some measure of security about his own identity: 'I followed him in the wildest amazement, resolute not to abandon a scrutiny in which I now felt an interest all-absorbing' (p.172).

The pursuit is circular, and returns to the hotel from whose safety the observer had ventured out. But, as in 'Wakefield', one action has changed the face of everything: the hotel 'no longer wore ... the same aspect' (p.170). The self-returning chase continues into a second evening, when like Edgar Huntly or Wringhim 'wearied unto death', the observer risks being himself observed and, 'stopping fully in front of the wanderer, gazed at him steadfastly in the face. He noticed me not, but resumed his solemn walk, while I, ceasing to follow, remained absorbed in contemplation' (p.173). The narrator is, to the other, invisible. The self-conscious observer's unnecessary concern to avoid detection in his own pursuit is the obverse of the observed man's obsessive seeking for anonymity and emptiness in the crowds. To observe from a distance is to be invisible; to be observed – to become interesting to another – is, for the provincial observer, to assume the secret of a forbidden knowledge. Participation without guilt, loss of self-consciousness without loss of selfhood: these are the hopeless desiderata of both puritan and provincial.

In both 'Wakefield' and 'The Man of the Crowd', the individual 'chosen' from the multitude has identity because he is being observed. Confident of God's watchful eye upon them, seventeenth-century puritans were assured that their lives had significance. In the absence of that certainty, the meaning – and finally the reality – of human actions became dependent upon self-observation and the observations of others. Signification had to be wrested from and imposed upon others through predatory espionage. The observer endows his quarry with both characteristics and identity, and in so doing creates a necessary role for himself, because as soon as he loses sight of the object of his pursuit the latter will melt back into the crowd and cease to exist. Thus the observing narrator of 'The Man of the Crowd' plays God with his character, dismissing him at the end of the story to non-being with a sententious aphorism: 'perhaps it is but one of the great mercies of God that "er lasst sich nicht lesen"' (p.173). When the narrator releases his character, both cease to have any reason for being.

When the spectator's interest in the scene he describes has dwindled to the alienated observations of a spy, and when spectral presence substitutes for involvement with the world, the scene itself begins to lose solidity, to become a 'cloud-capp'd vision' in the mind of the observer. The complete absence of participatory relation between the spectral observer and what he observes reduces it to a spectacle, a masquerade of surfaces which conceal an inaccessible significance.

Melville's Chola Widow in 'The Encantadas' (1854) watches the enactment of her destiny (the private tragedy which deprives her of husband and brother, her only relations and her source of support) by accident, almost idly, as a spectacle upon a stage:

> Before Hunilla's eyes they sank. The real woe of this event passed before her sight as some sham tragedy on the stage... the better to watch the adventure of those two hearts she loved, Hunilla had withdrawn the branches to one side, and held them so. They formed an oval frame, through which the bluely boundless sea rolled like a painted one. And there, the invisible painter painted to her view the wave-tossed and disjointed raft, its once level logs slantingly upheaved, as raking masts, and the four struggling arms undistinguishable among them; and then all subsided into smooth-flowing creamy waters, slowly drifting the splintered wreck; while first to last, no sound of any sort was heard. Death in a silent picture; a dream of the eye; such vanishing shapes as the mirage shows.[21]

Hunilla's absolute distance from this tableau staged by the invisible showman Destiny, and her absolute passivity, prevent her from establishing any relation to it:

> So instant was the scene, so trance-like its mild pictorial effect, so distant from her blasted bower and her common sense of things, that Hunilla gazed and gazed, nor raised a finger or a wail. But as good to sit thus dumb, in stupor staring on that dumb show, for all that otherwise might be done. (p.184)

All she can do is to deflect the quite incomprehensible 'meaning' of these deaths into 'art': she transforms them — to survive them — into objects of sentimental contemplation and ritualistic re-enactment. But once we see the widow herself viewing her tragedy as a spectacle on a stage, the whole way in which her tale is offered, and the relation in which the reader stands to it, become suspect. In a passage as rhetorically 'composed' as the vision of the sable form in 'Young Goodman Brown', the narrator appeals to the controlling hand of the 'invisible painter' with disingenuous fatalism. His self-consciously aesthetic manner evokes events as a static tableau; the reader becomes a voyeur, a distanced spectator of a sentimental tale:

> It is not artistic heartlessness, but I wish I could but draw in crayons; for this woman was a most touching sight; and crayons, tracing softly melancholy lines, would best depict the mournful image of the dark-damasked Chola Widow. (p.181)

Sympathy and distance are ruthlessly manipulated for effect.

In the *Treatise*, Hume used the image of observing a shipwreck to illustrate his ideas about 'sympathy' and its opposite, detached 'comparison': watch the wreck from too great a distance, he says, and it can have little effect, but go too close and it becomes a source of pain rather than of aesthetic pleasure:

> Suppose the ship to be driven so near me, that I can perceive distinctly the horror, painted on the countenance of the seamen and passengers, hear their lamentable cries, see the dearest friends give their last adieu, or embrace with a resolution to perish in each other's arms: No man has so savage a heart as to reap any pleasure from such a spectacle, or withstand the motions of the tenderest compassion and sympathy. 'Tis evident, therefore, there is a medium in this case; and that if the idea be too feint, it has no influence by comparison; and, on the other hand, if it be too strong, it operates on us entirely by sympathy, which is the contrary to comparison. (pp.594–5)

Moral and aesthetic gratification is the result, then, of observing from the 'correct' distance.

Just as the meaning of her own experience as the tragedy's spectator is withheld by the showman Destiny from Hunilla, so the narrator withholds from the reader the vital truth of the subsequent experience which would enable us to understand Hunilla herself:

> The half shall here remain untold. Those two unnamed events which befell Hunilla on this isle, let them abide between her and her God. In nature, as in law, it may be libelous to speak some truths. (p.188)

Our curiosity as readers to know the truth is reprimanded by the narrator's sententious mouthing of Calvinistic warnings about forbidden knowledge. The effect is very similar to the genteel platitudes of the narrator of 'Bartleby' or to the aphoristic curtain-closing of Poe's narrator in 'The Man of the Crowd': 'perhaps it is but one of the great mercies of God that "er lasst sich nicht lesen"'.

Thus arbitrarily excluded from the scene he observes, the reader is inclined to resist the 'explanatory' pageant of Hunilla which concludes the tale. The neat way in which she is made an icon of suffering, her tale an allegory of Christ's Passion with its punning 'seen'/scene is yet one more unmeaning spectacle presented to the spectator's alienated vision:

> The last seen of lone Hunilla she was passing into Payta town, riding upon a small gray ass; and before her on the ass's shoulders, she eyed the jointed workings of the beast's armorial cross. (p.193)

If the 'aesthetic' observer has no stake in the events he describes, he does in another sense have a crucial 'interest' in the scene he creates for the reader, for it is there that he comes into being at all, and there that he must persuade his audience to acquiesce in the 'covenant of meaning' which will allow him to establish relationships beyond his own perceiving consciousness. The observer's insistence on the emptiness of his self and its skill only to record but not to control the events it describes is akin to the wilful rhetoric of submission of the puritan autobiographies. These (as in Jonathan Edwards' *Personal Narrative*) put the self-questioning sinner at the centre of the stage, his own mind the theatre of God's unfolding plan for mankind. Obsessive self-consciousness divorces thought from action and enforces passivity: 'the Thought', Thomas Carlyle thundered, 'conduces not to the Deed; but in boundless chaos, self-devouring, engenders monstrosities, phantasms, fire-breathing chimeras'.[22]

George Santayana puts it that 'people can mimic only what they have not absorbed. They reconstruct and turn into an archaeological masquerade only what strikes them as outlandish.'[23] When men cease to know their relation to experience, they adopt its voices and forms as 'art' and play out their existence as self-projections on an artificial plane. Masquerade is the projection of the observer's lack of self-possession; it is the creation of a mind divorced from its own purposes and from its own past. Continuities through time are disrupted: the masquerade projects one flat plane back onto another, and the self-engendered vision loses all vital connection with the reality which may exist beyond it. The masquerade is a powerful image in Scottish and American fiction; it aptly describes both the provincial view of life itself and the literature which is created in the 'fallen' state of distance from experience. These will be the concern of the remainder of this chapter.

Poe's tale 'The Masque of the Red Death' (1840) suggests that the withdrawal to a fictional masquerade is not necessarily an indemnifying one. His author-showman stands not like Scott's, half-way between fiction and fact, committed both to the illusoriness of the one and the solidity of the other, but (as its creator and director) is firmly within the fiction. In this tale, the characters withdraw from the dangers of real life; guided by their artist-prince, they create a substitute reality in 'a masked ball of most unusual magnificence'.[24] The heavily symbolic description confirms that the Red Death – 'blood was its avatar and its seal' (p.326) – is present even in the entirely artificial inner world from which it has been consciously excluded. The prince's imagination has constructed his inner masquerade from the materials of outer life, and 'in the western, or black, chamber the effect of the firelight that streamed upon the dark hangings through the blood-tinted panes was ghastly in the extreme' (p.329). The Red Death, like Original Sin, is within the masqueraders even as they withdraw from life's tainted realities and attempt to establish a 'clean', innocent and observing relationship to it. In this respect they resemble the Blithedale Community in Hawthorne's romance.

A new masquerader, the Red Death personified, makes himself known in the artificial precinct, and the artist-prince is powerless to prevent the invasion: he creates and directs his puppets in the stage setting he has provided for them, but having thus abstracted them from reality, he cannot protect them against it. Prince Prospero and his private world, with all its fictional occupants, are destroyed by this spectral image of reality 'untenanted by any tangible form'. 'And Darkness and Decay and the Red Death held illimitable dominion over all' (p.335).

The vulnerability of Prince Prospero's stance is that of the provincial author who creates a fiction out of his sense of distance from reality – a sense at once defensive and self-righteous – but then has difficulty in controlling the precise relation in which his masquerade stands to that reality. The showman creates a masquerade and casts the reader in the puritan–provincial role of interpreter of inscrutable surfaces. Where, in Poe's teasing fiction about creating a fiction within a fiction, does the real repose?

A similar Chinese-box illusion of receding fictional frameworks is effected in Hogg's series on 'The Scottish Muses' in *The Spy*. A secondary *persona*, Mr Shuffleton, takes the stage from the empty spy. Mr Shuffleton is a showman whose masquerade is 'the most curious method imaginable for making each of [the modern Scottish poets] appear in their proper colours':

> He supposes every poet's muse his mistress ... and in this large mirror here, or rather in that magic area seemingly behind it, he makes these ladies to appear in their common wearing apparel, and walk about, and sing as long as we please: and what is more curious still, if any one of us choose to ask a question ... they will answer us. (p.9)

As in Poe's tale, the showman as artist within a fiction does not 'mirror' reality in his work; his art is a spectacle, a puppet-show which aims to delude the senses into accepting its illusory 'magic area' as real. Mr Shuffleton anticipates Melville's artist as confidence man and foreshadows the artist-showmen of Hawthorne's short tales, purveyors of words rather than things, who conjure up spectral scenes for a fictional audience. The shifting panorama of 'Main-street' (1849) offers a close analogy to Mr Shuffleton's methods:

> I have contrived a certain pictorial exhibition, somewhat in the nature of a puppet-show, by means of which I propose to call up the multiform and many-colored Past before the spectator, and show him the ghosts of his

forefathers, amid a succession of historic incidents, with no greater trouble than the turning of a crank.[25]

This is history as (in Santayana's words) an 'archaeological masquerade'; the spectres of the past are called up to amuse the present. The showman's advertisement of his 'pictorial exhibition' is strikingly similar to the lightly quizzical tone in which Hume advocates 'The Study of History' to a genteel feminine audience:

> what more agreeable entertainment to the mind, than ... to see all human race, from the beginning of time, pass, as it were, in review before us; appearing in their true colours, without any of those disguises, which, during their lifetime, so much perplexed the judgment of the beholders. What spectacle can be imagined, so magnificent, so varied, so interesting?[26]

The masquerade of history offers a 'succession' of incidents, apparently unconnected to each other or with the present; the distanced observer sees no chain of cause and effect leading back into the past. History is not a 'story', but a series of discrete tableaux.[27] But Hawthorne's showman in 'Main-street', again like Hume, suggests that from 'the proper point of view' his masquerade does contain meaning and that his audience can establish a relationship with these events. The burden of interpretation – and the power to refuse that role – rests upon the reader.

The showman presents 'the spectral image' of the 'Great Squaw Sachem' (p.51), the 'spectral representative' of Governor Winthrop (p.61), and the 'life-like images, – their spectres, if you choose so to call them' of the puritan fathers (p.60) for the amusement of his audience, but he cannot by himself make his spectacle meaningful. When challenged by 'an acidulous-looking gentlemen' with the manifest unreality of his masquerade, the artist-showman admits that he must 'now and then ask a little aid from the spectator's imagination'. But the irascible critic who 'make[s] it a point to see things precisely as they are' (p.52) refuses to acquiesce in the illusion. He obstinately adopts his own distance from the spectacle, thereby rendering the artist impotent and nullifying the effect of his art:

> 'But, sir, you have not the proper point of view', remarks the showman. 'You sit altogether too near to get the best effect of my pictorial exhibition. Pray, oblige me by removing to this other bench; and, I venture to assure you, the proper light and shadow will transform the spectacle into quite another thing.'
> 'Pshaw!' replies the critic: 'I want no other light and shade. I have already told you, that it is my business to see things just as they are'. (p.57)[28]

The showman who presents a spectacle whose reality is so completely dependent upon the acquiescence of its spectators, wants 'Spirits to enforce, art to enchant': he is passive both at the hands of his audience and of his spectral material. He has no prerogative to bestow meaning on it by interpretations of his own:

> Let us thank God for having given us such ancestors; and let each successive generation thank him, not less fervently, for being one step further from them in the march of ages.
> 'What is all this?' cries the critic. 'A sermon? If so, it is not in the bill.'
> 'Very true,' replies the showman; 'and I ask pardon of the audience' . . .
> 'Turn your crank, I say,' bellows the remorseless critic, 'and grind it out, whatever it be, without further preface!'
> The showman deems it best to comply. (pp.68, 73)

Like the tourist Hawthorne in England, whose distance from the scenes he viewed there stands as an epigraph to this chapter, the 'critic' tires quickly of a spectacle to which he can establish no personal relation.[29] He craves, like Poe's Man of the Crowd, other scenes in which he may lose his emptiness. The artist-showman is helpless before such egotistical demands for relation and meaning from his audience; his own mind, like that of a man caught between sleeping and waking, has 'a passive sensibility, but no active strength . . . the imagination is a mirror, imparting vividness to all ideas, without the power of selecting or controlling them'.[30]

Another of Hawthorne's 'masquerade' sketches, 'P's Correspondence' (1845), makes the crucial connection between the masquerade of life that art presents to puritan–provincial sensibility and the 'postures' of the perceiving mind itself, a connection which takes us back to Hume's sense that 'the mind is a kind of theatre' and the self-observations of the divided Calvinist consciousness. 'P' is a madman, whose 'haunted mind' creates spectral meetings with deceased literary figures, imagining them as they would now be if still alive. The crazed showman presents his spectacle provisionally, for completion and realisation in the acquiescence of its unknown audience. If this assent is denied, as the reader is bound to deny the reality of 'P's fantasies, or as the acidulous gentlemen denies the showman's masquerade in 'Main-street', the artist's vision of life remains a solipsistic show; his showman's frame collapses, and he finds himself the sole spectator of a self-generated spectacle. This (*if* we grant the 'Ideality' of the Universe) may, as Emerson suggests, be a fate awaiting more than the madman: 'How long before our masquerade will end its noise of tambourines, laughter, and shouting, and we shall find it was a solitary performance?'.[31] The provincial voice, borrowing the Addisonian mantle, tries to confer reality on its milieu but succeeds only in demonstrating the failure of relationship between consciousness and the objects of contemplation.

The postures of 'P's mind have collapsed chronology; as there is no difference to him between inner and outer, so he makes no distinctions between past and present, the dead and the living. Consequently, neither is real to the observer of his masquerade. But 'P's mental reality, which exists in the extinction of time, is not so different from the 'Ideality' of the Calvinist or Transcendentalist, upon which it may be a comment. For Teufelsdröckh in Carlyle's *Sartor Resartus* (1831), for example, the desideratum is to 'Pierce through the Time-element, glance into the Eternal'.[32] To discover meaning camouflaged by appearances, the distancing 'Phantasms, TIME and SPACE' (p.203) must be obliterated:

> These, as spun and woven for us from before Birth itself, to clothe our celestial ME for dwelling here, and yet to blind it, – lie all-embracing, as the universal canvas, or warp and woof, whereby all minor Illusions, in this Phantasm Existence, weave and paint themselves. In vain, while here on earth, shall you endeavour to strip them off; you can, at best, but rend them asunder for moments, and look through. (p.207)

Where Scott's masque-presenters (who insist on time as one of the conditions of the illusion) make *themselves* spectral in order to invest their characters with imaginative solidity, Teufelsdröckh's obsessive idealism makes *all* appearances spectral:

> Are we not Spirits, that are shaped into a body, into an Appearance; and that fade away again into air and Invisibility? This is no metaphor, it is a simple scientific *fact*: we start out of Nothingness, take figure, and are Apparitions; round us, as round the veriest spectre, is Eternity. (p.211)

He hopes by the very intensity of his observation to melt Nature's masking surfaces. Carlyle's mind, as he evokes the rapt vision of Teufelsdröckh, is filled with images from *The Tempest*; the chapter ('Natural Supernaturalism') ends with a slightly misremembered quotation from the showman Prospero's dismissal of the masque of Juno and Ceres.

In August 1834, Carlyle wrote to Emerson acknowledging the American's criticism of *Sartor Resartus* and explaining his decision to leave Craigenputtock and Scotland and to reside in London. Defending *Sartor*'s idiosyncrasy, Carlyle describes its stylistic levity as a sign of the times: when (he suggests) the central style has become through imitation decadent and theatrical, only a deliberately *e*ccentric voice can claim assent and assume the burden of meaning:

> You say well that I take up that attitude because I have no known public, am *alone* under the Heavens, speaking into friendly or unfriendly space; add only that . . . at last we have lived to see all manner of Poetics and Rhetorics and Sermonics, and one may say generally all manner of *Pulpits* for addressing mankind from, as good as broken and abolished: alas, yes; if you have any earnest meaning, which demands to be not only listened to but *believed* and

> *done*, you cannot (at least I cannot) utter it *there*, but the sound sticks in my throat, as when a Solemnity were *felt* to have become a Mummery; and so one leaves the pasteboard coulisses, and three unities, and Blairs lectures, quite behind; and feels only that there is *nothing sacred*, then but the *Speech of Man* to believing Men![33]

This is a new note of positive confidence in the eccentric voice's ability to perceive and communicate truth. But the voice is a lowly one, speaking in a hostile or indifferent crowd. Of his new metropolitan residence, Carlyle goes on to say, 'A strange element this; and I as good as an Alien in it . . . much as I can speak and hear, I am alone, alone'. Finally, he tells Emerson of a 'queer production', 'The Diamond Necklace', which he intends to publish soon (p.105).

This little-known novella has some importance in the literature of provincialism. 'The Diamond Necklace' was an attempt 'to make Reality Ideal'. Its truth must be founded on faith, both on the part of the author and of the reader: 'what a man *does not believe* can never at bottom be of true interest to him'.[34] In the Calvinist universe a man without faith becomes a spectator and the world a distanced spectacle with which he cannot engage. Carlyle, like Hawthorne, transposes the puritan–provincial dilemma of distance onto an artistic canvas: the observer who cannot suspend disbelief in the masquerade fails to participate in (and thereby to continue) the process of meaning initiated by the showman. And an unmeaning spectacle, as we have seen, threatens the identity of the observer.

But Hawthorne's showman learned to his cost that the spectator's assent to the terms of his enterprise – the attempt to 'make Reality Ideal' – is a necessary condition of its power to hold him. As long as the audience either believes in the symbolising structure of Calvinist perception, or is uncomfortable in its disbelief, the puritan–provincial masquerade will command attention; only he who does *not* believe that the Ideal lies behind and separate from the Real or that meaning resides in interpretation cannot be threatened by an inscrutable pageant of surfaces. Carlyle's narrator tries from the beginning to establish a covenant of meaning with the reader, to adjust the viewpoint of his posited spectator to the 'correct' distance from which meaning can become apparent:

> As in looking at a finished Drama, it were nowise meet that the spectator first of all got behind the scenes, and saw the burnt-corks, brayed-resin, thunder-barrels, and withered hunger-bitten men and women, of which such heroic work was made: so here with the reader. A peep into the side-scenes shall be granted him, from time to time. But, on the whole, repress, O reader, that too insatiable scientific curiosity of thine; let thy *aesthetic* feeling first have play; and witness what a Prospero's-grotto poor Eminence Rohan is led into.[35]

The covenant of meaning allows the reader a certain measure of initiative, but as we saw in chapter 4, there may be certain secrets which are better prudently left mysterious. Distance and faith in the showman (so he promises) will together give the pageant a semblance of reality and shareable meaning.

'The Diamond Necklace' is about a political and sexual intrigue which took place at the French court on the eve of the Revolution, and in whose events and outcome Carlyle saw a premonition of that apocalypse. As with the fictions of Scott and Hawthorne's 'Main-street', the 'truth' of the past is approached through the controlled postures of a masquerade. The plot involves the machinations of the milliner Lamotte – the 'Artist', as Carlyle dubs her – who plays on the vanity of her dupes to create a masquerade which they in their self-centred blindness take for reality. This 'great creative Dramaturgist' sits 'at the heart of the whole mystery, [with] a clear belief founded on completest insight' and pulls the strings of her puppets, the jeweller Boehmer and the Duc de Rohan, whose 'clear belief [is] founded on stupidity' (p.373).

The mechanics of Lamotte's masquerade are laid bare by a narrator-showman who exhibits the dramatist and her illusion at a distance which controls both scepticism and the reader's gullible wish to participate in the illusion as though it were truth: 'Good reader, thou surely art not a Partridge the Schoolmaster, or a Monseigneur de Rohan, to mistake the stage for a reality!' (p.372). The mind of the showman Lamotte is only visible through her creation, the masquerade; she stands clear of her spectacle and can 'justly retort: Who saw me in it?' (p.377). Her thoughts remain opaque to the speculations of the narrator who presents *her* as a puppet in *his* masquerade. She is without substance or belief and exists only in the ventriloquistic mimicry of her show: 'her grand quality is rather to be reckoned negative' (p.387).

Gradually, as Lamotte overstretches her desire to reshape reality into a fiction, the limits of her control (like those of Poe's Prince Prospero) become apparent: another, higher, artist – 'Destiny itself' – has all the time been directing her actions in its own cosmic dramatic spectacle (p.384). The 'Fourth, final Scenic Exhibition, composed by Destiny' (p.389) exposes her illusion for the sham and corruption of reality it is and culminates in the Jeremaic denunciations of the 'arch-quack' Cagliostro: 'O Lamotte, has thy *Hypocrisia* ended, then? Thy many characters were all acted. Here at last thou actest not, but art what thou seemest; a mangled squelch of gore, confusion and abomination' (p.397). Cagliostro's rhetoric rises to prophetic heights, openly parodying the coercive emotionalism of revivalist preaching:

> 'For it is the End of the Dominion of IMPOSTURE (which is Darkness and opaque Firedamp); and the burning-up, with unquenchable fire, of all the Gigs

that are in the Earth'! – Here the Prophet paused, fetching a deep sigh; and the Cardinal uttered a kind of faint, tremulous Hem! (p.400)

For all the disproportion of rhetoric to meaning, the eccentric voice of the confidence trickster Cagliostro does seem to speak for Carlyle himself. He reveals the 'plain conclusion that Sham is indispensable to Reality, as Lying to Living' (p.394). The problem which has proved Lamotte's downfall, and which he undertakes to solve for the reader, is to find a relationship between sham and reality, lying and living:

> Wonderously, indeed, do Truth and Delusion play into one another; Reality rests on Dream. Truth is but the *skin* of the bottomless Untrue: and ever, from time to time, the Untrue *sheds* it; is clear again; and the superannuated True itself becomes a Fable. (p.394)

Cagliostro's is indeed a Tale of a Tub, but the very canting theatricality of his rhetoric redeems it from the Addisonian decorum of 'the three unities, and Blairs lectures'; it claims to be, in a strange way, 'the *Speech of Man* to believing Men!'. The eccentricity of the voice – Spy and Confidence Man rolled into one – seems to lend authority to its words. A 'sympathetic' observer of Lamotte's masquerade, Cagliostro derives its meaning for the mystified reader: 'this little Business, like a little cloud, bodied itself forth in skies clear to the unobservant: but with such hues of deep-tinted villany [sic], dissoluteness and general delirium as, to the observant, betokened it electric' (p.402). Behind the surface of the masquerade there apparently lurks portentous significance. Cagliostro's apocalyptic call to faith completes the apotheosis by which 'this poor opaque Intrigue of *The Diamond Necklace* might become quite translucent between us; transfigured, lifted up into the serene of Universal-History' (p.330). His attempt to make reality Ideal establishes the symbolising hierarchy of the Calvinist temper: the fallen observer sees only the surfaces; the regenerate seer penetrates to significance. In this respect, Carlyle seems close to Emerson's Transcendental belief that to fathom the meaning of reality is to see the visible world as an insubstantial spectacle constantly about to dissolve in the Ideal, and that the man able to make this transition from signs to significance is the true poet.

Carlyle's tale itself tends to unsettle the reader's confidence in its interpreter's integrity. The narrator's admiration for Lamotte's technical virtuosity, his inquiry into the details of her craft and his generalising description of her attributes all tend to suggest that Lamotte is the artist personified. If in the end she is merely a paltry hack to be upstaged by the greater canting theatricality of Cagliostro, then the reader has been duped by the narrator just as thoroughly as Lamotte duped the pasteboard figures whose self-seeking blindness we despised in the masquerade. The whole tale then empties of significance and is reduced to an elaborate confidence trick played on the gullible reader. And Cagliostro himself, who seems to carry the burden of interpretation in 'The Diamond Necklace', is a showman whose rhetoric creates just another version of reality for effect. What kind of credence is due to this 'Arch-Quack' if he does speak for Carlyle as the artist who reveals the meaning of the past and our relation to it? At what point, if any, does this series of distancing perspectives rest in a 'real' experience, past or present? Must we too disappear into Poe's maelstrom of empty voices which deny relation even as they colonise attention, or is there (in 'Destiny itself', perhaps) a final guarantor of meaning lurking behind the scenes like the Calvinist God or Cooper's 'Mr Harper'?

Exploiting the deracinated effects of the moment to rhetorical effect, 'The Diamond Necklace' seems to exemplify – and to expose – the creative process Poe analyses in 'The Philosophy of Composition' (1846). Rejecting in turn 'history', 'narrative' and 'incidents of the day' as suitable starting points for a story, Poe declared his preference for 'commencing with the consideration of an effect' and took delight in dismantling the machinery of artistic creation. His theatrical image tantalisingly echoes Carlyle's own (see above, p.127):

> Most writers ... would positively shudder at letting the public take a peep behind the scenes ... at the wheels and pinions – the tackle for scene-shifting – the step-ladders and demon-traps – the cock's feathers, the red paint and the black patches, which, in ninety-nine cases out of the hundred, constitute the properties of the literary histrio.[36]

But, as 'The Diamond Necklace' shows, flaying the story alive tends to alter its person for the worse and takes the reader no closer at all to the heart of the matter. Unmasking the performance exposes tawdry props rather than 'truth'. 'The Diamond Necklace' is an unsatisfying evocation of the distance between appearance and meaning, not just because the past is mysterious and events do finally remain inscrutable to observation, but because the reader cannot touch the existence of a real – even though alien – past at all through the self-conscious posturings of the showman's voice. There is no access to anything beyond the theatre of the mind, obsessively interpreting and bestowing meaning on its own phantasms. The peculiarly excessive Carlylese of this piece, coercing attention to the voice at the expense of its subject, makes interpretation by the reader at once essential and futile. Just as we resist the showman-narrator's self-indulgent interpretation of the Chola Widow but have no access to the 'real' facts, so the canting rhetoric of Cagliostro effectively blocks the possibility of there ever being a meaning for the present in the historical events of 'The Diamond Necklace'.

Melville is probably Carlyle's only true literary heir. From the overwriting in *Moby-Dick* which turns the character of Ahab into a pastiche of borrowed voices, a one-man 'archaeological masquerade' of tragic postures, Melville's writing seems progressively to lose confidence in the possibility of stable or communicable relationships between past and present, or, analogously, between language and experience. As with Carlyle, there are two distinguishable aspects to this scepticism; these are embodied in two of the works Melville wrote after *Moby-Dick*: 'Benito Cereno' (1855), and *The Confidence-Man: His Masquerade* (1857).

'Benito Cereno' is presented as a masquerade of ambiguous appearances which demand interpretation. The naive American observer Amasa Delano is mystified by a manifestation of European guilt; the showman-narrator directs attention to surfaces and incites both protagonist and reader to fathom the reality beneath. From Amasa Delano's first sight of the Spanish ship San Dominick, the narrative constantly insists on the scene's equivocality; the vocabulary of masks and masquerades is liberally, almost excessively sprinkled throughout the tale:

> the living spectacle [the ship] contains, upon its sudden and complete disclosure, has, in contrast with the blank ocean which zones it, something of the effect of enchantment. The ship seems unreal; these strange costumes, gestures, and faces, but a shadowy tableau just emerged from the deep, which directly must receive back what it gave.[37]

To the American captain's observing eye, the ship is festooned with the fascinating but inscrutable iconography of the Old World:

> the principle relic of faded grandeur was the ample oval of the shield-like stern-piece, intricately carved with the arms of Castile and Leon, medallioned about by groups of mythological or symbolical devices; uppermost and central of which was a dark satyr in a mask, holding his foot on the prostrate neck of a writhing figure, likewise masked. (p.58)

The 'central' past intrudes into the 'provincial' present, but the meanings which would establish relationship are lost to the observer. Delano is taken in by the 'spectacle of fidelity . . . and confidence' (p.68) which seems to mark the relationship between the Spanish Captain Benito Cereno and his black slave Babo; later, when contradictory appearances arouse his suspicions, he sees a rather different masquerade being acted out between them, but still one that to his alienated eye is disturbingly superficial:

> there was something so hollow in the Spaniard's manner, with apparently some reciprocal hollowness in the servant's dusky comment of silence, that the

idea flashed across him, that possibly master and man, for some unknown purpose, were acting out, both in word and deed... some juggling play before him... At last, regarding the notion as a whimsy, insensibly suggested, perhaps, by the theatrical aspect of Don Benito in his harlequin ensign, Captain Delano speedily banished it. (p.104)

In these hints – presented as the evanescent suspicions that float across the candid mind of the observer – the narrator insinuates a particular reading of appearances which undermines Delano's 'singular guilelessness' (p.79) in wanting always to take things at face value. Like Delano, the reader seems to have landed in a world of inscrutable clues which must be interpreted. The narrator asserts power over both by providing an 'explanation': appended legal documents purport to establish the 'facts' in the mystery, as these emerge in the trial for mutiny and murder of Babo and his black confederates. Much is made of the moment when, the 'mask torn away' (p.119), 'across the long-benighted mind of Captain Delano, a flash of revelation swept, illuminating, in unanticipated clearness... every enigmatic event of the day, as well as the entire past voyage of the San Dominick' (p.118). The moment of enlightenment re-enacts the 'conversion experience' of the puritan autobiographers and claims to establish a meaning which relates past and present events. But the revelation's very inclusiveness is suspect: many contradictory and incomplete aspects remain in the narrative. The showman himself casts doubt on the adequacy of the documents which reveal the 'truth'; perhaps Amasa Delano's extreme reluctance to cast about for a meaning beyond the surface appearances of events was right after all. The showman-narrator chides his observer for failing to adopt 'the proper point of view' in regarding the spectacle, but the conflicting nature of the evidence suggests that there may be no point of view which could reconcile them. Right to the end, when Benito Cereno totters away on the arm of his new *alter ego*, the monk Infelez (whose unpropitious name harps back uneasily to Delano's first impression of the ship as being peopled by 'throngs of dark cowls... dark moving figures... as of Black Friars pacing the cloisters' [p.57]), we seem still to be spectators of an inscrutable masquerade.

The otherness of these events finally evades not only the explanations of the narrator and his 'objective' legal evidence but also any other interpretation supplied by the reader. But Melville's tale itself is not nullified by its inscrutability; this past may not be colonised by possessing its meaning, but it retains a powerful though alien pull on the mind. There is no doubt that *something* took place, that Guilt and Innocence have been locked in conflict, and that the outcome, although its 'significance' may not be clear, does bear some important relationship to the reader's experience. We have no prerogative to interpret – but there is a solidity and a completeness in what took place on the San Dominick which exceeds a masquerade of surfaces. In its confident reticence this tale belongs more with Scott's 'Highland Widow' than with the infinitely regressing refractions of a Poe tale.

Melville's final novel, *The Confidence-Man: His Masquerade* (1857), is a procession of incidents which coalesce around successive avatars of an artist who conjures himself into existence in a series of masquerading appearances. The Confidence Man himself has no continuity of identity through time; the covenant of meaning both between the author and the reader and within the book itself has become a purely fictional one: characters exist as and for how long the observer believes – has faith – in their reality. The sustained pun on 'confidence' casts an ironic light on the quality required by Hawthorne and Carlyle for their fictions to signify; it suggests that faith is merely a fiction by which the controlling artist – be he God, showman or con-man – subjects his audience to the capricious exercise of his will.

The Confidence-Man may, then, be the ultimate satire on puritan–provincial society, and, behind it, the Calvinist state of mind itself. In terms of the content of its individual scenes, the book is 'about' corruption in mid-nineteenth-century America: it anticipates the satire of Mark Twain and Charles Dudley Warner in its attack on the 'gilded age' of the con-man/entrepreneur out to fleece his gullible fellow-citizens. Aboard the Mississippi steamer *Fidèle* is every sort of American con-man, from the card sharper to the herb doctor, from the speculator to the Transcendentalist. The interpretation of the book as satirical of puritan–provincial society is supported by Gary Lindberg's view (from a different angle) that it projects 'a culture without authority. The absolute has been absolutely severed from the human', and 'the discrepancy between belief and behavior comes to characterize a whole social world'.[38] But the whole notion of interpretation, as we have seen, is suspect in a context where the guarantor of meaning – the authority behind the words – has made itself invisible. Interpretative procedures may persist, but their end, significance, cannot be verified. A look at one of the supposedly satiric tableaux of *The Confidence-Man* exposes how futile Melville renders the interpretative acts which his method inveigles the reader into performing.

The Transcendentalists, as we seem to view them in the spectres of Emerson ('Mark Winsome') and Thoreau (his disciple 'Egbert Oliver') who discourse with the equally spectral Confidence Man, are apparently criticised for their cold distance from the world. Just as Winsome 'loves wine' so much that he leaves it 'in the lasting condition of an untried abstraction', so all his speculations are unexperienced, based on a complete absence of involvement with their objects. The Eidolon of

Emerson sits 'purely and coldly radiant as a prism', discoursing eloquently and elusively on every subject offered to him, elevating 'whim' and decrying 'consistency'.[39] Melville appears to direct his criticism specifically against the Transcendentalists' elevation of disengagement and their institutionalising of genteel emptiness; not only the emotional inhumanity but also the moral naivety of Emerson and his disciples emerge. But Melville's fiction refuses the reader the comfort and confidence of 'a foolish consistency'[40], and Winsome's discourse is subjected to the same paralysing relativism which characterises all colloquy with the Confidence Man: '"a pleasing belief", rejoined the Cosmopolitan' (p.266). The shifting perspectives involved in the transience of the Cosmopolitan's own 'identity' give no anchoring point to satire, which moves – like the other seemingly significant episodes in the book – towards pure word play.

The provincial's self-conscious adoption of an alien cosmopolitan stance here becomes an absolute separation of voice and content: every compact of meaning between author and reader, as between Winsome and the Cosmopolitan, becomes a transaction of 'faith', provisional and momentary, without duration or stability. Each new scene – indeed each new statement – requires an act of self-conscious assent for it to spring into being: structure and identity, reality itself (so Melville seems to imply) are matters of belief rather than of ontological existence. In his presentation of Emerson/Winsome ('toning the whole man, was one-knows-not-what of shrewdness and mythiness, strangely jumbled . . . he seemed a kind of cross between a Yankee peddler and a Tartar priest' [p.265]), Melville seems for the moment to have provided the reader with what Coleridge called 'a human interest and a semblance of truth sufficient to procure for these shadows of imagination that willing suspension of disbelief . . . which constitutes poetic faith'.[41] But *The Confidence-Man* does not rest content with demonstrating the conditions of what Coleridge called 'Stage Illusion'.[42] Its scepticism is radical. The words entice interpretation by signalling symbolic content; the verbal surface excites involvement by the promise of meaning, then leaves the reader ungratified as the shifting farrago of voices moves on without delivering its secrets. This, the book implies, is true not only of fictional or 'poetic' faith, but characterises all the compacts of meaning which constitute what we agree to call reality. Just as Adam's downfall, according to Calvin, was a failure of faith, so in reading or in living (so Melville implies) a loss of confidence is a Fall which immediately renders the world into structureless fragments.

This might well be so in a world where language and experience have become estranged to the point where a verbal continuity (the recurrent 'avatar', for example) guarantees nothing about content unless or until the reader wills it into existence (our desire to recognise the Confidence Man as a 'character' with identity and extension across episodes). But Melville turns identity itself into a game played by the Confidence Man; three 'authorial' interchapters on 'The Art of Fiction' expose how we all, in reading a book as in life, put in our stake and want it to be 'real'. The reader, like Hume's Sceptic,

> is always a sublime philosopher, when he needs not; that is, as long as nothing disturbs him or rouzes his affections. While others play, he wonders at their keenness and ardour; but he no sooner puts in his own stake, than he is commonly transported with the same passions, that he had so much condemned, while he remained a simple spectator.[43]

The game is a game of faith – confidence – in which we all engage; only the sceptic-as-confidence-man remains aloof and *plays* it rather than finding his existence within it. He is also, for both Melville and Hume, a showman whose game is to *make* and to *show* character. It is quite motiveless, as 'he' is quite character-less; the difference is that Hume does not believe that life is really lived this way: even the Sceptic throws in his lot and becomes an actor rather than an observer. Melville's scepticism is complete, and in *The Confidence-Man* Hume's 'theatre of the mind' becomes a masquerade of postures in which ac*tion* becomes ac*ting*:

> 'How? Does all the world act? Am *I*, for instance, an actor? Is my revered friend here, too, a performer?'
> 'Yes, don't you both perform acts? To do is to act; so all doers are actors'.
> (p.47)

The Confidence-Man deliberately shatters the illusion of reality which sustained the mysterious impenetrability of 'Benito Cereno'. It is not that 'Benito Cereno' has a source in historical records – that, in some sense, it 'really happened' – while *The Confidence-Man* is patently and aggressively a fiction; the difference lies, rather, in the depth of Melville's scepticism about experience. *The Confidence-Man* represents a radical failure of confidence which is simultaneously a scathing satirical indictment of the puritan–provincial temper of American society and itself the ultimate embodiment of that temper. It demonstrates the hollowness of the symbolising state of mind in a fiction that can only be 'read' symbolically.

Despite Melville's evident dislike of the Transcendentalist con-trick, the verbal virtuosity of *The Confidence-Man* shares its gnomic opacity with much of Emerson's writing. Skating always on rhetorical surfaces, Melville's book is spinning round a central emptiness. The puritan–provincial temper, which his fiction evades or holds in steady contemplation up to this point, eventually overtakes and subsumes it. Melville's Masquerade embodies precisely those consequences of unmitigated scepticism which Hume's writing works always to elude: the loss of a sense of identity (however shaky its philosophical basis), of natural relationship between temporal moments, and of communal values.

In George Santayana's 'Dialogue' on Walt Whitman, one of his speakers makes the ethical case against the puritan–provincial stance of detached observation: 'it isn't immoral,' he says, 'to call a spade a spade, but it is immoral to treat life as a masquerade, as a magic pantomime in which acts have no consequences and happiness and misery don't exist'. His antagonist ('Van Tender') responds:

> Ah, but Whitman is nothing if not a spectator, a cosmic poet to whom the whole world is a play. And good and evil, although not equally pleasant to experience, are equally interesting to look at. Is it wrong to enjoy our misery when its distance from us makes contemplation of it possible?[44]

Hawthorne's *The Blithedale Romance* (1852) is narrated by a very minor 'cosmic poet' and describes (like Melville's novel) an attempt 'to treat life as a masquerade'. It is based on the real Transcendentalist community at Brook Farm where Hawthorne himself had stayed for a time, but with his characteristic mixture of defensiveness and self-deprecation he declares that his

> present concern with the Socialist Community is merely to establish a theatre, a little removed from the highway of ordinary travel, where the creatures of his brain may play their phantasmagorical antics, without exposing them to too close a comparison with the actual events of real lives.[45]

'The mind', as Hume said, 'is a kind of theatre'. What, then, is the play being shown on this fictional stage? *The Blithedale Romance* conjures up a group of Transcendental idealists who attempt to establish a regenerate life apart from corrupt society. These reformers are self-consciously proud 'descendants of the Pilgrims, whose high enterprise, as we sometimes flattered ourselves, we had taken up, and were carrying it onward and aloft, to a point which they never dreamed of attaining' (p.117). Their secession from the conventions and restrictions of ordinary life combines, in the mind of the book's narrator Coverdale, the imagery of radical, revolutionary Calvinism with Arcadian pastoral withdrawal. 'We had left the rusty iron framework of society behind us. We had broken through many hindrances that are powerful enough to keep most people on the weary treadmill of the established system' (p.19).[46] The attempt to live the fictional life of pastoral in reality emphasises the *un*reality of the whole enterprise; it is in their distance from, and antagonism to, life as lived by most people that the Blithedale reformers most resemble their puritan ancestors:

> as regarded society at large, we stood in a position of new hostility, rather than new brotherhood . . . Constituting so pitiful a minority as now, we were inevitably estranged from the rest of mankind, in pretty fair proportion with the strictness of our mutual bond among ourselves. (pp.20–21)

In their sense of a special mission, and their self-definition by opposition, they do indeed relive the action of the Pilgrim Fathers; but the burden of the past is theirs too: the covenant that unites them in this fallen state is, Coverdale thinks, 'not affirmative but negative' (p.63). The shadow of their illustrious ancestors hangs over them and mocks their imitative exercise, which is, finally, only 'a show of novelty' achieved by 'projecting [their] minds outward' on a soil 'fathom-deep with the dust of deluded generations' (p.128). Everything is a faithless imitation of what had once had significance. When (to recall William Wirt's words) 'the curtain of ceremony is drawn up to the very sky' at Blithedale, all that is revealed is another stage behind it. *The Blithedale Romance* demonstrates the provincial predicament: cast in the puritan mould, but distanced from its Calvinist certainties, it seems doomed to re-enact an empty masquerade.

The characters (and the narrator Coverdale) all live self-conscious lives of artifice, as though beyond appearances lay the Ideal; but the Calvinist faith in transcendence has gone rotten from within. In the absence of the confirming, controlling divine presence, the glimpses of a real beyond the tangible are all sham, and their showmen charlatans: the masquerade of Blithedale itself is introduced by Coverdale's account of his attendance at the spectacle of the 'Veiled Lady', whom he questioned about the future only to get a response 'of the true Sybilline stamp, nonsensical in its first aspect, yet, on closer study, unfolding a variety of interpretations, one of which has certainly accorded with the event' (p.6). The Ideal is an empty dimension which renders all the action of the reformers staged and stagey; their masquerade is seen through the 'fallen' vision of Coverdale, who has the empty ego of the puritan–provincial observer. Blithedale's playing at Edenic simplicity and Coverdale's desire for knowledge about the subjects he observes are different aspects of the same distance from experience. The pasteboard characters he presents are pastiches of puritan postures: Hollingsworth the reformer becomes to his vision the Calvinist minister preaching to the faithful on a Sunday from the outdoor forum they call 'Eliot's pulpit', and, later, he will become the stern puritan judge, absolute as destiny in his sentence on Zenobia. Hollingsworth is obsessed with sin and totally committed to ideas; Coverdale feels the threat of his 'tremendous concentrativeness and indomitable will' (p.135), which offers no half measures: '"Be with me", said Hollingsworth, "Or be against me! There is no third choice for you"' (p.135).

The other spectres in the theatre of Coverdale's mind are Zenobia, Priscilla, Westervelt and himself. Zenobia – the enchantress, the actress, the witch – is to Coverdale the fascinating possessor of 'knowledge' and experience; her full-blown presence 'caused our heroic enterprise to show like an illusion, a masquerade, a pastoral, a counterfeit Arcadia, in which we grown-up men and women were making a play-day of the years that were given us to live in' (p.21).

Priscilla is the most insubstantial of all the spectres. She is the 'Veiled Lady', the will-less self who is the victim of the power struggle between the other characters. She is 'blown about like a leaf' (p.171), but she has (as none of the others do) absolute faith, against which nothing can prevail. It gives her a self-possession that seems strangely absolute to the insecure Common Sense criteria of Coverdale's analysis:

> Hollingsworth could have no fault. That was the one principle at the centre of the universe. And the doubtful guilt or possible integrity of other people, appearances, self-evident facts, the testimony of her own senses ... would have weighed not the value of a mote of thistle-down, on the other side.
>
> (pp.220–1)

She is the true daughter of the puritans, Hollingsworth her God; she needs none of the aids to belief (self-evident facts, or the testimony of her own senses) of an age whose faith is foundering.

Westervelt is the most stagey puppet in Coverdale's masquerade: he is the wizard, the devil of 'Young Goodman Brown' who carries a staff in the shape of a wriggling serpent (p.92) transposed to the familiar guise of gentility, ingratiating himself by his intelligence, urbanity and rationality. He is the devil as magician, the artist in illusion, the con-man. Like Hogg's Gil-Martin, he has uncanny perceptive powers, 'a cat-like circumspection; and though precisely the most unspiritual quality in the world, it was almost as effective as spiritual insight, in making him acquainted with whatever it suited him to discover' (p.158). This enables him to detect Coverdale at his 'post of observation' in a Boston hotel window. Westervelt is himself a showman, the manipulator of the 'Veiled Lady', and he exerts a mysterious sway over the imperious Zenobia; he has strong and suggestive affinities with Coverdale himself.

This, then, is the puritan–provincial cast which Coverdale assembles in the theatre of his mind. Like the showman of 'Main-street', he exhibits them to the reader in a series of postures, static tableaux which recall the scenes of the puritan past:

> as my eyes wandered from one of the group to another, I saw in Hollingsworth all that an artist could desire for the grim portrait of a Puritan magistrate, holding inquest of life and death in a case of witchcraft; – in Zenobia, the sorceress herself, not aged, wrinkled, and decrepit, but fair enough to tempt Satan with a force reciprocal to his own; – and, in Priscilla, the pale victim,

> whose soul and body had been wasted by her spells. Had a pile of faggots been heaped against the rock, this hint of impending doom would have completed the suggestive picture. (p.214)

Coverdale's dramatisation of himself as an observer of such scenes makes him an empty spy who participates vicariously in the lives of his victims. As an observer, he is like Westervelt (and like the satanic Gil-Martin) a parasite on the lives of others, creating and composing their actions in his own private masquerade. Like many of Hawthorne's narrators, Coverdale does not 'possess' reality, but always seems to be in the process of acquiring it. This acquisition is not a movement outwards from self towards what lies beyond it, but an appropriation of observed events to the chimeras of the mind. He meditates self-justifyingly on

> that quality of the intellect and the heart, which impelled me (often against my own will, and to the detriment of my own comfort) to live in other lives, and to endeavour – by generous sympathies, by delicate intuitions, by taking note of things too slight for record, and by bringing my human spirit into manifold accordance with the companions whom God assigned me – to learn the secret which was hidden even from themselves. (p.160)

Coverdale, like many of the narrators discussed in this chapter, is a bachelor without either human attachments or a calling in life: he has nothing to do, 'unless to make pretty verses, and play a part, with Zenobia and the rest of the amateurs, in our pastoral. It seems but an unsubstantial sort of business' (p.43). But in abstracting himself even from this minor attachment, Coverdale finds (like Wakefield) that he has committed an irrevocable act. When he returns from Boston, it is as a houseless spectre: 'resolving to spy out the posture of the community I would go wandering about the outskirts of the farm, and, perhaps catching sight of a solitary acquaintance would approach him amid the brown shadows of the trees, (a kind of medium fit for spirits departed and revisitant, like myself) and entreat him to tell me how all things were' (p.207). It is a compromise between absence and presence, action and passivity, which he relishes: in his Boston hotel, like Poe's 'Man of the Crowd', he 'felt a hesitation about plunging into this muddy tide of human activity and pastime. It suited me better, for the present, to linger on the brink, or hover in the air above it' (p.147).

As he muses on his delightful detachment from life, there appears on the stage of the window opposite – which is also his mental stage – another tableau in his masquerade, as Westervelt, Zenobia and Priscilla act out a dumb-show before him:

> I began to long for a catastrophe... Let it all come! As for me, I would look on, as it seemed my part to do, understandingly, if my intellect could fathom the meaning and the moral, and, at all events, reverently and sadly. The curtain

> fallen, I would pass onward with my poor individual life, which was now attenuated of much of its proper substance, and diffused among many alien interests. (p.157)

But when the curtain does fall, it is not at his own instigation. He is deeply humiliated as Zenobia negates his right to observe by shutting him out of the scene. Once the puppets in the theatre of the mind start directing the show themselves, the full impotence of the showman becomes gallingly plain to the spectators. His self-justifying guilt and embarrassment at being perceived as a spy is now familiar:

> I had a keen, revengeful sense of the insult inflicted by Zenobia's scornful recognition, and more particularly by her letting down the curtain; as if such were the proper barrier to be interposed between a character like hers, and a perceptive faculty like mine. (p.160)

Coverdale sees his role in their drama as that of an indispensable assistant to Destiny ('the most skilful of stage-managers') – a secondary place (p.97). But the self-conscious self-effacement which he practises before his audience is a measure of his egotism. The story exists only as and when he chooses to present it to his audience, and the masque-presenter can always arrange to give himself the last word:

> It remains only to say a few words about myself... I have made but a poor and dim figure in my own narrative, establishing no separate interest, and suffering my colorless life to take its hue from other lives. But one still retains some little consideration for one's self; so I keep these last two or three pages for my individual and sole behoof. (p.245)

But as the narrative constantly suggests, egotism and emptiness are not antithetical in the puritan–provincial framework. The showman finally lacks the resources to make anything real to the reader except the perplexities of his own observing consciousness. Like the puritan autobiographer, Coverdale is at the centre of his own stage, his own mind the theatre of every event.

Coverdale's plight as showman-spy is at once the source and the reflection of the *ersatz*, alienated existence of the puppets in his masquerade. The prevailing atmosphere of sham, artifice and manipulation which envelopes all the events of the book exposes the empty Idealism of the Transcendentalists and their decadent version of puritan spirituality. There is a good deal of direct criticism of the Brook Farm experiment based on Hawthorne's own experiences as participant/observer, but Henry James's comment in his book on Hawthorne that 'there is no satire whatever in the Romance; the quality is almost conspicuous by its absence' (p.90) finally seems the right note. Against all expectation, and like Melville's *Confidence-Man*, *The Blithedale Romance* is not, despite its many implied criticisms of American society, ultimately satiric. Hawthorne is not a skilful mimic, and strikes false notes with the figure of Silas Foster (the 'earthy' character who exists to show up the fantastic behaviour of the Blithedale reformers) when he attempts to root him in literary reality as a Shakespearian clown at the moment of Zenobia's death: 'Heigh-ho! –well – life and death together make sad work for us all. Then, I was a boy, bobbing for fish; and now I am getting to be an old fellow, and here I be, groping for a dead body!' (p.232). Far from grounding the event in reality, this merely emphasises further the displaced theatricality of the whole affair. Hawthorne is no more able than Melville to sustain the illusion of life through the assumption of the voices of his European literary heritage. To this extent, the 'emptiness' of *The Blithedale Romance* is similar to the masquerade of *The Confidence-Man*: the satiric stances adopted within it remain ventriloquistic poses which self-consciously declare their distance from anything outside the fiction.

But the primary reason why *Blithedale* is not a satire distinguishes it from Melville's novel: it is that Hawthorne's analysis of the predicament of mid-century America has a *historical* dimension. He sees the Transcendental enterprise as merely a particular manifestation of the declension from the certainties of the Founding Fathers which has led to the degeneration of puritanism into provincialism. The book recapitulates Coverdale's plight obsessively: in the figure of Theodore in Zenobia's fable of the 'Veiled Lady', whose 'natural tendency towards scepticism' (p.113) leads him to fail the test of faith and condemns him to live out his life in hopeless longing for an unattainable ideal; in the satanic showman Westervelt; and in Old Moodie, who as 'Fauntleroy', 'a man of show',

> had laid no real touch on any mortal's heart. Being a mere image, an optical delusion, created by the sunshine of prosperity, it was his law to vanish into the shadow of the first intervening cloud. He seemed to leave no vacancy; a phenomenon which, like many others that attended his brief career, went far to prove the illusiveness of his existence. (p.183)

The final variation or avatar seems to have been recognised by Hawthorne in himself; in 1840 he had described his own earlier disconnected state in a letter to Longfellow:

> there is no fate in the world so horrible as to have no share in either its joys or sorrows. For the last ten years I have not lived, but only dreamed of living . . . I have seen so little of the world that I have nothing but thin air to concoct my stories of, and it is not easy to give a life-like semblance to such shadowy stuff. Sometimes, through a peephole, I have caught a glimpse of the real world, and the two or three articles in which I have portrayed these glimpses please me better than the others.[47]

This self-portrait of the artist as showman-spy seems to support the connection of Coverdale's activities with Hawthorne's account in *Blithedale*'s preface of 'establishing a theatre ... where the creatures of his brain may play their phantasmagorical antics' (p.1), but by 1852 Hawthorne was in his own life no longer a self-alienated bachelor-spy but the father of children and husband of a real wife (as opposed to the allegorically-conceived 'Faith' of 'Young Goodman Brown' in 1835). And there is sufficient evidence within *The Blithedale Romance* to suggest that Coverdale is a more-or-less dramatised version of the alienated observer, not a transparent mouthpiece for his author. However, quantifying the 'more-or-less' proves – as often in Hawthorne's writing – the insoluble crux. The final relationship between narrator and author, showman and spectacle, remains equivocal and unplaceable. It simply is not possible to ascertain the relative degrees of identification and projection which would enable us to say for certain whether or not Coverdale should be regarded as a character within the fiction.

Whatever the truth here (and it may finally be immaterial), James's description of Hawthorne's *aesthetic* relationship to the theological realities of his Calvinist forebears suggests something very like Coverdale's aesthetic sublimation of his fallen state; both establish the relationship between the puritan past and the provincial present as one which has inescapable consequences for the American writer and his audience:

> Nothing is more curious and interesting than this almost exclusively imported character of the sense of sin in Hawthorne's mind; it seems to exist there merely for an artistic or literary purpose. He had ample cognisance of the Puritan conscience; it was his national heritage; it was reproduced in him; looking into his soul, he found it there. But his relation to it was only, as one may say, intellectual; it was not moral and theological. He played with it and used it as a pigment; he treated it, as the metaphysicians say, objectively.
>
> (*Hawthorne*, p.67)

The Confidence-Man severs historical and narrative continuity and reduces art to the con-man's preying upon his gull; the book seems to reject satire because no values survive unviolated in the faithless, rootless state of its aggressively episodic discontinuities. *The Blithedale Romance* rebuffs satire's centrally tending perspectives for different reasons. Hawthorne's exploration of the relationship between the showman-spy, his spectacle and its spectators establishes such a strong *connection* between past and present that the world seems to present similar enigmas to the observer, be he seventeenth-century puritan or nineteenth-century provincial. The temper of mind which debated the credibility of 'spectre evidence' in the Salem witch trials readily translated into Coverdale's puzzlement about how to construct the 'truth' of the relationship between Zenobia and Priscilla from the evident influence which one exerts over the other, or into the reader's uncertainty about what may be deduced about Coverdale's 'real' motives from the account of Theodore's 'fictional' story. Problems of interpretation, of action and passivity, election and reprobation, Hawthorne suggests, remain constant through time; what is lacking in the provincial state is not the real as such, but the faith to perceive it. Satire is inappropriate not because of the dissolution of identity (as in *The Confidence-Man*) but because the allegorising mode has become regressive and repetitive. The attenuating cycles of puritan–provincial experience allow for nothing contingent, adventitious or, therefore, new. The book seems pessimistic about the possibility of a regenerating faith which will recover action from passivity, participation from observation, Ideal from Appearance, but it does hold to the division between them.

There is no possibility of a decisive breaking of the pattern in *The Blithedale Romance*; this means that the book's historical dimension is not itself a liberation (although it may release us from the confinement of Coverdale's individual self-consciousness), because the book as a whole remains trapped in the repetitive pattern of puritan–provincial history. The scepticism of *The Confidence-Man*, on the other hand, is absolute: reality has become entirely inaccessible in an ever-receding series of masks behind masks. Both works are committed to a version of the puritan polarities whose inevitable end is 'the alienation of the intellect from the milieu'.[48] The main difference, finally, is that by recognising a temporal dimension, Hawthorne's fiction is able to point the reader away from itself and himself towards a reality (the puritan past) which anchors the masquerade just sufficiently to halt the infinite regression of meaning (although not to envisage new possibilities), while Melville's *Confidence-Man* encloses itself within the obsessively self-referential world of the reprobate mind where symbols are forever distanced from significance. It is, literally, an 'unreadable' book, in which 'meaning' is a trick played by the author on the confidence of the reader. It is against this background that the greater historical freedoms of *The Scarlet Letter* and *The Heart of Midlothian* will be considered in chapter 6.

Puritan–provincial fiction is characteristically static: the story of the Fall is replaced by the evocation of the fallen condition, and events lose their temporal dimension. Narrative becomes tableaux in series, not dramatic development. In *The Blithedale Romance* Hawthorne suggests that the drama of puritan life becomes theatrical in the provincial mind as action is replaced by re-enactment. Significantly, transition from the third-person voice of the preface, which establishes the 'theatre', to the first person of Coverdale's narrative, does not signal a transformation of the theatrical into the dramatic. The realities of the provincial mind are all gleaned at second-hand, from observation or from books. This explains not only the emptiness of voices adopted at a remove from experience but also the theatricality of poses which are established to express a pre-existing idea. 'The drama', as Enid Welsford writes, 'is a story with crisis and denouement; the masque is an invention moving upon a hinge . . . it is the logical working out of an idea which has to be taken for granted.'[49]

Behind all the provincial fictions discussed in this chapter – as 'Prince Prospero' in 'The Masque of the Red Death', as 'Prospero's-grotto' in 'The Diamond Necklace', as Scott's magician breaking his wand and burying his book, in the misquotations of Carlyle's Teufelsdröckh and as the showmen Shuffleton, Westervelt and Coverdale – lies the inspiration of *The Tempest*. It is the play which Emerson thinks of, over and over again, to characterise the activity of the Transcendental mind of the Poet who dissolves the Real in the Ideal, and it is the part of Shakespeare Hawthorne wants to evoke in the reader's mind when he describes (in the preface to *Blithedale*) the romancer 'seeking an atmosphere of strange enchantment' (p.2) and sends his narrator off to the magic island of Blithedale in a 'tempest' (p.10). It makes sense to ask why this play is so important to these writers, why it is that they seek there an image of the double consciousness which attempts to look through the Real to the Ideal. A.C. Bradley perhaps describes best the qualities which, making *The Tempest* 'uncharacteristic' of Shakespeare, actually tend to align it with the eccentric and polarising impulses of the puritan–provincial imagination as I have described them:

> the tendency which . . . produced Ariel and Caliban, [is] the tendency of imagination to analyse and abstract, to decompose human nature into its constituent factors, and then to construct beings in whom one or more of these factors is absent or atrophied or only incipient. This, of course, is a tendency which produces symbols, allegories, personifications of qualities and abstract ideas; and we are accustomed to think it quite foreign to Shakespeare's genius, which was in the highest degree concrete.[50]

The allegorising or symbolising frame of mind which abstracts the idea from its embodiment produces such projections of Prospero's divided self as Ariel and Caliban, his 'brave spirit' and 'thing of darkness'; it also makes *The Tempest* Shakespeare's most undramatic, most masque-like play.[51] The pastoral framework dislocates it to the timeless and placeless realm of Prospero's island; it introduces a programmatic – though temporary – abstraction from 'life'. Leo Marx suggests that 'the topography of *The Tempest* anticipates the moral geography of the American imagination'; looking back on the play from the puritan–provincial perspectives established in this chapter, we may suggest that the world-dissolving spirit of the masque creates a 'universe of the imagination', a world created and sustained in the theatre of the mind.[52] The play's action exists as an idea in the mind of Prospero – an idea of revenge and retribution to which he gives body and form through the agency of his creative spirit, Ariel. Prospero's is the only will present: he is a showman-spy, both masque-presenter and a character in the performance he directs. The other characters move, or cease to move, like puppets at his command. In his absolute power and inscrutability Prospero has the characteristics of the Calvinist God; but the truer analogy is perhaps with the theatrical mind of the fallen puritan or the distanced provincial: Prospero, deposed Duke of Milan, lost his 'state' through abstracting himself from reality; now exiled from the centre of power he manipulates his puppets in a series of spectacles designed at once to validate and to restore his sense of the 'real' state of things.

Prospero's estrangement from the past gives him a manipulative power over the disjunction between the Real and the Ideal within which the play's masque-like action operates. Like the Emersonian poet, he dispels by an act of mind the apparent to the realms of the insubstantial:

> These our actors,
> As I foretold you, were all spirits, and
> Are melted into air, into thin air:
> And, like the baseless fabric of this vision,
> The cloud-capp'd towers, the gorgeous palaces,
> The solemn temples, the great globe itself,
> Yea, all which it inherit, shall dissolve,
> And, like this insubstantial pageant faded,
> Leave not a rack behind. We are such stuff
> As dreams are made on; and our little life
> Is rounded with a sleep.   (IV.i.148–58)

The beauty of the poetry deliberately unanchors itself from reality and floats upwards towards the Ideal: within the play, every 'level' of reality is shown to be an evanescent mask of the Ideal. Prospero's Epilogue seems to suggest that the whole spectacle can only be lent substance by the assent and confidence of the audience:

> Gentle breath of yours my sails
> Must fill, or else my project fails,
> Which was to please. Now I want
> Spirits to enforce, Art to enchant;
> And my ending is despair,
> Unless I be reliev'd by prayer.   (Epilogue, 11–16)

In these features, then, *The Tempest* seems to reveal qualities of mind very similar to those displayed by the puritan–provincial temper. But there is something more. The centring of action in the creating mind of the observer – which corresponds to the movement from the dramatic to the theatrical – seems also to signal a reversion from the public to the private, from the stage of the world to the theatre of the mind. Not in the presentation of the works as such: clearly in performance, the masque of *The Tempest* is as public as the play of *A Midsummer Night's Dream*, and *The Blithedale Romance* as available as *Mansfield Park*. The difference lies rather in a certain obliquity, in what we might call the quality of the reticence displayed by these works. Chapter 4 described a certain otherness which is always preserved by Scott's descriptions of experience – an otherness which does not exclude the reader from some meaning which is presumed to lie there, but which preserves the integrity and the uniqueness of experience and respects what Hawthorne calls the 'mystery of the human heart'. An absence of anxiety, either on the part of the author or (as created by the author) in the reader, about the otherness of the other is characteristic of the 'central' mind. Many things remain a mystery in *Mansfield Park* and in *A Midsummer Night's Dream*; but these enigmas do not threaten the audience, which partakes, fully, of what is publicly available, and understands the impertinence, the lack of literary tact, which would be involved in proceeding further.

In the self-projected worlds of *The Blithedale Romance* and *The Tempest*, on the other hand, the boundaries between the private and the public, the shareable and the inaccessible, blur until the realms are often disturbingly indistinguishable. There is a deliberate lack of care on the part of the artist to accommodate the audience's desire to know where these boundary lines are; there are more clues which suggest meaning than there is available action to embody it. Prospero, for example, is at the centre of such action as *The Tempest* contains and presents himself more fully – verbally – than anyone else in the play, and yet because his voice cannot be related to a 'self' which has a public existence, the audience seems to eavesdrop on his emotions; the anger, the frustrations, the satisfaction he displays must tell us something about the man, but we have no access to what this might be. The play keeps its secrets absolutely but teasingly lets us know that there *are* secrets. The effect of this self-conscious 'privateness' is to induce an interpretative anxiety in the audience, a symbolising zeal to strike through the pasteboard mask which is the re-creation in the reader of the puritan–provincial dilemma. In different ways, these masque-like fictions all banish time and recreate the past as an 'archaeological masquerade'. It now remains to consider how the puritan–provincial writer may put the moment in time back into relation both with the contingent sequences of life and with the timeless continuities which intersect them.

6

'Is anything central?'

> The dweller in the capital knows that his city however large it may be, is only one point of the cosmos, a decentralised corner of it. He knows, further, that the world has no centre, and that it is therefore necessary, in all our judgements, to discount the peculiar perspective that reality offers when it is looked at from our own point of view. This is the reason why the provincial always thinks his neighbor of the great city a sceptic, though the fact is that the latter is only better informed.
> (José Ortega y Gasset)

> ... the phenomenon of oblique reference. Whether as humour or as allegory, this phenomenon is the same in all American writers: they walk all round the circumference of a subject and imagine they have been at the centre.
> (Herbert Read)

> London is the epitome of our times, and the Rome of to-day.
> (R.W. Emerson)[1]

In 1743, the English painter George Stubbs travelled to Rome, the cultural centre of Europe. Ozias Humphry, the British miniaturist who recorded this journey, says that it was made 'to convince himself that nature was, and is always, superior to art, whether Greek or Roman; and having received this impression he immediately resolved on returning home'.[2] What Henry James might have called the 'exquisite provincialism' of this anecdote is manifest in three features which recur in Scottish and American nineteenth-century fiction: the provincial's need to test his own values against the absolutes of the centre, the complacency with which he confirms his presuppositions and returns unscathed to the province, and the recounting of his journey by the artist, a fellow-provincial who may or may not relish its absurdity.[3] The naive opposition of Nature and Art associates itself with the polarised points of view of province versus centre.

Scottish and American writers searched for a point of view from which to overcome these polarising tendencies: by investigating the nature of provincialism they attempted to endow it with a status which is not dependent on opposition to, or defence against, a 'centre'. Such a position would see differences not as paradoxes and oppositions; it would find a viable relation between self and other and accept what James calls 'the possible other case', not as a threat but as a measure of existence.[4]

The fictional account of the provincial's 'journey to the centre' translates distance out of the realm of self-consciousness to the spatial and temporal dimensions of narrated events. The journey to the centre – from Edinburgh or Glasgow or Boston or New York to London – was a reality of provincial life for the Scot or the American of the eighteenth and nineteenth centuries. This journey, and the report which the observer made of life at the centre to a provincial audience avid for edification or for self-congratulation, was an obvious subject for provincial fiction; its evocation of the provincial state resonated with the Augustinian and Calvinist versions of the Christian pilgrimage. Travel is the characteristic puritan–provincial metaphor for life.

In the *City of God*, St Augustine opposes those who are 'at home' in the present world to those who are 'on their way' home to the better world of heaven:

> When those two cities started on their course through the succession of birth and death, the first to be born was a citizen of this world, and later appeared one who was a pilgrim and stranger in the world, belonging as he did to the City of God. He was predestined by grace, and chosen by grace, by grace a pilgrim below, and by grace a citizen above.[5]

After Calvin had elaborated this Pauline view in his *Institutes* as a description of fallen man's alienation from meaning, the image of the 'pilgrim and stranger', the 'sojourner in a strange country' became an essential trope of the kind of puritan writing represented by Edwards' 'The Christian Pilgrim'.[6] It shapes the puritan spiritual autobiography, and, in Bunyan's hands, becomes the allegorical narrative of *A Pilgrim's Progress*, in which (the goal being assured) the passage is everything. This translation of the *state* of alienation and distance to the *narrative* of becoming is one of the ways in which the provincial redeems action from passivity and discovers a dramatic relationship to the centre. It is a way also of 'stretching out' the critical, revolutionary moment which is the impetus of puritanism to a livable lifetime: it gives a meaning in time to an impulse of the soul.

In an essay on provincialism in art, Kenneth Clark suggests that the provincial painter escapes the dominance of the central style in one of two ways. The first is by anecdote, or narrative: 'When there is a story to tell, the pressure of style can be relaxed.'[7] Illustration and anecdote are not merely escape routes from dependence on the centre; they are the provincial's necessary anchors to reality: 'The artist of the perimeter who empties his work of its element of illustration is almost certainly condemned to high-minded vacuity. Still worse if he empties it of fact. Provincial art is surest of success when it is concrete' (p.53). But, Clark goes on, 'the plain man, and lover of fact, is not the only type of artist who flourishes in isolation and gains by remoteness. There is also the poet. Provincial painting is at its best when it is . . . lyrical painting. The word lyrical . . . can be applied to a work which expresses a single mood or emotion, complete in itself, lasting only as long as the emotion lasts. And secondly it implies that the work, like a song, does not aspire to pure form, but is a blending of two elements: or in other words that the associations which give the work its poignancy are not hidden within the form, but openly confessed' (p.55).

Emerging in the shadow of a strongly central eighteenth-century English literature, where the 'pressure on style' was great, the provincial literature of nineteenth-century Scotland and America answers readily to these formulations. In the first (or anecdotal) type we may recognise the narrative expansiveness of Scott and Melville, with the present danger of 'high-minded vacuity' when the writer aspires from the concrete to the abstract. The compression and intensity of Hawthorne's and Poe's methods associate them with the lyrical or poetic artist whose art is the most difficult to hold, for as Kenneth Clark puts it, 'in the art of the perimeter, poetical painting leads a precarious existence. It is, in the main, visionary painting, and when vision loses its compulsive intensity, there is no orderly contact with the outer world to sustain it' (p.56). If Scott's *The Heart of Midlothian* is the greatest narrative or 'anecdote' of the period, Hawthorne's *The Scarlet Letter* is provincialism's greatest poetic fiction.

Scott and Hawthorne stand apart from Melville and Poe and from all other Scots and Americans writing at this time by their peculiar grasp of the relationship between past and present. For both authors a sense of the past gives access to the continuous scale which plays between what the Calvinist sees as irreconcilable oppositions and thus to a recognition of 'the possible other case'. As Ortega y Gasset puts it,

> the divergence between the worlds of two subjective entities does not involve the falsity of one of them. On the contrary, precisely because what each one sees is a reality, not a fiction, its aspect must be distinct from what the other

perceives. The divergence is not a contradiction, but a complement. If the universe had presented an identical appearance to the eyes of a Greek of Socrates' time and to those of a Yankee we should have to suppose that true reality, independent of subjective entities, does not reside in the universe.[8]

Scott's and Hawthorne's historical fiction contains a recognition of the complementary and continuous realities of past and present which rescues them from extreme provincial polarisation. Their writing assumes neither that its own viewpoint is the sole source of reality nor that (since viewpoints are relative to one another) absolute scepticism is the only resting point.[9] It is in this sense that Scott and Hawthorne are, with Hume, writers who find a way of writing non-provincially about being provincial, writers whose grasp of relationship turns distance – between past and present, between province and centre – from a source of alienation to one of measure and proportion. Their writing shows that the narrative of the 'journey to the centre' is a quest not merely for meaning but for a viable means of expression, a literary quest for an idiom which is neither alienated imitation nor provincial idiosyncrasy.

The problems of being in the provinces when metropolitan culture is strongly in demand are well illustrated by the early numbers of *Blackwood's Edinburgh Magazine*. *Blackwood's* exploded on the Edinburgh literary scene in October 1817 with the 'Chaldee Manuscript', an outrageous biblical spoof which lampooned local personalities. The magazine's provocative style soon won it the wider reputation coveted by its ambitious provincial contributors, who included Lockhart, John Wilson and Galt. English readers were fascinated but frankly puzzled by much of what they found in *Blackwood's* and suggested that some awareness of metropolitan affairs would be an asset to its pages:

> Some of your finest strokes of satire have lost their point with us, from being of too local a nature: it will be but fair to give *us* a hit now and then which we Londoners can fully enter into the spirit of. As in this sort of ChitChat I shall generally give you my authority, you can use it as occasion may serve. You ought to have the earliest intelligence of what is stirring in the literary world as it is called – of London![10]

The 'ChitChat' thus supplied from London by Alaric Watts was worked up (probably by Lockhart) and became the first number of the magazine's most successful self-consciously local series. Blackwood himself wrote triumphantly, 'The Noctes Ambrosianae are prodigiously liked in London, and nothing can be a better vehicle for giving all manner of fun, criticism, or information'.[11] News of the centre was good for the magazine, because it amused the London audience to read about themselves in the provincial pages of *Blackwood's*; but – equally importantly – the Edinburgh audience was desperate for 'information' about the events and the fashions of the metropolis.

It was in this context that John Galt, one of Blackwood's 'expatriate' contributors then working in London, wrote to the publisher in 1820:

> I send you the first part of "*The Ayrshire Legatees*" which I have called my London sketches. It was necessary, in order to prepare the reader for the tone of the observations that I mean to ascribe to the several characters, to frame somewhat more of a story than I at first intended. This however will not diminish the interest of the work, – but it has forced me to make as it were an earlier beginning; but having now got the parties in London, and engaged in the objects of their journey, we shall proceed with a freer rein. Perhaps I ought to warn you that whatever change I may give to names and professions the persons described are all portraits, and I doubt not that some of those in the first[?] part will be recognised by your Ayrshire readers.[12]

The Ayrshire Legatees is, Galt suggests, both a supremely local work and one which will amuse a London audience with accessible satirical 'hits'. It aspires, too, to overcome its provincial readership's sense of distance from the centre by providing 'information'. The double purpose is built into the journey of the Reverend Pringle and his family from Ayrshire to London to collect their inheritance, as this is described in their letters back from the centre to Garnock's avid readership. Mrs Pringle writes to inform the seamstress Miss Nanny Eydent of the latest metropolitan fashions so that she may copy them in her own creations; Rev. Pringle writes to the schoolmaster and 'Session-clerk' Mr Micklewham about the state of the church and the condition of public worship; their son Andrew writes to his college friend Charles Snodgrass about society and the fashionable life of the clubs; the daughter Rachel writes to her confidante Isabella Todd genteel letters about love, manners and accomplishments.

The parochialism of these responses is exaggerated archly to amuse both the provincial and cosmopolitan sectors of the audience, but the 'information' conveyed is never obscured by this humour:

> you will be surprised to hear, that no such thing as whusky is to be had in the public-houses, where they drink only a dead sort of beer; and that a bottle of true jennyinn London porter is rarely to be seen in the whole town.
>
> (Mrs Pringle)[13]

The correspondents give between them complementary accounts of such interesting topical events as the funeral of George III and the trial and divorce proceedings against the Queen. The *Legatees'* transmission of ephemeral 'information' to a provincial readership is typical of the early nineteenth-century Scottish and American periodicals.[14] But another aspect of the book underlies the humorous provincialism of form and treatment, and combines with it to suggest something more interesting about the nature of this journey to the centre for the provincial Scot.

Zachariah Pringle is a Presbyterian minister; for him, his family's trip to London comes to seem less a pleasure jaunt than a pilgrimage through perilous and treacherous terrain. In this context, the notion of inheritance acquires a new suggestiveness. His is the most interesting of the letters which describe the dangers of the 'momentous journey' (p.7):

> Well, indeed, is it ordained that we should pray for those who go down to the sea in ships, and do business on the great deep; for what me and mine have come through is unspeakable, and the hand of Providence was visibly manifested.
>
> On the day of our embarkation at Leith, a fair wind took us onward at a blithe rate for some time, but in the course of that night, the bridle of the tempest was slackened, and the curb of the billows loosened, and the ship reeled to and fro like a drunken man, and no one could stand therein. My wife and daughter lay at the point of death; Andrew Pringle, my son, also was prostrated with the grievous affliction; and the very soul within me, was as if it would have been cast out of the body . . . on the morning of the seventh day of our departure, we cast anchor near a town called Gravesend, where, to our exceeding great joy, it pleased HIM, in whom alone there is salvation, to allow us once more to put our foot on the dry land. (pp.27–9)

Dr Pringle's biblical rhetoric is a harmless bit of mock-heroic which amuses the reader with the minister's simplicity: such disproportionate importance attached to the routine voyage of the Leith smack! And yet it creates a new emotional context; for the journey is far from routine to Pringle and his family, and the reader is reminded – as Irving and Melville will also suggest – that no voyage, no journey from home to the unknown, is without its uncertainties and danger. The dignity with which the minister's voice invokes the biblical tone lends a momentary strength and resonance to this flimsy fiction; we glimpse for a second the world of the Calvinist castaway, where the tempestuous voyage is but an image of spiritual abandonment. At the beginning of the *Treatise*, Hume, on the verge of his 'voyage' into the world of speculation, the 'immense depths of philosophy', pauses for a moment to ponder the perilousness of his enterprise:

> Methinks I am like a man, who having struck on many shoals, and having narrowly escap'd ship-wreck in passing a small frith, has yet the temerity to put out to sea in the same leaky weather-beaten vessel, and even carries his ambition so far as to think of compassing the globe under these disadvantageous circumstances . . . The wretched condition, weakness, and disorder of the faculties, I must employ in my enquiries, encreases my apprehensions . . . reduces me almost to despair, and makes me resolve to perish on the barren rock, on which I am at present, rather than venture myself upon that boundless ocean, which runs out into immensity.[15]

Calvin himself applies the image to the perilous freedoms of thought which tempt man to overstep his lawful and accustomed boundaries:

> there is scarcely a mind in which the thought does not sometimes rise, Whence your salvation but from the Election of God? But what proof have you of your election? When once this thought has taken possession of any individual, it keeps him perpetually miserable . . . Therefore, as we dread shipwreck, we must avoid this rock, which is fatal to every one who strikes upon it. And though the discussion of predestination is regarded as a perilous sea, yet in sailing over it the navigation is calm and safe, nay, pleasant, provided we do not voluntarily court danger . . .
>
> Hence unhappy consciences find no rest, but are vexed and driven about by a dire whirlwind, feeling as if torn by an angry God, pierced through with deadly darts, terrified by his thunderbolt, and crushed by the weight of his hand; so that it were easier to plunge into abysses and whirlpools than endure these terrors for a moment.[16]

The Pringles are indeed cast adrift in London: displaced from the associations and relationships which guarantee their identity and the sureness of their responses, they are all, in their different ways, at sea. Andrew Pringle, who (despite Galt's disavowal) probably represents most closely the author's reflections on his own condition as an expatriate provincial lodging at the centre, describes this sense of isolation in terms which once again link the plight of the provincial with that of the Calvinist:

> in London, the feeling of self-importance is totally lost and suppressed in the bosom of a stranger. A painful conviction of insignificance – of nothingness, I may say – is sunk upon his heart, and murmured in his ear by the million who divide with him that consequence which he unconsciously before supposed he possessed in a general estimate of the world. While elbowing my way through the unknown multitude that flows between Charing-Cross and the Royal-Exchange, this mortifying sense of my own insignificance has often come upon me with the energy of a pang; and I have thought, that after all we can say of any man, the effect of the greatest influence of an individual on society at large, is but as that of a pebble thrown into the sea. (pp.21–2)[17]

Galt's command of the puritan–provincial rhetoric of unrelatedness raises *The Ayrshire Legatees* just sufficiently above itself for the implications of the journey to the centre to penetrate its cheerfully provincial intentions.

As he put together the first of the 'Noctes Ambrosianae' from the information sent to Blackwood about events in London, J.G. Lockhart included a brief notice of *The Ayrshire Legatees*. The previous year – 1821 – he too had published a novel about the journey of a provincial to the centre. *Valerius, A Roman Story* transposes the theme from a contemporary British setting to Rome, viewed at the moment when European civilisation's most 'central' culture was passing from maturity to decadence. Valerius, a provincial Roman youth, travels from his home in Britain to Rome to claim his inheritance and returns to the purity and peace of the province. This choice of date and setting is a stroke of genius on Lockhart's part. It enables him to take advantage of Scott's example in *Ivanhoe* (1819) to write a period tale of manners and 'information' which is perhaps the first Roman novel in English and which displays Lockhart's Oxonian command of the classical background. More importantly, it also makes available the thinking which underlies every Scotsman's or American's visit to London in the eighteenth and nineteenth centuries. The whole province–centre debate in this period is formulated around a belief in the consummate centrality of Augustan Rome and the question of whether or not it had been possible to recapture this quality in eighteenth-century England.

The plot closely resembles that of *The Ayrshire Legatees*. Valerius, living far from the centre of the Empire, looks forward impatiently to his journey to knowledge and experience:

> Instead of moving here among the ill-cemented and motley fabric of an insulated colony, and seeing only the sullen submission of barbarians, on the one hand, or the paltry vanity of provincial deputies on the other, I shall tread the same ground with the rulers of the earth, and wear, among native Romans, the gown of my ancestors . . . I shall gaze upon the antique majesty of temples and palaces, and open my eyes on all that art and nature have been able to heap together through eight long centuries, for the ornament of the chosen seat of wisdom and valour.[18]

Once in Rome, Valerius takes in all the sights of the centre. Public oratory, feasts, carnivals, gladiatorial combats pass in succession before him; he is entertained royally, but (like the Pringles in London) finds himself an isolated and insignificant observer amidst the splendour: 'alone, I might almost say to myself, in the greatest city of the world – not one of whose inhabitants I have ever, so far as I know, conversed with . . . Alas! were I to be swallowed up this moment in the waves of the Tiber, not one of all these lights would be dimmed by reason of my calamity' (I, 52–3).

Valerius quickly becomes sated with marvels, and the cruelty and evil underlying the magnificence emerges as he is involved in a series of melodramatic events: plots, druggings, imprisonment, bloody sacrifices and the incantations of malevolent witches. At the crisis of the novel, he contrasts his unhappy condition as a prisoner threatened with execution with 'the strong and light hopes' (II, 204) with which he had approached Rome for the first time only a few days before:

> What new emotions had arisen within my breast in the interval! How had every sense been gratified! how had every dream of imagination been exceeded! Yet what a void had been created within – what a void felt – not, alas, filled! – Alas! said I to myself at one moment, why is it that I have been

subjected to all these novelties? Had I not done better to have remained, after all, where life flowed ever calmly – where affection hung over me like a protecting buckler, and my soul could sleep in the security of unbroken faith!

(II, 204–5)

This is exactly the implicit question behind Hawthorne's tale 'My Kinsman, Major Molineux' (1832); but where Hawthorne leaves the consequences of young Robin's journey to the centre and his initiation into its secrets entirely equivocal – to the point that we cannot be sure whether or not he could return even as an alien to his province – Lockhart must assure his reader that Valerius has really escaped unscathed from his experiences, that the provincial is not himself endangered by contact with corruption. He gives up nothing, apparently, not even his innocence, and is allowed to return from the centre to 'the quiet valleys of [his] far off island' (III, 219) with his integrity intact, a new Christian faith, his inheritance, and the beautiful Athanasia as his bride. The end of the novel returns to a pastoral innocence which dissolves the uncomfortable realities which have intervened into an airy pageant: 'the bark skimmed the calm surface of the waters like a sea-bird. The sailors whistled joyously to the prospering gale . . . the blue shores of Italy lay behind us like the shadows of a dream' (III, 303).

The evasiveness of this ending is quite different in character from the obscurity which surrounds the *dénouement* of Hawthorne's 'Roman' novel, *The Marble Faun* (1860), but the source of the difficulty is similar. Both novelists have worked themselves into an impossible ideological corner in which the internal logic of the fiction cannot be made to square with the artists' refusal unequivocally to countenance the implications of the journey to the centre as a journey from innocence to experience. At the end of *The Marble Faun*, Hilda – that 'daughter of the Puritans', as she calls herself – ceases to tend the lamp before the Virgin's shrine, comes down from the tower which had held her above the corruptions of Rome and consents to return with Kenyon to America as his bride: 'now that life had so much human promise in it, they resolved to go back to their own land; because the years, after all, have a kind of emptiness, when we spend too many of them on a foreign shore'.[19]

The 'human promise' that life now offers must be – as it is too for Valerius and his bride as they leave for Britain – something gathered from the events they have witnessed at the centre, events which, if they have manifested human magnificence and achievement, have shown no less of evil, cruelty and anarchy. Hilda is left a wedding gift from Miriam, the book's darkly experienced heroine: 'a bracelet, evidently of great cost, being composed of seven ancient Etruscan gems, dug out of seven sepulchres, and each one of them the signet of some princely personage, who had lived an immemorial time ago' (p.462). This symbol connects the new bride to experience, establishes her relationship with the past and removes her from the peripheral innocence of the province to the knowledge of the centre. And yet Hilda seems untouched by Rome to the end, and Hawthorne refuses to allow the reader even to gauge the quality of her resolute provincialism; she regards as blasphemous Kenyon's suggestion that the Fall may have been 'fortunate':

> 'Here comes my perplexity', continued Kenyon. 'Sin has educated Donatello, and elevated him. Is Sin, then – which we deem such a dreadful blackness in the Universe – is it, like Sorrow, merely an element of human education, through which we struggle to a higher and purer state than we could otherwise have attained. Did Adam fall, that we might ultimately rise to a far loftier Paradise than his?' (p.460)

Hilda's untouchability puts her outside time, and yet the narrative that gives her existence is a temporal sequence which insists on the succession of events. Both *The Marble Faun* and *Valerius* are very much concerned with time and with history, but both fail to enlist a 'sense of the past' which includes the historical continuities of time, or to elucidate the relationship between innocence and guilt, past and present, and province and centre as a continuum of perception which might reconstruct these not as polarities but as possibilities for life. The story of the journey to the centre draws them in the direction of 'human promise', of the interrelatedness of loss and gain, sacrifice and value; but the polarised symbolism of province and centre refuses to allow this shading and insists against all the pulls of time and sequence that Hilda and Valerius may return to the province loaded with the benefits of the centre but serenely untouched by their experience of it.

Valerius was apparently mistaken by a reviewer for 'a religious tale by an American': the error is strangely and significantly understandable.[20] The effect of Lockhart's attempt to introduce local colour into *Valerius* is always that of 'information' gleaned from books, not of 'facts' which proclaim their own solidity; it is reminiscent of Hawthorne's revealing, semi-apologetic headnote to 'The May-pole of Merry Mount', written when he too was an apprentice to Scott's grasp of the past: 'Authority on these points may be found in Strutt's book of English Sports and Pastimes.'[21]

Lockhart's parallel between London and Rome tells a story: Valerius' journey to the centre embodies a spatial and temporal recognition of what it means to be distanced from the places where action and outlook are generated. But, as in many puritan–provincial works on this theme, the 'centre' is both the Eternal City and Vanity Fair, its ripe civilisation rotting to decadence and corruption. In *Valerius*, this contradiction is further complicated by Lockhart's Romantic sense of Scotland's provinciality not only in relation to England but also with respect to her own independent national past. The parallel between London and Rome is complemented by another between Edinburgh and Rome.

The sense of affinity with Augustan Rome which was so important to England in the first half of the eighteenth century took on a talismanic significance for provincial – and nationalistic – writers in Scotland and America at the beginning of the nineteenth century. Broadly speaking, Americans saw a Roman future ahead of them, while Scots had to be content with preserving a 'classical' past. For Lockhart, this sense of departed national greatness was not merely nostalgia but a matter of cultural theory. The most critically sophisticated of all the Scottish writers, he was well versed in German Romantic nationalism and had himself in 1818 translated Friedrich Schlegel's *Lectures on the History of Literature, Ancient and Modern* (1812). Two passages on the decline of great classical literatures suggest what Lockhart found in Schlegel to alert Scotland to the importance of preserving her independent national past:

> [The poetry of Greece] depended . . . on the mythology, the popular belief, the traditional tales, and the ancient modes of life of the country; after the national manners had become relaxed and corrupted, it exhibited merely a faint echo of what it had formerly been . . .

> [Rome's] writers both neglected the ancient and national traditions of their own country; and bestowed much unprofitable labour on the imitation of foreign modes of writing – which, as soon as they are transplanted from their native soil, for the most part assume the appearance of unproductiveness, coldness and death, – or, at best, protract a lingering and inefficient life, like the sickly exotics of a green-house.[22]

In 1819 Lockhart put some of the lessons he had learned from Schlegel into a directly Scottish context in *Peter's Letters to his Kinsfolk*. It reverses the structure of *The Ayrshire Legatees*: a Welsh visitor to Edinburgh describes the manners of 'the Athens of the North' to his correspondent. Peter discovers everywhere on his journey matter for regret in the dissolution of old Scots customs and the gradual blurring of national idiosyncrasies; he finds the law courts to be one of the last bastions of independent Scottishness. Even here signs of decadence are evident: comparing Cockburn's language with the 'Doric dialect' of an older lawyer, Peter cannot restrain his doubts:

> He uses the Scottish dialect – always its music, and not unfrequently its words – quite as broadly as Mr. Clerk, and perhaps, at first hearing, with rather more vulgarity of effect – for he is a young man, and I have already hinted, that no young man can speak Scotch with the same impunity as an old one.[23]

In a similar way, Rome's decadence first strikes the provincial visitor Valerius as a decadence of language: words have come to be used to deceive by the great orators in the Forum; the formulae are empty of meaning and no longer communicate truth (81). Drawing the parallel between Edinburgh and Rome, Lockhart gives a Schlegelian view of a great independent national civilisation in decline: this is the 'lyrical' or poetic theme of *Valerius*. Its method is metaphorical and impressionistic, and puts great emotional pressure on words like 'purity' and 'preservation'. It is a warning of impending fate which has no narrative dimension and demands of the reader an instantaneous recognition of, and assent to, its implied analogies.

For all Lockhart's intuition of the possibilities of elucidating the dilemmas of the present by considering them in the context of the past, *Valerius* remains 'provincial', unable to relate past and present in continuously sequential time. The story of the journey emphasises here dislocation rather than continuity; it plays between poles which are too abstractly and too statically conceived to be mutually illuminating. Scotland and Rome remain places, not 'present real possibilities of being'.[24] It is the result, sadly, of Lockhart's doomed attempt to rejuvenate national literature by injecting it with what he referred to elsewhere as 'a spirit of system': like Addison's Roman play *Cato* in the moment of England's Augustan aspirations, it is a work which knows what it is doing, has all the 'right' ideas abut classicism and all the dullness of its good intentions. Despite Lockhart's strong endorsement of Schlegel's pronouncements on the importance of a 'national and independent language', the novel signally fails to find a distinctive idiom which, perceiving the connection between the spiritual abandonment of the puritan and the provincial's disorientated oscillations around the centre, might suggest a literary continuity with the national past. Lockhart's self-consciously correct prose confirms his provincial unrelatedness. Its distanced effect is well caught in Noah Webster's description of the Scottish rhetoricians, who 'now stand almost the first for erudition; but perhaps no man can write a foreign language with genuin [sic] purity'.[25]

Washington Irving's *The Sketch Book of Geoffrey Crayon, Gent.* (America, 1819; England, 1820) was the first internationally popular work of fiction by an American author. Its success with both American and English audiences lies in the peculiar balance of urbanity and alienation which Irving's style achieves, a balance which suggests an alternative to Lockhart's stylistic nullity in exploiting the tension generated between the 'central' and 'provincial' impulses.[26]

The quest for an inheritance which galvanised the journeys to the centre of Valerius and the Ayrshire Legatees becomes in *The Sketch Book* an overtly immaterial odyssey: Irving's protagonist goes in search of his roots and his spiritual home. The first sketch, 'The Voyage', which dramatises the distance travelled by the provincial in order to reach the centre, also sets the voice of Geoffrey Crayon stylistically and imagistically adrift at the beginning of his work: 'to an American visiting Europe the long voyage he has to make is an excellent preparative. The temporary absence of worldly scenes and employments produces a state of mind peculiarly fitted to receive new and vivid impressions. The vast space of waters, that separates the hemispheres is like a blank page in existence.'[27] The ocean is a limbo between one phase of existence and another; it is also the scene of dislocation, where relationships are severed, and shipwreck threatened:

> In travelling by land there is a continuity of scene and a connected succession of persons and incidents, that carry on the story of life, and lessen the effect of absence and separation. We drag, it is true, 'a lengthening chain' at each remove of our pilgrimage; but the chain is unbroken – we can trace it back link by link; and we feel that the last still grapples us to home. But a wide sea voyage severs us at once. – It makes us conscious of being cast loose from the secure anchorage of settled life and sent adrift upon a doubtful world. It interposes a gulph, not merely imaginary, but real, between us and our homes – a gulph subject to tempest and fear and uncertainty, rendering distance palpable and return precarious. (p.11)

The Calvinist rhetoric of spiritual abandonment lurks like a rock just beneath the untroubled surface of Geoffrey Crayon's genteel prose. It is typical of Irving's method that the impending shipwreck does not happen to Geoffrey Crayon himself, but is the spectacle of someone else's experience, which (like Hunilla in Melville's 'Encantadas') he observes from a distance as matter for melancholy meditation: 'What sighs have been wafted after that ship; what prayers offered up at the deserted fireside of home' (p.13).

So Geoffrey Crayon arrives unscathed, but his quest for the centre continues as he travels on in search of experience. His 'poetical pilgrimage' (p.209) is a journey *around* the centre. From a moving stage coach he observes life being unselfconsciously lived about him. He watches some ebullient schoolboys descending from the coach at their home:

> I looked after them with a feeling in which I do not know whether pleasure or melancholy predominated; for I was reminded of those days when, like them, I had neither known care nor sorrow, and a holyday was the summit of earthly felicity ... I could just distinguish the forms of a lady and two young girls in the portico, and I saw my little comrades, with Bantam, Carlo, and old John, trooping along the carriage road. I leaned out of the coach window, in hopes of witnessing the happy meeting, but a grove of trees shut it from my sight.
> (p.156)

The journey puts him in touch with his past, only to emphasise how alienated he is from it. It is, like the 'shifting panorama' of Hawthorne's 'Main-street', not only unrecapturable, but somehow vitally unrelated to the observing consciousness. In this respect it resembles even more closely Hawthorne's description of the train journey of Hepzibah and Clifford Pyncheon at the end of *The House of the Seven Gables* (1851), where the scenery of contemporary America flashes past too fast for their disorientated minds to comprehend.[28]

In each case the reader is involved not with the scene itself but with its effect on the observer's sensibilities; Geoffrey Crayon is like Miles Coverdale or a Henry James hero, a professional tourist who cannot stop to 'belong'. He introduces himself at the beginning of *The Sketch Book* – with an air of ingenuous egotism – as a wandering spirit, desirous of association but chary of involvement. His is the voice of *The Spectator*, but attenuated to the point of whimsy by his inability to participate in the scenes he observes:

> I have wandered through different countries and witnessed many of the shifting scenes of life. I cannot say that I have studied them with the eye of a philosopher, but rather with the sauntering gaze with which humble lovers of the picturesque stroll from the window of one print shop to another. (p.9)

The theatrical image of the 'shifting scenes' and the pose of the 'picturesque traveller' who studies a landscape for its composition rather than its content reveal that the responses of Geoffrey Crayon to experience will always be self-consciously aesthetic. And indeed, the only 'reality' in sketches like 'The Broken Heart' is the gently throbbing sensibility of the observer. No wonder, then, given his literary antecedents, that stepping upon the home of his forefathers, Geoffrey Crayon finds himself 'a stranger in the land' (p.15).

But he is not merely one more incarnation of the alienated voice of the observer-spy. For (recalling Herbert Read's comment that American writers march all round a subject and imagine they have been at the centre) what Irving dramatises in the narrative journey of Geoffrey Crayon is the literary quest of the provincial for centrality. Geoffrey Crayon is a figure acceptable to the centre who feels at a distance from it. He is, in his own words, a '*literary* pilgrim' (p.224, emphasis added), and the centre he seeks is a stylistic one whose 'realities' are all verbal. He visits Stratford-upon-Avon and tries to reconstruct episodes in Shakespeare's life from his plays; he builds another sketch around the work of 'A Royal Poet', and his tribute to 'The Angler' is an extended meditation on 'the seductive pages of honest Izaak Walton' in which Crayon is content to read Walton while his companions actually catch fish (p.264).

The most extended example of the 'literariness' of *The Sketch Book* is the 'Christmas' sketches, which were often reprinted as a group in nostalgic tribute to the traditional conduct of English festivities. There is, however, nothing remotely naturalistic about Geoffrey Crayon's account; the scenes he describes come from the English poetic tradition: they are the poems of Herrick, Suckling and Ben Jonson reconstructed by the provincial as a substitute for direct realities. And just as Geoffrey Crayon's place in these festive scenes is peripheral – he is the visitor, the invited guest at the family centre – so his fanciful rendering of tradition is stylistically distanced from possession:

> The irruption of this motley crew, with beat of drum, according to ancient custom, was the consummation of uproar and merriment. Master Simon covered himself with glory by the stateliness with which, as Ancient Christmas, he walked a minuet with the peerless, though giggling, Dame Mince Pie. It was followed by a dance of all the characters, which, from its medley of costumes, seemed as though the old family portraits had skipped down from their frames to join in the sport. Different centuries were figuring at cross hands and right and left; the dark ages were cutting pirouettes and rigadoons; and the days of Queen Bess jigging merrily down the middle, through a line of succeeding generations. (p.190)

The fancy is pure Hawthorne: such a passage could have been lifted straight from 'the masques, mummeries, and festive customs' of 'The May-pole of Merry Mount' – or indeed from any number of Hawthorne's 'colonial' sketches.[29] The narrative version of the literary pilgrimage which connects the sketches of Geoffrey Crayon makes clear – in a way that 'The May-pole' (or *Valerius*) cannot – the *process* by which the provincial acquires reality starting from the distanced account of it he has found in books, and the inevitably peculiar version of experience which such a perspective will give him. *The Scarlet Letter*'s dramatic evocation of the puritan–provincial mind is latent here. In *The Sketch Book* the narrative image of the provincial writer's poetical pilgrimage to the centre of his literary tradition throws outward onto the consciousness of Geoffrey Crayon a mode of perception which is completely absorbed into the complex voice of the later novel.

The journey to the centre liberates the genteel provincial voice of Geoffrey Crayon; it gives him an occasion to 'open an intercourse with the world' – of literature. Visiting the reading room of the British Museum, he falls into a daydream in which he communicates with books as though they were people; a similar fantasy occurs in Westminster Abbey, where he hopes for access to the opinions and the realities of the past through conversation with one of its neglected tomes, whose remarks 'were couched in such intolerably antiquated terms' that Geoffrey Crayon has 'infinite difficulty in rendering them into modern phraseology' (p.103). His communication with the past persuades him that its continuities with the present are minimal.

Geoffrey Crayon's status as a visiting pilgrim also allows him to align himself with the central literary tradition by retelling (in 'Rip Van Winkle', 'The Spectre Bridegroom' and 'The Legend of Sleepy Hollow') its folk tales. These stories sit strangely amid the guidebook observations of the genteel tourist, and Irving goes to some pains to make it clear to the reader that they are not original; they are imitations of works with which the world of the centre has long amused itself. But despite the calculated air of arbitrary appropriation, the tales as Irving retells them do not bear a random relationship to the book's concerns: 'The Legend of Sleepy Hollow' and 'Rip Van Winkle' (the two which he transposes from a European to an American setting) belong respectively to the realm of the 'pursuer pursued' and that of the distanced observer or 'spy'.

Irving's literary pilgrim travels in 'easy faith' (p.210), believing readily the most unlikely tales spun by the natives of the classic spots he visits. This is at once a free choice and an inevitability, for – despite their unlikelihood – these stories are his only access to what might have been the truth. Armed with the stories of the centre, the provincial goes in search of the realities which he supposes to lie 'behind' them; like the Calvinist, he assumes that the world holds the key to the meaning of the thing and seeks the truth through the sign. But one of the consequences of knowing the literature apart from – and before – the world which produced it is that this world when visited by the literary pilgrim seems disappointing and even unreal by comparison. A sense of loss inevitably accompanies the provincial's arrival at what he takes to be the centre when he finds that knowledge of the one does not guarantee possession of the other. This would become the central irony of Redburn and *his* guidebook.

In *The Sketch Book* the recognition is more muted and the sense of desolation so restrained that it is scarcely allowed to break the surface of the reader's consciousness, but it does entail stylistic consequences. Isolation or detachment is both the predicament and the solution: it is a pose which Irving cultivated in his own life in Europe as an expatriate bachelor and through his literary *personae*. In *Bracebridge Hall* (1822) which followed *The Sketch Book*, the preliminary sketch of 'The Author' makes clearer the position of Geoffrey Crayon with respect to this literary material; he is now an avowedly provincial *persona* seeking the centre: 'England is as classic ground to an American as Italy is to an Englishman; and old London teems with as much historical association as mighty Rome'.[30]

Geoffrey Crayon avows his provinciality in order to accept it, and Irving remains a provincial writer because of the incompleteness with which he recognises the implications of his narrator's journey to the centre. Geoffrey Crayon's failure to experience or to belong to the realities of his literary heritage remains suspended in the prose as a kind of wistfulness which retreats easily into whimsy. The polarised categories of 'province' and 'centre' remain inviolate and opposed, and time is a dimension of discontinuity rather than relationship. Irving fails to exploit the recognition — which requires this journey or pilgrimage for its formulation — that for the American there can be finally no centre, no resting place in a priori certainties. Hawthorne in *Our Old Home* describes his family as 'pilgrims and dusty wayfarers' who find a *temporary* resting place in 'A London Suburb' — just beyond the coveted precincts:

> Within so trifling a distance of the central spot of all the world (which, as Americans have at present no centre of their own, we may allow to be somewhere in the vicinity, we will say, of Saint Paul's Cathedral), it might have seemed natural that I should be tossed about by the turbulence of the vast London whirlpool. But I had drifted into a still eddy, where conflicting movements made a repose, and, wearied with a good deal of uncongenial activity, I found the quiet of my temporary haven more attractive than anything that the great town could offer.[31]

The most remarkable thing about Hawthorne's preoccupation with 'centres' of any kind — London, Rome, Boston, Shakespeare, 'experience' — is its ambivalence. This is not merely the equivocation of *Valerius* as to the relative merits of centre against province, an equivocation which assumes a partition of values between them. It is, rather, an ambivalence about the very nature of experience for the mind which approaches it at second-hand. Chapter 5 noted Hawthorne's self-confessed propensity to retreat from experience; faced with the irreducible, absolute presence of the experienced past in London, and in Rome, he recognised its claims on him but recoiled from the kind of relationship it seemed to demand. He wrote on leaving Rome in 1850:

> I looked at everything as if for the last time; nor do I wish ever to see any of these objects again, though no place ever took so strong a hold of my being, as Rome, nor ever seemed so close to me, and so strangely familiar. I seem to know it better than my birth place, and to have known it longer; and though I have been very miserable there, and languid with the effects of the atmosphere, and disgusted with a thousand things in daily life, still I cannot say I hate it — perhaps might fairly own a love for it. But (life being too short for such questionable and troublesome enjoyments) I desire never to set eyes on it again.[32]

One might fairly ask what 'life' is this, for which Hawthorne is so carefully saving himself from experience?

When he came in *The Marble Faun* to ask how the American, situated both geographically and culturally on the edge of history, might establish a right relation to the centre, Hawthorne failed to integrate the story of his provincials' discovery of the centre – their initiation into experience – with a sense of what this experience might be in terms of the Roman past. The result is an enigmatic story whose 'significance' is ominously bodied forth in obtrusive puritan overtones, and is also – quite gratuitously – a picturesque guidebook. Time and place fail to connect in the narrative. *The Marble Faun* seems to confirm Geoffrey Crayon's conclusion that the provincial only has access to the past and to its literature as a sentimental tourist who looks always at the spectacle of the centre with the aid of a manual. It was, however, a conclusion which Melville had already treated with vigorous scepticism.

Redburn: His First Voyage (1849) takes direct issue with *The Sketch Book of Geoffrey Crayon* and with all books which profess to guide the reader to possession of experience. This challenge (as Melville recognises implicitly with an early and good-natured touch of that irony towards his audience which later came to dominate *The Confidence-Man*) extends to his own novel insofar as it might claim to communicate the life of a sailor: 'nearly all literature, in one sense, is made up of guide-books', and guidebooks, as Redburn discovers, are useless.[33]

Redburn, a callow youth, embarks on a voyage from his native American village to the centre. Melville deftly sketches the provinciality of his background in a few touches: the bound copies of *The Spectator* reverently locked up in the library case; the pretensions to culture in the evenings spent poring over portfolios of French prints; the 'continual dwelling upon foreign associations' (p.7). Young Redburn, seeking a clue to 'life', is fascinated by a ship in a glass bottle; like Hawthorne's Surveyor when he comes upon the ancient scarlet letter in the attic of the Custom House, he scrutinises an obscure symbol which, rightly interpreted, will be a key to knowledge:

> often I used to try to peep in at the portholes, to see what else was inside; but the holes were so small, and it looked so very dark indoors, that I could discover little or nothing; though, when I was very little, I made no doubt, that if I could but once pry open the hull, and break the glass all to pieces, I would infallibly light upon something wonderful, perhaps some gold guineas, of which I have always been in want, ever since I could remember. (p.8)

Redburn is abandoned in the world and cheated of his genteel inheritance by his father's bankruptcy. This father, who has 'fallen' and died dishonoured in obscurity, is to Redburn the pattern in whose footsteps he desires to follow. This compulsion to travel the road from innocence to experience sends Redburn on his pilgrimage to England, for his father before him had gone to Europe and brought back tales of a wonderful land beyond the sea, 'full of mossy cathedrals and churches, and long, narrow, crooked streets without side-walks, and lined with strange houses' (p.5). Like Caleb Williams or Geoffrey Crayon, Redburn has lived life at a distance; his experiences have come second-hand from books. He leaves home to see for himself those objects in which, by association, he has come to locate the 'meaning' of England, the centre. Like Geoffrey Crayon and Valerius (for whom too reading had preceded reality), he is inevitably disappointed, for it appears that England is not after all composed of reified associations:

> But where are the old abbeys, and the York Minsters, and the lord mayors, and coronations, and the May-poles, and fox-hunters, and Derby races, and the dukes and duchesses, and the Count d'Orsays, which, from all my reading, I had been in the habit of associating with England? Not the most distant glimpse of them was to be seen. (p.133)

Redburn takes with him on his voyage his father's old guidebook to Liverpool, the 'Stranger's Guide', as it is subtitled (p.146). He resolves to quote 'information' from this for the reader's benefit, since his own paraphrase as the book's distanced inheritor could only be a poor imitation: 'with regard to a matter, concerning which I myself am wholly ignorant, it is far better to quote my old friend verbatim, than to mince his substantial baron-of-beef of information into a flimsy ragout of my own; and so, pass it off as original' (p.149). Finally, however, he refrains on the grounds that such quotation could not convey to the reader 'all the pleasant associations which the original carries to me!' (p.149). The whole episode reads like a deliberately comic misprision of *The Sketch Book*. Where Irving dramatises the American writer's quest for literary centrality, Melville satirises the provincialism of such aspirations. As he put it in his famous review of Hawthorne's *Mosses from an Old Manse*, 'there is no hope for us in these smooth, pleasing writers that know their powers ... we want no American Goldsmiths ... Let us boldly condemn all imitation ... and foster all originality'.[34]

But Melville also has more serious purposes for Redburn's guidebook, purposes which suggest a way out of the attenuated gentility of the distanced provincial voice. Recognising and reappropriating its strong Calvinist origins, Melville finds an idiom live enough to charge his fiction with the energy to fight back against its exclusion from the centre. Redburn's guidebook is both his Bible and his history: its text and the additional personal marks made by his younger self and his father are Redburn's connections to the past. In retracing his father's footsteps through Liverpool, Redburn hopes to take immediate possession of both his ancestral heritage and the secrets of the centre:

> Great was my boyish delight at the prospect of visiting a place, the infallible clew to all whose intricacies I held in my hand ... For I was determined to make the whole subject my own; and not be content with a mere smattering of the thing, as is too much the custom with most students of guide-books ... I could not but think that I was building myself up in an unerring knowledge of Liverpool; especially as I had familiarized myself with the map, and could turn sharp corners on it, with marvelous confidence and celerity ... I began to think I had been born in Liverpool, so familiar seemed all the features of the map.
>
> (pp.151–2)

So he begins his 'filial pilgrimage' along the predestined route marked out 'according to the dotted lines in the diagram' (p.154). The very act of following the same path as his father had once taken brings home to young Redburn a self-pitying sense of his absolute aloneness in the universe: 'Poor, poor Wellingborough! thought I, miserable boy! you are indeed friendless and folorn. Here you wander a stranger in a strange town' (p.154).

Redburn's faith in his ability to recover his past with the aid of the guidebook is shaken when the map and the reality fail to coincide. The 'precious book' of 'fine old family associations' is useless as a guide to the present: 'the thing that had guided the father could not guide the son' (p.157). Redburn's discovery that the past carries no messages to the present is one with his realisation that there neither is nor can be a fixed, unchanging 'centre': this, he says to himself, 'is a moving world; its Riddough's Hotels are forever being pulled down; it never stands still; and its sands are forever shifting' (p.157). For Melville's alienated provincial there is no continuity, only change.

The novel's wisdom is, however, by no means limited to Redburn's discovery of the failure of relation. The hero's immediate response to his inability to possess his English heritage is an aggressive nationalism which, denying one parent, claims for the American a 'universal paternity': 'we are the heirs of all time, and with all nations we divide our inheritance' (p.169). To replace nothing by everything: this is to fall prey to the Whitmanesque provincialism of extremes. But the novel does find between these polarities a means of projecting James' 'possible other case, the case rich and edifying where the actuality is pretentious and vain'; it does, that is, gain access to that continuous scale of possibilities which plays between the irreconcilable oppositions of the Calvinist mentality. Melville achieves this by tapping the narrative energies of the story, and his method suggests the less quoted, more complex understanding of the relationship between tradition and innovation which complements the passage already cited from his 'Mosses' essay: 'imitation is often the first charge brought against originality ... You must have plenty of sea-room to tell the Truth in; especially when it seems to have an aspect of newness.'[35] Melville's language is not only more decisively charged with Calvinist undertones than Irving's; it is also more strongly focused at the points of contact between the static imagery of the puritan–provincial condition and the dynamic of the pilgrim's progression through life. The forward movement of events connected sequentially creates a relationship between successive moments which does not claim to be one of cause and effect but of continuity through time. This is concrete, 'narrative' provincial art: it tells of what it is like to be on a journey to the centre. The structure of Melville's novel articulates clearly the difference between *being* 'at home' and *getting there*, which makes this story of the pilgrim's journey a peculiarly appropriate form for the puritan–provincial writer. The *rite de passage* structuring the voyages of the Ayrshire Legatees and Geoffrey Crayon becomes here an explicit process of disorientation which transforms the native into a pilgrim and a stranger:

> People who have never gone to sea for the first time as sailors, can not imagine how puzzling and confounding it is. It must be like going into a barbarous country, where they speak a strange dialect, and dress in strange clothes, and live in strange houses. For sailors have their own names, even for things that are familiar ashore; and if you call a thing by its shore name, you are laughed at for an ignoramus and a land-lubber. (p.65)

Redburn is 'at sea' in every sense: his physical state is an emblem of his spiritual condition. Hume had used the same image to describe man's inability to be at home with 'theological reasonings':

> We are like foreigners in a strange country, to whom everything must seem suspicious, and who are in danger every moment of transgressing against the laws and customs of the people with whom they live and converse.[36]

To inquire into affairs beyond the scope of one's knowledge and competence is to risk being set adrift and even shipwrecked on the rocks of uncertainty. Where Calvin at this point – recognising that 'there is scarcely a mind in which the thought does not sometimes rise' – urges man to draw back from the 'abysses and whirlpools' to the safe harbour of unquestioning faith in God's providence, Hume and Melville accept that it is a property of the human mind to speculate beyond the knowable and are willing to voyage a little further towards scepticism. Hume's passage continues:

> We know not how far we ought to trust our vulgar methods of reasoning in such a subject; since, even in common life and in that province which is peculiarly appropriated to them, we cannot account for them, and are entirely guided by a kind of instinct or necessity in employing them.

The voyage to a strange land teaches that we have all along been strangers in our own country. Hume's great achievement in the *Dialogues Concerning Natural Religion* is to make it possible to be 'at home' with this puritan–provincial state of distance, uncertainty and impenetrability, to find a provisional place for the speculative mind within a life which is necessarily lived on assumptions of the knowable:

> All sceptics pretend, that, if reason be considered in an abstract view, it furnishes invincible arguments against itself, and that we could never retain any conviction or assurance, on any subject, were not the sceptical reasonings so refined and subtile, that they are not able to counterpoise the more solid and more natural arguments, derived from the senses and experience. But it is evident, whenever our arguments lose this advantage, and run wide of common life, that the most refined scepticism comes to be on a footing with them, and is able to oppose and counterbalance them. The one has no more weight than the other. The mind must remain in suspense between them; and it is that very suspense or balance, which is the triumph of scepticism.
> (pp.135–6)

Melville's first attempt to cast off the anchors which tied him to experience was a disastrous failure as fiction. In *Mardi, and A Voyage Thither*, which was published earlier in the same year as *Redburn*, he allowed the exhilaration of free-floating speculative thought to blow him hither and thither across a private mental ocean in a narrative which shipwrecks itself on a proliferating reef of uninterpretable symbols. The narrator Taji's half-desolate, half-exultant cry, 'Oh, reader, list! I've chartless voyaged', makes the pilgrim a castaway indeed:

> Those who boldly launch, cast off all cables; and turning from the common breeze, that's fair for all, with their own breath, fill their own sails. Hug the shore, naught new is seen; and 'Land Ho!' at last was sung, when a new world was sought.
> That voyager steered his bark through seas, untracked before; ploughed his own path mid jeers; though with a heart that oft was heavy with the thought, that he might only be too bold, and grope where land was none.
> So I . . . better to sink in boundless deeps, than float on vulgar shoals; and give me, ye gods, an utter wreck, if wreck I do.[37]

Taji's final fate is to become a defiant reprobate in flight from eternal vengeance: 'And thus, pursuers and pursued flew on, over an endless sea' (p.654). The allegorical pole of this journey or quest predominates over the 'real' to the extent that the work becomes literally tautological: a quest for a quest, a symbol of symbolising. The problem of interpretability becomes paramount, overriding any possibility of the story revealing – and being – its own meaning.

Hume never 'turns from the common breeze' as Melville does in *Mardi*; if he does not hug the shore, neither does he lose sight of land altogether, for 'to whatever length any one may push his speculative principles of scepticism, [the philosopher] must act, I own, and live, and converse like other men; and for this conduct he is not obliged to give any other reason than the absolute necessity he lies under of so doing' (*Dialogues*, p.134). This requires a kind of faith, or confidence, in the mind's ability to maintain the 'suspense or balance' which can hold the claims of the world in tension with its own. It is a faith which Melville, discovering in *Mardi* the excitements of speculative thought, fails to value as a communicable bridge between private and public. The result is what Kenneth Clark calls the 'high-minded vacuity' of provincial art which rejects the potential of narrative to ground it in reality.

Redburn was written in the wake of the public's dismissal of *Mardi*. Melville was short of cash, and professed scorn of his 'little nursery tale'.[38] Yet it is just this retrenchment to the familiar realms of the story, the 'common breeze' of shared experience, which allows Melville to capture in *Redburn* something of Hume's – or Scott's – poise between the chartless voyage of the mind and the predestined pilgrimage of a human life. *Redburn* is a novel unafraid to rest part of its case on 'information'. By anchoring his fable of the puritan–provincial state to history and a story in the narrative of an individual journey to the centre, Melville at once concedes the claims of knowable, shareable experience, and is able (like Hume and Scott) to suggest their provisionality.

It is this faith in the story as a bridge between the 'facts' of living and speculative thought which enables Melville to deploy his Calvinist rhetoric strongly and effectively without allowing it to float off into the realm of unanchored symbols. Thus Redburn, on his first voyage, finds himself 'about sunset . . . thrust out of the world' (p.36) in a ship's company of outcasts and reprobates. At first, burdened like Bunyan's Christian with egotistical vanity, Redburn sets himself apart from the crew and assumes that he is under the paternal care of the ship's captain. His first inkling that the strongly centripetal tendencies of his puritan–provincial perceptions may be crumbling under pressure from experience comes with the realisation that he is *not* specially chosen and that Captain Riga is no more than a confidence-man, 'but a shabby fellow after all . . . a sort of imposter; and while ashore, a gentleman on false pretences' (p.71). The bright red shooting-jacket which is the emblem of Redburn's burden of vanity and which sets him apart from the rest of the crew begins about this time to disintegrate upon his back from the rigours of the voyage. As he gains in experience as a common sailor, Redburn finds a place in the democracy of shipboard life. With the questioning of his special status as one of the elect amongst the reprobate, Redburn (like the reader) is being prepared for the discovery that the 'centre' he seeks does not exist. His existence begins to take on 'that lasting temper of all true, candid men – a seeker, not a finder yet'.[39]

After his disillusioning attempt to try to get to know Liverpool through the guidebook, Redburn abandons second-hand knowledge and wanders freely through the streets on his own initative. Casting the anchors which tie him to the genteel tradition, he opens his mind to experiences that lie beyond the predestined route of the dotted line on the diagram. He now comes into direct contact with degradation and corruption and attempts to help the starving family of Lancelott's-Hey. After this experience, the distancing veil of self-consciousness interposed between the observer and the scene is lifted: Redburn's revised description of Liverpool is clear, and chilling, in its refusal to divorce 'fact' from 'implication':

> The pestilent lanes and alleys which ... go by the names of Rotten-row, Gibraltar-place, and Booble-alley, are putrid with vice and crime; to which, perhaps, the round globe does not furnish a parallel. The sooty and begrimed bricks of the very houses have a reeking, Sodom-like, and murderous look; and well may the shroud of coal-smoke, which hangs over this part of the town, more than any other, attempt to hide the enormities here practiced. These are the haunts from which sailors sometimes disappear forever; or issue in the morning, robbed naked, from the broken door-ways. These are the haunts in which cursing, gambling, pickpocketing, and common iniquities, are virtues too lofty for the infected gorgons and hydras to practice... They seem leagued together, a company of miscreant misanthropes, bent upon doing all the malice to mankind in their power. With sulphur and brimstone they ought to be burned out of their arches like vermin. (p.191)

Every word of this acknowledges the primacy of experience, however unbearable; the language looks steadily at its subject, lit by real horror and real anger, not by the glancing taper of the picturesque tourist. In such terms Redburn throws off his provincial complacency and commits himself to reality, and Melville earns the authority to depict a vision of hell which aligns him – as a companion, not an imitator – with Dickens and Hogarth, and with Dante. The imaginative freedoms of this idiom are different in kind from the free-floating speculations of Babbalanja in *Mardi*, or even from the Poesque evocation of corruption in which Melville indulges later in *Redburn* when the hero attends Harry Bolton to London (p.233). The highly specific emotional charge balances the immediate claims of the observed particular with the sceptical mind's refusal to accept this evidence as the final truth about reality. The freedom of the language brings it closest, perhaps, to the peroration of Hawthorne's 'sable figure' which is the climax of the nightmare vision of Young Goodman Brown. In both passages the poise is maintained in the incalculable relationship between the literary realities displayed upon the surface and the physical or psychological reality which informs these. It is a relationship of disproportion as much as of congruence; but rhetoric and meaning are not alienated one from another, and their affinity lends a tension to the prose which is quite lacking from the 'merely' literary surfaces of Geoffrey Crayon.

The connective strength of the information about the sailor's life or about conditions in Liverpool which the story of Redburn imparts turns an image of abandonment and spiritual isolation into a quest for mental freedom that comprehends the provincial writer's search for a viable idiom. Redburn's journey to the centre is a story of alienation and thwarted ambitions, yet through Melville's confident handling of narrative it releases a strong sense of 'the possible other case'. Exclusion and distance from the certainties of knowledge which are presumed to lie at the centre liberate Melville's prose to a position where it may freely assert that 'all knowledge is knowledge from a point of view'.[40]

Scott's *The Heart of Midlothian* (1818) is at once a masterpiece of narrative art and fiction's most sympathetic understanding of the puritan–provincial mind. The union of these qualities comes from Scott's refusal to repine at the conditions which stultified all provincial attempts to create 'central', dramatic literature. Chapter 5 showed Carlyle and Hawthorne recording regretfully how the dramatic in puritan–provincial hands slides unstably into a theatrical spectacle, with the actor a distanced spectator of his own actions. The final effect of all fiction which adopts the 'central' stance from an alienated point of view is to dissolve the external spectacle and to focus reality in the mind of the observer. Scott's revolutionary perception was that the appropriate fictional form for the Calvinist mind was not dramatic (where it always looks inauthentically stagey and eccentric) but narrative, taking the theological concepts of predestination, guilt and salvation out of the obsessively self-referential psyche and endowing them with spatial and historical extension. The result, in *The Heart of Midlothian*, is a work of immense historical intelligence and imaginative self-possession.

The opening of *The Heart of Midlothian* depicts a country which has lost confidence in itself and in its rulers. This failure of faith in Scotland is – according to the comic voices which provide a kind of choric commentary on the action – a consequence of the country's loss of independence through the Union of Parliaments in 1707:

> 'And as for the lords of state,' said Miss Damahoy, 'ye suld mind the riding o' the Parliament, Mr. Saddletree, in the gude auld time before the Union, – a year's rent o' mony a gude estate gaed for horse-graith and harnessing, forby broidered robes and foot-mantles, that wad hae stude by their lane wi' gold brocade, and that were muckle in my ain line.'
> 'Aye, and then the lusty banqueting, with sweetmeats and comfits wet and dry, and dried fruits of divers sorts,' said Plumdamas. 'But Scotland was Scotland in these days.'
> 'I'll tell ye what it is, neighbours,' said Mrs. Howden, 'I'll ne'er believe Scotland is Scotland ony mair, if our kindly Scots sit doun wi' the affront they hae gien us this day.'[41]

The Union, in this view, is a kind of fall which has terminated the golden age of peace and plenty and inaugurated the harsh rule of a distanced and authoritarian centre.

A historical incident launches the story: the last-minute reprieve granted by the English Crown to Captain Porteous of the Edinburgh City Guard, who had been condemned to death for firing into the crowd at the execution of a locally popular criminal. Fixing on this demonstration of provincial impotence (the reprieve is a direct revocation of Scots law by the superior powers in England), Scott imagines his way into the subject of provincialism. He is engagingly candid about the process of story-telling; his prose conceals no secrets of effect, and one of the major pleasures of reading *The Heart of Midlothian* is to assist at the flowering of the story from its seed in the historical moment. The fourth chapter of the novel perfectly illustrates this imaginative growth: it begins by describing the event – the Edinburgh crowd's anticipation of Porteous' execution – then withdraws from the scene to fill in the background, to suggest the likelihood of a reprieve and to speculate on what this would mean to the provincial populace. As this possibility becomes a reality, Scott gives his disappointed crowd a collective voice which is the rebellious response to arbitrary power from the centre, then abruptly narrows his focus to a single, representative conversation. This is the moment when 'history' becomes a 'story':

> 'I am judging,' said Mr. Plumdamas, 'that this reprieve wadna stand gude in the auld Scots law, when the kingdom was a kingdom.'
> 'I dinna ken muckle about the law,' answered Mrs. Howden; 'but I ken, when we had a king, and a chancellor, and parliament-men o' our ain, we could aye peeble them wi' stanes when they werena gude bairns – But naebody's nails can reach the length o' Lunnon.' (p.43)

By the union with England, it seems, Scotland has subjected itself to the absolute decrees of an alien power. Its people, like the Calvinist reprobate, are reduced to muttering rebelliously against a destiny they feel impotent to affect. But the comic exuberance of the Scots speakers itself vitally denies the determinism under which they seem to labour. The solidity of these characters who evoke the historical dilemma in terms of their own self-interest testifies to a continuing undercurrent of life unsubdued by dogma, be it political or theological. It is the life of Eastcheap Tavern continuing through the troubled reign of Henry IV, and the light that glimmers in the darkest moments of *Macbeth* in the grumblings of the Porter roused from his bed. The vitality of such speech cuts across the predetermined events to tap the energies of story which are not subdued to order or meaning by any narrative line.

In this atmosphere of unrest and high feeling, a band of citizens led by the dead smuggler's associate Geordie Robertson takes the law violently into their own hands, seize Porteous from the Tolbooth and execute him unceremoniously on the gallows from which he has so lately been reprieved. While storming the Tolbooth, Robertson pauses to urge escape on another unhappy inmate, and we glimpse a connection between the publicly motivated events of the night and a private victim of the same arbitrary and distant rule of the centre. The prisoner in whom Robertson is interested is Effie Deans, awaiting trial for child murder; Robertson himself later emerges as the father of the missing infant.

Scott has already introduced the Deans family at their home on the outskirts of Edinburgh. The first conversation between Effie and her sister reveals a vital failure of faith: Effie, fearing the wrath of their strict Cameronian father, fails to trust in Jeanie and thereby seals her own fate:

> The objurgation of David Deans, however well meant, was unhappily timed. It created a division of feelings in Effie's bosom, and deterred her from her intended confidence in her sister. 'She wad haud me nae better than the dirt below her feet,' said Effie to herself, 'were I to confess I hae danced wi' him four times on the green down by . . . and she'll maybe hing it ower my head that she'll tell my father, and then she wad be mistress and mair.' (p.118)

The chance nature of this initial failure of confidence is stressed by Scott in the coincidence which provoked it; but it is at the same time inevitable, predestined in the characters presented by the story-teller: Effie proud, spoilt and wilful; Jeanie righteous but mistrusting her sister's giddiness and attractiveness; Davie Deans the abrupt unbending adherent of the Law. Once the moment of confidence has passed unprofited, Effie's fall is inevitable. She becomes pregnant, disappears at the time of her confinement and on her reappearance is arrested for the murder of her child under a statute which takes failure to confide her condition to another as presumption of guilt. The harshness and arbitrariness of this law are universally admitted, but in the absence of the child or its father (now in hiding after his part in the Porteous affair), Effie cannot hope for acquittal unless Jeanie will say that she knew of the pregnancy. But Effie did not trust her sister, and Jeanie will not stand perjured before the law; so Effie is condemned to death – in effect, for a failure of faith. No hope is held of a reprieve from England, because the Queen is said to be so angered by her Scottish subjects' rebellion in the affair of Porteous that she will countenance no mercy towards any individual amongst them.

Scott offers several courses of action to Scotsman facing these arbitrary decrees of justice from the distant centre. The first is familiar: non-action, or passivity. For Davie Deans the strict Calvinist, guilt is guilt, despite his doubts about the justifiability of man-made law as a surrogate for God's law; Effie stands condemned as a murderess, and must endure her fate.

He, like the 'Roman' he resembles (p.231), insists on living in an absolute relation to the absolute. Nothing therefore is to be done but to accept the decree with submission:

> 'if telling down my haill substance could hae saved her frae this black snare, I wad hae walked out wi' naething but my bonnet and my staff to beg an awmous for God's sake, and ca'd mysell an happy man – But if a dollar, or a plack, or the nineteenth part of a boddle, wad save her open guilt and open shame frae open punishment, that purchase wad David Deans never make! – Na, na; an eye for an eye, a tooth for a tooth, life for life, blood for blood – it's the law of man, and it's the law of God. – Leave me, sirs – leave me – I maun warstle wi' this trial in privacy and on my knees.' (p.125)

Deans' proud fatalism is such that he can thus resign his daughter before her case has even come to trial in the courts of men.

The second alternative, rebellious denial of the law, is the way of the reprobate, of those who transport Porteous to his death in the face of his reprieve, and of Ratcliffe, Effie's gaoler, who would have Jeanie subvert the law and save her sister by swearing to an untruth:

> 'it's d—d hard, when three words of your mouth would give the girl the chance to nick Moll Blood [the gallows], that you make such scrupling about rapping to them. D—n me, if they would take me, if I would not rap to all whatd'yecallum's – Hyssop's Fables, for her life – I am us'd to't, b—t me, for less matters. Why, I have smacked calf-skin fifty times in England for a keg of brandy.' (p.245)

Thirdly, there is the way of faith, Jeanie's way as she undertakes a journey to the centre confident that there is mercy as well as justice in its law. 'Strongly persuaded that... she would be called upon, and directed, to work out her sister's deliverance' (p.211), Jeanie's faith in herself as an instrument of Providence gives her courage to exert her will and act. She goes to London not to deny the Union or to evade its laws, but to beg for mercy within the bounds of justice; not to have Effie declared innocent, but to have her pardoned. Her heart is great, and her faith simple in its conviction that predestination does not cancel out the free act of the faithful individual.

In the story of Jeanie's journey to the centre and its consequences, Scott makes outward and accessible the distance between the polarities which structure the thought of the puritan and the provincial. Jeanie's expedition is a real and (as Scott is careful to point out) in those days a dangerous enterprise; it is also a dramatic and sympathetic embodiment of the mind of the Calvinist elect. She travels in faith, and her instinctive literal-mindedness gives her confidence to act *within* her sense of predestination at a point when her father's comparative theological sophistication paralyses him under the law: 'My weird maun be fulfilled', she says, 'my life and my safety are in God's hands, but I'll not spare to risk either of them on the errand I am gaun to do' (p.142). It is finally this confidence which itself procures the pardon for her sister; the story of Jeanie's journey is therefore not about *whether* she will get there, but about the *process* of doing so, about the business of living in relation to what is already known.[42] It evades, through faith, the immobilising consequences of the paradox of freedom and predestination.

In most provincial fiction the journey itself becomes secondary to the provincial's account of life 'at' the centre. *The Heart of Midlothian* reverses these proportions and reverts to the strong, 'active' Calvinist position which finds the significance of living to lie not in the disclosure of the centre's mystery but in the striving of the elect soul in time. Scott is able to re-enact and to make available the puritan paradoxes through Jeanie's journey, without recourse to theological or (as in *Guy Mannering*) astrological terms which inhibit imaginative understanding.

Instead, Scott grasps the shape and the meaning of Jeanie's journey by association with Bunyan's *Pilgrim's Progress*. The way the analogy is first suggested and then drawn out is important for the conduct and credibility of the story; it points to an essential difference between Scott's and Melville's understandings of the relationship between the real and the ideal. For Scott, the ideal exists as an idea held in the realm of the real; it is not a *possible* other realm of existence, but a mental flexibility which enriches this life by viewing the immediate as a context rather than an absolute. The connection between Jeanie's journey to the centre and that of Bunyan's Christian is made not by Jeanie herself – this would be for her to entertain a sense of her own special importance which is quite alien to her self-denying mission – or by the narrator, which (as in *Redburn*) would tend to force an allegorical 'interpretation' onto her story. It comes instead by a chance appropriateness from within the story, in the wayward ramblings of the madwoman Madge Wildfire who dances attendance on the most treacherous parts of Jeanie's journey. 'And you shall be the woman Christiana, and I will be the maiden, Mercy – for ye ken Mercy was of the fairer countenance ... and if I had my little messan dog here, it would be Great-heart, their guide, ye ken' (p.358).

Once the association of their enterprise with Bunyan's tale has taken hold of Madge's wavering intellect, she grasps it with childlike enthusiasm as a game of make-believe. She is released from her miserable, demented condition for a few moments as she follows the play of her fancy into an imaginative world:

> Ye see, there was an auld carle wi' a bit land, and a gude clat o' siller besides, just the very picture of old Mr. Feeblemind or Mr. Ready-to-halt, that Great-heart delivered from Slaygood the giant, when he was rifling him and about to pick his bones, for Slaygood was of the nature of the flesh-eaters – and Great-heart killed Giant Despair too – but I am doubting Giant Despair's come alive again, for a' the story-book – I find him busy at my heart whiles.   (p.359)

The lyrical rhythms of her speech hold fast to the poignancy with which the fable haunts her disordered mind; as Madge is momentarily possessed by her idea, the prose rises to that imaginative compression which marks the moments of greatness in Scott. These lines give information about Madge's own history and its connection with Jeanie's condemned sister Effie; they also illuminate the nature of Jeanie's quest and touch the heart of loss and despair and faith in every life. But this is by no means allegory: the strands are not separable, and the story holds its own wisdom.

The imaginative leap by which Madge associates Jeanie's journey with Bunyan's fable seems to have been a moment of vision for Scott himself: it is as though her voice so possessed him that in writing himself into her character she took on momentarily an autonomous existence and surprised him by pointing the way forward for the story. Madge's inspired association works from this point both forwards and backwards on the text: earlier events such as the gaoler Ratcliffe's gift of a 'scart o' ... guse feather' to protect Jeanie 'if ye fall among thieves, my precious' (pp.293–4) and Jeanie's discovery of its protective power when her safety and chastity are threatened on the road by highwaymen, gain fresh resonance in this new context:

> 'You must follow us off the road, young woman,' said the taller.
> 'For the love of God!' exclaimed Jeanie, 'as you were born of woman, dinna ask me to leave the road! rather take all I have in the world.' (pp.338–9)

The deviation of Christian's companions from the right road leads one to '*Danger*', and the other to '*Destruction*', 'where he stumbled and fell, and rose no more'.[43]

It is not only the reader who, given the hint, reads retrospectively into the nature of Jeanie's journey; Scott too, seems to see it in a new light. From this point it becomes a series of trials which search the extent and the quality of her self-possessed faith. As in Bunyan's fable, the burden of selfish doubt is not what must be overcome and flung to the ground: like Christian, whose burden falls away at the beginning of his pilgrimage, Jeanie's faith is being tried in the context of the known – what is already determined. The sufferings of the journey are undergone and understood *in the presence of* the roll of assurance which each grasps along the way. Besides the overt battles (like those Christian fought with Apollyon and Giant Despair) there are the subtler temptations to take an easier path. Jeanie's most serious seduction from the road occurs when Effie's seducer Robertson/Staunton offers her the means to obtain her sister's pardon in an easy and infallible way: by delivering him up to punishment as the leader of the Porteous mob. It is a solution which, in addition to saving Effie, would afford Jeanie some measure of personal vengeance against the unprincipled rake who caused her sister's downfall. After rigorous self-inquiry, Jeanie finally resolves to put herself in God's hands (p.410). She will not usurp the role of Providence in condemning Staunton to the fate she believes he deserves. Passivity is not an element here: her submission is a strenuous subjugation of self-interest and self-importance, born of faith.

When Jeanie arrives at the centre she surprises her provincial Scottish relatives by refusing to be (like the Ayrshire Legatees, or Geoffrey Crayon, or Redburn) a sentimental tourist in London. She is quite uninterested in seeing the sights and learning the ways of the metropolis, and secludes herself in her lodgings to await the call which will accomplish her quest. London is to her only a Vanity Fair, and she is proof against all its allurements. Her journey to the centre is not that of the provincial who seeks to shed eccentricity; the quest itself and what it reveals of her faith impress the Duke of Argyle and the Queen, and gain her sister's pardon. Throughout the story, Jeanie's centre is not without – somewhere she might travel *to* – but within, in the faith which allows her to 'possess her soul in quiet' (p.482) at moments of crisis.

Jeanie's journey to London transposes her Calvinist distance from perfection from a theological or metaphysical to a literal, narrative framework, and thereby makes it susceptible to the appeal of what Hume calls 'common sense and experience' (*Dialogues*, p.135). Her response to being a 'foreigner in a strange country' is practical and conciliatory:

> Hitherto she had been either among her own country-folk, or those to whom her bare feet and tartan screen were objects too familiar to attract much attention. But as she advanced, she perceived that both circumstances exposed her to sarcasm and taunts, which she might otherwise have escaped; and although in her heart she thought it unkind, and inhospitable, to sneer at a passing stranger on account of the fashion of her attire, yet she had the good sense to alter those parts of her dress which attracted ill-natured observation.
> (p.322)

Davie Deans (like his Cameronian ancestors), or the antinomian Robert Wringhim in Hogg's *Confessions*, would have delighted in the martyrdom of being different and would deliberately have drawn down the taunts of strangers to prove his own election. Hawthorne shows Hester Prynne, too, succumbing to the seductive dangers of opposition and exclusion, and James' Olive Chancellor eagerly embraces her sense of her own difference in *The Bostonians* (1886). But Scott suggests that true election is less self-regarding. Like Melville's Redburn, who learns to feel with rather than against the crew of strangers on the *Highlander* and so doing finds that they are not strangers after all, Jeanie Deans, by not insisting on her status as 'a stranger in a strange land', does away with the polarised opposition of province and centre. Her confidence in travelling the distance which separates them assures Jeanie of a spiritual home first in the Arcadia of Roseneath and eventually in heaven.

The Heart of Midlothian turns dogma into story. By lending solidity to intensely intellected Calvinist theology, the story shows how the doctrine can be lived and how ideas about predestination and reprobation may be located in the psychology of the self and in the relationship between past and present. The genius of Scott's appropriation of *The Pilgrim's Progress* for his puritan–provincial fable lies in Bunyan's vital human conversion of Calvin's doctrine through narrative. Here, first, is dogma, then story:

> Though purged by [Christ's] sanctification, we are still beset by many vices and much weakness, so long as we are enclosed in the prison of the body. Thus it is, that placed at a great distance from perfection, we must always be endeavouring to make some progress, and daily struggling with the evil by which we are entangled. (Calvin)

> ... and behold at a great distance he saw a most pleasant Mountainous Country, beautified with Woods, Vinyards, fruits of all sorts ... so far as this Valley reached, there was on the right hand a very deep Ditch ... The pathway was here also exceeding narrow, and therefore good Christian was the more put to it; for when he sought in the dark to shun the ditch on the one hand, he was ready to tip over into the mire on the other; also when he sought to escape the mire, without great carefulness he would be ready to fall into the ditch. Thus he went on, and I heard him here sigh bitterly: for ... the path way was here so dark, that oft times when he lift up his foot to set forward, he knew not where, or upon what he should set it next. (Bunyan)[44]

The Heart of Midlothian is a great work of art because Scott has found in the conduct of his story a literary equivalent for the religious faith which is its subject. This is not a matter which concerns Scott's personal beliefs (although all his writing is informed by a faith that 'province' and 'centre' are not opposed and incompatible, and that the word of one may successfully be 'read' by the other), but it does suggest the powerful continuum between Scott's puritan–provincial heritage and his narrative art. What Lionel Trilling describes as the source of the 'literary ideas' of Hawthorne and Melville is appropriate to Scott too:

> religion in its decline leaves a detritus of pieties, of strong assumptions, which afford a particularly fortunate condition for certain kinds of literature; these pieties carry a strong charge of intellect, or perhaps it would be more accurate to say that they tend to stimulate the mind in a powerful way. ...
>
> Hawthorne and Melville, for example, lived at a time when religion was in decline and they were not drawn to support it. But from religion they inherited a body of pieties, a body of issues, if you will, which engaged their hearts and their minds to the very bottom.[45]

If we add to this Kenneth Clark's description of the kind of provincial art in which 'the associations which give the work its poignancy are not hidden within the form, but openly confessed', it is possible to approach the convergence of the narrative and the lyrical in the provincial fiction of Scotland and America with an understanding of their shared puritan impetus.

The terms of the translation from a puritan–provincial mentality to an art which can comprehend that state in *The Heart of Midlothian* may be observed through one of Scott's own narrative *personae*. In chapter 1 of *The Bride of Lammermoor* (1819), the painter Dick Tinto describes

> that instant and vivid flash of conviction, which darts on the mind from seeing the happy and expressive combinations of a single scene, and which gathers from the position, attitude, and countenance of the moment, not only the history of the past lives of the personages represented, and the nature of the business on which they are immediately engaged, but lifts even the veil of futurity, and affords a shrewd guess at their future fortunes.[46]

It is a secular account of the critical pivot of Calvinist theology: that moment of conversion which gives meaning to the puritan's life and structures his spiritual autobiography. In Dick Tinto's terms, story-telling itself is an act of faith: faith in the effective relations of past, present and future, faith in the moment of vision which can reveal these relations and faith in their communicability from author to reader. The temporal extension which flows backwards and forwards from the moment's 'instant and vivid flash of conviction' is an act of historical imagination which perceives time in vital relation to the timeless. When Madge Wildfire grasps the magical dimension to Jeanie's quest, her moment of imaginative vision depends crucially for its effects on the solidity of the ground-bass, on Scott's prior success in persuading the reader of the temporal reality of the journey. These concentrative moments are timeless and placeless; they belong to a realm which suppresses causality and in which the hunger for explanation is assuaged.

At such moments the language takes on a stylised eloquence which bestows a luminous otherness upon the realistic facts of the story. These are the rhythms of fairy-tale and ballad, an impersonal space occupied by such other moments in Scott as Meg Merrilees' denunciation of Ellangown in *Guy Mannering*, or by Wandering Willie's Tale in *Redgauntlet*. Madge Wildfire's fitful hold on the fabulous element in Jeanie's journey bears the same sort of relationship to that journey as Wandering Willie's fable of the Redgauntlet family does to Darsie Latimer's search for his origins: both open the door to another world in a 'moment of vision' which possesses the subject and its meaning in unity. At the climax of the book Jeanie's address to the Queen, who has power to grant a pardon, rises to the eloquent impersonality which her prosaic character has hitherto shunned and discloses that critical intersection of time and timelessness which inspires the Calvinist faith:

> Oh, madam, if ever ye kend what it was to sorrow for and with a sinning and a suffering creature, whose mind is sae tossed that she can be neither ca'd fit to live or die, have some compassion on our misery! – Save an honest house from dishonour, and an unhappy girl, not eighteen years of age, from an early and dreadful death! Alas! it is not when we sleep soft and wake merrily ourselves that we think on other people's sufferings. Our hearts are waxed light within us then, and we are for righting our ain wrangs and fighting our ain battles. But when the hour of trouble comes to the mind or to the body – and seldom may it visit your Leddyship – and when the hour of death comes, that comes to high and low – lang and late may it be yours! – Oh, my Leddy, then it isna what we hae dune for oursells, but what we hae dune for others, that we think on maist pleasantly. And the thoughts that ye hae intervened to spare the puir thing's life will be sweeter in that hour, come when it may, than if a word of your mouth could hang the haill Porteous mob at the tail of ae tow.
>
> (p.451)

This focusing of the narrative into a moment of conviction, in which the workaday prose of the story gathers itself to a ballad-like compression, brings the temporal narrative into relation with the timeless lyric vision. The relation is, crucially, a literary one. T.S. Eliot, writing of Marvell's poetry, says 'suggestiveness is the aura around a bright clear centre ... you cannot have the aura alone'.[47] The 'bright clear centre' of *The Heart of Midlothian* is the story of Jeanie and Effie Deans, a story which keeps its own counsel and is, finally, uninterpretable. The 'suggestiveness' belongs to the stylistic concentration which allows the mind to expand beyond the narrative's concern with historical understanding, with explanations and with facts. The whole episode of Jeanie's relationship with the Duke of Argyle and her interview with the Queen belongs to the magical world. The Duke is a fairy prince who arranges everything with an infinite and benevolent power: 'With the third morning came the expected coach, with four servants clustered behind on the foot-board, in dark brown and yellow liveries; the Duke in person, with laced coat, gold-headed cane, star and garter, all, as the story-book says, very grand' (p.463). With its mixture of detailed description and time-honoured formulae, this is a world like that of Cinderella, with its own wondrous logic. It is a realm where the relation of cause and effect no longer creates anxiety, a realm of faith where the truth is known because it is believed in. The comfortingly fabulous aura of the Duke makes him precisely not a manipulative *deus ex machina* from beyond the fiction, unlike the absent presence of 'Harper', who at once sustained the plot and flawed the inner logic of Cooper's *The Spy*.

The timeless, eternal view is always in Scott's work understood in relation to time. In her plea to absolute authority that justice be combined with mercy, Jeanie's language itself achieves the 'centrality' which comes from the heart of her experience. But this, which is 'truth' for Jeanie, is not universal; to read it so would be to sentimentalise a scene which Scott deliberately gives a comic edge. The Queen treats Jeanie's truth as a rhetorical performance and rewards her with the favour of a needle-case. When it is set against the worldly considerations of court politics, Jeanie's view is evidently virtuous, but it is also simplistic. The answer to the question of whether the granting of Effie's pardon belongs to Providence or to politics depends, strictly speaking, upon point of view: if Jeanie's view finally carries conviction with the reader, it does so by virtue of the firmly comic understanding which roots it in the finite and the fallible. Scott, like Hume, is able both to confer reality on the whole range of human experience and to grant its provisionality without undermining its authenticity.

Of all the Scottish and American writers, Hawthorne is the most deeply steeped in the history and theology of puritanism. Its presence in his work is a critical commonplace, and little is to be gained by enumerating examples of his grasp of the puritan mind. In the single character of Dimmesdale, Hawthorne illustrates most of the attitudes described in chapter 1: it is a great achievement of historical imagination not merely to have given body to Calvinist doctrine, but, as he has in Dimmesdale, to see it as an expression of enduring states of the human soul. It is this that makes Hawthorne's work more than ordinarily hospitable to psychoanalytic reading. But Hawthorne's literary achievement, as the artist of puritanism, lies elsewhere. If Scott renders the puritan–provincial mind narratively, through a Shakespearian sympathy for the poignancy of its associations as these continued to operate in nineteenth-century Scotland, Hawthorne renders it lyrically, with a purity of intention and intensity of focus which makes it, for the time, inescapable. More than any other novel, it shows from the inside how the world looks to the Calvinist. Thus inwardly realised, the journey to the centre becomes a physical, metaphorical and metaphysical image of relationship between seventeenth-century puritan Boston and the experience of nineteenth-century provincial America.

Like *The Heart of Midlothian*, *The Scarlet Letter* considers the fundamental Calvinist situation: the breaking of a law and its apparently irrevocable consequences. Both novels, like Calvinism itself, pass immediately from a declaration of irrevocability to consider the possibilities for free will and action. To live as a Calvinist is to find oneself continually at the intersection of the temporal and the eternal: this is the plight which Hawthorne's story enacts in events while his style impresses it upon words. The scene near the beginning of the book where Hester Prynne displays the symbols of her adultery – the scarlet 'A', and its 'living hieroglyphic' the baby Pearl – publicly at the scaffold is such a moment as Scott describes, in which the reader is offered both the 'past lives of the personages represented' and a glimpse into futurity.[48] To Hester herself, it seems as though her life inevitably leads up to and away from this moment: 'the scaffold of the pillory was a point of view that revealed to Hester Prynne the entire track along which she had been treading, since her happy infancy' (p.58). The repetition of a scene on this spot at the centre of the book and again at its climax – each time involving the central triangle of characters – gives the reader, too, something of this sense of focused inevitability which persuades Hester 'that her whole orb of life, both before and after, was connected with this spot, as with the one point that gave it unity' (p.244).

But already, at the moment she acknowledges her fate, Hester struggles to adjust herself to the known and to declare a measure of freedom in the context of the inevitable. The beadle who executes the force of the law leads her out from confinement into the public glare, 'until, on the threshold of the prison-door, she repelled him, by an action marked with natural dignity and force of character, and stepped into the open air, as if by her own free-will' (p.52). The 'as if' renders the freedom of Hester's action not illusory, but provisional; for both spectators and reader her gesture turns the moment from a prepared spectacle set up by authority to a dramatic action – but an action which takes place in instant relation to the absolute.

For the Calvinist, the Law of the Old Testament is absolute: Justice decrees that all are damned in Adam's Fall. Mercy (the salvation of a few), which is taught by the New Testament, is found only in relation to the absolute Law of the Old. In *The Heart of Midlothian*, 'law' is of and from the 'centre'; in *The Scarlet Letter*, law *is* the centre, but the central *event*, the 'original sin' which called into being the judgement of the law, is absent from the narrative. *The Scarlet Letter* is in this sense a completely predetermined story. It is the perfect narrative of the condition of postlapsarian Calvinist existence analysed by Edwards and Hume: all consequence, all reaction against an action inaccessibly beyond the confines of the plot. In the absence of the experience, its significance can only be projected backwards on different unverifiable assumptions.

Amongst the puritans, Hawthorne tells us, 'religion and law were almost identical', and Hester is condemned by both 'the Scripture and the statute-book' (pp.50, 52). Hester, like Adam, broke the law, and in so doing she forfeited her freedom and has justly deserved her damnation. Has she been granted mercy? Already the book involves the reader in puritan modes of perception and interpretation: in the scaffold scene the onlookers take it for granted that the Scarlet 'A' is the visible emblem of Hester's reprobation and rejoice in the righteousness of the community which has brought it to light; but the narrator suggests another perspective on the spectacle which would enjoin a very different reading:

> Had there been a Papist among the crowd of Puritans, he might have seen in this beautiful woman, so picturesque in her attire and mien, and with the infant at her bosom, an object to remind him of the image of Divine Maternity, which so many illustrious painters have vied with one another to represent; something which should remind him, indeed, but only by contrast, of that sacred image of sinless motherhood, whose infant was to redeem the world.
>
> (p.56)

The purpose of this 'alternative possibility' is not merely to suggest that point of view may not be absolute and that the puritans may be in error to assume that their interpretation is necessarily the right one.[49] More than this, it enforces the presumption that Hester's status is not immediately available to perception but must be interpreted from visual, secondary and consequential evidence which may confuse or mislead. In the absence of the event itself (the original scene in the forest), the reader is denied the vital evidence which alone could guarantee proper judgement of its significance.

To ask such questions of the book as 'Is Hester damned?' (as Hawthorne surely means us to in chapters like 'Hester at her Needle' and 'Another view of Hester') is to become aware that one is reading the book as a puritan would 'read' life – as a crucial epistemological investigation of the truth behind the contradictory clues manifest to perception. 'Hester at her Needle' is a marvellous psychological portrayal of the dreary business of continuing life under sentence of the law after the sustaining moment of crisis has passed. It is Hawthorne's picture of the time when puritan certainties have become provincial doubts: is her distance and alienation from the centre of the community a sign of reprobation or of superior virtue? The free thoughts which her exclusion from the centre fosters may mark either salvation or downfall. Again, these are 'signs' whereby Hester's state may be inferred, not causes of that state, and the burden of interpretation is placed on the reader.

Hawthorne's rendering of the tortured unease of Hester's mind in these chapters has a subtlety and a flexibility matched only in the self-revelations of Browning's dramatic monologues or Pope's 'Eloisa to Abelard'. The dramatic situation of the latter is very similar, but comparison reveals both how differently (and in 'central' terms how *peculiarly*) Hawthorne makes us read, and how much finer a sense his reticence gives to the quality of a woman's mind. Eloisa's monologue proceeds in complete collusion with the reader, who identifies at once the emotional stage of pent-up passion upon which her fantasies are projected, and (knowing that their enactment can never be more than verbal) connives at their extravagant expression. 'Reality' preserves its chastity. 'Connives' seems the appropriate word for the quality of the reader's participation in her pain, for the self-indulgence with which she stokes it becomes the reader's when we take the innuendo of her desire to 'Pant on thy lip, and to thy heart be prest; / Give all thou canst – and let me dream the rest' for wit.[50] The fluctuations of her desires towards a carnal and a heavenly consummation are brilliantly rendered as the conflicting pulls which put a soul in torment, but, despite the language, there is very little that is religious about this anguish and nothing that leaves the reader wondering. Eloisa's extravagance is complete, and Pope's command of her state perfect – because it is conceived entirely in emotional rather than ontological terms. Thus the questions she puts are rhetorical not real, evidence of passionate instability not religious doubt:

> Ah wretch! believed the spouse of God in vain,
> Confess'd within the slave of love and man.
> Assist me heav'n! but whence arose that pray'r?
> Sprung it from piety, or from despair?
> Ev'n here, where frozen chastity retires,
> Love finds an altar for forbidden fires.   (lines 177–82)

When Hester Prynne feels the stirrings of the scarlet letter within her in response to something without, the questions are real and full of theological significance for herself and others:

> She shuddered to believe, yet could not help believing, that it gave her a sympathetic knowledge of the hidden sin in other hearts. She was terror-stricken by the revelations that were thus made. What were they? Could they be other than the insidious whispers of the bad angel, who would fain have persuaded the struggling woman, as yet only half his victim, that the outward guise of purity was but a lie, and that, if truth were everywhere to be shown, a scarlet letter would blaze forth on many a bosom besides Hester Prynne's? Or, must she receive those intimations – so obscure, yet so distinct – as truth?
> (p.86)

It is not merely that Hester is uncertain – really uncertain, where Eloisa is ambivalent – about the source of her feeling, but that each possibility requires to be interpreted, for each would 'mean' something very different about her own state and that of others. Either way, she risks following the footsteps of Young Goodman Brown into the forest.

Hawthorne at once suggests that the reader make the interpretative choice and that this be a conscious decision: the wry comment about Hester's shock at the 'irreverent inopportuneness' of her sensations of sympathy makes us aware of the puritan–provincial thought processes, but it does not transcend or circumvent them. The impeccable Calvinism of the 'moralising' interpretation of Hester's dilemma – 'Such loss of faith is ever one of the saddest results of sin' (that is, Hester is damned) – is immediately rendered uncertain again in the sequel: 'Be it accepted as a proof that all was not corrupt in this poor victim of her own frailty, and man's hard law, that Hester Prynne yet struggled to believe that no fellow mortal was guilty like herself' (that is, Hester may yet be saved; p.87). The whole episode is rendered as opaque and as pregnant of meaning as the centre observed from the province, or the world through corrupted perception. The state of mind of the reader – doubting, anxious, compulsively interrogating the words – is by this stage a good replica of the Calvinist consciousness.

Hawthorne's mode of presenting his characters corresponds in each case to the aspect of the puritan–provincial mind which they embody: that is, he describes each character's responses in such a way as to make the reader read these events as that character would 'read' life.[51] This is the highest form of the ventriloquism which allowed Galt and Lockhart, in their mimicry of the Calvinist rhetoric, to suggest what it might be like to see the world from the point of view of the 'pilgrim and stranger', ever distanced from and searching out the centre. Hawthorne's technique is immeasurably subtler, but his understanding of the puritan–provincial viewpoint is not essentially different. Hester's impulse is (like Jeanie Deans') to search out a route for free will within the absolute of predestination, and her 'journey to the centre' involves looking for mercy to temper justice. The reader is teased by the paradoxical combination of knowledge and possibility in her presentation – the *knowledge* that she has sinned (and sins again, in her mind) in a world where 'an evil deed invests itself with the character of doom' (p.211) – and the *possibility* that she is none the less saved, or may even save herself, by her acts of charity and mercy. Hester's scarlet letter is her 'burden' (p.79) as a pilgrim; it is (like Redburn's) both what isolates her, 'taking her out of the ordinary relations of humanity' (p.54), and what relates her to the community. Acknowledging it, as Dimmesdale fails to acknowledge his, turns the 'A' from Hester's burden to her roll of assurance. By it she is known and has a place, and 'had she fallen among thieves, it would have kept her safe' (p.163). Like Bunyan's Christian struggling on after his burden had dropped away, and Jeanie Deans' refusing to abandon her pilgrimage for the easily won prize of Staunton's surrender, Hester voluntarily reassumes the scarlet letter when others no longer require it of her. She is, then, the puritan as pilgrim, looking for mercy as well as justice at the centre, and finding it in the assumption of her place in time.

There is, however, no final endorsement of Hester's viewpoint, and it is directly contradicted by those of Chillingworth and Dimmesdale. Chillingworth is an absolute determinist who refuses to countenance anything but original causes and fatal consequences: 'by thy first step awry,' he tells Hester, 'thou didst plant the germ of evil; but, since that moment, it has all been a dark necessity . . . It is our fate. Let the black flower blossom as it may!' (p.174). Fatalism robs Chillingworth of the dimension of human possibility; he becomes a caricatured 'black man' who creeps ominously through the book gathering poisonous herbs and prying into the sacred mysteries of the human heart. He has no 'character', only function, and withers away when that function is fulfilled. The gothic language which describes Chillingworth shows (like Scott's Staunton) his functional nature; he is not however as Staunton is a device of the plot, designed to cast a clearer light on the qualities of the heroine, but an evocation of a means of perception and a way of reading.

Chillingworth is the obsessively truth-seeking puritan–provincial whose quest and whose fall concerned chapter 4; the parts of *The Scarlet Letter* which concern his story read like the lurid spiritual allegories of Edgar Huntly and Robert Wringhim. The motions of mind which Hawthorne reveals in Hester have in Chillingworth all been allegorised away into outward manifestations which make 'the state of the soul' into something abstract, universal and impersonal. Such is his sojourn among the Indians of the wilderness, for example, which locates the nightmares of his psyche in the alienated world of *Edgar Huntly*; as is the 'light which glimmered out of [his] eyes . . . like the reflection of a furnace, or, let us say, like one of those gleams of ghastly fire that darted from Bunyan's awful door-way in the hill-side, and quivered on the pilgrim's face' (p.129). Like Hester, he is a 'stranger' (p.61) in the world, a 'wanderer, and isolated from human interests' (p.76), but he is on no pilgrimage. His 'centre' is an inexorable nemesis, never to be approached, never to be put to the question. His is a world exaggerated, deformed, full of grim and secretive purpose: life as it appears to the alienated imagination. The interpretative passion overwhelms every other consideration in his life: 'Were it only for the art's sake, I must search this matter to the bottom' (p.138); in 'reading' *him* we search to know his meaning, not his identity.

Dimmesdale is the puritan as artist whose words (though we do not hear them) have power to move by their spiritual import. He, the holy preacher and tortured sinner, belongs with the pages of Jonathan Edwards' *Personal Narrative* and the hell-fire sermons of the orthodox Calvinist divines. His world is centred in self, and distorts perception with its monstrously self-abnegating egotism:

> But what shall we say, when an individual discovers a revelation, addressed to himself alone, on the same vast sheet of record! In such a case, it could only be

the symptom of a highly disordered mental state, when a man, rendered morbidly self-contemplative by long, intense, and secret pain, had extended his egotism over the whole expanse of nature, until the firmament itself should appear no more than a fitting page for his soul's history and fate. (p.155)

This is Hawthorne the historian of puritanism describing one manifestation of the puritan consciousness; his artistic success is to make the reader acquiesce in the inevitability of this point of view and its reality as an emotional state. The questions that arise with Dimmesdale are not of the same type as those which perplex the reader with Hester or with Chillingworth: to wonder, as we find ourselves doing, whether Dimmesdale 'really' has the 'A' branded on his breast is to ask a question of the same kind as whether Donatello in *The Marble Faun* really has furry ears. In the latter case, the question arises inopportunely and against the grain of the book: Hawthorne's method has betrayed itself here to the point where it is possible to suspect *him* of being a puritan–provincial symboliser. The same question asked of Dimmesdale is not inappropriate, because Hawthorne presents him so that the reader comes to expect that *if* he is guilty his sin *will* manifest itself visibly and that the disjunction between appearance and reality must make itself known.

Dimmesdale, like Chillingworth, seeks the absolute. Where Chillingworth denies his identity to search for the truth in a centre beyond himself, Dimmesdale seeks to expose the centre of truth within himself, to relieve it of its disguises of unreality. Dimmesdale also has no character, no illusion of freedom; his whole being is focused into the tortured conscience which renders everything beyond itself insubstantial and spectral. He is the victim of his own unreality, and his mind (like the spy's) is a theatre or stage upon which the showman Chillingworth can introduce his masquerade:

> He became, thenceforth, not a spectator only, but a chief actor, in the poor minister's interior world. He could play upon him as he chose. Would he arouse him with a throb of agony? The victim was for ever on the rack; it needed only to know the spring that controlled the engine; – and the physician knew it well! Would he startle him with sudden fear? As at the waving of a magician's wand, uprose a grisly phantom, – uprose a thousand phantoms, – in many shapes of death, or more awful shame, all flocking round-about the clergyman, and pointing with their fingers at his breast! (p.140)

Pearl has at once the most fully interpretable, the most clearly 'symbolic' existence in the book and the most complete otherness. Hester's question to her, 'Child, what art thou?' produces an answer which has all the pellucid opacity of the pearl itself: '"O, I am your little Pearl!" answered the child' (p.97). In her complete visual identification with the predestinating scarlet letter, Pearl paradoxically becomes human possibility incarnate, and the most perfectly realised child in

American literature before *Huckleberry Finn*.[52] She resists every attempt to capture, tame or impose meaning upon her, and finally evades the puritan nexus entirely by making the journey to Europe.

Hester's journey, on the other hand, is a more complex emblem of her religious status and of the book's purpose. Unlike Pearl, who is constantly at war with the restrictive community of her upbringing, Hester refuses the confrontation and conflict which characteristically justify puritan action; 'she never battled with the public, but submitted uncomplainingly to its worst usage' (p.160). Her rebellion is inward, insidious, highly dangerous to puritan Law and, possibly, to her own soul. It takes her into treacherous regions across the gulf of ocean which separates the dogmatic certainties of the new world from the sinful liberties of the old: 'she assumed a freedom of speculation, then common enough on the other side of the Atlantic, but which our forefathers, had they known of it, would have held to be a deadlier crime than that stigmatized by the scarlet letter' (p.164). Hester's 'errand into the wilderness' is, like Jeanie Deans' journey to London, at once a real, a spiritual and a metaphorical one.

However, despite Hawthorne's association of Hester with Bunyan's pilgrim, hers is not altogether the pilgrimage of the faithful soul whose ultimate goal is assured, but – as she voyages in her mind beyond the permitted boundaries of puritan thought – is also a venturing into the treacherous freedoms of unlicensed territory, with all its attendant risks of 'shipwreck' on the 'rock [of doubt], which is fatal to every one who strikes upon it' (Calvin, *Institutes*, II, 243). Hester

> wandered without a clew in the dark labyrinth of mind; now turned aside by an insurmountable precipice; now starting back from a deep chasm. There was wild and ghastly scenery all around her, and a home and comfort nowhere. At times, a fearful doubt strove to possess her soul . . . (p.166)

This is perhaps what led Hawthorne to describe *The Scarlet Letter* to his friend Horatio Bridge as 'positively a h—ll-fired story'.[53] In Hester's 'journey' Hawthorne brings into dramatic juxtaposition the spiritual autobiography and the 'unholy' voyage of speculation into forbidden waters. This equivocal combination of quests turns out to be Hester's story: a sanctioned pilgrimage and an unlawful passage co-ordinate her life as an uninterpretable compound of conflicting significances:

> It was as if a new birth, with stronger assimilations than the first, had converted the forest-land, still so uncongenial to every other pilgrim and wanderer, into Hester Prynne's wild and dreary, but life-long home. All other scenes of earth – even that village of rural England, where happy infancy and stainless maidenhood seemed yet to be in her mother's keeping, like garments put off long ago – were foreign to her, in comparison. (p.80)

The imagery extends to all Calvinist perception, finally to return again to a truth which is fuller than the psychoanalytic insight. It is the unknown-ness of what is 'at' the centre itself which renders the journey equivocal. The triumphant inwardness of Hawthorne's analysis of Hester exposes an awful imaginative truth: the Calvinist quest for unity with the divine heart of things (the sanctified spiritual autobiography) may not, finally, be absolutely distinguishable from the forbidden voyage in pursuit of unlawful knowledge.[54]

One of the fruits of Hester's inner voyage is her resolution to rescue Dimmesdale from his spiritual paralysis in the puritan–provincial state of self-alienation and distance from grace. To this end she acts, like Jeanie Deans, to reclaim a lost companion, and her journey into the wilderness takes on a physical dimension in 'A Forest Walk':

> The road . . . was no other than a footpath. It straggled onward into the mystery of the primeval forest. This hemmed it in so narrowly, and stood so black and dense on either side, and disclosed such imperfect glimpses of the sky above, that, to Hester's mind, it imaged not amiss the moral wilderness in which she had so long been wandering. (p.183)

There she accosts Dimmesdale, whose 'pathway through life was haunted . . . by a spectre that had stolen out from among his thoughts' (p.189), and tries to persuade him to venture out upon the historical, geographical and spiritual journey to freedom:

> 'Doth the universe lie within the compass of yonder town, which only a little time ago was but a leaf-strewn desert, as lonely as this around us? Whither leads yonder forest-track? Backward to the settlement, thou sayest! Yes; but onward, too! Deeper it goes, and deeper, into the wilderness, less plainly to be seen at every step; until, some few miles hence, the yellow leaves will show no vestige of the white man's tread. There thou art free! So brief a journey would bring thee from a world where thou hast been most wretched, to one where thou mayest still be happy! . . . Then there is the broad pathway of the sea! It brought thee hither. If thou so choose, it will bear thee back again. In our native land, whether in some remoted rural village or in vast London . . . in pleasant Italy, – thou wouldst be beyond his power and knowledge! And what hast thou to do with all these iron men, and their opinions? They have kept thy better part in bondage too long already!' (p.197)

It is the voyage to the centre which had seemed to Redburn to promise so much.

Hester, whose spirit is not in bondage to the past and who has her 'home, as it were, in desert places, where she roamed as freely as the wild Indian in his woods' (p.199), can make the prospect of this journey (which can only ever be a dream for Dimmesdale) into a reality. After Dimmesdale's death she voyages abroad with Pearl, and news of her returns, as from a shipwreck, 'like a shapeless piece of driftwood tost ashore, with the initials of a name upon it' (p.261). But, like these other voyagers in search of the centre, the Ayrshire Legatees, Geoffrey Crayon, Valerius, Redburn, Hilda and Kenyon, Hester returns to take up her burden and find her 'centre' not in a place to go *to*, but in a mode of being, in her accustomed way of life at the edge of the forest. Messages come to her here from afar, to indicate that she is 'the object of love and interest with some inhabitant of another land' (p.262). Pearl, the 'living hieroglyphic' and consequence of the original, displaced meaning of the tale, has become the symbolic though absent centre of the book's significance. Her personification of the scarlet letter takes on the heraldic mysteries of the old world, the 'armorial seals' and bearings which so puzzled Amasa Delano in 'Benito Cereno'.

But Hester's distance from the centre of such significance does not render her life shadowy or spectral:

> there was more real life for [her] here, in New England, than in that unknown region where Pearl had found a home. Here had been her sin; here, her sorrow; and here was yet to be her penitence. She had returned, therefore, and resumed, – of her own free will, for not the sternest magistrate of that iron period would have imposed it, – resumed the symbol of which we have related so dark a tale. (p.263)

Taking up thus the burden of her life in time, Hester becomes an object of veneration, comfort and counsel. Like Jeanie Deans she refuses the status of the puritan 'saint' and (unlike Goodman Brown) accepts her complicity with imperfect, stained humanity. 'Earlier in life, Hester had vainly imagined that she herself might be the destined prophetess, but had long since recognized the impossibility that any mission of divine and mysterious truth should be confided to a woman stained with sin, bowed down with shame or even burdened with a life-long sorrow' (p.263).

All the characters search through Pearl for the meaning of the central symbol around which their minds revolve. The scarlet letter itself is the known, its absolute truth is the inheritance which they seek at the centre. It is both temporal (in Pearl) and timeless (in the letter which is the mark of the Law), and the search involves not only the puritan characters but the provincial narrator of the Custom House Preface and his assumed audience:

> My eyes fastened themselves upon the old scarlet letter, and would not be turned aside. Certainly, there was some deep meaning in it, most worthy of interpretation, and which, as it were, streamed forth from the mystic symbol, subtly communicating itself to my sensibilities, but evading the analysis of my mind. (p.31)

The 'deep meaning' dimly discerned by the Surveyor never does emerge: the romance moves to enforce the opacity of the scarlet letter, until on the last page it gleams forth as a symbol only of its own symbolic-ness. It does not finally matter *what* the 'deep meaning' was: it is enough that the story of the letter establishes a vital connection between past and present. There is no doubt, though, that something *did* take place in the forest, and that Pearl and the scarlet 'A' are real consequences. Hester Prynne is the one figure in all of Hawthorne's work who has, unequivocally, been touched by experience, and has been brought to recognise a reality beyond herself. Her journey — towards others, or away from them, into the realms of speculation — is her 'centre': both the image of her destiny and the process of its enactment.

The multiplicity of viewpoints distances the reader, like the puritan–provincial, from a 'central' meaning: the central voice is absent from the narrative. *The Scarlet Letter* points out the error which is the source of the 'Main-street' showman's frustration: there *is* no 'proper point of view' from which the present can view the past to make it yield up its 'centre', or absolute meaning. The experience of that past is as completely inaccessible as the unregenerate Calvinist feels God to be. Time, like the Fall, introduces an inevitable distance between 'now' and 'then'; it is a barrier to certain knowledge. But *The Scarlet Letter* does not rest in disjunction and distance; it is a truly historical novel in the possibilities it offers for *relationship* between present and past. If we cannot 'know' it, it is nonetheless possible to establish a point of view which will link present experience to observation of the past. The line of relationship will not be a rigorous chain of cause and effect, but a sense of continuity which does not trap the contingent within the absolutes of historical determinism. Jeanie Deans and Hester Prynne search for a way of living in relation to the absolute Law which confronts them in its completeness. The historical imaginations of Scott and Hawthorne suggest how the reader of *The Heart of Midlothian* and *The Scarlet Letter* may establish a relationship with the absolute pastness of the past.

The scepticism which views all these realities as provisional is not what Hume would call 'pyrrhonism'; it does not deny the existence of reality as such, but rather suggests (as Hume does himself) that reality *as it may be perceived* is dependent on point of view. As Hester comes to recognise, knowledge of truth is tied to the limits of vision; the universal and absolute are not present to perception or livable in time. Like Hume's, Hawthorne's writing suggests not the relativity but the provisionality of every point of view. Like Scott, he gives the provisional viewpoint solidity, and meaning, by localising it in time and place. By showing that it is in time that the timeless is glimpsed, that the covenant of meaning may only operate when perception is held in its surroundings, Scott and

Hawthorne engage imaginative realms beyond the confines of the known without casting off to the treacherous free-floating language of *Mardi*. It is a shared characteristic of their writing to perceive temporal and eternal not as disjunct planes, but as different aspects of a single continuum.

Calvinism is a religion of absolutes, of crises, of 'moments' such as that experienced by Hester in her first vigil at the scaffold or the glorious persecution of the Covenanters which defines all Davie Deans' subsequent responses. The problem for the second and all subsequent moments and generations (as shown in Hester's dreary life as the wearer of the scarlet letter, and by Jeanie and Effie Deans who inherit the covenanting burden) is to find a way of continuing in relation to a crisis which has passed. The greater the distance from the 'centre' of the crisis, the more its solidity of significance tends to dissolve into myriad interpretative possibilities.

The Calvinist lives in relation to the inscrutable, omnipotent Divine will, with every action a sign of meaning on a different plane of apprehension; provincials define themselves in relation to a distant, inaccessible and absolute centre. To 'live in an absolute relation to the absolute' is to place oneself beyond the realm of criticism or of art. The provincial writer attempts to find a perspective in which the alternative to the inaccessible absolute (the possession of one exclusive truth, held to in the uniqueness of the critical moment) is not the moral defeat represented by relativism. Chapter 4 considered the puritan–provincial's compulsive pursuit of absolute knowledge; chapter 5 examined the world-dissolving consequences of relativism. This chapter has looked at how the provincial's isolation and sense of distance from meaning may be used to evolve the relation between provincial and puritan predicaments. The story of the faithful pilgrim's journey towards his or her inheritance establishes in the surpassing versions of Scott and Hawthorne a point of view which commands assent but does not claim exclusivity. Their art refuses both the relative and the transcendent, but finds instead confidence to exist in relation to the finite. It 'solidifies' experience in terms of history, not of eternity. Hawthorne and Scott have very different imaginative grasps of the puritan perceptions of Bunyan's *Pilgrim's Progress*, but both derive from his narrative a similar solidity of temporal relation which acts as an analogy for the continuity of finite and eternal. Their confidence reaches back towards earlier certainties; Melville, in both his strengths and weaknesses, is a more 'modern' writer than either: his writing finally lacks faith in the provisional stances from which the mind is able to hold the claims of the world in tension with its own. As Hawthorne's Custom House Preface puts it, 'thoughts are frozen and utterance benumbed, unless the speaker stand in some true relation with his audience' (p.4).

St Augustine, as he wrote to dispute the absoluteness of Rome's claim to centrality, established the utter separateness of the Eternal City from the finite one. The inhabitant of the 'centre' in heaven, he says, can only be in the relation of 'pilgrim and stranger' to the temporal city on earth. Alienated provincials think of the centre as a place from which they are excluded and to which their existence is peripheral. But the centre is finally, as *The Heart of Midlothian* and *The Scarlet Letter* show, not a place to go *to*, but a mode of being. The self finds its own centre not within itself (as Dimmesdale, for example, does), or in a place beyond itself (Rome, or London), but in the process of living. Curiously enough, one of the most explicit statements of this principle of centrality is to be found in Poe's uniquely *in*human 'cosmic poem', *Eureka* (1849), itself a compendium of puritan–provincial postures:

> Each atom, forming one of a generally uniform globe of atoms, finds more atoms in the direction of the centre, of course, than in any other, and in that direction, therefore, is impelled – but is *not* thus impelled because the centre is *the point of its origin*. It is not to any *point* that the atoms are allied. It is not any *locality*, either in the concrete or the abstract, to which I suppose them bound. Nothing like *location* was conceived as their origin. Their source lies in the principle, *Unity. This* is their lost parent. This they seek always.[55]

The centre is the ability to live from or beyond oneself, and the 'middle way' represented by the journey is not a compromise position between the extremes of antinomian absolutism and arminian relativism, but a commitment to the full range of experience through time. 'Faithful' living involves confident progression outwards from the self towards others; it resists the Calvinistic attraction towards the logical conclusion and the ineluctable certainty of 'arrival'.

We may wonder as much about the nature of Pearl's 'human promise' as we do about that of Hilda in *The Marble Faun*, but *The Scarlet Letter*, like *The Heart of Midlothian*, comprehends 'the present real possibilities of being' as existing in time in a way that the alienated mind of the puritan–provincial cannot admit. The point is not that Pearl (or Hester, or Jeanie Deans) exists as a character who might belong in a novel by George Eliot or Hardy, but rather that Scott and Hawthorne, like Hume, have forged an idiom in which to speak non-provincially about the temporal provisionality of every life. Their writing emerges from the puritan–provincial rhetoric of distance to rediscover in the contingent of historical relation a position where mind and spirit are not at enmity within the self, and whose stylistic consequences are neither alienated imitation nor egocentric idiosyncrasy.

The result is an art which does not mistake itself or attempt to be a substitute for reality, but is, as Scott would put it, 'permitted to dismiss [its] spectres as [it] raise[s] them, amidst the shadowy and indistinct light so favourable to the exhibition of phantasmagoria, without compelling them into broad daylight'.[56] It does not, by this, lose contact or relation with reality because (so Scott continues) the 'painter of actual life . . . is entitled to leave something in shade, when the natural course of events conceals so many incidents in total darkness'. Not everything can be said, but something may be; for, as Henry James suggests, discussing the artistic problem of how to present evil in 'The Turn of the Screw' (1898): 'There is for such a case no eligible *absolute* of the wrong; it remains relative to fifty other elements, a matter of appreciation, speculation, imagination – these things moreover quite exactly in the light of the spectator's, the critic's, the reader's experience'.[57]

Notes

1 CALVIN'S THEOLOGY AND THE PURITAN MIND

1 Quoting Leon Kellner, in 'Puritanism as a Literary Force', *A Book of Prefaces*, fourth edition (London, 1922), p.197.
2 *Institutes of the Christian Religion* (1559), translated by Henry Beveridge, 2 volumes (Grand Rapids, Michigan, 1979), I, 213. Subsequent references to this edition are in the text.
3 *Letters of John Calvin*, compiled and edited by J. Bonnet, 4 volumes (New York, 1972), II, 189.
4 Robert Bruce (1554–1631), 'The Fourt Sermon', quoted by Gordon Marshall in *Presbyteries and Profits: Calvinism and the Development of Capitalism in Scotland, 1560–1707* (Oxford, 1980), p.56.
5 *A History of the Work of Redemption*, in *The Works of Jonathan Edwards*, with a memoir by Sereno E. Dwight; revised and corrected by Edward Hickman (1834), 2 volumes (Edinburgh, 1979), I, 548.
6 'The Way of Life' (1641), in *The Puritans*, edited by Perry Miller and T.H. Johnson, second edition, 2 volumes (New York, 1963), I, 319–27.
7 Perry Miller, 'The Marrow of Puritan Divinity', in *Errand into the Wilderness* (Cambridge, Mass., 1978), p.93.
8 John Gauden, *Ecclesiae Anglicanae Suspiria*... (1659), in *Anglicanism*, edited by Paul E. More and F.L. Cross (London, 1935), p.81; St Augustine, *City of God*, translated by Henry Bettenson (Harmondsworth, 1981), p.595.
9 John Milton, *Areopagitica* (1644), *The Complete Prose Works of John Milton*, general editor Don M. Wolfe, 8 volumes (London, 1953–80), II (1959), 514–15.
10 *The Folger Library Edition of the Works of Richard Hooker*, general editor W. Speed Hill, 4 volumes (Cambridge, Mass., 1977–82), I (1977), 336, 338. Subsequent references to this edition are identified in the text by volume and page number.
11 *A Compleat Body of Divinity*... (1726), cited by E.B. Lowrie in *The Shape of The Puritan Mind: The Thought of Samuel Willard* (New Haven, 1974), p.110.
12 Quoted by H.R. McAdoo in *The Structure of Caroline Moral Theology* (London, 1949), p.17.
13 *Letters of Calvin*, III, 455. To the Earl of Arran, 1 August 1558.
14 John Donne, 'La Corona', *The Divine Poems of John Donne*, edited by Helen Gardner; second edition (Oxford, 1982), p.2.

15 *Letters of Calvin*, I, 211. To Guillaume Farel, 27 October 1540.
16 Hebrews 11.13; see, for example, *City of God*, pp.573, 596; Calvin's support in Geneva was largely drawn from Frenchmen exiled from their native land, a fact which may have influenced both his ideas and his rhetoric. See also *Works of Hooker*, I, 20 on the Calvinists as self-designated aliens.
17 'Experience', *Emerson's Complete Works*, Riverside Edition, 11 volumes (Boston, 1885–6), II, 76.
18 John Cotton, quoted by Perry Miller in *The New England Mind*, volume I, *The Seventeenth Century* (Boston, 1965), p.56; Robert Bruce in Marshall, *Presbyteries and Profits*, p.81.
19 *Compleat Body . . .*, quoted by Lowrie in *The Shape of the Puritan Mind* pp.123–4.
20 *American Colonial Prose: John Smith to Thomas Jefferson*, edited by M.A. Radzinowicz (Cambridge, 1984), p.188. See also Patricia Caldwell, *The Puritan Conversion Narrative: The Beginning of American Expression* (Cambridge, 1983), to which I am indebted at this point.
21 James Fraser (a Scottish minister), *Memoirs . . .* (1738), quoted by Owen Watkins in *The Puritan Experience* (London, 1972), p.40.
22 *Nature*, *Emerson's Complete Works*, Riverside Edition, 11 volumes (Boston, 1885–6), I, 31.
23 *Journals of R.W. Emerson*, edited by E.W. Emerson and W.E. Forbes, 10 volumes (London and Boston, 1909–14), X, 171. As William Carlos Williams describes it, 'A most confusing thing in American History . . . is the nearly universal lack of scale': *In the American Grain* (Harmondsworth, 1971), p.90.
24 John Cosin, *Historia Transubstantiationis* (1675), in More and Cross, *Anglicanism*, p.469.
25 James Ussher, 'A Sermon' (1621), in More and Cross, *Anglicanism*, p.488 (my emphasis).
26 *The Table Talk of John Selden*, edited by Samuel H. Reynolds (Oxford, 1892), p.164.
27 *The Pilgrim's Progress from this World to that which is to come* (1678), edited by Roger Sharrock (London, 1966), p.173. See below, chapter 6.
28 The precariousness of the 'middle way' trodden in Massachusetts is shown in the fact that it was the sermons of John Cotton which inspired the thinking of Anne Hutchinson. There was little to distinguish their doctrinal positions, but Cotton (mindful always of human frailty and of the dangers of trusting the natural impulses of fallen man) refused to make an absolute distinction between faith and works; Anne Hutchinson upheld the purity of the heart's responses and renounced works entirely. See R.T. Kendall, 'John Cotton and the Antinomian Controversy in America (1636–1638)', in *Calvin and English Calvinism to 1649* (Oxford, 1981) and Larzar Ziff, *The Career of John Cotton: Puritanism and American Experience* (Princeton, New Jersey, 1962).
29 'The British Church', *The Works of George Herbert*, edited by F.E. Hutchinson (Oxford, 1941), p.109.
30 Quoted in J.D. Mackie, *A History of Scotland*, second edition, revised and edited by Bruce Lenman and Geoffrey Parker (Harmondsworth, 1978), p.77.
31 Perry Miller, quoting a sermon of Samuel Danforth (1670) in *Errand into the Wilderness*, p.2; Benjamin Woodbridge, elegy 'Upon the Tomb of . . . John Cotton', quoted by Sacvan Bercovitch in *The Puritan Origins of the American Self* (New Haven, 1976), p.122; T.J. Wertenbaker, 'The Fall of the Wilderness Zion', in *Puritanism in Early America*, edited by George M. Waller, Problems in American Civilisation Series (Lexington, Mass., 1950), p.24.
32 Quoted by David Levin in *Cotton Mather: The Young Life of the Lord's Remembrancer* (Cambridge, Mass., 1978), p.205. Mather was one of those who questioned the value

of spectre evidence throughout the witchcraft trials. Christina Larner, *Enemies of God: The Witch-hunt in Scotland* (London, 1981), p.170. Witchcraft was frequently believed to take the form of demonic inversions of the Covenant and of the Sacraments.
33 Robert Kirk, *The Secret Common-Wealth* (1692), in *Scottish Prose 1550–1700*, edited by R.D.S. Jack (London, 1971), pp.189–90. For Scott's 'sportful ape', Major Weir, in 'Wandering Willie's Tale', see below, chapter 4.
34 *Memorable Providences*, quoted by David Levin in *Cotton Mather*, p.152.
35 As recent research has shown, New England society became adept at accommodating witch trials, and indeed witches themselves, into continuing social life. See John Demos, *Entertaining Satan: Witchcraft and The Culture of Early New England* (New York, 1982) and David Levin, 'The Form and Sources of Cultural History', *Early American Literature*, 18 (1983), 95–101.

2 AFTER ARMAGEDDON

1 *The Life and Character of Reverend Mr Jonathan Edwards* (1765), in *Jonathan Edwards: A Profile*, edited by David Levin (New York, 1969), p.52.
2 Jonathan Edwards, 'A Narrative of Surprising Conversions' (1736), in *Jonathan Edwards on Revival* (Edinburgh, 1984), p.19.
3 *The Works of Jonathan Edwards* with a memoir by Sereno E. Dwight, revised and corrected by Edward Hickman (1834), 2 volumes (Edinburgh, 1979), II, 9.
4 *Works*, II, 243–44.
5 Edwards' concern is always to discover the beauty as well as the correctness of a doctrine through its direct impact on the senses. In his *Personal Narrative* he describes how he came to a 'delightful conviction' of God's sovereignty, and only then was able to trust his belief in it: *American Colonial Prose*, edited by M.A. Radzinowicz (Cambridge, 1984), p.180.
6 'A Faithful Narrative . . . of the Surprising Work of God', *The Great Awakening*, edited by C.C. Goen, *The Works of Jonathan Edwards*, volume IV (New Haven, 1972), p.189.
7 *Jonathan Edwards: Representative Selections*, edited by Clarence H. Faust and Thomas H. Johnson, revised edition (New York, 1962), p.107.
8 Radzinowicz, *American Colonial Prose*, p.186.
9 *Religion and the Rise of Capitalism*, 2nd edition 1938; rpt (Harmondsworth, 1980), p.201.
10 'Words were first formed to express external things', and, therefore, language is inadequate to express the truths of the soul, religious truths. See Edwards' *The Freedom of the Will*, edited by Paul Ramsey, in *The Works of Jonathan Edwards*, volume I (New Haven, 1957), p.376.
11 *Moby-Dick: or, The Whale* (1851), edited by Harrison Hayford, Hershel Parker and G. Thomas Tanselle, *The Writings of Herman Melville*, Northwestern-Newberry Edition, volume VI (Evanston and Chicago, 1988), p.164.
12 *Religious Affections*, edited by John E. Smith, in *The Works of Jonathan Edwards*, volume II (New Haven, 1959), p.215. Subsequent references are incorporated into the text.
13 *An Essay Concerning Human Understanding* (1689), edited by Peter H. Nidditch (Oxford, 1979), p.115.
14 As Norman Fiering puts it, 'the division may be understood as that between ratiocinative and practical knowledge, with the latter necessarily God-given. In ethics the situation is exactly the same': *Jonathan Edwards's Moral Thought and Its British Context* (Chapel Hill, North Carolina, 1981), p.88.

15 Quoted by Perry Miller, 'The Rhetoric of Sensation', in *Errand into the Wilderness* (Cambridge, Mass., 1978), pp.177–8.
16 Faust and Johnson, *Representative Selections*, p.xxxv (my emphasis).
17 Review of *A Free Enquiry into the Nature and Origin of Evil* (1757), in Mona Wilson, ed., *Johnson: Prose and Poetry*, second edition (Oxford, 1970), p.368.
18 *The Nature of True Virtue* (1765), ed. William K. Frankena (Ann Arbor, Michigan, 1960), p.64.
19 Ibid., pp.66–7.
20 'Lectures on Eloquence, IV', *The Works of the Rev. John Witherspoon, D.D.*, 9 volumes (Edinburgh, 1815), VII, 187.
21 *Freedom of the Will*, edited by Paul Ramsey, in *The Works of Jonathan Edwards*, volume II (New Haven, 1957) pp.427, 428. Subsequent references are incorporated in the text.
22 *A Treatise of Human Nature*, edited by L.A. Selby-Bigge, second edition, text revised by P.H. Nidditch (Oxford, 1978), pp.72, 87, 67–8. Subsequent references are incorporated in the text.
23 Hume, *Dialogues Concerning Natural Religion* (1779), edited by Norman Kemp Smith, second edition (London, 1947), p.136.
24 Samuel Johnson, quoted by James Boswell in *The Life of Samuel Johnson* (1791), 2 volumes (London, 1906; rpt. 1973), II, 210.
25 Hume, 'An Abstract of a Book lately Published, Entituled, A Treatise of Human Nature, etc', *Treatise*, p.652.
26 *Enquiries Concerning Human Understanding and Concerning the Principles of Morals* (1777), edited by L.A. Selby-Bigge, third edition, revised by P.H. Nidditch (Oxford, 1979), p.73.
27 'Of the Study of History', in *Essays, Moral, Political and Literary*, edited by T.H. Green and T.H. Grose, 2 volumes (London, 1875), II, 389–90.
28 Ibid., p.391.
29 'Of the Standard of Taste', *Essays*, I, 276–7.
30 The writings of Hume's teacher Francis Hutcheson (1694–1746), a liberal Church of Scotland minister and Professor of Moral Philosophy at the University of Glasgow, represent the middle term which established the continuities between English empirical moral sense and the thought of Edwards. Hutcheson's *Inquiry Concerning the Original of Our Ideas of Virtue or Moral Good* (1725) and *Essay on the Nature and Conduct of the Passions and Affections, with Illustrations on the Moral Sense* (1728) posited natural benevolence and intuitive perception of objective ethical values; sympathy with good and aversion from evil rendered man capable of moral action. Edwards, committed to the corruption of unregenerate natural man, made 'true sympathy' the possession of the elect alone, as against the merely intellectual (and therefore fallible and tainted) moral knowledge of the natural man. (I am indebted to Norman Fiering at this point.) Hume, too – leaving supernaturalist 'election' out of account – would take the view that natural affective moral response was imperfect, being based only on the untestable evidence of the senses and not (as Hutcheson and the later Common Sense writers would protest) on direct intuitive perception of objective realities; but nonetheless inescapable. 'Nature' and 'Reason' are opposed, but inseparable: 'Nature is obstinate, and will not quit the field, however strongly attack'd by reason; and at the same time reason is so clear in the point, that there is no possibility of disguising her' (*Treatise*, p.215).
31 It is striking how frequently Hume finds the relationship of province and centre an appropriate analogy to explicate his Calvinist-influenced philosophy of mind. See, for example, also *Treatise*, p.342.

32 'The Sceptic', *Essays*, I, 227; 'Of the Dignity or Meanness of Human Nature', *Essays*, I, 153.
33 *The Letters of David Hume*, edited by J.Y.T. Grieg, 2 volumes (Oxford, 1932), I, 32–3.
34 S.T. Coleridge, *Biographia Literaria* (1817), edited by James Engell and W.J. Bate, *The Collected Works of Samuel Taylor Coleridge*, general editor Kathleen Coburn (Princeton, New Jersey, 1980–), 7 (1983), II. 16.
35 *Essays*, I, 231. Compare the accusation which Hawthorne imagines his Calvinist ancestors putting to him: 'What is he?' murmurs one gray shadow of my forefathers to the other. 'A writer of story-books! What kind of a business in life, – what mode of glorifying God, or being serviceable to mankind in his day and generation, – may that be? Why, the degenerate fellow might as well have been a fiddler!' *The Scarlet Letter* (1850), *The Centenary Edition of the Works of Nathaniel Hawthorne*, ed. by William Charvat and Roy Harvey Pearce (Columbus, Ohio, 1962–), I (1978), p.10.
36 'Epistle to Miss Blount, With the Works of Voiture' (1712), *The Twickenham Edition of The Poems of Alexander Pope*, general editor John Butt, 11 volumes (London, 1939–69), volume VI, *Minor Poems*, edited by Norman Ault (1954), p.62.
37 See above, chapter 1, pp.2, 8–9. See also chapter 6 below.
38 The phrase is spoken by a figure in Hawthorne's sketch 'The Intelligence Office', and subsequently borrowed by Melville to characterise Hawthorne's own writing in 'Hawthorne and His Mosses', *The Literary World* (1850), reprinted in *The Shock of Recognition*, edited by Edmund Wilson, second edition (New York, 1956), p.200.

3 FROM PURITANISM TO PROVINCIALISM

1 Robert Lowell, 'Jonathan Edwards in Western Massachusetts', in *For the Union Dead* (London, 1970), p.40.
2 *The Theory of Moral Sentiments*, edited by D.D. Raphael and A.L. MacFie, *The Glasgow Edition of the Works and Correspondence of Adam Smith*, 6 volumes (Oxford, 1976), I, pp.190–1. Subsequent references are in the text.
3 D.D. Raphael, 'The Impartial Spectator', *Proceedings of the British Academy*, 58 (London, 1974), p.342.
4 (London, 1774), p.172.
5 'To a Louse, on Seeing one on a Lady's Bonnet at Church' (1786), *The Kilmarnock Poems*, edited by Donald A. Low (London, 1985), p.106.
6 Letter to Benjamin Bailey, 22 November 1817, *The Letters of John Keats, 1814–1821*, edited by H.E. Rollins, 2 volumes (Oxford, 1958), I, 184 (my emphasis).
7 Smith's later work, *The Wealth of Nations* (1776) provides a gloss: 'In all great countries which are united under one uniform government, the spirit of party commonly prevails less in the remote provinces than in the centre of the empire. The distance of those provinces from the capital, from the principal seat of the great scramble of faction and ambition, makes them enter less into the views of any of the contending parties, and renders them more indifferent and impartial spectators of the conduct of all. The spirit of party prevails less in Scotland than in England'. (*An Inquiry into the Nature and Causes of the Wealth of Nations*, edited by R.H. Campbell and A.S. Skinner, *The Glasgow Edition of The Works and Correspondence of Adam Smith* (Oxford, 1976), II, 945).
8 *The Papers of Benjamin Franklin*, edited by L.W. Labaree et al. (New Haven, 1959–), III (1961), 13; *North-American Review*, 24 (1827), 463.
9 Number 5 (1781), reprinted in *The Beginnings of American English*, edited by M.M. Mathews, (Chicago, 1931), pp.17, 15.
10 'The Druid', p.17.

11 *Lectures on Rhetoric and Belles Lettres*, edited by J.C. Bryce, *Works*, volume IV (1983), p.42.
12 Hume, quoted by Douglas Young in *Edinburgh in the Age of Sir Walter Scott* (Norman, Oklahoma, 1965), p.115. Beattie, letter to Sylvester Douglas, 5 January 1778, in Sir William Forbes, *An Account of the Life and Writings of James Beattie LL.D*, 2 volumes (Edinburgh, 1806), II, 17.
13 *The Mirror*, fourth edition, 3 volumes (London, 1782), III, 75.
14 *Dissertations on the English Language* (1789), edited by Harry R. Warfel (Gainesville, Florida, 1951), pp.20–1.
15 [Jared Sparks], 'Professor Everett's Orations', *North American Review*, 20, no.47 (April 1825), 439. See also Walter Channing, writing in the *North American Review*, 1, no.3 (September 1815), 312.
16 'Bogland', *Selected Poems 1965–75* (London, 1980), p.54. James Joyce, *A Portrait of the Artist as a Young Man* (1916; rpt London, 1983), p.172.
17 Letter from Reid to Hume, 18 March 1763, in *The Story of Scottish Philosophy: A Compendium of Selections from the Writings of Nine Pre-eminent Scottish Philosophers, with Bibliographical Essays*, edited by D.S. Robinson (Westport, Connecticut, 1979), p.133.
18 *An Inquiry into the Human Mind, on the Principles of Common Sense* (St Andrews, 1823), p.vii.
19 Reid, *Essays on the Active Powers of the Human Mind* (1788), edited by Baruch A. Brody (Cambridge, Mass., 1969), p.29.
20 *Inquiry*, p.29.
21 *Culture and Anarchy*, edited by R.H. Super, *The Complete Prose Works of Matthew Arnold*, 11 volumes (Ann Arbor, Michigan, 1960–77), V (1965), 237–49.
22 See above, chapter 2, pp.42–3, and note 30. I am convinced by David Fate Norton's argument that Hume's scepticism in the *Treatise* is confined to his epistemological analysis, and that in discussing morality he too resorts to a 'common sense' to rescue ethical judgements from total subjectivity. See *David Hume: Common-Sense Moralist, Sceptical Metaphysician* (Princeton, New Jersey, 1982).
23 *Realistic Philosophy, Defended in a Philosophic Series*, 2 volumes (London, 1887), II, 181–3 (emphasis in the original).
24 *Notes on the State of Virginia* (1787 edition), edited by William Peden (New York, 1972), p.48.
25 Letter to Adams, 14 March 1820, in *The Adams-Jefferson Letters, The Complete Correspondence between Thomas Jefferson and Abigail and John Adams* edited by Lester J. Cappon, 2 volumes (Chapel Hill, North Carolina, 1959), II, 562. Jefferson is alluding to Montaigne's essay 'Experience'; see *The Essayes of Michael, Lord of Montaigne*, translated by John Florio (1603), introduced by Thomas Seccombe, 3 volumes (London, 1908), III, 414. See below, p.68.
26 Letter to Henry Lee, 8 May 1825, in *The Life and Selected Writings of Thomas Jefferson*, edited by Adrienne Koch and William Peden (New York, 1944), p.719.
27 Throughout the battle against the British, Jefferson was adroit in eliciting a coherent national response from the disunited colonists by appealing to the familiar rhetoric of the puritan sermon and by reviving the old ritual of the communal fast. See Emory Elliott, 'The Puritan Roots of American Whig Rhetoric', in *Puritan Influences in American Literature*, edited by Emory Elliott (Urbana, Illinois, 1979), p.112. See also Alan Heimert, *Religion and the American Mind: From the Great Awakening to the Revolution* (Cambridge, Mass., 1966); Edmund Morgan, 'The Puritan Ethic and the American Revolution', *William and Mary Quarterly*, series 3, 24, no.1 (1967), 3–43;

Barry Ray Bell, 'The Ideology and Rhetoric of the American Revolution' (PhD Dissertation, University of Virginia, 1977). Two recent studies of the 'Declaration', those of Garry Wills in *Inventing America: Jefferson's Declaration of Independence* (New York, 1979) and of Stephen Fender in *American Literature In Context, 1620–1830* (London and New York, 1983), offer challenging analyses of its language and antecedents. In his *Prodigals and Pilgrims: The American Revolution Against Patriarchal Authority 1750–1800* (Cambridge, 1984), Jay Fliegelman discusses how non-coercive Lockean and Common Sense views of parent/child relationships mitigated the absolutism of the authoritarian Calvinist model. My emphasis on underlying *continuities* of conception and expression takes account of the rather different aims of intellectual history which inform his discussion.

28 *The Papers of Thomas Jefferson*, general editor Julian P. Boyd (Princeton, New Jersey, 1950–), I, 423 (Jefferson's draft). Subsequent references are in the text.
29 'The United States Elevated to Glory and Honor', in *The Pulpit of the American Revolution*, edited by John Wingate Thornton (Boston, 1860), p.441.
30 In 1838 John Quincy Adams, celebrating 'The Jubilee of the Constitution', could declare with perfect orthodoxy, 'Fellow citizens, the ark of your covenant is the Declaration of Independence': quoted by John J. McWilliams, Jr., *Hawthorne, Melville and the American Character* (Cambridge, 1984), p.133.
31 Jay Fliegelman, *Patriots and Pilgrims*, p.83.
32 Facsimile edition, edited by V.H. Paltsits (New York, 1971), p.155.
33 See Heimert, *Religion and the American Mind*, p.548.
34 'The Genteel Tradition in American Philosophy', in *Selected Critical Writings of George Santayana*, edited by Norman Henfrey, 2 volumes (Cambridge, 1968), II, 96.
35 *Emerson's Complete Works*, Riverside Edition, 11 volumes (Boston, 1885–6), II, 49. Subsequent references are in the text.
36 'Genteel Tradition', p.91.
37 *Complete Works*, I, 315.
38 'Experience', *Complete Works*, III, 76–7.
39 *The Journals and Miscellaneous Notebooks of R.W. Emerson*, edited by W.H. Gilman and others, 16 volumes (Cambridge, Mass., 1960–82), IV (1964), 274.
40 'The Transcendentalist', *Complete Works*, I, 332–4.
41 *Emerson in His Journals*, edited by Joel Porte (Cambridge, Mass., 1982), p.543.
42 'Fate', *Complete Works*, VI, 49–51.
43 'Poetry and Imagination', *Complete Works*, VIII, 23, 45.
44 *Nature*, *Complete Works*, I, 60. Subsequent references are in the text.
45 *Journals*, edited by Edward W. Emerson and W.E. Forbes, 10 volumes (Boston and London, 1909–14), X, 171.
46 *Complete Works*, IX, 13.
47 *Sartor Resartus* (1831), in *The Works of Thomas Carlyle*, Edinburgh Edition, 30 volumes (New York, 1903–4), I, 175.
48 'The Hero as Poet', in *Heroes and Hero-Worship* (1841), *Works*, V, 81.
49 'Experience', p.86.
50 *The Essayes of Michael, Lord of Montaigne*, III, 467.
51 Ibid, p.414.
52 *Representative Men* (1850), *Complete Works*, IV, 148. Subsequent references are in the text.
53 The American critic Constance Rourke, defining comedy in *American Humor: A Study of the National Character* (New York, 1959), p.268.

4 THE PURSUIT OF THE DOUBLE

1 Calvin, *Institutes of the Christian Religion*, translated by Henry Beveridge, 2 volumes (Grand Rapids, Michigan, 1979), II, 243; Luther quoted by Erik Erikson in *Young Man Luther: A Study in Psychoanalysis and History* (London, 1959), p.252; *The Journals and Miscellaneous Notebooks of R.W. Emerson*, edited by W.H. Gilman and others, 16 volumes (Cambridge, Mass., 1960–82), V (1965), 475.
2 *Caleb Williams*, edited by David McCracken (London and New York, 1977), pp.130, 133. Subsequent references are in the text.
3 William Hazlitt, *The Spirit of the Age, or Contemporary Portraits* (1825), facsimile edition (London, 1971), p.50.
4 *Essays Religious and Mixed, The Complete Prose Works of Matthew Arnold*, edited by R.H. Super, 11 volumes (Ann Arbor, Michigan, 1960–77), VIII (1972), 198. This desire to know forbidden secrets, and the self-destroying consequences of such knowledge, inform Hawthorne's most powerful short stories.
5 See above, chapter 1, p.16; chapter 2, pp.26–37.
6 Arnold, p.200.
7 Journal entry of 1795, cited by David Lee Clark in *Charles Brockden Brown: Pioneer Voice of America* (Durham, North Carolina, 1952), p.157.
8 *Edgar Huntly; or Memoirs of a Sleepwalker*, edited by David Stineback (New Haven, 1973), p.29. Subsequent references are in the text.
9 Cited by David Lee Clark in *The Monthly Magazine*, (June 1799), 313.
10 Compare this passage from Hawthorne's sketch 'The Haunted Mind' (1835): 'In the depths of every heart there is a tomb and a dungeon ... sometimes, and oftenest at midnight, those dark receptacles are flung wide open. In an hour like this, when the mind has a passive sensibility, but no active strength; when the imagination is a mirror, imparting vividness to all ideas, without the power of selecting or controlling them; then pray that your griefs may slumber, and the brotherhood of remorse not break their chain. It is too late! A funeral train comes gliding by your bed, in which Passion and Feeling assume bodily shape, and things of the mind become dim spectres to the eye!' (*Twice-Told Tales, The Centenary Edition of the Works of Nathaniel Hawthorne*, edited by William Charvat and Roy Harvey Pearce (Columbus, Ohio, 1962–), IX (1974), 306.
11 This shortcoming throws light on the unsatisfactoriness of Poe's single long fiction, *The Narrative of Arthur Gordon Pym of Nantucket* (1837), in comparison with the short stories in which he found the perfect vehicle for similar states (rather than stories) of mind.
12 'Memoir of Charles Brockden Brown, the American Novelist', reprinted from *The North American Review* in Prescott's *Biographical and Critical Miscellanies* (Philadelphia, 1875), p.23.
13 *The Private Memoirs and Confessions of a Justified Sinner*, edited by John Carey (Oxford, 1970), p.12. Subsequent references are in the text.
14 October 1824; quoted by Carey in *Private Memoirs*, p.257.
15 Compare the assertive context established by Melville's 'Call me Ishmael' at the beginning of *Moby-Dick* (1851).
16 *Institutes*, II, 20.
17 *Selected Stories and Sketches*, edited by Douglas S. Mack (Edinburgh, 1982), pp.101–2; *The Tales of James Hogg, The Ettrick Shepherd*, 2 volumes (London, 1884), II, 302.
18 Yvor Winters, 'Maule's Curse' (1938), in *In Defense of Reason* (London, 1960), p.170.
19 See James Cox, 'Edgar Poe: Style as Pose', *Virginia Quarterly Review*, 44, no.1 (Winter, 1968), 81.

20 *The Complete Works of Edgar Allan Poe*, 10 volumes (New York, 1902), III, 317. Subsequent references in the text are to this edition, except where otherwise noted.
21 Pages 344–345. The emphasis is not in *Works*, but appears in *Edgar Allan Poe: Selected Writings*, edited by David Galloway (Harmondsworth, 1967), p.175, which follows the text revised by Poe for the *Broadway Journal* (August, 1845).
22 *Mosses from an Old Manse, Centenary Edition*, X, (1974), 166.
23 *Complete Works*, III, 317 prints 'spectre' as 'sceptre'; see *Selected Writings*, p.158.
24 See the discussion of 'The Masque of the Red Death' below, chapter 5, pp.122–3.
25 Again I follow here the more emphatic version of *Selected Writings*, p.166.
26 *Selected Writings*, p.178.
27 *Quarterly Review*, X, 463, reprinted in *British Criticisms of American Writings 1783–1815: A Contribution to the Study of Anglo-American Literary Relationships*, University of Wisconsin Studies in Language and Literature, no.1, edited by W.B. Cairns (Madison, Wisconsin, 1918), p.34.
28 The phrase is Joseph Wood Krutch's in his *Edgar Allan Poe: a Study in Genius* (London, 1926), p.217.
29 I find support from Kathryn Sutherland's recent introduction to *Redgauntlet* (Oxford, 1985), which appeared after my own account was composed. Amongst her suggestive comments on the novel, she remarks that '*Redgauntlet* is concerned with ... problematic formulations of identity and of the relation between a sense of fiction and a sense of self' (p.ix), and 'the novel's "true centre" turns out to be storytelling itself – how stories are told and received. Significantly, it is a subject only understood in the withholding of the ultimate story' (p.xv).
30 Review of Godwin's *Fleetwood*, in *The Edinburgh Review* (1805), reprinted in *Sir Walter Scott on Novelists and Fiction*, edited by Ioan Williams (New York, 1968), pp.193–4.
31 *Redgauntlet* (Oxford, 1912), p.25. Subsequent references to this edition are incorporated in the text.
32 The 'border' or boundary between the familiar and the strange, the accepted and the forbidden, is an important location for Scott. G.M. Young writes, 'it is impossible to imagine Scott as anything but a Borderer, imbued from infancy with that sense of contrast, that feeling of something beyond, something mysteriously or magnetically different': 'Scott and the Historians', in *Sir Walter Scott Lectures, 1940–1948*, introduced by W.L. Renwick (Edinburgh, 1950), p.84.
33 Anonymous review of *Tales of my Landlord*, published in *The Quarterly Review* (1817), reprinted in *The Prose Works of Sir Walter Scott, Bart.*, 28 volumes (Edinburgh, 1834–6), XIX, 4–5.
34 Ibid., p.5.
35 *Sir Walter Scott* (London, 1932), p.265.
36 *Waverley* (1814; Oxford, 1912), p.2.
37 'The Highland Widow', in *Chronicles of the Canongate, First Series* (1827; Oxford, 1912), pp.84–5.
38 *Mosses From an Old Manse*, p.349. Subsequent references are in the text.
39 Review of Byron's *Childe Harold*, Canto IV (*Quarterly Review*, 1818), reprinted in *Prose Works*, XVII, 359.
40 'Preface' to *Twice-Told Tales, Centenary Edition*, IX (1974), 6.
41 Q.D. Leavis calls it 'a dramatic poem of the Calvinist experience in New England': 'Hawthorne as Poet', *Sewanee Review*, 59 (1951), 197.
42 *Centenary Edition*, I (1978), 243.
43 *Poetical Works*, edited by Douglas Bush (London, 1969), Book V, 30–5. Subsequent references are by book and line number in the text.

44   how disturbed
       This night the human pair, how he designs
       In them at once to ruin all mankind.   (v, 226–8)
45 *The Piazza Tales* (1857), edited by Egbert S. Oliver (New York, 1962), p.28. Subsequent references are in the text.
46 Hawthorne, Letter to William D. Ticknor (1855), quoted by Henry Nash Smith in *Democracy and the Novel: Popular Resistance to Classic American Writers* (New York, 1978), p.7.
47 'The Genteel Tradition in American Philosophy', in *Selected Writings of George Santayana*, edited by Norman Henfrey, 2 volumes (Cambridge, 1968), II, 89.
48 *Mosses*, p.192; Santayana, p.90. Santayana describes Poe and Hawthorne (Melville is not mentioned) as exemplars of the 'genteel tradition'; my analysis here suggests how these writers (in Santayana's words) may 'half-escape' their puritan–provincial heritage by making it the subject of their fiction.
49 *Moby-Dick*, edited by Harrison Hayford, Hershel Parker and G. Thomas Tanselle, *The Writings of Herman Melville*, The Northwestern-Newberry Edition, volume VI (Evanston and Chicago, 1988), p.195.

5 SPECTATORS, SPIES AND SPECTRES

1 Hume, *A Treatise of Human Nature*, edited by L.A. Selby-Bigge, second edition, text revised by P.H. Nidditch (Oxford, 1978), p.253; *The Journal of Sir Walter Scott*, edited by W.E.K. Anderson (Oxford, 1972), pp.127–8; Hawthorne, *The English Notebooks*, edited by Randall Stewart (London, 1941), p.184 (entry for 30 July 1855).
2 'The Life of Addison' (1779), in *Lives of the English Poets*, 2 volumes (London, 1977), I, 449.
3 Scott, *Waverley* (Oxford, 1912), p.528; Franklin's *Letters of Silence Dogood* (1722) were modelled on *The Spectator*, and he tells us in his *Autobiography* how his style was formed in imitation of Addison. One of Caleb Williams' disguises in his flight from Falkland was as a writer of *Spectator*-like essays.
4 Southern Literary Classics Series, facsimile of the 1832 edition (Chapel Hill, North Carolina, 1970), p.242. Subsequent references are in the text.
5 *The Letters of Jonathan Oldstyle, Gent.* and *Salmagundi*, edited by Bruce I. Granger and Martha Hartzog, in *The Complete Works of Washington Irving*, volume VI (Boston, 1977), p.3. Subsequent references are in the text.
6 The reviewers in *Blackwood's Edinburgh Magazine* also played with many bachelor-*personae*. Like Irving and the other *Salmagundi* authors, the perpetrators of these *personae* were all young provincial writers experimenting with tone and subject matter, simultaneously anxious to conceal their inexperience behind an authoritative voice and impatient of the literary conventions represented by that voice.
7 James Hogg, *Memoirs of the Author's Life*, edited by D.S. Mack (Edinburgh, 1972), p.19.
8 (Edinburgh, 1810), pp.1–2. The pagination of *The Spy* is erratic; page numbers in the text are cited throughout as they stand in the National Library of Scotland copy, LC1241. Hogg appeals directly to Addison's example in the final number, p.410. See also Emerson's *Journal* for February 1867: 'I am so purely a spectator that I have absolute confidence that all pure spectators will agree with me, whenever I make a careful report', *Journals*, edited by Edward W. Emerson and W.E. Forbes, 10 volumes (Boston and London, 1909–1914), X, 191.
9 *The Tempest*, edited by Frank Kermode, The Arden Shakespeare, sixth edition (London, 1980), V.1.82–3.

10 'Feathertop', *Mosses from an Old Manse*, *The Centenary Edition of the Works of Nathaniel Hawthorne*, edited by William Charvat and Roy Harvey Pearce (Columbus, Ohio, 1962–), x, (1974), 242–3.
11 'General Preface' (1829) to the Waverley Novels, *Waverley*, p.xxv.
12 'Chronicles of the Canongate', first series, in *The Betrothed* (1827; Oxford, 1912), p.51.
13 Introduction to 'Tales of My Landlord', first series, in *Old Mortality* (Oxford, 1912), p.xiii; Henry James, *Hawthorne* (1879), reissued with an introduction by Tony Tanner (London, 1967), p.42 (subsequent references to this work are in the text); *The Bride of Lammermoor* (Oxford, 1912), p.1.
14 'Advertisement' to *Rob Roy* (Oxford, 1912), p.ix; 'Introductory Epistle' to *The Fortunes of Nigel* (Oxford, 1912), p.xxii. Hawthorne's 'Feathertop' owes much to the whimsical humour of Scott's narrative *personae*.
15 Introduction to 'Chronicles of the Canongate', pp.xxii, xxxv.
16 'General Preface', p.xxviii.
17 *The Spy: A Tale of the Neutral Ground*, edited by J.E. Morpurgo, Classic American Texts Series (Oxford, 1968), p.67. Subsequent references are incorporated in the text. It is worth recalling the distinction frequently made in *Caleb Williams* between the superficial and the acute observer. Amongst the latter, Falkland is almost preternaturally acute as a penetrator of disguises.
18 See the entry from Scott's *Journal* quoted in the epigraph to this chapter. The vantage points of observation are carefully constructed in Scott's novels; see, for example, the Scots Jeanie Deans and the Duke of Argyle looking down upon the Thames Valley, the 'heart' of England, from Richmond Hill in chapter 36 of *The Heart of Midlothian*.
19 'Wakefield', *Twice-Told Tales, Centenary Edition of the Works of Nathaniel Hawthorne*, IX, (1974), 140. Subsequent references are in the text.
20 *The Complete Works of Edgar Allan Poe*, 10 volumes (New York, 1902), IV, 160. Subsequent references are in the text.
21 *The Piazza Tales* (1857), edited by Egbert S. Oliver (New York, 1962), pp.183–4. Subsequent references are in the text.
22 'Characteristics' (1831), *The Edinburgh Edition of the Works of Thomas Carlyle*, 30 volumes (New York, 1903–4), XXVIII, 27.
23 'Hints of Egotism in Goethe', *Selected Critical Writings of George Santayana*, edited by Norman Henfrey, 2 volumes (Cambridge, 1968), I, 183.
24 *Complete Works*, IV, 327. Subsequent references are in the text.
25 *The Snow-Image, Centenary Edition of the Works of Nathaniel Hawthorne*, XI (1974), 49. Subsequent references are in the text.
26 *Essays Moral, Political and Literary*, edited by T.H. Green and T.H. Grose, 2 volumes (London, 1875), II, 389–90.
27 'The masques, mummeries and festive customs describes in the text, are in accordance with the manners of the age,' as Hawthorne had put it in a typically distanced 'authorial' headnote to his early 'slight sketch', 'The May-pole of Merry Mount' (*Twice-Told Tales*, p.54). In its allegorical confrontation between carefree 'old world' revellers and the 'new world' puritans, this tale anticipates Poe's account of a self-enclosed world of masquerade being invaded by harsh reality. The allegory polarises the forces of youth and age, innocence and experience, 'jollity' and 'gloom' into frozen states; only at the end is the possibility of development and continuing life suggested, and here again it is conceived in literary terms borrowed from *Paradise Lost*.
28 In the teasing prefaces to his novels, Scott too plays with the difficulties experienced by his various showmen-spies as they persuade their audiences to adopt 'the proper

point of view' which will reveal the meaning of the scene presented. See, for example, chapter 1 of *The Bride of Lammermoor*.
29 Hawthorne testified to his sense of being a traitor or 'spy' in England in his *English Notebooks*, pp.91–2.
30 'The Haunted Mind', *Twice-Told Tales*, p.306.
31 'Experience', *Emerson's Complete Works*, Riverside edition, 11 volumes (Boston, 1885–6), III, 81.
32 *Edinburgh Edition*, I, 208. Subsequent references to this volume are incorporated in the text.
33 *The Correspondence of Emerson and Carlyle*, edited by Joseph Slater (New York, 1964), pp.103–4.
34 Letter of 24 December 1833, *The Collected Letters of Thomas and Jane Welsh Carlyle*, The Duke-Edinburgh Edition, edited by C.R. Sanders and K.J. Fielding (Durham, North Carolina, 1970–), VII (1977), 61.
35 *Edinburgh Edition*, XXVIII, 359–60. Subsequent references to this volume are incorporated in the text.
36 *Poe: Essays and Reviews*, edited by G.R. Thompson, *Library of America* (New York and London, 1984), pp.13, 14.
37 'Benito Cereno', *The Piazza Tales*, p.59. Subsequent references are in the text.
38 *The Confidence Man in American Literature* (New York and Oxford, 1982), p.18.
39 *The Confidence-Man: His Masquerade*, edited by H. Bruce Franklin (Indianapolis and New York, 1967), p.270. Subsequent references are in the text.
40 Emerson, 'Self-Reliance', *Complete Works*, II, 58.
41 *Biographia Literaria* (1817), edited by James Engell and W.J. Bate, *The Collected Works of Samuel Taylor Coleridge*, general editor Kathleen Coburn (Princeton, New Jersey, 1980–), 7 volumes (1983), II, 6.
42 Letter to Stuart, quoted in *Biographia Literaria*, II, 7.
43 Hume, 'The Sceptic', *Essays Moral, Political, and Literary*, edited by T.H. Green and T.H. Grose, 2 volumes (London, 1875), I, 227–8.
44 'Walt Whitman: A Dialogue', in *Santayana on America: Essays, Notes, and Letters on American Life, Literature and Philosophy*, edited by R.C. Lyon (New York, 1968), p.290.
45 *The Blithedale Romance and Fanshawe*, Centenary Edition, III (1964), p.1. Subsequent references to this edition are in the text.
46 It is an enterprise paralleled by the circumvention of the iron gate at Sotherton in Jane Austen's *Mansfield Park* (1814). However, in *Mansfield Park* the rebellion against social constraint is shown to unleash passions whose reality is not in doubt but which would be better kept in check, whereas in Hawthorne's romance of provincialism the separation from society constitutes a withdrawal from 'life'. The 'free' society of Blithedale turns out to be as artificial as anything the rebels have left behind.
47 Quoted by James, *Hawthorne*, p.64.
48 Santayana, describing the 'destructive element' in the writing of Henry James, in a letter to Daniel Cory cited by Lyon in *Santayana on America*, p.xiv.
49 *The Court Masque: A Study in the Relationship between Poetry and the Revels* (Cambridge, 1927), p.256.
50 *Shakespearian Tragedy*, second edition (London, 1974), p.216.
51 *The Tempest*, I.ii.206, V.i.275. Subsequent references are in the text. In *The Machine in the Garden: Technology and the Pastoral Ideal* (London, 1978), Leo Marx has described *The Tempest* as 'Shakespeare's American Fable', on the basis of its pastoral debate (which he finds appropriate to the 'New World' context) between nature and nurture, savagery and civilisation, innocence and experience. I would suggest that

these oppositions are specific instances of the many divisions which structure the play and that it is rather the frame of mind which perceives life as a series of paradoxes or polarities which makes *The Tempest*, if it is such, an 'American' play. It is, however, a play which is hospitable to any 'interpretation' (another consequence of its 'symbolising' origin in the mind of the playwright?); my discussion intends merely to suggest why *The Tempest* should have come so readily to the hands of puritan–provincial writers as they explored the disjunction between the Real and the Ideal.

52 Marx, *The Machine in the Garden*, p.72; Hume, *Treatise*, p.68. See above, chapter 2, p.38.

6 'IS ANYTHING CENTRAL?'

1 'Is anything central?', John Ashbery, 'The One Thing That Can Save America', in *Self-Portrait in a Convex Mirror* (New York, 1975), p.44; Ortega Y Gasset, *The Modern Theme*, translated by James Cleugh (New York, 1961), p.140; Read, 'Hawthorne', in *Essays on Literary Criticism: Particular Studies* (London, 1969), p.141; Emerson, *English Traits*, *Emerson's Complete Works*, Riverside Edition, 11 volumes (Boston, 1885–6), V, 283.
2 Quoted by Kenneth Clark, 'Provincialism', in *Moments of Vision* (London, 1981), p.54.
3 James uses the phrase of Poe's critical essays, in *Hawthorne* (1879), reissued with an introduction by Tony Tanner (London, 1967), p.71. Hawthorne himself is described as 'exquisitely and consistently provincial' on p.137.
4 'Preface' to 'The Lesson of the Master', in *The Art of the Novel: Critical Prefaces*, introduced by R.P. Blackmur (New York, 1962), p.222.
5 Translated by Henry Bettenson (Harmondsworth, 1981), p.596.
6 Epistle to the Hebrews 11.13; *Institutes of the Christian Religion*, translated by Henry Beveridge, 2 volumes (Grand Rapids, Michigan, 1979), I, 471; for Edwards' sermon see above, chapter 2. In *Magnalia Christi Americana*, Cotton Mather adopts the metaphor extensively to describe the spiritual journey of the early colonists, who landed, as he put it, in a world 'in which they found they must live like strangers and pilgrims' (quoted by Cecilia Tichi, 'Spiritual Biography and the Lord's Remembrancers' in *The American Puritan Imagination: Essays in Revaluation*, edited by Sacvan Bercovitch (Cambridge, 1974), p.66. The puritan image of the journey of the world's outcast away from a material centre, a 'place', and towards a spiritual centre is dogma in the writings of St Paul and St Augustine. It becomes narrative, a story, in Bunyan's *Pilgrim's Progress*. It is the form of the puritan–provincial quest enacted by, for example, Cooper's Ishmael Bush in *The Prairie* (1827) and Melville's Ishmael in *Moby-Dick*.
7 Clark 'Provincialism', p.53. Subsequent references to this essay are in the text.
8 Ortega Y Gasset, *The Modern Theme*, p.91.
9 The view that Melville's *Moby-Dick* seems to move towards, and which *The Confidence-Man* finds inescapable.
10 Alaric Watts, letter to Blackwood, 29 January 1822, quoted by Claire Cartmell in 'The Age of Politics, Personalities, and Periodicals: The Early Nineteenth-Century World of the "Noctes Ambrosianae" of *Blackwood's Edinburgh Magazine*' (unpublished Ph.D. dissertation, University of Leeds, 1974), p.103.
11 Letter to William Maginn, 24 May 1822, National Library of Scotland ACC. 5643: B2, fo.318.
12 National Library of Scotland MS 4005, f.82. After the success of *The Ayrshire Legatees*, Blackwood wrote to Galt (23 January 1821), 'I wish much you would begin

a new series of any kind which would give sketches of London men and things. Every one is anxious to hear what is going on in the great world' (quoted by Erik Frykman in *John Galt's Scottish Stories 1820–1823* (Uppsala, 1959), pp.35–6).

13 *The Ayrshire Legatees, or, The Pringle Family* (Edinburgh, 1821), p.85. Subsequent references are in the text.

14 See, for example, 'The Scotchman in London', *Blackwood's*, 4, no.31 (October, 1819), 64–6.

15 *A Treatise of Human Nature*, edited by L.A. Selby-Bigge, second edition, text revised by P.H. Nidditch (Oxford, 1978), pp.263–4.

16 Calvin, *Institutes*, II, 243, 276. The ventriloquistic assumption of the Scottish religious voice, Galt's greatest strength as a writer, is at its most sustained in the Reverend Micah Balwhidder in *Annals of the Parish* (1821) and in *Ringan Gilhaize* (1823), a narrative of the Covenanting wars told from the point of view of a Covenanter who is driven by circumstances to fanaticism. On the significance of this rhetorical assumption of voices for the puritan–provincial viewpoint, see above, chapter 5.

17 Galt's *Autobiography* (1833) describes his own first days in London in similar terms; the forlorn, isolated plight of the provincial on his arrival in the centre is a repeated situation in his fiction: see, for example, *Sir Andrew Wylie, of that Ilk* (1822) and *The Stolen Child* (1833).

18 *Valerius, A Roman Story*, 3 volumes (Edinburgh, 1821), I, 14–15. Subsequent references are in the text.

19 *The Marble Faun: or, The Romance of Monte Beni*, The Centenary Edition of the Works of Nathaniel Hawthorne, edited by William Charvat and others (Columbus, Ohio, 1962–), IV (1971), p.461. Subsequent references are in the text.

20 Andrew Lang, *The Life and Letters of John Gibson Lockhart*, 2 volumes (London, 1897), I, 289 fn.

21 *Twice-Told Tales*, Centenary Edition, IX (1974), 54. See above, chapter 5, p.124. Contrast with this meticulous declaration of sources Scott's cavalier assertion in the 'Dedicatory Epistle' to *Ivanhoe*: 'I neither can nor do pretend to complete accuracy, even in matters of outward costume, much less in the more important points of language and manners' (Oxford, 1912), p.xxv.

22 2 volumes (Edinburgh, 1818), I, 95, 114.

23 *Peter's Letters to His Kinsfolk*, third edition, 3 volumes (Edinburgh, 1819), II, 68. This often-repeated sorrow for the declining purity of spoken Scots is paralleled in the American Jeremiads' lament for the declension in piety from the high purpose of the Puritan fathers to the subsequent generations of New England. Both become frequently rehearsed tropes of puritan–provincial fiction.

24 E.B. Lowrie, *The Shape of the Puritan Mind: The Thought of Samuel Willard* (New Haven, 1974), p.125.

25 For Lockhart's views on the 'systematic' rejuvenation of literature, see his 'Thoughts on Novel Writing', *Blackwood's*, 4 (January 1819), p.396; Noah Webster, *Dissertations on the English Language* (1789), edited by Harry R. Warfel (Gainesville, Florida, 1951), p.33.

26 Irving's letters at the time he was working on *The Sketch Book* show his acute concern with the potential readership, both in England and America, and his awareness of the different expectations peculiar to each group. See, for example, *Life and Letters of Washington Irving*, 4 volumes (London, 1862–4), I, 373–4, and a letter of 13 August 1820 to Scott, National Library of Scotland MS 3891, f.120.

27 *The Sketch Book of Geoffrey Crayon, Gent.*, edited by Haskell Springer, *The Complete Works of Washington Irving*, volume VIII (Boston, 1978), p.11. Subsequent references are in the text.

28 'Main-street', *The Snow-Image and Uncollected Tales, Centenary Edition*, XI (1974), p.49; *The House of the Seven Gables, Centenary Edition*, II, (1965; rpt. 1971), p.256.
29 *Twice-Told Tales*, p.54. *Centenary Edition*, XIV (1980), 524.
30 *Bracebridge Hall, Complete Works*, IX (Boston, 1977), p.4.
31 *Our Old Home: A Series of English Sketches, Centenary Edition*, V (1970), 214. James describes the book as 'the work of an outsider, of a stranger, of a man who remains to the end a mere spectator (something less even than an observer), and always lacks the final initiation into the manners and nature of a people of whom it may most be said, among all the people of the earth, that to know them is to make discoveries'; *Hawthorne*, p.141).
32 *The French and Italian Notebooks*, edited by Thomas Woodson, *Centenary Edition*, XIV (1980), 524.
33 *Redburn, The Northwestern–Newberry Edition of the Writings of Herman Melville*, edited by Harrison Hayford and others (Evanston and Chicago, 1968–), IV (1969), 157. Subsequent references are in the text.
34 'Hawthorne and His Mosses' (1850), reprinted in *The Shock of Recognition, Recorded by the Men who made it*, edited by Edmund Wilson, second edition (New York and London, 1956), pp.197–8.
35 Ibid., p.195.
36 *Dialogues Concerning Natural Religion*, edited by Norman Kemp Smith, second edition (London, 1947), p.135. Subsequent references are in the text.
37 *Mardi, and A Voyage Thither, The Northwestern–Newberry Edition*, III (1970), pp.556–7. Subsequent references are in the text. For the 'modernity' of this, compare the voyaging speculative boldness of Robert Louis Stevenson's attitude to his art in 1883: 'O the height and depth of novelty and worth in any art! and O that I am privileged to swim and shoulder through such oceans! Could one get out of sight of land – all in the blue? Alas not, being anchored here in flesh, and the bonds of logic being still about us. But what a great space and a great air there is in these small shallows where alone we venture! and how new each sight, squall, calm, or sunrise!' *The Letters of Robert Louis Stevenson to his Family and Friends*, edited by Sidney Colvin, 2 volumes (London, 1899), I, 273–4.
38 Letter to R.H. Dana, Jr, 6 October 1849, in *The Letters of Herman Melville*, edited by Merrell R. Davis and William H. Gilman (New Haven, 1960), p.93.
39 'Hawthorne and His Mosses', p.200.
40 Ortega y Gasset, *The Modern Theme*, p.90.
41 *The Heart of Midlothian* (Oxford, 1912), p.46. Subsequent references are incorporated in the text.
42 See Perry Miller, 'John Bunyan's Pilgrim's Progress', in *The Responsibility of Mind in a Civilisation of Machines: Essays* (Amherst, Mass., 1979), p.69.
43 *The Pilgrim's Progress from this World to that which is to come* (1678, 1684), edited by Roger Sharrock (London, 1966), p.173.
44 Calvin, *Institutes*, I, 520; *The Pilgrim's Progress*, pp.183, 189–90.
45 'The Meaning of a Literary Idea', in *The Liberal Imagination: Essays on Literature and Society* (New York, 1976), p.300.
46 *The Bride of Lammermoor* (Oxford, 1912), p.17.
47 'Andrew Marvell', in *Selected prose of T.S. Eliot*, edited by Frank Kermode (London, 1975), p.168.
48 *The Scarlet Letter, Centenary Edition*, I (1978), 207. Subsequent references are in the text.
49 On Hawthorne's use of 'the formula of alternative possibilities', see Yvor Winters, 'Maule's Curse', in *In Defense of Reason* (London, 1960), p.170.

50 *The Twickenham Edition of the Works of Alexander Pope*, general editor John Butt, 11 volumes (London, 1939–1969), II, *The Rape of the Lock and other poems*, edited by Geoffrey Tillotson, second edition (1954), p.309, lines 123–4. Subsequent references are by line number in the text.
51 See Richard Brodhead, *Hawthorne, Melville and the Novel* (Chicago and London, 1977), pp.62–3, to whose writing I am indebted for this thought.
52 Unlike the other characters, who exist as powerful products of Hawthorne's imaginative intellect, Pearl has a 'real' source in Hawthorne's observation of his own daughter Una. See *The American Notebooks*, edited by Claude M. Simpson, *Centenary Edition*, VIII (1972), pp.413–5, 430–1.
53 Quoted by Arlin Turner, *Nathaniel Hawthorne: A Biography* (New York and Oxford, 1980), p.210.
54 See above, chapter 1: 'Calvin's Theology'.
55 *Edgar Allan Poe: Poetry and Tales*, edited by Patrick F. Quinn, *Library of America* (Cambridge, 1984), p.1287.
56 On the novelist Ann Radcliffe, collected in *Sir Walter Scott on Novelists and Fiction*, edited by Ioan Williams (London, 1968), pp.115–6.
57 *The Novels and Tales of Henry James*, New York Edition, 24 volumes (New York, 1907–9), XII (1908), xxi.

Bibliography

MANUSCRIPT AND UNPUBLISHED MATERIAL

Blackwood Papers, National Library of Scotland
Cartmell, Claire, 'The Age of Politics, Personalities, and Periodicals: The Early Nineteenth-Century World of the "Noctes Ambrosianae" of *Blackwood's Edinburgh Magazine* (unpublished Ph.D. dissertation, University of Leeds, 1974)
Garside, P.D., 'Intellectual Origins of Scott's View of History in the Waverley Novels' (unpublished Ph.D. dissertation, University of Cambridge, 1970)
Meehan, Michael, 'Liberty and Creativity: Political Models in English Literary Theory, 1709–1767' (unpublished Ph.D. dissertation, University of Cambridge, 1977)
National Library of Scotland, manuscript letters of Scott, Hogg, Galt, Lockhart and the Blackwood Group
Osborne, Robert Stevens, 'A Study of Washington Irving's Development as a Man of Letters to 1825' (unpublished Ph.D. dissertation, University of North Carolina, 1947)
Swann, C.S.B., 'Fictions of Past and Present: Some Ideas of History and of the Past in Certain Novels of the Nineteenth Century' (unpublished Ph.D. dissertation, University of Cambridge, 1975)
Strout, Alan Lang, unpublished MS of vol. II of *The Life and Letters of James Hogg the Ettrick Shepherd* (National Library of Scotland)

PUBLISHED WORKS

Aberdein, Jennie W., *John Galt* (London, 1936)
Abrams, M.H., *The Mirror and the Lamp: Romantic Theory and the Critical Tradition* (1953; rpt. Oxford, 1974)
　Natural Supernaturalism: Tradition and Revolution in Romantic Literature (1971; rpt. New York, 1973)
Adair, John, *Founding Fathers: The Puritans in England and America* (London, 1982)
Adams, James T., *The American: The Making of a New Man* (New York, 1943)
Adams, John, and Thomas Jefferson, *The Adams–Jefferson Letters, The Complete Correspondence between Thomas Jefferson and Abigail and John Adams*, ed. by Lester J. Cappon, 2 vols. (Chapel Hill, North Carolina, 1959)
Adams, Percy G., *Travelers and Travel Liars 1600–1800* (Berkeley, Calif., 1962)

Addison, Joseph, and Sir Richard Steele, *The Spectator*, ed. by Donald F. Bond, 5 vols (Oxford, 1965)
Akers, Charles W., 'Calvinism and the American Revolution', in *The Heritage of John Calvin*, Heritage Hall Lectures 1960–70, ed. by John H. Bratt (Grand Rapids, Mich., 1973)
Alexander, J.H., '"Only Connect": The Passionate Style of Walter Scott', *Scottish Literary Journal*, 6, no. 2 (December 1979), 37–54
Alison, Archibald, *Essays on the Nature and Principles of Taste*, 5th edn, 2 vols. (Edinburgh, 1817)
Allan, George, [and William Weir], *Life of Sir Walter Scott, Bart., With Critical Notices of His Writings* (Edinburgh, 1832–4)
Allen, Michael, *Poe and the British Magazine Tradition* (New York, 1969)
Alterton, Margaret, *Origins of Poe's Critical Theory*, University of Iowa Humanistic Studies, 2, no. 3 (April 1925)
Anderson, James, 'Sir Walter Scott as Historical Novelist', 6 parts, *Studies in Scottish Literature*, from vol. 4, no. 1 (July 1966) to vol. 5, no. 3 (January 1968)
Anderson, Quentin, *The Imperial Self: An Essay in American Literary and Cultural History* (New York, 1971)
Andrewes, Lancelot, *Ninety-Six Sermons*, ed. by J.P. Wilson, 5 vols. (Oxford, 1841–3)
Arnold, Matthew, *The Complete Prose Works of Matthew Arnold*, ed. by R.H. Super, 11 vols. (Ann Arbor, Mich., 1960–77)
Arvin, Newton, *Herman Melville*, The American Men of Letters Series (London, 1950)
Ashbery, John, *Self-Portrait in a Convex Mirror* (New York, 1975)
Ashton, Rosemary, *The German Idea: Four English Writers and the Reception of German Thought, 1800–1860* (Cambridge, 1980)
Augustine of Hippo, St, *The Confessions of Saint Augustine*, trans. by F.J. Sheed (1944; rpt. London, 1978)
  City of God, trans. by Henry Bettenson (1972; rpt. Harmondsworth, 1981)
Austen, Jane, *Mansfield Park*, ed. by R.W. Chapman, *The Oxford Illustrated Jane Austen*, vol. III (Oxford, 1978)
Ayer, A.J., *Hume*, Oxford Past Masters Series (Oxford, 1980)
Bald, R.C., *John Donne: A Life*, completed and ed. by W. Milgate (Oxford, 1970)
Bancroft, George, 'Review of Mrs Hemans's Poems', *North American Review*, 24 (1827), 443–63
Barrell, John, *English Literature in History 1730–80: An Equal, Wide Survey* (London, 1983)
Bate, Walter Jackson, 'The Sympathetic Imagination in Eighteenth-Century English Criticism', *English Literary History*, 12 (1945), 144–64
  The Burden of the Past and the English Poet (London, 1971)
Batho, Edith C., *The Ettrick Shepherd* (Cambridge, 1927)
Baym, Nina, *The Shape of Hawthorne's Career* (New York, 1976)
Becker, Carl L., *The Declaration of Independence: A Study in the History of Political Ideas* (New York, 1922; rpt. 1956)
  The Heavenly City of the Eighteenth-Century Philosophers, Yale University Storrs Lectures, 1931 (1932; rpt. New Haven, Conn., 1952)
Beers, Henry A., *The Connecticut Wits and Other Essays* (New Haven, Conn., 1920)
Behnken, Eloise M., *Thomas Carlyle: 'Calvinist without the Theology'*, University of Missouri Studies, 66 (London, 1978)
Bell, Alan, ed., *Scott Bicentenary Essays* (Edinburgh, 1973)
Bell, Michael D., *Hawthorne and the Historical Romance of New England* (Princeton, N.J., 1970)
  The Development of American Romance: The Sacrifice of Relation (Chicago, 1980)

Bibliography

Benjamin, Walter, *Illuminations*, ed. and introd. by H. Arendt, trans. by Harry Zohn (1970; rpt. London, 1973)
Bercovitch, Sacvan, *The Puritan Origins of the American Self* (New Haven, Conn., 1975; rpt. 1976)
  The American Jeremiad (Madison, Wis., 1978)
Bercovitch, Sacvan, ed., *The American Puritan Imagination: Essays in Revaluation* (Cambridge, 1974)
Berlin, Isaiah, *Vico and Herder: Two Studies in the History of Ideas* (1976; rpt. London, 1980)
  Against the Current: Essays in the History of Ideas, ed. by Henry Hardy (1979; rpt. Oxford, 1981)
Berlin, Isaiah, ed., *The Age of Enlightenment: The Eighteenth Century Philosophers* (1956; rpt. Oxford, 1979)
Berthoff, Werner, '"A Lesson on Concealment": Brockden Brown's Method in Fiction', *Philological Quarterly*, 37, no. 1 (January 1958), 45–57
  The Example of Melville (Princeton, N.J., 1962)
Bettenson, Henry, ed., *Documents of the Christian Church*, 2nd edn (Oxford, 1963; rpt. 1967)
Bevilacqua, Vincent M., 'James Beattie's theory of Rhetoric', *Speech Monographs*, 34, no. 2 (June 1967), 109–24
Bewley, Marius, *The Complex Fate: Hawthorne, Henry James and some other American Writers* (London, 1952)
  The Eccentric Design: Form in the Classic American Novel (London, 1959)
Birkhead, Edith, *The Tale of Terror: A Study of the Gothic Romance* (London, 1921)
Black, George Fraser, *Scotland's Mark on America* (New York, 1921)
  Macpherson's Ossian and the Ossianic Controversy (New York, 1926)
Black, Michael L., 'Bibliographical Problems in Washington Irving's Early Works', *Early American Literature*, 3, no. 3 (Winter 1968–9), 148–58
Blackwood's Edinburgh Magazine (Edinburgh, 1817–1980)
Blair, Hugh, *Lectures on Rhetoric and Belles Lettres*, 2 vols. (London, 1783)
Bloedé, Barbara R., 'James Hogg's *Private Memoirs and Confessions of a Justified Sinner*: The Genesis of the Double', *Etudes Anglaises*, 26, no. 2 (April–June 1973), 174–86
Bloom, Harold, *The Anxiety of Influence: A Theory of Poetry* (New York, 1973)
Bloom, Lillian, 'Addison's Popular Aesthetic: The Rhetoric of the *Paradise Lost* Papers', in *The Author in His Work: Essays on a Problem in Criticism*, ed. by Louis L. Martz and Aubrey Williams (New Haven, Conn., 1978), 263–81
Boorstin, Daniel J., *The Lost World of Thomas Jefferson* (New York, 1948)
  The Americans: The National Experience (New York, 1965)
  The Exploring Spirit: America and the World Experience, The Reith Lectures, 1975 (London, 1976)
Borland, R., introduction to Edith Batho's *James Hogg the Ettrick Shepherd, Memorial Volume* (Selkirk, Scotland, 1898)
Boswell, James, *The Life of Samuel Johnson* (1791), 2 vols. (London, 1906; rpt. 1973)
Boulger, James D., *The Calvinist Temper in English Poetry* (The Hague, 1980)
Bowen, Merlin, *The Long Encounter: Self and Experience in the Writings of Herman Melville* (London and Chicago, 1960)
Brackenridge, Hugh Henry, *Modern Chivalry, Containing the Adventures of Captain John Farrago and Teague O'Regan, his Servant*, ed. by Lewis Leary (New Haven, Conn., 1965)
Bradford, William, *History of the Plymouth Plantation*, introduction by S.E. Morison, new edn (New York, 1952)

Bradley, A.C., *Shakespearian Tragedy*, 2nd edn (1905; rpt. London, 1974)
Brevoort, Henry, *Letters of Henry Brevoort to Washington Irving*, together with other unpublished Brevoort Papers, ed. by George S. Hellman (New York, 1916)
Bridgman, Richard, *The Colloquial Style in America* (New York, 1966)
Brodhead, Richard H., *Hawthorne, Melville and the Novel* (Chicago and London, 1976; rpt. 1977)
Brogan, D.W., *The American Character*, 2nd edn (1956; rpt. New York, 1959)
Bronson, Bertrand Harris, *Facets of the Enlightenment* (Berkeley and Los Angeles, Calif., 1968)
Brooks, Van Wyck, *The Flowering of New England 1815–1865* (London, 1936)
  The World of Washington Irving (1945; rpt. London, 1947)
  The Writer in America, 2nd edn (New York, 1968)
Brown, Charles Brockden, *Wieland, or The Transformation* (New York, 1798; rpt. New Haven, Conn., 1968)
  Ormond (New York, 1799; rpt. New Haven, Conn., 1968)
  Edgar Huntly, or, Memoirs of a Sleepwalker, ed. by David Stinebeck (New Haven, Conn., 1973)
Brown, David, *Walter Scott and the Historical Imagination* (London, 1979)
Bruccoli, Matthew J., ed. *The Chief Glory of Every People: Essays on Classic American Writers* (London, 1973)
Bryson, Gladys, *Man and Society: The Scottish Inquiry of the Eighteenth Century* (Princeton, N.J., 1945)
Buber, Martin, *I and Thou*, trans. by Walter Kaufmann (Edinburgh, 1970)
Buchan, John, *Sir Walter Scott* (London, 1932)
Buckle, Henry Thomas, *On Scotland and the Scotch Intellect*, ed. by H.J. Hanham (Chicago and London, 1970)
Bunyan, John, *Grace Abounding to the Chief of Sinners*, and *The Pilgrim's Progress from this World to that which is to come*, ed. by Roger Sharrock (London, 1966)
Buranelli, Vincent, *Edgar Allan Poe*, Twayne's United States Authors Series, no. 4, 2nd edn (Boston, Mass., 1977)
Burke, Edmund, *A Philosophical Inquiry into the Origin of Our Ideas of the Sublime and the Beautiful*, ed. by J.T. Boulton (Notre Dame, Ind., and London, 1958)
  Reflections on the Revolution in France, and on the Proceedings in Certain Societies in London Relative to that Event, ed. by Conor Cruise O'Brien (1968; rpt. Harmondsworth, 1979)
Burns, Robert, *The Kilmarnock Poems*, ed. by Donald A. Low (London, 1985)
Butler, Marilyn, *Jane Austen and the War of Ideas* (Oxford, 1975)
  Romantics, Rebels and Reactionaries: English Literature and its Background 1760–1830 (Oxford, 1981)
Burwick, Frederick, 'Associationist Rhetoric and Scottish Prose Style', *Speech Monographs*, 34, no. 1 (March, 1967), 21–34
Buxbaum, Melvin H., 'Hume, Franklin and America: A Matter of Loyalties', *Enlightenment Essays*, 3, no. 2 (Summer 1972), 93–105
Cairns, William B., *British Criticisms of American Writings 1783–1815: A Contribution to the Study of Anglo–American Literary Relationships*, University of Wisconsin Studies in Language and Literature, no. 1 (Madison, Wisc., 1918)
  British Criticisms of American Writings 1815–1833: A Contribution to the Study of Anglo–American Literary Relationships, University of Wisconsin Studies in Language and Literature, no. 14 (Madison, Wisc., 1922)
Caldwell, Patricia, *The Puritan Conversion Narrative: The Beginning of American Expression* (Cambridge, 1983)

Bibliography

Calvin, John, *Letters of John Calvin*, compiled and ed. by J. Bonnet, 4 vols. (1858; rpt. New York, 1972)
   Institutes of the Christian Religion (1559), trans. by Henry Beveridge, 2 vols. (Grand Rapids, Mich., 1979)
   John Calvin, ed. by G.R. Potter and M. Greengrass, Documents of Modern History Series (London, 1983)
   The Christian Life, ed. by John H. Leith (Cambridge, Mass., 1984)
Camic, Charles, *Experience and Enlightenment: Socialization for Cultural Change in Eighteenth-Century Scotland* (Edinburgh, 1983)
Campbell, Ian, 'Author and Audience in Hogg's *Confessions of a Justified Sinner*', *Scottish Literary News*, 2, no. 4 (June 1972), 66–76
Campbell, Ian, ed., *Nineteenth-Century Scottish Fiction: Critical Essays* (Manchester, 1979)
Camus, Albert, *Selected Essays and Notebooks*, trans. and ed. by Philip Thody (Harmondsworth, 1970)
Carlyle, Alexander, *Anecdotes and Characters of the Times*, ed. by James Kinsley (London, 1973)
Carlyle, Thomas, *Reminiscences*, ed. by Charles Eliot Norton, 2 vols (London, 1887)
   Two Notebooks of Thomas Carlyle: from 23rd March, 1822 to 16th May, 1832, ed. by Charles Eliot Norton (1898; facsimile rpt. Mamaroneck, N.Y., 1972)
   The Edinburgh Edition of The Works of Thomas Carlyle, 30 vols. (New York, 1903–4)
   Correspondence between Goethe and Carlyle, ed. by Charles Eliot Norton (1932; rpt. London, 1972)
Carlyle, Thomas, *The Collected Letters of Thomas and Jane Welsh Carlyle*, ed. by C.R. Sanders and K.J. Fielding, The Duke–Edinburgh Edition (Durham, N.C., 1970–)
   The Correspondence of Emerson and Carlyle, ed. by Joseph Slater (London, 1964)
Carpenter, Frederic I., 'The Vogue of Ossian in America: A Study in Taste', *American Literature*, 2, no. 4 (January 1931), 405–17
Carswell, Donald, *Sir Walter: A Four-Part Study in Biography – Scott, Hogg, Lockhart, J. Baillie* (London, 1930)
Carton, Evan, 'Hawthorne and The Province of Romance', *English Literary History*, 47, no. 2 (Summer 1980), 331–54
Cassirer, Ernst, *The Philosophy of the Enlightenment*, trans. by Fritz Koelln and James P. Pettegrove (1951; rpt. Boston, 1964)
Catalogue of the Library of Abbotsford (Edinburgh, 1838)
Cawelti, John G., 'Some Notes on the Structure of *The Confidence-Man*,' *American Literature*, 29, no. 3 (November 1957), 278–88
Caws, Peter, ed., *Two Centuries of Philosophy in America*, Library of Philosophy, no. 7 (Oxford, 1980)
Chadwick, Owen, *The Reformation*, The Pelican History of the Church, vol. III (1964; rpt. Harmondsworth, 1982)
Chandler, Elizabeth Lathrop, *A Study of the Sources of the Tales and Romances Written by Nathaniel Hawthorne before 1853*, Smith College Studies in Modern Languages, 7, no. 4 (Northampton, Mass., 1926)
[Channing, Walter], 'Essay on American Language and Literature', *North American Review*, 1, no. 3 (September 1815), 307–14
Chapman, R.W., 'Blair on Ossian', *Review of English Studies*, 7, no. 25 (January 1931), 80–83
Charvat, William, *The Origins of American Critical Thought 1810–1835* (Philadelphia, Pa., and London, 1936)
   The Profession of Authorship in America 1800–1870, ed. by Matthew J. Bruccoli (Columbus, Ohio, 1968)

Chase, Richard, *Herman Melville: A Critical Study* (New York, 1949)
　The American Novel and its Tradition (New York, 1957)
Chesterton, G.K., *Twelve Types* (London, 1902)
Chitnis, Anand, *The Scottish Enlightenment: A Social History* (London, 1976)
Clark, David Lee, *Charles Brockden Brown: Pioneer Voice of America* (Durham, N.C., 1952)
Clark, Kenneth, *Moments of Vision* (London, 1981)
Clark, Stuart, 'Inversion, Misrule and the Meaning of Witchcraft', *Past and Present*, no. 87 (May 1980), 98–127
Clebsch, William A., *American Religious Thought: A History*, Chicago History of American Religion (Chicago and London, 1973)
Clive, John, *Scotch Reviewers: 'The Edinburgh Review' 1802–1815* (London, 1957)
Clive, John, and Bernard Bailyn, 'England's Cultural Provinces: Scotland and America', *William and Mary Quarterly*, 3rd series, 11, no. 2 (April 1954), 200–13
Clubbe, John, ed., *Carlyle and His Contemporaries*, Essays in Honour of Charles Richard Sanders (Durham, N.C., 1976)
Cobb, Joann P., 'Godwin's Novels and *Political Justice*', *Enlightenment Essays*, 4, no. 1 (Spring 1973), 15–28
Cobban, Alfred, *In Search of Humanity: The Role of the Enlightenment in Modern History* (London, 1960)
Cockburn, Henry, *Memorials of His Time* (Edinburgh, 1856)
Cockshut, A.O.J., *The Achievement of Walter Scott* (London, 1969)
Cohen, Hennig, ed., *The American Experience: Approaches to the Study of the United States* (Boston, Mass., 1968)
Cohen, Hennig, ed., *The American Culture: Approaches to the Study of the United States* (Boston, Mass., 1968)
Cohen, Ralph, 'The Rationale of Hume's Literary Inquiries', in *David Hume: Many-sided Genius*, ed. by Kenneth R. Merrill and Robert W. Shahan (Norman, Okla., 1976)
Colacurcio, Michael J., *The Province of Piety: Moral History in Hawthorne's Early Tales* (Cambridge, Mass., 1984)
Coleridge, Samuel Taylor, *Biographia Literaria* (1817), ed. by James Engell and W.J. Bate, *The Collected Works of Samuel Taylor Coleridge*, general ed. Kathleen Coburn (Princeton, N.J., 1980–), vol. VII (1983)
Collinson, Patrick, *The Religion of Protestants: The Church in English Society 1559–1625* (1982; rpt. Oxford, 1984)
Collis, John Stewart, *The Carlyles: A Biography of Thomas and Jane Carlyle* (London, 1971)
Conrad, Joseph, 'The Secret Sharer', in *'Twixt Land and Sea* (London, 1913)
Constable, Thomas, *Archibald Constable and His Literary Correspondents*, 3 vols. (Edinburgh, 1873)
Cooney, Seamus, 'Scott's Anonymity: Its Motives and Consequences', *Studies in Scottish Literature*, 10, no. 4 (April 1973), 207–19
Cooper, Anthony Ashley, 3rd Earl of Shaftesbury, *Characteristicks of Men, Manners, Opinions, Times, etc* (1711), ed. by J.M. Robertson, 2 vols. (London, 1900)
Cooper, James Fenimore, *The Travelling Bachelor; or, Notions of the Americans*, 2nd edn, 2 vols. in 1 (New York, 1852)
　The Works of J. Fenimore Cooper, 10 vols. (1891–2; rpt. New York, 1969)
　Gleanings in Europe: Volume Two; England, ed. by Robert E. Spiller (New York, 1930)
　The Letters and Journals of James Fenimore Cooper, ed. by J.F. Beard, 6 vols. (Cambridge, Mass., 1960–8)
　The Spy: A Tale of the Neutral Ground, ed. by J.E. Morpurgo, Classic American Texts Series (Oxford, 1968)

The American Democrat, ed. by George Dekker and Larry Johnston (Harmondsworth, 1969)
Corson, James C., 'Lockhart the Scorpion: an Unpublished Manuscript', *Studies in Scottish Literature*, 1, no. 3 (January 1964), 197–201
Costain, Keith M., 'The Community of Man: Galt and Eighteenth-Century Scottish Realism', *Scottish Literary Journal*, 8, no. 1 (May 1981), 10–29
Cottom, Daniel, 'The Waverley Novels: Superstition and the Enchanted Reader', *English Literary History*, 47, no. 1 (Spring 1980), 80–102
Cournos, John, introd., *American Short Stories of the Nineteenth Century* (London, 1930)
Cox, James M., 'Edgar Poe: Style as Pose', *Virginia Quarterly Review*, 44, no. 1 (Winter 1968), 67–89
Cox, R.G., 'The Great Reviews', *Scrutiny*, 6, no. 1 (June 1937), 2–20; no. 2 (September 1937), 155–75
Craig, David, *Scottish Literature and the Scottish People 1680–1830* (London, 1961)
Crèvecoeur, J. Hector St-John de, *Letters from an American Farmer* (1782; rpt. New York, 1904)
Crews, Frederick, *The Sins of the Fathers: Hawthorne's Psychological Themes* (1966; rpt. London, 1970)
Crosland, T.W., *The Unspeakable Scot* (London, 1902)
Cunliffe, Marcus, *The Nation Takes Shape: 1789–1837*, Chicago History of American Civilisation (1959; rpt. Chicago, 1969)
The Literature of the United States, 3rd edn (1967; rpt. Harmondsworth, 1976)
Cunningham, Valentine, *Everywhere Spoken Against: Dissent in the Victorian Novel* (Oxford, 1975)
Daiches, David, *Literary Essays* (Edinburgh, 1956)
'Scott's *Redgauntlet*', in *From Jane Austen to Joseph Conrad, Essays Collected in Memory of James T. Hillhouse*, ed. by Robert C. Rathburn and Martin Steinmann, Jr (1958; rpt. Minneapolis, Minn., 1967), 46–59
The Paradox of Scottish Culture: The Eighteenth-Century Experience (London, 1964)
Scotland and the Union (London, 1977)
Literature and Gentility in Scotland (Edinburgh, 1982)
Dangerfield, George, *The Awakening of American Nationalism 1815–1828*, The New American Nation Series (New York, 1965)
Dauber, Kenneth, *Rediscovering Hawthorne* (Princeton, N.J., 1977)
Davidson, Edward H., *Jonathan Edwards: The Narrative of a Puritan Mind* (Cambridge, Mass., 1968)
Davie, Donald, *The Heyday of Sir Walter Scott* (London, 1961)
'The Poetry of Sir Walter Scott', *Proceedings of the British Academy*, 47 (1961), 61–75
A Gathered Church: The Literature of the English Dissenting Interest, 1700–1930, The Clark Lectures, 1976 (London and Henley, 1978)
Davie, George Elder, *The Democratic Intellect: Scotland and her Universities in the Nineteenth Century*, 2nd edn (Edinburgh, 1964)
The Scottish Enlightenment, The Historical Association, General Series, no. 99 (London, 1981)
Davies, Horton, *Worship and Theology in England*, vol. II, *From Andrewes to Baxter* (Princeton, N.J., 1975); vol. III, *From Watts and Wesley to Maurice, 1690–1850* (Princeton, N.J., 1961–75)
Davies, Hugh Sykes, and George Watson, eds., *The English Mind: Studies in the English Moralists* (Cambridge, 1964)
Davis, Richard Beale, 'Poe and William Wirt', *American Literature*, 16 (1944–5), 212–20
Dekker, George, *James Fenimore Cooper the Novelist* (London, 1967)
The American Historical Romance (Cambridge, 1987)

Dekker, George, and J.P. Williams, eds., *Fenimore Cooper: The Critical Heritage* (London, 1973)
Demos, John, *Entertaining Satan: Witchcraft and the Culture of Early New England* (New York, 1982)
Denny, Margaret, and William Gilman, eds., *The American Writer and the European Tradition* (Minneapolis, Minn., 1950)
Devlin, D.D., ed., *Walter Scott*, Modern Judgments series (London, 1969)
Dillingham, William B., *Melville's Short Fiction 1853–1856* (Athens, Ga., 1977)
Donaldson, Gordon, *The Scottish Reformation* (Cambridge, 1960)
  Scotland: Church and Nation through Sixteen Centuries, 2nd edn (Edinburgh, 1972)
Donne, John, *Sermons on the Psalms and Gospels, with a Selection of Prayers and Meditations*, ed. and with an introduction by Evelyn M. Simpson (Berkeley, Calif., 1963)
  The Divine Poems of John Donne, ed. and introduced by Helen Gardner, 2nd edn (Oxford, 1978; rpt. 1982)
Doubleday, Neal Frank, 'Hawthorne and Literary Nationalism', *American Literature*, 12 (1940–1), 447–53
  Hawthorne's Early Tales, a Critical Study (Durham, N.C., 1972)
  Variety of Attempt: British and American Fiction in the Early Nineteenth Century (Lincoln, Neb., 1976)
Douglas, George, *James Hogg*, Famous Scots Series (Edinburgh, 1899)
Dowden, Edward, *Puritan and Anglican: Studies in Literature* (London, 1900)
Dryden, Edgar A., *Melville's Thematics of Form: The Great Art of Telling the Truth* (Baltimore, Md., 1968)
Dubler, Walter, 'Theme and Structure in Melville's *The Confidence-Man*', *American Literature*, 33, no. 3 (November 1961), 307–19
Duckworth, Alistair, 'Scott's Fiction and the Migration of Settings', *Scottish Literary Journal*, 7, no. 1 (May 1980), 97–112
Dussinger, John, *The Discourse of Mind in Eighteenth-Century Fiction*, Studies in English Literature, no. 80 (The Hague, 1974)
Eakin, Paul John, 'Poe's Sense of an Ending', *American Literature*, 45, no. 1 (March 1973), 1–22
Eberwein, Jane Donahue, ed., *Early American Poetry: Selections from Bradstreet, Taylor, Dwight, Freneau, and Bryant,* (Madison, Wis. 1978)
Edwards, Jonathan, *Freedom of the Will*, ed. by Paul Ramsey, *The Works of Jonathan Edwards*, vol. I (New Haven, Conn., 1957)
  Religious Affections, ed. by John E. Smith, *The Works of Jonathan Edwards*, vol. II (New Haven, Conn., 1959)
  The Nature of True Virtue (1765), ed. by William K. Frankena (Ann Arbor, Mich., 1960)
  Jonathan Edwards: Representative Selections, ed. by Clarence H. Faust and Thomas H. Johnson, revised edn (New York, 1962)
  The Great Awakening, ed. by C.C. Goen, *The Works of Jonathan Edwards*, vol. IV (New Haven, Conn., 1972)
  'A Narrative of Surprising Conversions' (1736), in *Jonathan Edwards on Revival* (Edinburgh, 1965; rpt. 1984)
  The Works of Jonathan Edwards, with a Memoir by Sereno E. Dwight; revised and corrected by Edward Hickman (1834), 2 vols. (Edinburgh, 1974; rpt. 1979)
Edwards, Owen Dudley, and George Shepperson, eds., *Scotland, Europe and the American Revolution*, Essays Presented at the Scottish Universities American Bicentennial Conference, 1976 (Edinburgh, 1976)

Eggenschwiler, David, 'James Hogg's *Confessions* and the Fall into Division', *Studies in Scottish Literature*, 9, no. 1 (July 1971–April 1972), 26–39
Eliot, T.S., *Selected Essays* (London, 1932)
 Selected Prose of T.S. Eliot, ed. by Frank Kermode (London, 1975)
Elliott, Emory, ed., *Puritan Influences in American Literature*, Illinois Studies in Language and Literature, no. 65 (Urbana, Ill., 1979)
Emerson, Everett, *Puritanism in America 1620–1750* (Boston, Mass., 1977)
Emerson, Ralph Waldo, *Emerson's Complete Works*, Riverside Edition, 11 vols. (Boston, Mass., 1885–6)
 Journals, ed. Edward W. Emerson and W.E. Forbes, 10 vols. (Boston, Mass., and London, 1909–14)
 The Journals and Miscellaneous Notebooks of R.W. Emerson, ed. by W.H. Gilman and others, 16 vols. (Cambridge, Mass., 1960–82)
 Emerson in His Journals, ed. by Joel Porte (Cambridge, Mass., 1982)
Erämetsä, Erik, *A Study of the Word 'Sentimental' and of other Linguistic Characteristics of Eighteenth-Century Sentimentalism in England* (Helsinki, 1951)
Erikson, Erik, *Young Man Luther: A Study in Psychoanalysis and History* (London, 1959)
Fagin, N. Bryllion, *The Histrionic Mr. Poe* (Baltimore, Md., 1949)
Fairbanks, Henry G., 'Sin, Free Will and "Pessimism" in Hawthorne', *PMLA*, 71 (1956), 975–89
Fairchild, Hoxie Neale, *Religious Trends in English Poetry*, 6 vols. (New York, 1939–68)
Falk, Robert, ed., *Literature and Ideas in America: Essays in Memory of Harry Hayden Clark* (Columbus, Ohio, 1975)
Farrell, John P., *Revolution as Tragedy: The Dilemma of the Moderate from Scott to Arnold* (Ithaca, N.Y. and London, 1980)
Fay, C.R., 'Burke and Adam Smith', Lecture delivered at Queen's University, Belfast, 1956
Feidelson, Charles, *Symbolism in American Literature* (Chicago, 1953; rpt. 1959)
Fender, Stephen, *Plotting the Golden West: American Literature and the Rhetoric of the California Trail* (Cambridge, 1981)
 American Literature in Context, 1620–1830 (London and New York, 1983)
Ferguson, Adam, *The History of the Progress and Termination of the Roman Republic*, 3 vols. (London, 1783)
 An Essay on the History of Civil Society (1767), ed. by Duncan Forbes (Edinburgh, 1966)
Ferguson, William, *Scotland: 1689 to the Present*, The Edinburgh History of Scotland, vol. IV (1968; rpt. Edinburgh, 1978)
Fiedler, Leslie, *Love and Death in the American Novel*, rev. edn (New York, 1975)
Fields, James T., *Yesterdays with Authors* (Boston, Mass., 1900; facsimile rpt. New York, 1970)
Fiering, Norman, *Jonathan Edwards's Moral Thought and Its British Context* (Chapel Hill, N.C., 1981)
Fish, Stanley E., ed., *Seventeenth-Century Prose: Modern Essays in Criticism* (New York, 1971)
 Self-Consuming Artifacts: The Experience of Seventeenth-Century Literature (Berkeley, Calif., 1972)
Fisher, P.F., 'Providence, Fate, and the Historical Imagination in Scott's *Heart of Midlothian*', *Nineteenth-Century Fiction*, 10, no. 2 (September 1955), 99–104
Flibbert, Joseph, *Melville and the Art of Burlesque* (Amsterdam, 1974)
Fliegelman, Jay, *Prodigals and Pilgrims: The American Revolution Against Patriarchal Authority 1750–1800* (Cambridge, 1982; rpt. 1984)

Folsom, James K., *Man's Accidents and God's Purposes: Multiplicity in Hawthorne's Fiction* (New Haven, Conn., 1963)
Forbes, Duncan, 'The Rationalism of Sir Walter Scott', *Cambridge Journal*, 7, no. 1 (October 1953), 20–35
Forbes, William, *An Account of the Life and Writings of James Beattie, LL.D.*, 2 vols. (Edinburgh, 1806)
Franklin, Benjamin, *The Papers of Benjamin Franklin*, ed. by L.W. Labaree and others (New Haven, Conn., 1959–)
  The Autobiography of Benjamin Franklin, ed. by L.W. Labaree and others (New Haven, Conn., 1964)
Franklin, H. Bruce, *The Wake of the Gods: Melville's Mythology* (1963; rpt. Stanford, Calif., 1966)
Frazer, Allan, ed., *Sir Walter Scott 1771–1832: An Edinburgh Keepsake* (Edinburgh, 1971)
Friedrich, Carl J., and Robert G. McCloskey, eds., *From the Declaration of Independence to The Constitution: The Roots of American Constitutionalism*, The American Heritage Series, 6 (New York, 1954)
Fritz, Paul, and David Williams, eds., *City and Society in the Eighteenth Century*, Publications of the McMaster University Association for 18th-Century Studies, vol. III (Toronto, 1973)
Frothingham, Octavius Brooks, *Transcendentalism in New England: A History* (1876; rpt. New York, 1959)
Froude, James Anthony, *Thomas Carlyle: A History of the First Forty Years of His Life 1795–1835*, 2 vols. (London, 1882)
Frykman, Erik, *John Galt's Scottish Stories 1820–1823* (Uppsala, 1959)
Fuller, Margaret, *Woman in the Nineteenth Century*, 1855 edn, introduction by Bernard Rosenthal (New York, 1971)
Furst, Lillian R., *Romanticism in Perspective: A Comparative Study of Aspects of the Romantic Movements in England, France and Germany* (London, 1969)
Furst, Lillian R., compiler, *European Romanticism: Self-Definition: an Anthology* (London, 1980)
Fussell, Edwin, *Frontier: American Literature and the American West* (Princeton, N.J., 1965)
Galt, John, 'Life of John Wilson', in *Scottish Descriptive Poems*, ed. by John Leyden (Edinburgh, 1803)
  The Ayrshire Legatees, or, The Pringle Family (Edinburgh, 1821)
  Sir Andrew Wylie, of that Ilk, 3 vols. (Edinburgh, 1822)
  The Entail; or, the Lairds of Grippy, 3 vols. (Edinburgh, 1823)
  Lawrie Todd; or The Settlers in the Woods, 3 vols. (Edinburgh, 1830)
  Bogle Corbet; or, the Emigrants, 3 vols. (London, 1831)
  Autobiography, 2 vols. (London, 1833)
  Eben Erskine, or, The Traveller, 3 vols. (London, 1833)
  The Literary Life and Miscellanies of John Galt, 3 vols. (Edinburgh, 1834)
  The Stolen Child (1833; rpt. London, 1837)
  The Gathering of the West, ed. by Bradford Allen Booth (Baltimore, Md., 1939)
  Ringan Gilhaize, ed. by Sir George Douglas (London, 1899)
  The Howdie and Other Tales, ed. by William Roughead (Edinburgh, 1923)
  A Rich Man and Other Stories, ed. by William Roughead (Edinburgh, 1925)
  Annals of the Parish, ed. by James Kinsley, Oxford English Novels (London, 1967)
  The Entail, ed. by Ian A. Gordon, Oxford English Novels (London, 1970)
  The Provost, ed. by Ian A. Gordon, Oxford English Novels (London, 1973)
  The Member, an Autobiography, ed. by Ian A. Gordon (Edinburgh, 1975)
  The Last of the Lairds, ed. by Ian A. Gordon (Edinburgh, 1976)
  Selected Short Stories, ed. by Ian A. Gordon (Edinburgh, 1978)

Garden, Mrs, ed., *Memorials of James Hogg, the Ettrick Shepherd* (Paisley and London, n.d.)
Gay, Peter, *A Loss of Mastery: Puritan Historians in Colonial America* (Berkeley and Los Angeles, Calif., 1966)
Gellner, Ernest, *Thought and Change*, Nature of Human Society Series (London, 1965)
Gerard, Alexander, *An Essay on Genius* (London, 1774)
Gifford, Douglas, *James Hogg* (Edinburgh, 1976)
[Gillies, R.P.], *Recollections of Sir Walter Scott, Bart.* (London, 1837)
   Memoirs of a Literary Veteran, 3 vols. (London, 1851)
Gilmore, Michael T., *The Middle Way: Puritanism and Ideology in American Romantic Fiction* (New Brunswick, N.J., 1977)
Godwin, William, *Enquiry Concerning Political Justice and its Influence on Modern Morals and Happenings* (1793), ed. by Isaac Kramnick (Harmondsworth, 1976)
   Caleb Williams, ed. by David McCracken (1970; rpt. New York, 1977)
Gohdes, Clarence, *American Literature in Nineteenth-Century England* (New York, 1944)
Goldberg, M.A., *Smollett and the Scottish School: Studies in Eighteenth-Century Thought* (Albuquerque, N.M., 1959)
Goldsmith, Oliver, *The Citizen of the World*, ed. by Arthur Friedman, The Collected Works of Oliver Goldsmith, vol. 2 (Oxford, 1966)
Gordon, George Stewart, *John Gibson Lockhart*, Commemoration Address delivered in the University of Glasgow, 1930 (Glasgow, 1944)
Gordon, Ian A., *John Galt: The Life of a Writer* (Edinburgh, 1972)
Gordon, Mrs, *'Christopher North'; A Memoir of John Wilson*, 2 vols. (Edinburgh, 1862)
Gordon, R.K., *John Galt* (Toronto, 1920)
Gordon, Robert C., *Under Which King? A Study of the Scottish Waverley Novels* (Edinburgh and London, 1969)
Grabo, Norman S., 'Ideology and the Early American Frontier', *Early American Literature*, 22, no. 3 (1987), 274–90
Graham, H.G., *Scottish Men of Letters in the Eighteenth Century* (London, 1901)
Graham, Ian C., *Colonists from Scotland: Emigration to North America, 1707–1783* (Ithaca, N.Y., 1956)
Graham, Walter, *English Literary Periodicals* (1930; rpt. London and New York, 1966)
Grave, S.A., *The Scottish Philosophy of Common Sense* (Oxford, 1960)
Greenlaw, Edwin, 'Washington Irving's Comedy of Politics', *Texas Review*, 1 (April 1916), 291–306
Grierson, H.J.C., *Sir Walter Scott, Bart: A New Life Supplementary to, and Corrective of, Lockhart's Biography* (London, 1938)
   'Lang, Lockhart and Biography', Andrew Lang Lecture, St Andrews University, 1933, in *Concerning Andrew Lang*, Lang Lectures 1927–37 (Oxford, 1949)
Grierson, H.J.C., ed., *Edinburgh Essays on Scots Literature* (Edinburgh, 1933)
Griswold, Rufus Wilmot, *The Prose Writers of America: With a Survey of the Intellectual History, Condition, and Prospects of the Country*. 4th edn, revised (Philadelphia, 1857)
Gross, Harvey, 'The Pursuer and the Pursued: A Study of *Caleb Williams*', *Texas Studies in Literature and Language*, 1, no. 3 (Autumn 1959), 401–11
Gross, John, *The Rise and Fall of the Man of Letters: Aspects of English Literary Life Since 1800* (London, 1969)
Grossman, James, *James Fenimore Cooper* (1949; rpt. Stanford, Calif., 1967)
Haller, William, *The Rise of Puritanism* (New York, 1938)
[Hamilton, Basil], *Men and Manners in America*, 2 vols. (Edinburgh and London, 1833)
Hamowy, Roland, 'Jefferson and the Scottish Enlightenment: A Critique of Garry Wills's *Inventing America: Jefferson's Declaration of Independence*', *The William and

Mary Quarterly, 3rd series, 36, no. 4 (October 1979), 503–23
Hampson, Norman, The Enlightenment (1968; rpt. Harmondsworth, 1976)
Hanham, H.J., 'Mid-Century Scottish Nationalism: Romantic and Radical', in Ideas and Institutions of Victorian Britain, Essays in Honour of George Kitson Clark, ed. by Robert Robson (London, 1967), 143–79
  Scottish Nationalism (London, 1969)
Hardy, Barbara, The Appropriate Form: An Essay on the Novel (London, 1964)
  'Towards a Poetic of Fiction: 3, An Approach through Narrative', Novel: A Forum on Fiction, 2, no. 1 (Fall 1968), 5–14
Harris, Kenneth Marc, Carlyle and Emerson: Their Long Debate (Cambridge, Mass., and London, 1978)
Harrold, C.F., Carlyle and German Thought: 1819–1834, Yale Studies in English (1934; rpt. Hamden, Conn., and London, 1963)
Hart, Francis R., Scott's Novels: The Plotting of Historic Survival (Charlottesville, Va., 1966)
  Lockhart as Romantic Biographer (Edinburgh, 1971)
  The Scottish Novel: A Critical Survey (London, 1978)
Hartman, Geoffrey H., Beyond Formalism: Literary Essays 1958–1970 (New Haven, Conn., and London, 1970)
Harvie, Christopher, Scotland and Nationalism: Scottish Society and Politics 1707–1977 (London, 1977)
Hawthorne, Nathaniel, The Complete Writings of Nathaniel Hawthorne, Old Manse Edition, 22 vols. (Boston, Mass., and New York, 1900)
  The English Notebooks, ed. by Randall Stewart (London, 1941)
  The Centenary Edition of the Works of Nathaniel Hawthorne, ed. by William Charvat and Roy Harvey Pearce (Columbus, Ohio, 1962–)
Hayden, John O., The Romantic Reviewers 1802–1824 (London, 1969)
Hayden, John O., ed., Scott: The Critical Heritage (London, 1970)
Hazard, Paul, European Thought in the Eighteenth Century: From Montesquieu to Lessing, trans. by J. Lewis May (London, 1954)
Hazlitt, William, Lectures on the English Comic Writers (1818), 3rd edn (London, 1841)
  The Spirit of the Age, or Contemporary Portraits (1825), facsimile edn (London, 1971)
Heaney, Seamus, Preoccupations: Selected Prose 1968–78 (London, 1980)
  Selected Poems 1965–75 (London, 1980)
Hedges, William L., 'Knickerbocker, Bolingbroke and the Fiction of History', Journal of the History of Ideas, 20, no. 3 (1959), 317–28
  Washington Irving: An American Study, 1802–1832, Goucher College Series (Baltimore, Md., 1965)
Heimert, Alan, Religion and the American Mind: From the Great Awakening to the Revolution (Cambridge, Mass., 1966)
Hellman, G.S., Washington Irving, Esquire, Ambassador at Large from the New World to the Old (London, 1924)
Herbert, George, The Works of George Herbert, ed. by F.E. Hutchinson (Oxford, 1941)
Hewitt, David, and J.H. Alexander, eds., Scott and His Influence: The Papers of the Scott Conference, 1982 (Aberdeen, 1983)
Hilles, Frederick W., and Harold Bloom, eds., From Sensibility to Romanticism, Essays Presented to Frederick A. Pottle (New York, 1965)
Hoeveler, J. David, Jr, James McCosh and the Scottish Intellectual Tradition: From Glasgow to Princeton (Princeton, N.J., 1981)
Hoffman, Daniel G., 'Irving's Use of American Folklore in "The Legend of Sleepy Hollow"', PMLA, 68, no. 3 (June, 1953), 425–35

Form and Fable in American Fiction (New York, 1961)
Poe Poe Poe Poe Poe Poe Poe (1972; rpt. New York, 1978)
Hogg, James, *The Tales of James Hogg, The Ettrick Shepherd*, 2 vols. (London, 1884)
The Shepherd's Guide (Edinburgh, 1807)
The Spy (Edinburgh, 1810–11)
Tales and Sketches by the Ettrick Shepherd, 6 vols. (Glasgow, 1835–8)
The Poetical Mirror, ed. by T. Earle Welby (London, 1929)
The Private Memoirs and Confessions of a Justified Sinner, ed. by John Carey (Oxford, 1970)
Selected Poems, ed. by Douglas Mack (Oxford, 1970)
Memoirs of the Author's Life and *Familiar Anecdotes of Sir Walter Scott*, ed. by Douglas Mack (Edinburgh and London, 1972)
The Three Perils of Man: War, Women and Witchcraft, ed. by Douglas Gifford (Edinburgh, 1972)
The Brownie of Bodsbeck, ed. by Douglas Mack (Edinburgh and London, 1976)
Selected Stories and Sketches, ed. by Douglas Mack (Edinburgh, 1982)
Holloway, Christopher John, *The Victorian Sage: Studies in Argument* (1953; rpt. Hamden, 1962)
Hook, Andrew, 'Carlyle and America', Carlyle Society Occasional Papers, no. 3 (Edinburgh, 1970)
Scotland and America: A Study of Cultural Relations 1750–1835 (Glasgow and London, 1975)
'Hogg, Melville and the Scottish Enlightenment', *Scottish Literary Journal*, 4, no. 2 (December 1977), 25–39
Hook, Andrew, ed., *The History of Scottish Literature*, vol. II, 1660–1800 (Aberdeen, 1987)
Hooker, Richard, *Of the Laws of Ecclesiastical Polity*, The Folger Library Edition of the Works of Richard Hooker, general editor W. Speed Hill, 4 vols. (Cambridge, Mass., 1977–82)
House, Kay Seymour, *Cooper's Americans* (Columbus, Ohio, 1965)
Howard, David, John Lucas and John Goode, eds., *Tradition and Tolerance in Nineteenth-Century Fiction: Critical Essays on Some English and American Novels* (London, 1966)
Hughes, Mrs, *Letters and Recollections of Sir Walter Scott*, ed. by Horace G. Hutchinson (London, n.d.)
Huizinga, J., *Erasmus of Rotterdam*, trans. by F. Hopman (London, 1952)
America, trans. by H.H. Rowen (New York, 1972)
Hume, David, *A Treatise of Human Nature*, ed. by L.A. Selby-Bigge, 2nd edn, text revised by P.H. Nidditch (Oxford, 1978)
Enquiries Concerning Human Understanding and Concerning the Principles of Morals, ed. by L.A. Selby-Bigge, 3rd edn, revised by P.H. Nidditch (1975; rpt. Oxford, 1979)
Dialogues Concerning Natural Religion, ed. by Norman Kemp Smith, 2nd edn (London, 1947)
Essays, Moral, Political and Literary, ed. by T.H. Green and T.H. Grose, 2 vols. (London, 1875)
The Letters of David Hume, ed. by J.Y.T. Grieg, 2 vols. (Oxford, 1932)
Hutcheson, Francis, *Inquiry into the Original of Our Ideas of Beauty and Virtue*, 2nd edn (London, 1726)
Illustrations on the Moral Sense, ed. by Bernard Peach (Cambridge, Mass., 1971)
Insh, George Pratt, *The Scottish Jacobite Movement: A Study in Economic and Social Forces* (Edinburgh, 1952)
Irving, Pierre M., *Life and Letters of Washington Irving*, 4 vols. (London, 1862–4)

Irving, Washington, *Tales of a Traveller* (1824; rpt. London, 1868)
  Woolfert's Roost and Other Papers, Constable's Miscellany of Foreign Literature, vol. IV (Edinburgh, 1855)
  Biographies and Miscellaneous Papers, collected by P.M. Irving (London, 1867)
  Notes While Preparing Sketch Book &c 1817, ed. by Stanley T. Williams (New Haven, Conn., 1927)
  Tour In Scotland 1817, and other Manuscript Notes, ed. by Stanley T. Williams (New Haven, Conn., 1927)
  Washington Irving and the Storrows: Letters from England and the Continent 1821–1828, ed. by Stanley T. Williams (Cambridge, Mass., 1933)
  Representative Selections, ed. by Henry A. Pochmann (New York, 1934)
  The Western Journals of Washington Irving, ed. by John Francis McDermott (Norman, Okla., 1944)
  A Tour on the Prairies, ed. by John Francis McDermott (Norman, Okla., 1956)
  A History of New York, ed. by Edwin T. Bowden, 1812 edn (New Haven, Conn., 1964)
  'Washington Irving to Walter Scott: 2 Unpublished Letters', ed. by Ben Harris McClary, *Studies in Scottish Literature*, 3, no. 2 (October 1965), 114–18
  Washington Irving's Contributions to 'The Corrector', introduction by Martin Roth, Minnesota Monographs in the Humanities, 3 (Minneapolis, Minn., 1968)
  The Complete Works of Washington Irving, general editor Henry A. Pochmann (Madison, Wis., then Boston, Mass., 1969–)
Jack, Ronald D.S., ed., *Scottish Prose 1550–1700* (London, 1971)
James, Henry, *The Novels and Tales of Henry James*, New York Edition, 24 vols. (New York, 1907–9)
  The Art of the Novel: Critical Prefaces, introduction by R.P. Blackmur (1934; rpt. New York, 1962)
  Henry James and Robert Louis Stevenson: A Record of Friendship and Criticism, ed. by Janet Adam Smith (London, 1948)
  Hawthorne (1879), reissued with an introduction by Tony Tanner (London, 1967)
  English Hours, ed. by Leon Edel (Oxford, 1981)
James, William, *The Will to Believe, and Other Essays in Popular Philosophy* (New York, 1897; rpt. 1903)
  The Varieties of Religious Experience: A Study in Human Nature, ed. by Martin E. Marty (Harmondsworth, 1982)
Jefferson, Thomas, *The Life and Selected Writings of Thomas Jefferson*, ed. by Adrienne Koch and William Peden (New York, 1944)
  The Papers of Thomas Jefferson, general editor Julian P. Boyd (Princeton, New Jersey, 1950–)
  Notes on the State of Virginia (1787), ed. by William Peden (1954; rpt. New York, 1972)
Johnson, Edgar, *Sir Walter Scott: The Great Unknown*, 2 vols. (London, 1970)
Johnson, Samuel, *Lives of the English Poets*, 2 vols. (1906; rpt. London, 1977)
  Prose and Poetry, ed. by Mona Wilson, 2nd edn (Oxford, 1975; rpt. 1970)
Johnson, W.S., *Thomas Carlyle: A Study of his Literary Apprenticeship 1814–1831* (New Haven, Conn., 1911)
Jones, Howard Mumford, *O Strange New World: American Culture: The Formative Years* (1952; rpt. New York, 1964)
  The Theory of American Literature, 2nd edn (Ithaca, N.Y., 1965)
Jones, Maldwyn A., *The Limits of Liberty: American History 1607–1980*, The Short Oxford History of the Modern World (Oxford, 1983)

Joyce, James, *A Portrait of the Artist as a Young Man* (1916; rpt. London, 1983)
Jung, Karl Gustav, *Modern Man in Search of a Soul*, trans. by W.S. Dell and Cary F. Baynes (London, 1933)
Kames, Henry Home, Lord, *Elements of Criticism* (1762), 11th edn, with the Author's Last Corrections and Additions (London, 1840)
Karcher, Carolyn Lury, 'The Story of Charlemont. A Dramatization of Melville's Concepts of Fiction in *The Confidence-Man: His Masquerade*', *Nineteenth-Century Fiction*, 21, no. 1 (June 1966), 73–84
Kaul, A.N., *The American Vision: Actual and Ideal Society in Nineteenth-Century Fiction* (1963; rpt. New Haven, Conn., and London, 1964)
Kearns, Michael S., 'Intuition and Narration in James Hogg's *Confessions*', *Studies in Scottish Literature*, 13 (1978), 81–91
Keats, John, *The Letters of John Keats, 1814–1821*, ed. by H.E. Rollins, 2 vols. (Oxford, 1958)
Kelly, Gary, *The English Jacobin Novel 1780–1805* (Oxford, 1976)
Kemp, John C., 'Historians Manqués: Irving's Apologetic Personae', *American Transcendental Quarterly*, no. 24, Supplement 2 (1974), 15–19
Kendall, R.T., *Calvin and English Calvinism to 1649* (1979; rpt. Oxford, 1981)
Kermode, Frank, *The Classic*, T.S. Eliot Memorial Lectures, 1973 (London, 1975)
Ketterer, David, *The Rationale of Deception in Poe* (Baton Rouge, La., 1979)
Kieckhefer, Richard, *European Witch Trials. Their Foundations in Popular and Learned Culture, 1300–1500* (London, 1976)
Kiely, Robert, *The Romantic Novel in England* (Cambridge, Mass., 1972)
Kierkegaard, Soren, *Selections*, ed. by W.H. Auden (London, 1955)
Kinsley, James, ed., *Scottish Poetry: A Critical Survey* (London, 1955)
Knight, Charles A., 'The Created World of the Edinburgh Periodicals', *Scottish Literary Journal*, 6, no. 2 (December 1979), 20–36
Knights, L.C., *Public Voices: Literature and Politics with Special Reference to the Seventeenth Century*, The Clark Lectures, 1970–1 (London, 1971)
 Selected Essays in Criticism (Cambridge, 1981)
Knox, John, *The History of the Reformation of Religion within the Realm of Scotland*, ed. by C.J. Guthrie (Edinburgh, 1982)
Kohn, Hans, *American Nationalism: An Interpretative Essay* (New York, 1957)
Krapp, George Phillip, *The English Language in America*, 2 vols. (New York, 1925)
Kroeber, Karl, *Romantic Narrative Art* (Madison, Wis., 1960)
Krutch, Joseph Wood, *Edgar Allan Poe: A Study in Genius* (London, 1926)
Kuhns, Richard, *Literature and Philosophy: Structures of Experience* (London, 1971)
Kwiat, Joseph J., and Mary C. Turpie, eds. *Studies in American Culture: Dominant Ideas and Images* (Minneapolis, Minn., 1960)
Lamb, G.F., 'Some Anglo–American Literary Contacts', *Quarterly Review*, 285, no. 572 (April 1947), 247–58
Lamont, William, *Godly Rule: Politics and Religion 1603–1660* (London, 1969)
Lamont, William, and Sybil Oldfield, eds., *Politics, Religion and Literature in The Seventeenth Century* (London, 1975)
Lang, Andrew, *The Life and Letters of John Gibson Lockhart*, 2 vols. (London, 1897)
Langbaum, Robert, *The Poetry of Experience: The Dramatic Monologue in Modern Literary Tradition* (1957; rpt. New York, 1971)
Larner, Christina, *Enemies of God: The Witch-hunt in Scotland* (London, 1981)
Lascelles, Mary, *The Story-teller Retrieves the Past: Historical Fiction and Fictitious History in the Art of Scott, Stevenson, Kipling and some others* (Oxford, 1980)
Lathrop, George Parsons, *A Study of Hawthorne* (Boston, Mass., 1876)

Lawrence, D.H., *Studies in Classic American Literature* (1924; rpt. Harmondsworth, 1971)
Lease, Benjamin, *Anglo–American Encounters: England and the Rise of American Literature* (Cambridge, 1981)
Leavis, F.R., *The Great Tradition* (London, 1948)
'Anna Karenina' and Other Essays (1967; rpt. London, 1973)
Leavis, Q.D., *Fiction and the Reading Public* (1932; rpt. Harmondsworth, 1979)
'Hawthorne as Poet', *Sewanee Review*, 59 (1951), 179–205, 426–58
Lee, L.L., 'The Devil's Figure: James Hogg's *Justified Sinner*', *Studies in Scottish Literature*, 3, no. 4 (April 1966), 230–9
Leech, Clifford, *Shakespeare's Tragedies and Other Studies in Seventeenth-Century Drama* (London, 1950)
Lehmann, William C., *Scottish and Scotch–Irish Contributions to Early American Life and Culture* (Port Washington, N.Y. and London, 1978)
Lenman, Bruce, *Integration, Enlightenment, and Industrialisation: Scotland 1746–1832*, The New History of Scotland, vol. VI (London, 1981)
Leslie, C.R., *Autobiographical Recollections*, ed. by Tom Taylor, 2 vols. (London, 1860)
Leverenz, David, *The Language of Puritan Feeling: An Exploration in Literature, Psychology and Social History* (New Brunswick, N.J., 1980)
Levin, David, *In Defense of Historical Literature: Essays on American History, Autobiography, Drama, and Fiction* (New York, 1967)
Emerson: Prophecy, Metamorphosis, and Influence, Selected Papers from the English Institute (New York, 1975)
Cotton Mather: The Young Life of the Lord's Remembrancer (Cambridge, Mass., 1978)
'The Form and Sources of Cultural History', *Early American Literature*, 18 (1983), 95–101
Levin, David, ed., *Jonathan Edwards: A Profile* (New York, 1969)
Levin, Harry, *The Power of Blackness: Hawthorne, Poe, Melville* (London, 1958)
Levine, George L., and William Madden, eds., *The Art of Victorian Prose* (New York, 1968)
The Boundaries of Fiction: Carlyle, Macaulay, Newman (Princeton, N.J., 1968)
Levine, Paul, 'The American Novel Begins', *The American Scholar*, 35, no. 1 (Winter 1965–6), 134–48
Lewis R.W.B., *The American Adam: Innocence, Tragedy and Tradition in the Nineteenth Century* (Chicago, 1955)
Leyda, Jay, *The Melville Log: A Documentary Life of Herman Melville 1819–1891*, 2 vols. (New York, 1951)
Liebman, Sheldon W., 'The Origins of Emerson's Early Poetics: His Reading in the Scottish Common Sense Critics', *American Literature*, 45, no. 1 (March 1973), 23–33
Lindberg, Gary, *The Confidence Man in American Literature* (New York and Oxford, 1982)
Lindsay, Maurice, *History of Scottish Literature* (London, 1977)
Lochhead, Marion, *John Gibson Lockhart* (London, 1954)
Locke, Don, *A Fantasy of Reason: The Life and Thought of William Godwin* (London, 1980)
Locke, John, *Two Treatises of Civil Government* (1689), ed by Peter Laslett, 2nd edn (Cambridge, 1967; rpt. 1970)
An Essay Concerning Human Understanding (1689), ed. by Peter Nidditch (1975; rpt. Oxford, 1979)
Lockhart, J.G., *Peter's Letters to His Kinsfolk*, 3rd [2nd] edn, 3 vols. (Edinburgh, 1819)
Letter to the Right Honourable Lord Byron (London, 1821)
Valerius, A Roman Story, 3 vols. (Edinburgh, 1821)
Reginald Dalton, 3 vols. (Edinburgh, 1823)

The History of Matthew Wald (Edinburgh, 1824)

'Remarks on the Novel of *Reginald Dalton*, with *Extracts from that Work*, illustrative of *Life in Oxford*' (Oxford, 1824)

The Life of Robert Burns (1828; rpt. London, 1904)

'Abbotsford', in *The Anniversary, or, Poetry and Prose for 1829*, ed. by Allan Cunningham (London, 1829)

Lockhart's Literary Criticism, ed. by M. Clive Hildeyard (Oxford, 1931)

Memoirs of the Life of Sir Walter Scott, Bart., 7 vols. (Edinburgh, 1836–7)

The Ballantyne-Humbug, Handled, In a Letter to Adam Fergusson (Edinburgh, 1839)

Long, Orie W., *Literary Pioneers: Early American Explorers of European Culture* (Cambridge, Mass., 1935)

Lowell, James R., 'Carlyle', *The Works of J.R. Lowell*, Standard Library edn. 11 vols. (Boston, Mass., 1890), vol. II, 78–119

Among My Books (London, 1870)

Lowell, Robert, *For the Union Dead* (1965; rpt. London, 1970)

Lowrie, Ernest Benson, *The Shape of The Puritan Mind: The Thought of Samuel Willard* (New Haven, 1974)

Lucas, F.L., *The Art of Living: Four Eighteenth-Century Minds; Hume, Horace Walpole, Burke, Benjamin Franklin* (London, 1959)

Lundblad, Jane, *Nathaniel Hawthorne and European Literary Tradition*, Essays and Studies on American Language and Literature, no. 6 (Cambridge, Mass., 1947)

Lynen, John F., *The Design of the Present: Essays on Time and Form in American Literature* (New Haven, Conn., and London, 1969)

Lyons, John O., *The Invention of the Self: The Hinge of Consciousness in the Eighteenth Century* (Carbondale, Ill. and London, 1978)

McAdoo, H.R., *The Structure of Caroline Moral Theology* (London, 1949)

MacBeth, Gilbert, *John Gibson Lockhart: A Critical Study*, Illinois Studies in Language and Literature, no. 26 (Urbana, Ill., 1935)

McClary, Ben Harris, 'Ichabod Crane's Scottish Origin', *Notes and Queries*, n.s., 15, no. 1 (January 1968), 29

Washington Irving and the House of Murray: Geoffrey Crayon Charms the British 1817–1856 (Knoxville, Tenn., 1969)

McCosh, James, *Realistic Philosophy, Defended in a Philosophic Series*, 2 vols. (London, 1887)

McCracken, David, 'Godwin's *Caleb Williams*: A Fictional Rebuttal of Burke', *Studies in Burke and His Time*, 11, no. 2 (Winter 1969–70), 1442–52

McCracken, David, ed., *Caleb Williams* (London and New York, 1977)

Mack, Douglas, 'Hogg's Religion and *The Confessions of a Justified Sinner*', *Studies in Scottish Literature*, 7, no. 4 (April 1970), 272–5

MacKenzie, Agnes Mure, *Scotland in Modern Times: 1720–1939* (London, 1941)

Mackenzie, Henry, *The Mirror*, 4th edn, 3 vols. (London, 1782)

The Man of Feeling, ed. by Brian Vickers (London, 1970)

Mackie, J.D., *A History of Scotland*, 2nd edn, revised and ed. by Bruce Lenman and Geoffrey Parker (Harmondsworth, 1978)

Mackie, J.L., *Hume's Moral Theory* (London, 1980)

Maclean, Kenneth, *John Locke and English Literature of the Eighteenth Century* (1936; rpt. New York, 1962)

MacLeod, John, *Scottish Theology in Relation to Church History Since the Reformation*, 3rd edn (1946; rpt. Edinburgh, 1974)

McMaster, Graham, *Scott and Society* (Cambridge, 1981)

McNeill, John T., *The History and Character of Calvinism* (New York, 1954)

MacPherson, James, *The Poems of Ossian, Translated by James MacPherson, Esq.*, with

Dissertations on the Era and Poems of Ossian, and Dr. Blair's Critical Dissertation (London, n.d.)

Fragments of Ancient Poetry, Collected in the Highlands of Scotland, and Translated from the Galic [sic] or Erse Language (1760; rpt. Edinburgh, 1917)

MacQueen, John, *Progress and Poetry*, Part 1 of *The Enlightenment and Scottish Literature* (Edinburgh, 1982)

McWilliams, John J., Jr, *Hawthorne, Melville and the American Character* (Cambridge, 1984)

Manspeaker, Nancy, *Jonathan Edwards: Bibliographical Synopses* (New York, 1981)

Marshall, Gordon, *Presbyteries and Profits: Calvinism and the Development of Capitalism in Scotland, 1560–1707* (Oxford, 1980)

Martin, Harold C., 'The Development of Style in Nineteenth-Century American Fiction', in *Style in Prose Fiction*, ed. by H.C. Martin, English Institute Essays, 1958 (New York, 1959)

Martin, Terence, 'Social Institutions in the Early American Novel', *American Quarterly*, 9, no. 1 (Spring 1957), 72–84

The Instructed Vision: Scottish Common Sense Philosophy and the Origins of American Fiction (Bloomington, Ind., 1961)

Marx, Leo, *The Machine in the Garden: Technology and the Pastoral Idea in America*, (1964; rpt. London and New York, 1978)

Mather, Cotton, *Selections*, ed. by Kenneth B. Murdock, American Author Series, Haffner Library of Classics, 4th edn (New York, 1973)

Mathews, M.M., ed., *The Beginnings of American English* (Chicago, 1931)

Matthiessen, F.O., *American Renaissance: Art and Expression in the Age of Emerson and Whitman* (1941; rpt. London and New York, 1977)

May, Henry F., *The Enlightenment in America* (New York, 1976)

Mayhead, Robin, '*The Heart of Midlothian*: Scott as Artist', *Essays in Criticism*, 6, no. 3 (July 1956), 266–77

Mason, Michael Y., 'The Three Burials in Hogg's *Justified Sinner*', *Studies in Scottish Literature*, 13 (1978), 15–23

Mechie, Stewart, *The Church and Scottish Social Development, 1780–1870*, Cunningham Lectures, 1957 (London, 1960)

Melville, Herman, *The Piazza Tales* (1857), ed. by Egbert S. Oliver (New York, 1948; rpt. 1962)

Journal of a Visit to London and the Continent 1849–1850, ed. by Eleanor Melville Metcalf (London, 1949)

The Letters of Herman Melville, ed. by Merrell R. Davis and William H. Gilman (New Haven, Conn., 1960)

The Confidence-Man: His Masquerade, ed. by H. Bruce Franklin (Indianapolis, Ind., and New York, 1967)

The Writings of Herman Melville, general editor Harrison Hayford, The Northwestern–Newberry Edition (Evanston, Ill., and Chicago, 1968–)

Moby-Dick; or, The Whale (1951), ed. by Harold Beaver (Harmondsworth, 1972)

Mencken, H.L., *A Book of Prefaces*, 4th edn (London, 1922)

The American Language: An Inquiry into the Development of English in the United States, 4th edn, abridged and ed. by Raven I. McDavid, Jr (New York, 1979)

Merrill, Kenneth R. and Robert W. Shahan, eds., *David Hume: Many-sided Genius* (Norman, Okla, 1976)

Meyer, D.H., *The Instructed Conscience: The Shaping of the American National Ethic* (Philadelphia, Penn., 1974)

Middlekauf, Robert, 'Piety and Intellect in Puritanism', *William and Mary Quarterly*, 3rd series, 22, no. 3 (July 1965), 457–70
Miller, James E., Jr, '*The Confidence-Man*: His Guises', *PMLA*, 74 no. 1 (March 1959), 102–11
Miller, Karl, *Doubles: Studies in Literary History* (Oxford, 1985)
Miller, Perry, *The New England Mind: 1, The Seventeenth Century* (1939; rpt. Boston, 1965)
  Jonathan Edwards, The American Men of Letters Series ([New York], 1949)
  The Raven and the Whale: The War of Words and Wits in the Era of Poe and Melville (New York, 1956)
  The American Transcendentalists: Their Prose and Poetry (Garden City, N.Y., 1957)
  The New England Mind: 2, From Colony to Province (1953; rpt. Boston, 1966)
  Errand into the Wilderness (1956; rpt. Cambridge, Mass., 1978)
  The Life of the Mind in America: From the Revolution to the Civil War, Books 1–3 (London, 1966)
  The Responsibility of Mind in a Civilization of Machines: Essays (Amherst, Mass., 1979)
Miller, Perry, ed., *The American Puritans: Their Prose and Poetry* (New York, 1956)
  The Transcendentalists: An Anthology (1950; rpt. Cambridge, Mass., 1979)
Miller, Perry, and Thomas H. Johnson, eds., *The Puritans*, 2nd edn, 2 vols. (New York, 1963)
Mills, Barriss, 'Hawthorne and Puritanism', *New England Quarterly*, 21 (March 1948), 78–102
Mills, Nicolaus, *American and English Fiction in the Nineteenth Century: An Antigenre Critique and Comparison* (Bloomington, Ind., 1973)
Milton, John, *Areopagitica* (1644), *The Complete Prose Works of John Milton*, general editor Don M. Wolfe, 8 vols. (New Haven and London, 1953–1982), vol. II, 1643–8 (1959), 480–570
  Poetical Works, ed. by Douglas Bush (1966; rpt. London, 1969)
Miyoshi, Masao, *The Divided Self: A Perspective on the Literature of the Victorians* (New York, 1969)
Moir, D.M., *Biographical Memoir of John Galt* (Edinburgh, 1841)
Montaigne, Michel de, *The Essayes of Michael Lord of Montaigne*, trans. by John Florio (1603), introduction by Thomas Seccombe, 3 vols. (London, 1908)
Moore, Arthur K., *The Frontier Mind* (1957; rpt. New York and London, 1963)
More, Paul Elmer, and Frank Leslie Cross, eds., *Anglicanism: The Thought and Practice of the Church of England, Illustrated from the Religious Literature of the Seventeenth Century* (London, 1935)
Morgan, Edmund S., *Visible Saints: The History of a Puritan Idea* (Ithaca, N.Y., and London, 1963; rpt. 1971)
  'The Puritan Ethic and the American Revolution', *William and Mary Quarterly*, 3rd series, 24, no. 1 (January 1967), 3–43
Morice, G.P., ed., *David Hume: Bicentenary Papers* (Edinburgh, 1977)
Morris, John N., *Versions of the Self: Studies in English Autobiography from John Bunyan to John Stuart Mill* (New York, 1966)
Morrisroe, Michael, Jr, 'Characterization as Rhetorical Device in Hume's *Dialogues Concerning Natural Religion*', *Enlightenment Essays*, 1, no. 2 (Summer 1970), 95–107
Mossner, Ernest Campbell, *The Life of David Hume*, 2nd edn (Oxford, 1980)
Mott, Frank Luther, 'Carlyle's American Public', *Philological Quarterly*, 4, no. 3 (July 1925), 245–64
[Mudie, Robert], *The Modern Athens: A Dissection and Demonstration of Men and Things in the Scotch Capital. By a Modern Greek* (London, 1825)

Muir, Edwin, *Scott and Scotland: The Predicament of the Scottish Writer*, The Voice of Scotland (London, 1936)

Mullan, John, *Sentiment and Sociability: The Language of Feeling in the Eighteenth Century* (Oxford, 1988)

New, John F.H., *Anglican and Puritan: The Basis of their Opposition 1558–1640* (London, 1964)

Newey, Vincent, ed., *'The Pilgrim's Progress': Critical and Historical Views* (Liverpool, 1980)

Norton, David Fate, *David Hume; Common-Sense Moralist, Sceptical Metaphysician* (Princeton, N.J., 1982)

Nye, R.B., *The Cultural Life of the New Nation 1776–1830*, The New American Nation Series (1960; rpt. New York, 1963)

   Society and Culture in America 1830–1860, The New American Nation Series (New York, 1974)

O'Gorman, Edmundo, *The Invention of America* (Bloomington, Ind., 1961)

Oliphant, Margaret, ed., *Annals of a Publishing House: William Blackwood and His Sons: Their Magazine and Friends*, 2 vols. (Edinburgh, 1897)

Ong, Walter J., *Ramus; Method, and the Decay of Dialogue* (Cambridge, Mass., 1958)

Orians, G. Harrison, 'The Romance Ferment after *Waverley*', *American Literature*, 3, no. 4 (January 1932), 408–31

   'Scott and Hawthorne's *Fanshawe*', *New England Quarterly*, 11 (June 1938), 388–94

Ortega y Gasset, José, *The Modern Theme*, trans. by James Cleugh (1931; rpt. New York, 1961)

   The Dehumanization of Art and Other Essays on Art, Culture and Literature, trans. by H. Weyl and others (Princeton, N.J., 1968)

Osterweis, Rollin G., *Romanticism and Nationalism in the Old South* (New Haven, Conn., 1949)

Ousby, Ian, *Bloodhounds of Heaven: The Detective in English Fiction from Godwin to Doyle* (Cambridge, Mass., 1976)

Parker, William M., *Susan Ferrier and John Galt*, Writers and Their Work Series, no. 185 (London, 1965)

Parrington, Vernon Louis, *Main Currents in American Thought: An Interpretation of American Literature from the Beginnings to 1920*, 3 vols. in 1 (New York, 1927; rpt. 1930)

Parsons, Coleman O., *Witchcraft and Demonology in Scott's Fiction* (Edinburgh, 1964)

Pattee, Fred Lewis, *The Development of the American Short Story: An Historical Survey* (New York, 1923)

Peach, Linden, *British Influences on the Birth of American Literature* (London, 1982)

Pearce, Roy Harvey, 'The Eighteenth-Century Scottish Primitivists: Some Reconsiderations', *English Literary History*, 12 (1945), 203–20

   The Continuity of American Poetry (Princeton, N.J., 1961)

Pearce, Roy Harvey, ed., *Hawthorne Centenary Essays* (Columbus, Ohio, 1964)

Peck, H. Daniel, *A World by Itself: The Pastoral Moment in Cooper's Fiction* (New Haven, Conn., and London, 1977)

Petrie, Charles, *The Jacobite Movement: The Last Phase, 1716–1807*, 3rd edn, revised (London, 1959)

Phillips, Margaret Mann, *Erasmus and the Northern Renaissance* (London, 1949)

Phillipson, N.T., 'Nationalism and Ideology', in *Government and Nationalism in Scotland*, ed. by J.N. Wolfe (Edinburgh, 1969)

   'Towards a Definition of the Scottish Enlightenment', in *City and Society in the Eighteenth Century*, ed. by P. Fritz and D. Williams, McMaster University Assoc. for Eighteenth-Century Studies publications, vol. III (Toronto, 1973)

'The Export of Enlightenment', *The Times Literary Supplement* (2 July 1976), 823-4
Phillipson, N.T., and R. Mitchison, eds., *Scotland in the Age of Improvement: Essays in Scottish History in the Eighteenth Century* (Edinburgh, 1970)
Pickering, James H., ed., *The World Turned Upside Down: Prose and Poetry of The American Revolution* (Port Washington, N.Y., 1975)
Pocock, J.G.A., *Politics, Language and Time: Essays on Political Thought and History* (1971; rpt. London, 1972)
— *The Machiavellian Moment: Florentine Public Thought and the Atlantic Republican Tradition* (Princeton, N.J., 1975)
Poe, Edgar Allan, *Complete Works of Edgar Allan Poe*, 10 vols. (New York, 1902)
— *The Letters of Edgar Allan Poe*, edited by John Ward Ostrom, 2 vols. (Cambridge, Mass., 1948)
— *Selected Prose, Poetry and 'Eureka'*, ed. by W.H. Auden (New York, 1950)
— *Selected Writings*, ed. by David Galloway (Harmondsworth, 1967)
— *The Unknown Poe: An Anthology of Fugitive Writings by Edgar Allan Poe*, ed. by Raymond Foye (San Francisco, Calif., 1980)
— *Essays and Reviews*, edited by G.R. Thompson, Library of America (Cambridge, 1984)
— *Poetry and Tales*, edited by Patrick F. Quinn, Library of America (Cambridge, 1984)
Poirier, Richard, *A World Elsewhere: The Place of Style in American Literature* (London, 1967)
Pollin, Burton R., 'Poe and Godwin', *Nineteenth-Century Fiction*, 20, no. 3 (December 1965), 237-53
Pope, Alexander, *The Twickenham Edition of the Poems of Alexander Pope*, general editor John Butt, 11 vols. (London, 1939-1969), vol. II, *The Rape of the Lock and other poems*, ed. by Geoffrey Tillotson, 2nd edn (1954); vol. VI, *Minor Poems*, ed. by Norman Ault (1954)
Porte, Joel, *The Romance in America: Studies in Cooper, Poe, Hawthorne, Melville and James* (Middletown, Conn., 1969)
— *Representative Man: Ralph Waldo Emerson in His Time* (New York, 1979)
Porter, Roy, and Mikulas Teich, eds., *The Enlightenment in National Context* (Cambridge, 1981)
Prescott, William H., *Biographical and Critical Miscellanies* (Philadelphia, 1845; 1875)
Price, H.H., *Hume's Theory of the External World* (Oxford, 1940)
Price, John Vladimir, *David Hume*, Twayne's English Authors Series, 77 (New York, 1969)
Price, Martin, *To the Palace of Wisdom: Studies in Order and Energy from Dryden to Blake* (1965; rpt. Carbondale, Ill., 1970)
Pritchett, V.S., *The Living Novel* (London, 1946)
Pryde, George S., *The Scottish Universities and the Colleges of Colonial America* (Glasgow, 1957)
Punter, David, *The Literature of Terror: A History of Gothic Fictions from 1765 to the Present Day* (London, 1980)
Quinn, Arthur Hobson, *Edgar Allan Poe: A Critical Biography* (1941; rpt. New York, 1963)
Radzinowicz, M.A., ed., *American Colonial Prose: John Smith to Thomas Jefferson*, Cambridge English Prose Texts (Cambridge, 1984)
Railton, Stephen, *Fenimore Cooper: A Study of his Life and Imagination* (Princeton, N.J., 1978)
Raphael, D.D., *The Moral Sense* (Oxford, 1947)
— 'The Impartial Spectator', *Proceedings of the British Academy*, 58 (1972; rpt. London, 1974) 335-54
— *Adam Smith*, Oxford Past Masters Series (Oxford, 1985)

Raphael, D.D., ed., *British Moralists 1650–1800*, 2 vols. (Oxford, 1969)
Read, Herbert, *Essays on Literary Criticism: Particular Studies* (1938 as Part II of *Collected Essays in Literary Criticism*; rpt. London, 1969)
Regan, Robert, ed., *Poe: A Collection of Critical Essays* (Englewood Cliffs, N.J., 1967)
Reid, David, ed., *The Party-Coloured Mind: Prose Relating to the Conflict of Church and State in Seventeenth-Century Scotland* (Edinburgh, 1982)
Reid, Thomas, *An Inquiry into the Human Mind, on the Principles of Common Sense* (1763; rpt. St Andrews, 1823)
  Essays on the Active Powers of the Human Mind (1788), ed. by Baruch A. Brody (Cambridge, Mass., 1969)
Reid, W. Stanford, *Trumpeter of God: A Biography of John Knox* (New York, 1974)
Rendall, Jane, compiler, *The Origins of the Scottish Enlightenment* (London, 1978)
Renwick, W.L., introd., *Sir Walter Scott Lectures, 1940–1948* (Edinburgh, 1950)
Ridley, Jasper, *John Knox* (Oxford, 1968)
Rieger, James, *The Mutiny Within: The Heresies of Percy Bysshe Shelley* (New York, 1967)
Robertson, Archibald, *The Reformation* (London, 1960)
Robinson, Daniel Sommer, compiler and ed., *The Story of Scottish Philosophy: A Compendium of Selections from the Writings of Nine Pre-eminent Scottish Philosophers, with Bibliographical Essays* (1961; rpt. Westport, Conn., 1979)
Rosenberry, Edward H., *Melville and the Comic Spirit* (Cambridge, Mass., 1955)
Ross, John D., *Scottish Poets in America*, with Biographical and Critical Notices (New York, 1889)
Ross, Peter, *The Scot in America* (New York, 1896)
Roth, Martin, *Comedy and America: The Lost World of Washington Irving* (Port Washington, N.Y., 1976)
Rourke, Constance, *American Humor: A Study of the National Character* (1931; rpt. New York, 1959)
  The Roots of American Culture and Other Essays, ed. by Van Wyck Brooks (New York, 1942)
Russell, Bertrand, *The History of Western Philosophy, and its Connection with Political and Social Circumstances from the Earliest Times to the Present Day* (London, 1946)
Rust, Richard D., 'Coverdale's Confession: A Key to Meaning in *The Blithedale Romance*', in *Literature and Ideas in America*, ed. by Robert Falk (Columbus, Ohio, 1975), 96–110
Rutman, Darrett B., *American Puritanism: Faith and Practice* (Philadelphia, Penn., 1970)
Santayana, George, *Santayana on America: Essays, Notes, and Letters on American Life, Literature and Philosophy*, ed. by Richard C. Lyon (New York, 1968)
  Selected Critical Writings of George Santayana, ed. by Norman Henfrey, 2 vols. (Cambridge, 1968)
  George Santayana's America; Essays on Literature and Culture, comp. by James Ballowe (1967; rpt. Urbana, Ill., and London, 1969)
Sayre, Robert F., *The Examined Self: Benjamin Franklin, Henry Adams, Henry James* (Princeton, N.J., 1964)
Scheick, William J., *The Will and the Word: The Poetry of Edward Taylor* (Athens, Ga., 1974)
  The Writings of Jonathan Edwards: Theme, Motif and Style (College Station, Tex., 1975)
Schlegel, Friedrich, *Lectures on the History of Literature, Ancient and Modern* (1812), trans. by J.G. Lockhart, 2 vols. (Edinburgh, 1818)
Schlereth, Thomas J., *The Cosmopolitan Ideal in Enlightenment Thought: Its Form and Function in the Ideas of Franklin, Hume and Voltaire, 1694–1790* (Notre Dame, Ind., 1977)

Schwartz, Joseph, 'Three Aspects of Hawthorne's Puritanism', *New England Quarterly*, 36 (June 1963), 192–208
Scott, Walter, *The Prose Works of Sir Walter Scott, Bart.*, 28 vols. (Edinburgh, 1834–6)
Poetical Works (Edinburgh, 1855)
The Complete Novels, 24 vols. (Oxford, 1912)
The Letters of Sir Walter Scott, ed. by H.J.C. Grierson and others, 12 vols. (London, 1932–7)
Sir Walter Scott on Novelists and Fiction, ed. by Ioan Williams (London, 1968)
The Journal of Sir Walter Scott, ed. by W.E.K. Anderson (Oxford, 1972)
Scott on Himself, ed. by D.S. Hewitt (Edinburgh, 1981)
Redgauntlet, ed. and with an introduction by Kathryn Sutherland (Oxford, 1985)
Seigel, Jules Paul, ed., *Thomas Carlyle: The Critical Heritage* (New York, 1971)
Selden, John, *The Table Talk of John Selden*, ed. by Samuel H. Reynolds (Oxford, 1892)
Shafer, Boyd C., *Nationalism: Myth and Reality* (London, 1955)
Shain, Charles E., 'John Galt's America', *American Quarterly*, 8, no. 3 (Fall 1956), 254–63
Shakespeare, William, *The Tempest*, ed. by Frank Kermode, The Arden Shakespeare, 6th edn (1958; rpt. London, 1980)
Measure for Measure, ed. by J.W. Leaver, The Arden Shakespeare (1956; rpt. London, 1984)
Sharrock, Roger, ed., *Bunyan, 'The Pilgrim's Progress': A Casebook* (London, 1976)
Shea, Daniel B., Jr, *Spiritual Autobiography in Early America* (Princeton, N.J., 1968)
Sherman, Stuart P., *Points of View* (New York and London, 1924)
Shine, Hill, *Carlyle's Early Reading, to 1834, with an Introductory Essay on His Intellectual Development*, University of Kentucky Libraries, Occasional Contribution, no. 57 (Lexington, Ky., 1953)
Simpson, Louis, *James Hogg: A Critical Study* (Edinburgh, 1962)
Sinclair, David, *Edgar Allan Poe* (London, 1977)
Sitter, John, *Literary Loneliness in Mid-Eighteenth-Century England* (Ithaca, N.Y. and London, 1982)
Sloan, Douglas, *The Scottish Enlightenment and the American College Ideal* (New York, 1971)
Small, Christopher, *Ariel Like a Harpy: Shelley, Mary and 'Frankenstein'* (London, 1972)
Smart, J.S., *James Macpherson: An Episode in Literature* (London, 1905)
Smith, Adam, *The Theory of Moral Sentiments*, ed. by D.D. Raphael and A.L. MacFie, *The Glasgow Edition of the Works and Correspondence of Adam Smith*, 6 vols., (Oxford, 1976–83), vol. I (1976)
An Inquiry into the Nature and Causes of the Wealth of Nations, ed. by R.H. Campbell and A.S. Skinner, *The Glasgow Edition of the Works and Correspondence of Adam Smith* (Oxford, 1976–83), vol. II (1976)
Essays on Philosophical Subjects, ed. by W.P.D. Wightman, J.C. Bryce and J.S. Ross, *The Glasgow Edition of the Works and Correspondence of Adam Smith* (Oxford, 1976–83), vol. III (1980)
Lectures on Rhetoric and Belles Lettres, ed. by J.C. Bryce, *The Glasgow Edition of the Works and Correspondence of Adam Smith* (Oxford, 1976–83), vol. IV (1983)
Smith, Elbert B., *The Death of Slavery: The United States, 1837–65* (Chicago, 1967)
Smith, Henry Nash, *Virgin Land: The American West as Symbol and Myth* (Cambridge, Mass., 1950)
'The Scribbling Women and the Cosmic Success Story', *Critical Inquiry*, 1, no. 1 (September 1974), 47–70
Democracy and the Novel: Popular Resistance to Classic American Writers (New York, 1978)
Smith, Janet Adam, 'Scott and the Idea of Scotland', The Sir Walter Scott Lectures for

1963, *University of Edinburgh Journal*, 21, nos. 3 and 4 (Spring and Autumn 1964), 198–209, 290–8

Smollett, Tobias, *The Expedition of Humphry Clinker*, ed. and introd. by A. Parreaux, Riverside Edition (Boston, Mass., 1968)

Smout, T.C., *A History of the Scottish People 1560–1830*, 2nd edn (London, 1970)

[Sparks, Jared], 'Professor Everett's Orations', *North American Review*, 20, no. 47 (April 1825), 417–40

Speirs, John, *The Scots Literary Tradition: An Essay in Criticism*, rev. edn (London, 1962)

Spencer, Benjamin, *The Quest for Nationality: An American Literary Campaign* (Syracuse, N.Y., 1957)

Spender, Stephen, *Love–Hate Relations: A Study of Anglo–American Sensibilities* (London, 1974)

Spengemann, William C., *The Forms of Autobiography: Episodes in the History of a Literary Genre* (London, 1980)

Spiller, Robert E., *The American in England During the First Half Century of Independence* (New York, 1926)

The Cycle of American Literature: An Essay in Historical Criticism, 2nd edn (New York and London, 1967)

Stanford, Donald E., *Edward Taylor* (Minneapolis, Minn., 1965)

Starr, George A., *Defoe and Spiritual Autobiography* (Princeton, N.J., 1965)

Stein, William Bysshe, *Hawthorne's Faust: A Study of the Devil Archetype* (Hamden, Conn., 1968)

Steiner, George, *Tolstoy or Dostoevsky* (1959; rpt. Harmondsworth, 1960, 1967)

Stephen, Leslie, *Hours in a Library*, 2nd edn. 3 vols. (London, 1877)

Stephenson, Henry Thew, *The Ettrick Shepherd: A Biography*, Indiana University Studies, 9, no. 54 (Bloomington, Ind. 1922)

Stevenson, David, 'Major Weir: A Justified Sinner?', *Scottish Studies*, 16, part 1 (1972), 161–73

Stevenson, Robert Louis, *Familiar Studies of Men and Books* (London, 1882)

Memories and Portraits (London, 1887)

Letters to his Family and Friends, ed. by Sidney Colvin, 2 vols. (London, 1899)

Essays Literary and Critical (London, 1924)

Stewart, Dugald, 'Account of the Life and Writings of Adam Smith, LL.D', in *Essays on Philosophical Subjects*, ed. by W.P.D. Wightman, J.C. Bryce and I.S. Ross, *The Glasgow Edition of the Works and Correspondence of Adam Smith*, 6 vols., (Oxford, 1976–83), III (1980)

Stockley, Violet, *German Literature as Known in England 1750–1830* (London, 1929)

Stokoe, F.W., *German Influence in the English Romantic Period 1788–1818, with Special Reference to Scott, Coleridge, Shelley and Byron* (Cambridge, 1926)

Stolnitz, Jerome, 'On the Origins of Aesthetic Disinterestedness', *The Journal of Aesthetics and Art Criticism*, 20, no. 2 (Winter 1961), 131–43

Storch, Rudolf, 'Metaphors of Private Guilt and Social Rebellion in Godwin's *Caleb Williams*', *English Literary History*, 34, no. 1 (March 1967), 188–207

Strout, A.L., 'Concerning the *Noctes Ambrosianae*', *Modern Language Notes*, 51, no. 8 (December 1936), 493–504

'The *Noctes Ambrosianae* and James Hogg', *Review of English Studies*, 13, no. 49 (January 1937), 46–63; no. 50 (April 1937), 177–89

The Life and Letters of James Hogg the Ettrick Shepherd, Volume 1: 1770–1825, Texas Technical College Research Publications, no. 15 (Lubbock, Tex., 1946)

'James Hogg's "Chaldee Manuscript"', *PMLA*, 65, no. 5 (September 1950), 695–718

'Writers on German Literature in *Blackwood's Magazine*, with a Footnote on Thomas Carlyle', *The Library*, 5th series, 9, no.1 (March 1954), 35–44

'The First Twenty-Three Numbers of the *Noctes Ambrosianae*: Excerpts from the Blackwood Papers in the National Library of Scotland', *The Library*, 5th series, 12, no. 1 (March 1957), 108–18

A Bibliography of Articles in Blackwood's Magazine: Vols. 1 through 18, 1817–1825 (Lubbock, Tex., 1959)

Strout, Cushing, *The New Heavens and New Earth: Political Religion in America* (New York, 1974)

Sultana, Donald E., *'The Siege of Malta' Rediscovered: An Account of Sir Walter Scott's Mediterranean Journey and His Last Novel* (Edinburgh, 1977)

Symons, Julian, *Bloody Murder: From the Detective Story to the Crime Novel: A History* (London, 1972)

Tanner, Tony, *The Reign of Wonder: Naivety and Reality in American Literature* (Cambridge, 1965)

Tawney, R.H., *Religion and the Rise of Capitalism*, 2nd edn (1938; rpt. Harmondsworth, 1980)

Tennyson, G.B., *'Sartor' called 'Resartus': The Genesis, Structure and Style of Thomas Carlyle's First Major Work* (Princeton, N.J., 1965)

Thistlethwaite, Frank, 'What is Un-American?', *The Cambridge Journal*, 5, no. 4 (January 1952), 211–24

Thompson, Gary R., *Poe's Fiction: Romantic Irony in the Gothic Tales* (Madison, Wis., 1973)

Thompson, Lawrance, *Melville's Quarrel with God* (Princeton, N.J., 1952)

Thoreau, Henry David, *Walden and Civil Disobedience*, ed. by Owen Thomas (New York, 1966)

Thornton, John Wingate, ed., *The Pulpit of the American Revolution* (Boston, Mass., 1860)

Tocqueville, Alexis de, *Democracy in America*, trans. by Henry Reeve, revised by Francis Bowen, ed. by Phillips Bradley, 2 vols. (New York, 1945)

Todd, William B., ed., *Hume and the Enlightenment: Essays Presented to Ernest Campbell Mossner* (Edinburgh and Austin, Tex., 1974)

Tomas, Vincent, 'The Modernity of Jonathan Edwards', *New England Quarterly*, 25 (1952), 60–84

Tracy, Joseph, *The Great Awakening: A History of the Revival of Religion in the Time of Edwards and Whitefield* (1842; rpt. Edinburgh, 1976)

Trevor-Roper, Hugh, 'The Scottish Enlightenment', *Studies on Voltaire and the Eighteenth Century*, Transactions of the Second International Congress on the Enlightenment, 58 (Geneva, 1967), 1635–8

Trilling, Lionel, *The Liberal Imagination: Essays on Literature and Society* (1950; rpt. New York, 1976)

The Opposing Self (London, 1955)

Turner, Arlin, 'Hawthorne's Literary Borrowings', *PMLA*, 51, no. 2 (June 1936), 543–62

Nathaniel Hawthorne: A Biography (New York and Oxford, 1980)

Tuttleton, James W., 'The Devil and John Barleycorn: Comic Diablerie in Scott and Burns', *Studies in Scottish Literature*, 1, no. 4 (April 1964), 259–64

The Novel of Manners in America (Chapel Hill, N.C., 1972)

Tuveson, Ernest Lee, *The Imagination as a Means of Grace: Locke and the Aesthetics of Romanticism* (Berkeley, Calif., 1960)

Twain, Mark (S.L. Clemens), *The Adventures of Huckleberry Finn* (London, 1884)

Uphaus, Robert W., *The Impossible Observer: Reason and the Reader in Eighteenth-Century Prose* (Lexington, Ky., 1979)

Van Doren, Carl, *The American Novel 1789–1939*, rev. and enlarged edn (New York, 1940)
Van Ghent, Dorothy, *The English Novel: Form and Function* (1953; rpt. New York, 1961)
Vaughan, A.T., and Bremer, Francis J., eds., *Puritan New England: Essays on Religion, Society and Culture* (New York, 1977)
Vincent, Howard P., ed., *Melville and Hawthorne in the Berkshires: A Symposium* (Kent, Ohio, 1968)
Vogel, Stanley M., *German Literary Influences on the American Transcendentalists*, Yale Studies in English, 127 (New Haven, Conn., 1955)
Von Frank, Albert J., *The Sacred Game: Provincialism and Frontier Consciousness in American Literature 1630–1860* (Cambridge, 1985)
Wadlington, Warwick, *The Confidence Game in American Literature* (Princeton, N.J., 1975)
Wagenknecht, Edward, *Washington Irving: Moderation Displayed* (New York, 1962)
Waller, George M., ed., *Puritanism in Early America*, Problems in American Civilisation series (Lexington, Mass., 1950)
Warfel, Harry R., *Noah Webster: Schoolmaster to America* (New York, 1936)
  Charles Brockden Brown: American Gothic Novelist (1949; rpt. New York, 1974)
Warner, Charles Dudley, *Washington Irving*, American Men of Letters Series (London, 1882)
Washington, George, 'Farewell Address, 1796', in facsimile, ed. by V.H. Paltsits (New York, 1935; rpt. 1971)
Wasserman, Earl R., 'The Sympathetic Imagination in Eighteenth Century Theories of Acting', *Journal of English and Germanic Philology*, 46 (1947), 264–72
Waswo, Richard, 'Story as Historiography in the Waverley Novels', *English Literary History*, 47, no. 2 (Summer 1980), 304–30
Watkins, Owen C., *The Puritan Experience* (London, 1972)
Watson, John, *The Scot of the Eighteenth Century – His Religion and His Life* (London, 1907)
Webber, Joan, *The Eloquent 'I': Style and Self in Seventeenth-Century Prose* (Madison, Wis., 1968)
Webster, Noah, *Dissertations on the English Language* (1789), ed. by Harry R. Warfel (Gainesville, Fla., 1951)
Wellek, René, *Confrontations* (Princeton, N.J., 1965)
Welsford, Enid, *The Court Masque: A Study in the Relationship between Poetry and the Revels* (Cambridge, 1927)
Welsh, Alexander, *The Hero of the Waverley Novels* (New Haven, Conn., 1963)
Wendel, François, *Calvin: the Origins and Development of His Religious Thought*, trans. by Philip Mairet (1963; rpt. London, 1980)
Werner, John M., 'David Hume and America', *Journal of the History of Ideas*, 33, no. 3 (July–September 1972), 439–56
Wesley, John, *The Journal of John Wesley*, 4 vols. (London, 1827)
Weymouth, Lally, ed., *Thomas Jefferson: The Man, His World, His Influence* (London, 1973)
Whale, J.S., *The Protestant Tradition: An Essay in Interpretation* (Cambridge, 1935; rpt. 1962)
White, Morton, *The Philosophy of the American Revolution* (1978; rpt. Oxford, 1981)
Whitman, Walt, *Leaves of Grass* (1855), ed. by Malcolm Cowley (1959; rpt. Harmondsworth, 1978)
Willey, Basil, *The Eighteenth-Century Background: Studies on the Idea of Nature in the Thought of the Period* (London, 1940)
  Nineteenth-Century Studies: Coleridge to Matthew Arnold (London, 1949)

Williams, Charles, *Witchcraft* (1941; rpt. London, 1980)
Williams, S.T., *The Life of Washington Irving*, 2 vols. (New York, 1935)
Williams, William Carlos, *In The American Grain* (1925; rpt. Harmondsworth, 1971)
Wills, Garry, *Inventing America; Jefferson's Declaration of Independence* (1978; rpt. New York, 1979)
Wilson, A.N., *The Laird of Abbotsford: A View of Sir Walter Scott* (Oxford, 1980)
Wilson, Edmund, ed., *The Shock of Recognition: The Development of Literature in the United States, Recorded by the Men who made it*, 2nd edn (New York and London, 1956)
Wilson, James D., ed., *Tradition and Imagination in Colonial American Literature*, Studies in the Literary Imagination, 9, no. 2 (Fall 1976)
Wilson, John, *Noctes Ambrosianae*, ed. by Professor Ferrier, 4 vols. (Edinburgh and London, 1876)
Winters, Yvor, *In Defense of Reason* (London, 1960)
Wirt, William, *The Letters of the British Spy*, Southern Literary Classics Series, 1832 edn, facsimile rpt. (Chapel Hill, N.C., 1970)
Witherspoon, John, *The Works of John Witherspoon, D.D.*, 9 vols. (Edinburgh, 1815)
Wittig, Kurt, *The Scottish Tradition in Literature* (Edinburgh, 1958; rpt. 1973)
Wolf, William J., ed., *The Spirit of Anglicanism: Hooker, Maurice, Temple* (Wilton, Conn., 1979)
Wolfe, J.N., ed., *Government and Nationalism in Scotland: An Enquiry by Members of the University of Edinburgh* (Edinburgh, 1969)
Woodberry, George Edward, 'Knickerbocker Era of American Letters', *Harper's Monthly Magazine*, 105, no. 629 (October 1902), 677–83
Woodhouse, A.S.P., 'Romanticism and the History of Ideas', in *English Studies Today*, 1st series, ed. by C.L. Wrenn and G. Bullough (Oxford, 1951), 120–40
Wormald, Jenny, *Court, Kirk, and Community: Scotland 1470–1625*, The New History of Scotland, 6 vols. vol. IV (London, 1981)
Yeats, W.B., *Essays and Introductions* (London, 1961)
Young, Douglas, *Edinburgh in the Age of Sir Walter Scott* (Norman, Okla., 1965)
Young, Douglas, and others, *Edinburgh in the Age of Reason* (Edinburgh, 1967) *Scotland* (London, 1971)
Youngson, A.J., *Beyond the Highland Line: [Extracts from] Three Journals of Travel in Eighteenth-Century Scotland* (London, 1974)
Zelinsky, Wilbur, *The Cultural Geography of the United States* (Englewood Cliffs, N.J., 1973)
Ziff, Larzer, *The Career of John Cotton: Puritanism and the American Experience* (Princeton, N.J., 1962)
 Puritanism in America: New Culture in a New World (New York, 1973)
 Literary Democracy: The Declaration of Cultural Independence in America (1981; rpt. Harmondsworth, 1982)

Index

'Abyss, the', 2, 13, 66, 91, 97, 105, 167
Adams, John, 57
Addison, Joseph, 107–9, 158
alienation, 28, 34, 73, 106–7, 158–9, 166, 189; America, 51–3, 61–2; from the centre, 20; from fellow-men, 48–9; from God, 3–4, 9, 12; Hume, 43–4; from Nature, 7–9; and observation, 34, 99; Scotland, 51–3; *see also* observation; provincialism
Alison, Archibald, 62
America: civil war, 58, 115; Declaration of Independence, 58–61, 78; language, 52–3; literature, vii–ix, 49, 51, 71–2, 107, *see also under individual authors*; political rhetoric, 51, 57–61; provincialism, 51–3, 61–2, 148, 164; puritanism, 18–25, 66; witch hunts, 21–5, 99, 107
Andrewes, Lancelot, 8
Antinomianism, 17, 193
Arbroath, Declaration of, 18
Arminianism, 17, 36, 193
Arnold, Matthew, 55, 74
Augustine of Hippo, St, ix, 6, 8, 9, 148, 193
'Awakenings', 17, 26–9, 33
Ayrshire Legatees (Galt), 151–3

Bancroft, George, 51
'Bartleby the Scrivener' (Melville), 102–5
Beattie, James, 52
'Benito Cereno' (Melville), 105, 131–2, 135
Blackwood's Edinburgh Magazine, 150–1
Blair, Hugh, 62, 108
Blithedale Romance, The (Hawthorne), 136–43, 146
Bradford, William, 5
Bradley, A.C., 144
British Spy, The (Wirt), 108–9
Brown, Charles Brockden, 76–80, 83–4, 112; *Edgar Huntly*, 76–80, 83–4, 186; *Wieland*, 79, 87, 112
Brown, Thomas, 54

Browning, Robert, 183
Bruce, Robert, 3
Buchan, John, 93
Bunyan, John, 16–17, 148, 175–6, 178, 185, 186, 192
Burns, Robert, 49
Butler, Joseph, Bishop, 42

Caleb Williams (Godwin), 72–6, 88, 92
Calvin, John, vii–viii, 1, 11, 167; theology, ix, 1–5, 62
Calvinism, 192–3; conversion, 11–12, 16–17; determinism, 3, 8, 12, 19, 36, 72–3, 76; doubt, 13, 44–5, 66, 70, 148, 152–3, 167, 185, 188; egocentrism, 15–16; election, 2–4, 8, 11, 115, 119; exclusivity, 5–6, 8, 19; faith, 2–5, 14–15, 39; Fall, 2–4, 7–9, 12, 37–8, 62, 107; in literature, 73, 76; persecution, 18–21, 58; pilgrimage, 16–17, 178, 188; reason, 9–11, 16, 26–7, 39; reprobation, 2, 7–8; salvation, 2–5, 8, 17; search for knowledge, 9, 13, 45, 70, 71, 152–3, 189; signs, 14–15, 22, 34, 66, 68, 162, 183; will, 8, 12, 32–3
Carlyle, Thomas, 66, 69, 122, 133; 'Diamond Necklace', 127–30; *Sartor Resartus*, 84, 126–7
Catholic Church, 3, 5
'Celestial Rail-Road, The' (Hawthorne), 104
centre, 9, 26, 37, 70, 75, 107, 147–94; *Geoffrey Crayon*, 158–63; *Heart of Midlothian*, 171–81, 191, 192–3; *Marble Faun*, 155–6, 163–4; and provincialism, 147–53; *Redburn*, 164–70; *Scarlet Letter*, 181–93; *Valerius*, 153–5, 156–8; *see also* provincialism
Clark, Kenneth, 149, 168, 179
Coleridge, Samuel Taylor, 49, 134
Colman, Benjamin, 28
'Common Sense' philosophy, 53–8, 62–3, 74; in literature, 81, 100, 104, 138, 177
community, puritan, 15–18

Index

Confessions of a Justified Sinner (Hogg), viii, 17, 78, 80–4, 94
confidence, 3, 5, 6, 8–9, 13–14, 42, 73; in literature, 135; loss of, 13–14, 127, 173, 184
Confidence-Man, The (Melville), 132–5, 140, 142, 143
Congregationalism, 19–25
conscience, 11, 35–6, 49–50, 63, 71, 86; Smith, 49–50
conversion, 11–12, 16–17, 31–5, 132
Cooper, James Fenimore, 55, 114–16, 130, 180
Cotton, John, 5
covenant theology, 4–5, 13–14, 18–19, 27, 63, 66–7; Covenant of Grace, 4, 37; Half-Way Covenant, 27; Covenant of meaning, 14–15, 37, 61–2, 72, 106, 121–2, 128; Covenant of Works, 4
crisis, 6, 58, 191

determinism, 3, 8, 12, 19, 36, 72–3, 76, 93; *see also* free will
'Diamond Necklace, The' (Carlyle), 127–30
distance *see* alienation; *see also* observation; provincialism
division *see* Fall, consequences of
Donne, John, 8
doppelgänger, 23, 84; *see also* double
double, the, 70–105; 'Bartleby the Scrivener', 102–5; *Caleb Williams*, 72–6, 88, 92; *Confessions of a Justified Sinner*, 80–4; *Edgar Huntly*, 76–80, 83–4; pursuit of knowledge, 70–1; *Redgauntlet*, 88–96; 'William Wilson', 84–8; 'Young Goodman Brown', 97–101
'double consciousness', 64–5
doubt, 13, 44–5, 66, 70, 148, 152–3, 167, 188; *see also* scepticism

Ecclesiastical Polity (Hooker), 7–16
Edgar Huntly (Brockden Brown), 76–80, 83–4, 186
Edinburgh, 157–8
Edwards, Jonathan, 12–13, 26–38; faith, 61, 64; observation, 35–6, 56–7; pilgrimage, 27–8, 148; salvation, 4–5, 13; self-investigation, 34–5, 122, 186
egocentrism, 15–16
election, 2–4, 8, 11, 19, 115, 119
Eliot, T.S., 180
Emerson, Ralph Waldo, 62–8, 70; and Carlyle, 126–7; centrality, 147; facts, 12, 13, 66, 68, 125; self-investigation, 9, 68; Transcendentalism, 62–4, 129, 134, 143
'Encantadas, The' (Melville), 120–1
England: and America, 52–3, 59–61; literature, vii, 72, 107; and Scotland, 18–20, 172–4

Europe, and America, viii, 52–3, 61–2
evil, 83, 95, 194
exclusivity, 5–6, 8, 19, 27

'facts', 12, 13, 55–7, 66–8, 73, 74, 79–80, 89; *see also* 'Common Sense' philosophy
faith: Calvin, 2–5, 12, 14–15, 39, 174, 193; and confidence, 42; Edwards, 61, 64; literature, 127, 135, 179; loss of, 2, 13–14, 42, 127, 184; and narrative, 12; and reason, 16, 39
Fall, the, 2–4, 8, 12, 37, 62, 99, 101, 107, 143, 171, 182, 191; consequences of, 7–9, 12, 37–9, 63, 71, 107, 122, 144; flight/pursuit, 61, 71–2, 106; in literature, 76, 79–81, 85, 90, 98–9, 102, 119, 168
Franklin, Benjamin, 51, 108
free will, 36–9, 88, 181, 185; *see also* predestination
Freneau, Philip, 108

Galt, John, 150–3, 185
Gerard, Alexander, 48–9, 54
Godwin, William, ix, 72–6, 88; *Caleb Williams*, 72–6, 88, 92
grace, 4, 35–7
guilt, 70–1, 75, 79, 84, 91, 97

Half-Way Covenants, 27
Hawthorne, Nathaniel, 55, 69, 77, 84; *Blithedale Romance*, 136–43, 146; 'Celestial Rail-Road', 104; *House of the Seven Gables*, 160; 'Intelligence Office, The', 46; James on, 140, 141–2; 'Main-street', 123–5, 127, 160, 191; *The Marble Faun*, 155–6, 163–4, 187, 193; 'May-pole of Merry Mount', 156, 161; 'Monsieur du Miroir', 86; 'My Kinsman, Major Molineux', 155; observation, 34, 41–2, 106, 111–12; *Our Old Home*, 163; 'Roger Malvin's Burial', 97; *The Scarlet Letter*, 101, 149–50, 177, 181–93; 'Wakefield', 116–18, 119; 'Young Goodman Brown', 78, 97–101, 102, 138, 142, 170
Heaney, Seamus, 53
Heart of Midlothian, The (Scott), 149–50, 171–81, 191, 192–3
Herbert, George, 18
heresy, 17
Hogg, James, 55, 69; *Confessions of a Justified Sinner*, viii, 17, 78, 80–4, 94; *The Spy*, 110–13, 123
Hooker, Richard, 7–16
Hopkins, Samuel, 26
Hume, David, 26, 38–46, 177; double consciousness, 64–5; language, 52; mind, 39–40, 136, 167; observation, 40–4, 106,

124; reason, 38–40; scepticism, 44–6, 53–7, 69, 135, 167–9, 191; speculation, 152, 167–9; sympathy, 41–3, 121
Humphry, Ozias, 147
Hutcheson, Francis, 42, 43, 54, 56
Hutchinson, Anne, 17

Irving, Washington, 69, 109–10, 112; *Bracebridge Hall*, 162–3; *Sketch Book of Geoffrey Crayon, The*, 152, 158–63

James, Henry, 148, 166, 177, 194; on Hawthorne, 140, 142; provincialism, viii, 147–8, 166
Jefferson, Thomas, 57–61, 68, 78
Jenyns, Soame, 35
Johnson, Samuel, 33, 35, 39, 108
Joyce, James, 53

Kames, Henry Home, Lord, 62
Keats, John, 49–50
knowledge: forbidden, 2, 10, 44–5, 72, 75, 94, 106, 119, 188; search for, 9, 13, 44–6, 70, 73, 100, 106, 152–3, 188; *see also* double
Knox, John, 19

language, 51–3, 70, 108–9; Calvin, vii–viii, 11; literature, 76, 83, 87–8, 95, 101–4, 179
Law, 4–5, 13, 63, 172–4, 182, 183, 190, 191
Lawrence, D.H., viii
Lindberg, Gary, 133
Locke, John, 33–4, 37–8, 50, 82
Lockhart, J.G., 69, 150, 153–8, 185
London, as centre, 147–56, 162–3, 177, 193
Longfellow, Henry Wadsworth, 141
Lowell, Robert, 47
Luther, Martin, 10, 70
Lutheran Church, 3

McCosh, James, 56
Mackenzie, Henry, 52, 108
'Main-street' (Hawthorne), 123–5, 127, 159
'Man of the Crowd, The' (Poe), 118–19, 125
Mann, Thomas, 84
Marble Faun, The (Hawthorne), 155–6, 163–4, 187
Marx, Leo, 144
masks and masquerade, 33, 68, 113–15, 122–6, 128–35, 140, 144–66, 187
'Masque of the Red Death, The' (Poe), 122–3
Mather, Cotton, 5, 21–3, 107
Melville, Herman, 55, 66, 69, 192; 'Bartleby the Scrivener', 102–5; 'Benito Cereno', 105, 131–2, 135, 190; *The Confidence-Man*, 133–5, 140, 142, 143; 'The Encantadas', 120–1; *Mardi*, 61, 168, 170; *Moby-Dick*, 33, 131; *Redburn*, 152, 164–71, 175, 177
Mencken, H.L., 1

'Middle Way', 5, 16, 69, 78, 174, 177, 193
Milton, John, 6, 75, 101–2
monovalency, 16–17
Montaigne, Michel de, 68–9

narrative, 12, 31–2, 65, 71; *see also* observation

observation, 73, 106–46; 'Benito Cereno' 131–2; *Blithedale Romance*, 136–43, 146; *British Spy*, 108–9; *Confidence-Man*, 132–5, 140, 142, 143; 'Diamond Necklace', 127–30; Edwards, 35–6, 56–7; 'Encantadas', 120–1; Hawthorne, 34, 41–2, 106, 111–12; Hume, 40–4, 106, 124; Irving, 109–10, 112; 'Main-street', 123–5; 'Man of the Crowd', 118–19, 125; 'Masque of the Red Death', 122–3; puritanism, 9–10, 11; *Sartor Resartus*, 125–7; Scott, 106, 113–14; Smith, 48–9; *The Spy* (Cooper), 114–16; *The Spy* (Hogg), 110–13, 123; *The Tempest*, 126, 143–6; 'Wakefield', 116–18, 119; and witch hunts, 23–5
Original Sin *see* Fall
Ortega y Gasset, José, 147, 149–50

Paine, Tom, 59, 73
Paul, St, ix, 9, 15
Paulding, J.K., 87
persecution, 18–21, 58, 81
pilgrimage, 3–4, 16–17, 148, 152–3, 159, 160–1, 169, 175–8, 188
Pilgrim's Progress, The (Bunyan), 16–17, 148, 169, 175–6, 178, 192
Poe, Edgar Allan, ix, 55, 69, 77, 98; and *Edgar Huntly*, 77; *Eureka*, 193; 'Man of the Crowd', 118–19, 125, 139; 'Masque of the Red Death', 122–3; 'The Philosophy of Composition', 130; 'William Wilson', 84–8
polarities, 6–7, 38–9, 44, 70, 73, 149–50, 174
Pope, Alexander, 45, 183–4
possession, demonic *see* witch hunts
predestination, 3, 8, 12, 19, 36, 91, 182; *see also* free will
Presbyterianism, 18–25
Prescott, William H., 79
provincialism, 66, 71, 73, 147–9; in art, 41–2, 149, 162, 168, 178, 193–4; *Ayrshire Legatees*, 151–3; and centre, 147–53, 192–3; *Heart of Midlothian*, 149–50, 171–81, 191, 192–3; and literature, 147–50; and loss of confidence, 13–14; *Marble Faun*, 155–6, 163–4; puritan–prouncialism, 47–69; *Redburn*, 164–71; *Scarlet Letter*, 149–50, 177, 181–93; *Sketch Book of Geoffrey Crayon*, 158–62; *Valerius*, 153–5, 156–8
puritan–provincial mind, vii–x, 47–69, 161, 167, 192; the double, 70–105; observation, 106–46

Index

puritanism, 1, 71; and Calvinism, 6–15; church and community, 15–18; confidence, 3, 5, 8–9, 13; and the Fall, 60, 63–4; observation, 9–10, 11; relationships, 15–18, 24; in Scotland and America, 18–25

ratiocination, 9, 77, 83
Read, Herbert, 147, 160
realism, 12, 28–9, 33, 38–40, 67–8, 193–4; *see also* symbolism
reason, 71; Calvin, 10–11, 16, 26–7, 39; Edwards, 33–5; and faith, 16, 39; Hooker, 10, 16; Hume, 38–40
Redburn (Melville), 152, 164–71
Redgauntlet (Scott), 88–96
Reformation theology, 2–3, 6–7
Reid, Thomas, 53–7
reprobation, 2, 7–8, 32
Revivals, 17, 26–9, 33
Rome, 146, 153–8, 163, 192

Sacraments, the, 5, 14–15
salvation, 2–5, 8, 13, 17
Santayana, George, 62–3, 104, 122, 123–4, 136
Sartor Resartus (Carlyle), 84, 125–7
Scarlet Letter, The (Hawthorne), 101, 149–50, 177, 181–93
scepticism, 44–6, 53–7, 69, 134, 167–8, 191
Schlegel, Friedrich, 157–8
Scotland: and England, 18–20, 172–4; language, 51–2; literature, vii–ix, 49, 51–2, 71–2, 107, *see also under individual authors*; Presbyterianism, 18–25; provincialism, 51–3, 148; puritanism, 18–25; witch hunts, 21–5
Scott, Sir Walter, 55, 69, 193; *Bride of Lammermoor*, 179; *Heart of Midlothian*, 149–50, 171–81, 191, 192–3; 'Highland Widow', 96, 133; observation, 106, 113–14; *Redgauntlet*, 88–96, 179
Selden, John, 16
self, and other, 15–18, 71, 97, 106
self-consciousness, 78, 84, 89, 94, 122, 148, 169
self-investigation, 16, 71, 84; Edwards, 34–5, 122, 186; Emerson, 9, 68; Hume, 40–1; Smith, 49–50
Shaftesbury, Anthony Ashley Cooper, 3rd Earl of, 42
Shakespeare, William, 163; *The Tempest*, ix, 54, 114, 126, 144–6
shipwreck, 2, 22, 46, 120–1, 152–3, 159, 167–8, 188, 189
signs, 9, 14–15, 22, 34, 66, 107
Simson, John, 56
sin, 27, 72, 81, 86, 97, 182–5, 187; Original *see* Fall

Sketch Book of Geoffrey Crayon, The (Irving), 152, 158–62
Smith, Adam, 35, 42, 47–52, 74; conscience, 49–50; sympathy, 47–8
Sparks, Jared, 53
Spectator, The (Addison and Steele), 107–8
spectators *see* observation
'spectre evidence', 22, 33, 107, 142; in literature, 99, 117–18, 124, 139, 189
speculation, 55, 57, 152, 167–8, 194
Spy, The (Cooper), 114–16
Spy, The (Hogg), 110–13, 123
Steele, Sir Richard, 107
Stevenson, Robert Louis, viii
Stewart, Dugald, 54
Stiles, Ezra, 60–1
Stoddard, Solomon, 27
Stubbs, George, 147
symbolism, 12–13, 65–6, 144; in literature, 85, 131, 144, 155–6, 159, 190
sympathy: Edwards, 36, 42; Hume, 41–3, 121; power of, in literature, 74, 77, 82, 84–5, 91–2, 95, 100, 103, 106, 121; Smith, 47–8

Tawney, R.H., 32
Tempest, The (Shakespeare), ix, 54, 114, 126, 144–6
Thoreau, Henry David, 133
Tocqueville, Alexis, Comte de, 61
Transcendentalism, 62–4, 129, 133, 143
Trilling, Lionel, 178

Valerius (Lockhart), 153–5, 156–8
Voiture, Vincent de, 45

'Wakefield' (Hawthorne), 116–18, 119
Washington, George, 61–2
Watts, Alaric, 150
Webster, Noah, 52, 158
Welsford, Enid, 143
Whitefield, George, 27
will, 71, 88, 181; Calvin, 8, 12, 32–3; Edwards, 32–3, 36–7; Smith, 50
Willard, Samuel, 7, 11, 50
'William Wilson' (Poe), 84–8
Wilson, John, 150
Winthrop, John, 5
Wirt, William, 108–11, 137; *British Spy*, 108–9
witch hunts, 21–5, 27, 33, 99, 107, 142; in literature, 98, 99, 138
Witherspoon, John, 36, 51

'Young Goodman Brown' (Hawthorne), 78, 97–101, 102, 138, 142